Ah! 365 Yummy Lunch Recipes

(Ah! 365 Yummy Lunch Recipes - Volume 1)

Kathy Parker

Content

Chapter 1: No-Cook Lunch Recipes

***

1. "Fried" Chicken Salad

Serving: 1 | Prep: 15mins | Ready in:

Ingredients

- 3 ounces frozen lightly breaded chicken chunks
- 2 to 3 cups packaged chopped romaine lettuce
- 1 tablespoon white balsamic vinegar
- 1 teaspoon olive oil
- 1 teaspoon honey mustard
- 1 teaspoon honey
- ⅛ teaspoon ground black pepper
- 6 cherry tomatoes, halved (3 ounces)
- ¼ cup whole-grain large-cut croutons, coarsely crushed

Direction

- Microwave the chicken chunks following the package instructions.
- In the meantime, put the romaine in a medium bowl. To make the dressing, whisk together the pepper, honey, honey mustard, oil and vinegar in a tiny bowl, then drizzle the dressing on top of the romaine and toss until coated. Scoop the romaine mixture onto a big dinner plate.
- Put croutons, hot cooked chicken and cherry tomatoes on top of the salad.

Nutrition Information

- Calories: 346 calories;
- Sugar: 17
- Total Fat: 13
- Fiber: 5
- Cholesterol: 40
- Total Carbohydrate: 35
- Saturated Fat: 2
- Sodium: 593
- Protein: 21

2. Champion Chicken Pockets

Serving: 4 | Prep: 15mins | Ready in:

Ingredients

- ¼ cup plain low-fat yogurt
- ¼ cup bottled reduced-fat ranch salad dressing
- 1½ cups chopped cooked chicken or turkey
- ½ cup chopped broccoli
- ¼ cup shredded carrot
- ¼ cup chopped pecans or walnuts (optional)
- 2 (6 inch) 6- to 7-inch whole-wheat pita bread rounds, halved crosswise

Direction

- Mix ranch salad dressing and yogurt in a small bowl.
- Mix carrot, chicken, broccoli and, if wished, nuts. Put yogurt mixture over the chicken; toss to coat. Scoop the chicken mixture into pita halves. Use plastic wrap to wrap tightly and chill up to 24 hours. Place sandwiches in insulated containers and pack with ice packs.

Nutrition Information

- Calories: 231 calories;
- Total Fat: 8
- Saturated Fat: 1
- Sugar: 3
- Protein: 20
- Sodium: 392
- Fiber: 3

- Cholesterol: 53
- Total Carbohydrate: 21

3. Charcuterie Bistro Lunch Box

Serving: 1 | Prep: 5mins | Ready in:

Ingredients

- 1 slice prosciutto
- 1 mozzarella stick, halved
- 2 breadsticks, halved
- 2 dates
- ½ cup grapes
- 2 large radishes, halved or 4 slices English cucumber (¼-inch)

Direction

- Slice in half lengthwise the prosciutto, then around each piece of cheese, wrap a slice. In 4-cup divided sealable container, pile the radish or cucumber, grapes, dates, breadsticks and wrapped cheese. Store inside the refrigerator until serving time.

Nutrition Information

- Calories: 452 calories;
- Total Fat: 18
- Sodium: 597
- Fiber: 4
- Cholesterol: 26
- Sugar: 44
- Saturated Fat: 6
- Total Carbohydrate: 65
- Protein: 17

4. Chicken Focaccia Bread Sandwiches

Serving: 6 | Prep: 15mins | Ready in:

Ingredients

- 1 8-inch tomato or onion Italian flatbread (focaccia) or 1 loaf sourdough bread
- ⅓ cup light mayonnaise or salad dressing
- 1 cup lightly packed fresh basil leaves
- 2 cups sliced or shredded deli-roasted chicken
- ½ (7 ounce) jar roasted red peppers, drained and cut into strips (about ½ cup)

Direction

- Halve the bread horizontally using a long-serrated knife. Spread mayonnaise or dressing on the cut sides of the bread halves.
- Layer basil leaves, chicken and roasted peppers in between the bread halves, then slice it into six wedges.

Nutrition Information

- Calories: 263 calories;
- Sodium: 341
- Fiber: 1
- Total Carbohydrate: 27
- Sugar: 1
- Saturated Fat: 2
- Cholesterol: 51
- Protein: 19
- Total Fat: 10

5. Citrus Chicken Salad

Serving: 2 | Prep: 20mins | Ready in:

Ingredients

- 6 ounces cooked chicken breast, shredded, or one 6-ounce package refrigerated cooked chicken breast strips (see Test Kitchen Tip)

- 2 cups fresh baby spinach
- 1 (11 ounce) can mandarin orange sections, drained
- ½ cup loose-pack frozen whole kernel corn
- 2 tablespoons white wine vinegar or cider vinegar
- 1 tablespoon Dijon-style mustard
- 2 teaspoons snipped fresh oregano or ½ teaspoon dried oregano, crushed
- 2 teaspoons low-sugar or low-calorie orange marmalade
- 2 teaspoons salad oil
- ⅛ teaspoon salt
- ⅛ teaspoon ground black pepper

Direction

- Split chicken among 2 small resealable freezer bags; place in the freezer overnight.
- Split corn, mandarin oranges, and spinach among 2 airtight containers. Mix pepper, vinegar, salt, mustard, oil, oregano, and orange marmalade in a jar with screw-top; cover and shake thoroughly. Split the dressing among 2 small resealable plastic bags. Refrigerate the dressing and salads overnight.
- Store one bag of chicken, one bag of dressing, and a salad container, and an ice pack in an insulated lunch box for each serving. Serve salad within 5hrs.
- Toss the chicken and dressing to the spinach mixture to coat before serving. This recipe makes two, one and a half cup servings.

Nutrition Information

- Calories: 304 calories;
- Fiber: 3
- Total Carbohydrate: 28
- Sugar: 17
- Protein: 31
- Total Fat: 8
- Saturated Fat: 2
- Sodium: 422
- Cholesterol: 72

6. Classic House Salad

Serving: 4 | Prep: 15mins | Ready in:

Ingredients

- 5 cups shredded romaine lettuce
- 1 cup diced celery
- 1 cup sliced or julienned radishes
- 1 small red onion, thinly sliced

Direction

- In a large bowl, mix onion, radishes, lettuce, and celery and then lay out in between paper towels in an airtight container for storage.

Nutrition Information

- Calories: 26 calories;
- Sodium: 37
- Fiber: 2
- Total Carbohydrate: 5
- Protein: 1
- Total Fat: 0
- Saturated Fat: 0
- Cholesterol: 0
- Sugar: 2

7. Crab, Avocado Watercress Sandwiches

Serving: 12 | Prep: 20mins | Ready in:

Ingredients

- 3 tablespoons light mayonnaise or salad dressing
- 1 tablespoon snipped fresh chives, plus more for garnish
- 1 teaspoon lemon juice

- 1 cup chopped cooked fresh lump or jumbo crabmeat or drained pasteurized canned lump crabmeat, flaked and cartilage removed
- ⅛ teaspoon ground white pepper
- Dash salt
- 8 thin slices firm-texture white or wheat sandwich bread
- 2 tablespoons 40% to 50% vegetable oil spread
- 1 avocado, sliced
- ½ cup loosely packed watercress (thick stems discarded), rinsed and dried

Direction

- Mix lemon juice, chives and mayonnaise in a small bowl. Add crabmeat; mix to combine with a fork. Mix in salt and white pepper.
- Spread vegetable oil spread on 1 side of every bread slice; on 1/2 of buttered bread slices, put avocado slices. Put crab mixture over. Add watercress. Put leftover bread slices over, buttered sides down. Trim crusts from bread. Crosswise cut each sandwich to 3 pieces.
- Sprinkle extra chives; serve.

Nutrition Information

- Calories: 107 calories;
- Saturated Fat: 1
- Sodium: 178
- Fiber: 1
- Cholesterol: 13
- Total Carbohydrate: 10
- Total Fat: 6
- Sugar: 2
- Protein: 4

8. Crunchy Chicken Mango Salad

Serving: 4 | Prep: 20mins | Ready in:

Ingredients

- ⅓ cup orange juice

- 3 tablespoons rice vinegar
- 3 tablespoons less-sodium soy sauce
- 1 tablespoon toasted sesame oil
- 2 teaspoons sambal oelek (optional)
- 6 cups thinly sliced napa cabbage
- 2 cups sugar snap peas, thinly sliced diagonally
- 2 cups shredded cooked chicken breast
- 1 medium mango, sliced
- ½ cup coarsely chopped fresh mint
- ¼ cup sliced scallions
- 2 tablespoons toasted sesame seeds

Direction

- In a large bowl, whisk juice, sambal oelek (if using), vinegar, sesame oil and soy sauce. Add scallions, cabbage, mango, peas, mint, and chicken. Mix gently to coat. You can serve the salad sprinkled with sesame seeds.

Nutrition Information

- Calories: 285 calories;
- Total Fat: 9
- Saturated Fat: 1
- Sodium: 505
- Protein: 27
- Fiber: 5
- Cholesterol: 60
- Total Carbohydrate: 25
- Sugar: 16

9. Egg Salad Lettuce Wraps

Serving: 1 | Prep: 10mins | Ready in:

Ingredients

- ¼ cup plain nonfat Greek yogurt
- 1 tablespoon mayonnaise
- ½ teaspoon Dijon mustard
- Pinch of salt
- Ground pepper to taste

- 3 hard-boiled eggs, peeled
- 2 stalks celery, minced
- 2 tablespoons minced red onion
- 2 or 3 large iceberg lettuce leaves
- 1 tablespoon chopped fresh basil
- 2 carrots, peeled and cut into sticks

Direction

- In a medium bowl, combine pepper, yogurt, salt, mayonnaise, and mustard. Remove one egg yolk. Chop up left eggs and move to a bowl; stir in onion and celery until combined. Halve lettuce leaves and form two lettuce wraps by double-layering them. Split the egg salad between the wraps; add basil on top. Serve wraps with a side of carrot sticks.

Nutrition Information

- Calories: 436 calories;
- Total Fat: 27
- Cholesterol: 568
- Total Carbohydrate: 21
- Fiber: 5
- Sugar: 12
- Protein: 27
- Saturated Fat: 7
- Sodium: 624

10. Fresh Tuna Salad

Serving: 1 | Prep: 10mins | Ready in:

Ingredients

- 1 cup mixed salad greens
- ½ cup cherry tomatoes, halved
- 3 ounces flaked tuna (canned in water)
- 1 tablespoon fat-free mayonnaise
- ¼ cup chopped celery
- 4 pieces melba toast
- ½ cup chopped mango (optional)
- 1 cup fat-free milk (optional)

Direction

- Mix together cherry tomatoes and salad greens to make a simple side salad. Mix celery, mayonnaise and tuna to assemble tuna salad; eat it on its own or prepare two small sandwiches by arranging between slices of melba toast.
- To complete this balanced meal, serve accompanied with milk and mango.

Nutrition Information

- Calories: 224 calories;
- Total Fat: 3
- Saturated Fat: 1
- Sodium: 598
- Fiber: 4
- Total Carbohydrate: 23
- Protein: 24
- Cholesterol: 36
- Sugar: 4

11. Fruit Cheese Bistro Lunch Box

Serving: 1 | Prep: 5mins | Ready in:

Ingredients

- 2 or 3 whole-grain crispbreads or 6 whole-grain crackers
- 1 ounce Cheddar cheese, cubed or sliced
- 1 ounce goat cheese
- ¼ cup smoked almonds
- ½ apple, sliced
- 1 tablespoon fig jam
- ½ large carrot, peeled and cut into 4-inch sticks

Direction

- In a 4-cup divided sealable container, arrange carrot sticks, jam, apple, almonds, goat cheese, Cheddar, and crispbreads (or crackers). (You can keep separately the jam and almonds by using silicon baking cups to put them, if needed). Chill in the refrigerator until ready to enjoy.

Nutrition Information

- Calories: 557 calories;
- Saturated Fat: 11
- Sodium: 528
- Total Fat: 35
- Fiber: 7
- Cholesterol: 41
- Total Carbohydrate: 45
- Sugar: 25
- Protein: 21

12. Fruit, Veggie Cheese Plate

Serving: 4 | Prep: 10mins | Ready in:

Ingredients

- 1 (8 ounce) container avocado hummus (see Tip)
- 8 ounces Cheddar cheese
- 8 medium carrots, cut into sticks
- 1 green bell pepper, cut into strips
- 1 orange, cut into wedges
- 1 cup green grapes
- 20 whole-wheat crackers
- 4 (1 ounce) squares dark chocolate

Direction

- Split items evenly among 4 plates. Serve with a Pilsner-style beer if you want.

Nutrition Information

- Calories: 759 calories;
- Sugar: 29
- Protein: 23
- Cholesterol: 58
- Saturated Fat: 19

- Sodium: 732
- Fiber: 14
- Total Carbohydrate: 70
- Total Fat: 45

13. Ginger Tomato Salad

Serving: 4 | Prep: 15mins | Ready in:

Ingredients

- 2 tablespoons rice vinegar
- 1 tablespoon minced fresh ginger
- 1 tablespoon honey
- ⅛ teaspoon salt
- 2 cups cherry and/or grape tomatoes

Direction

- Whisk together the salt, honey, ginger and rice vinegar in a medium bowl, then add tomatoes; gently toss until coated. Put cover and let it chill until ready to serve.

Nutrition Information

- Calories: 37 calories;
- Saturated Fat: 0
- Sodium: 78
- Fiber: 1
- Total Carbohydrate: 8
- Sugar: 7
- Total Fat: 0
- Cholesterol: 0
- Protein: 1

14. Heirloom Tomato Salad With Tomato Vinaigrette

Serving: 8 | Prep: 10mins | Ready in:

Ingredients

- 2 pounds heirloom tomatoes, divided
- 2 tablespoons sherry vinegar
- 2 tablespoons extra-virgin olive oil
- 1 tablespoon minced shallot
- 1 teaspoon honey
- 1 teaspoon Dijon mustard
- ½ teaspoon salt
- 1 cup thinly sliced cucumber
- 4 ounces fresh mozzarella cheese, sliced
- ¼ cup chopped fresh basil
- Flaky salt for garnish

Direction

- Puree half cup chopped tomato, salt, vinegar, mustard, oil, honey, and shallot in a blender until smooth; scrape the sides down 1-2 times.
- Cut the remaining tomatoes. In a big serving platter, arrange the sliced tomatoes, mozzarella, and cucumber; pour the vinaigrette all over. Add basil on top. If desired, add flaky salt.

Nutrition Information

- Calories: 100 calories;
- Total Fat: 7
- Saturated Fat: 2
- Cholesterol: 11
- Protein: 4
- Sodium: 252
- Fiber: 1
- Total Carbohydrate: 6
- Sugar: 4

15. Hot Wing Salad

Serving: 1 | Prep: 5mins | Ready in:

Ingredients

- ½ of a heart of romaine, sliced
- ¾ cup coarsely chopped cooked chicken breast

- Buffalo wing sauce, such as Wing Time® brand (see Tip)
- 1 21-gram wedge light blue cheese, such as Laughing Cow® brand, crumbled
- ¼ teaspoon cracked black pepper
- 1 tablespoon bottled fat-free blue cheese salad dressing
- 1 teaspoon fat free milk
- 1 stalk celery, cut into 4 sticks

Direction

- In a bowl or on a plate, arrange the romaine. Mix wing sauce and chopped chicken together in a small microwaveable bowl. Put in the microwave for 40-50 seconds at 100 percent power (or high setting) until the chicken mixture is heated through.
- Put the chicken mixture on top of the romaine. Crumble cheese and sprinkle on top along with the pepper. Mix milk and salad dressing in a small bowl then sprinkle the mixture on top of the salad. Add in celery sticks then serve.

Nutrition Information

- Calories: 297 calories;
- Total Fat: 10
- Cholesterol: 99
- Total Carbohydrate: 13
- Saturated Fat: 3
- Sodium: 596
- Fiber: 3
- Sugar: 4
- Protein: 37

16. Mediterranean Chicken Salad

Serving: 4 | Prep: 10mins | Ready in:

Ingredients

- 1 1/2 cups sun-dried tomato and oregano salad dressing
- 4 skinless, boneless chicken breast halves
- 2 red bell peppers, halved and seeded
- 1 head romaine lettuce - rinsed, dried, and torn into bite-size pieces
- 1 cup black olives, drained
- 4 ounces feta cheese, crumbled
- 1/2 cup sun-dried tomato and oregano salad dressing

Direction

- Place chicken breasts in a shallow dish and evenly cover with 1 cup of salad dressing. Cover tightly and refrigerate for 20 minutes to 1 hour to marinate.
- Set grill to preheat to high heat. Meanwhile, place feta cheese, olives and lettuce in a salad bowl.
- Remove chicken from marinade and place on grill. Cook for 6 to 8 minutes each side. Place peppers on grill and baste with the reserved 1/2 cup dressing (remember not to use leftover marinade from chicken) Cook the peppers for a few minutes - keep an eye on them to avoid burning.
- Remove peppers and chicken from grill and allow to cool until save to handle. Slice into strips. Place peppers and chicken on top of salad and serve with remaining 1/2 cup of dressing.

Nutrition Information

- Calories: 720 calories;
- Total Fat: 51.5
- Sodium: 2213
- Total Carbohydrate: 23
- Cholesterol: 94
- Protein: 33.2

17. No Cook Black Bean Salad

Serving: 4 | Prep: 30mins | Ready in:

Ingredients

- ½ cup thinly sliced red onion
- 1 medium ripe avocado, pitted and roughly chopped
- ¼ cup cilantro leaves
- ¼ cup lime juice
- 2 tablespoons extra-virgin olive oil
- 1 clove garlic, minced
- ½ teaspoon salt
- 8 cups mixed salad greens
- 2 medium ears corn, kernels removed, or 2 cups frozen corn, thawed and patted dry
- 1 pint grape tomatoes, halved
- 1 (15 ounce) can black beans, rinsed

Direction

- Put the onion in a medium bowl and add enough water to cover. Set aside. In a mini food processor, mix avocado, salt, garlic, oil, cilantro, and lime juice and then process while scraping down the sides as needed until the resulting mixture is creamy and smooth.
- Before you serve, in a large bowl, mix beans, tomatoes, salad greens, and corn. Drain onions and add them in the bowl along with avocado dressing. Mix to coat.

Nutrition Information

- Calories: 322 calories;
- Protein: 11
- Saturated Fat: 2
- Cholesterol: 0
- Total Carbohydrate: 41
- Sugar: 11
- Total Fat: 16
- Sodium: 407
- Fiber: 13

18. Protein Bistro Lunch Box

Serving: 1 | Prep: 5mins | Ready in:

Ingredients

- 1 hard-boiled egg, peeled
- ½ cup edamame in shell, cooked
- 1½ tablespoons oil-cured black olives
- ¼ cup low-salt canned tuna in water (½ can), drained
- 2 (¼ inch thick) slices baguette
- 4 cherry tomatoes
- Lemon wedge

Direction

- In a 4-cup divided sealable container, arrange tuna, egg, olives, edamame, cherry tomatoes, baguette slices and lemon wedge. (olives and tuna can be kept separated by placing them in a silicone baking cup before arranging, if wanted). Refrigerate until ready to serve.

Nutrition Information

- Calories: 493 calories;
- Sugar: 4
- Sodium: 719
- Cholesterol: 211
- Saturated Fat: 2
- Fiber: 11
- Total Carbohydrate: 50
- Protein: 45
- Total Fat: 14

19. Quinoa Avocado Salad

Serving: 4 | Prep: 20mins | Ready in:

Ingredients

- 3 tablespoons lime juice
- 2 tablespoons avocado oil
- ¾ teaspoon garlic powder
- ½ teaspoon salt
- ¼ teaspoon ground pepper
- 3 cups cooked quinoa, cooled
- 2 medium avocados, chopped
- 1 cup grape tomatoes, halved
- 1 cup diced cucumber
- ½ cup chopped fresh cilantro
- 1 scallion, sliced

Direction

- In a medium bowl, mix together the pepper, salt, garlic powder, oil and lime juice. Then mix in the scallion, cilantro, cucumber, tomatoes, avocados and quinoa; gently mix until well combined.

Nutrition Information

- Calories: 414 calories;
- Sodium: 313
- Fiber: 12
- Protein: 9
- Total Fat: 25
- Total Carbohydrate: 44
- Sugar: 4
- Saturated Fat: 3
- Cholesterol: 0

20. Salmon Salad Stuffed Avocado

Serving: 1 | Prep: 10mins | Ready in:

Ingredients

- ⅓ cup canned salmon
- 1 tablespoon pesto
- 1 tablespoon nonfat plain Greek yogurt
- 2 teaspoons minced shallot
- ½ avocado
- 1 cup baby spinach
- 5 thin wheat crackers

Direction

- Mix shallot, pesto, salmon, and yogurt. Arrange it over avocado and baby spinach with crackers on the side before serving.

Nutrition Information

- Calories: 322 calories;
- Total Fat: 22
- Fiber: 7
- Cholesterol: 27
- Sugar: 2
- Protein: 22
- Saturated Fat: 3
- Sodium: 449
- Total Carbohydrate: 11

---

21. Smoked Salmon Avocado Spring Rolls

Serving: 3 | Prep: 25mins | Ready in:

Ingredients

- 2 tablespoons avocado oil
- 1 tablespoon rice vinegar
- 2 teaspoons white miso
- ¼ teaspoon garlic powder
- 4 cups baby arugula
- 6 spring roll wrappers
- 2 ounces sliced smoked salmon
- 1 avocado, sliced

Direction

- In a large bowl, mix together garlic powder, vinegar, miso and oil. Stir in arugula, tossing well to coat.
- Place hot water in a shallow dish and soak the wrapper for 20-30 seconds until softened, one wrapper at a time. Lift it out and let the excess water drip off. Lay it on a clean, dry cutting board.
- Lay out 1/6 of the salmon and avocado slices across the center of the wrapper and top it

with about half cup of the arugula. Fold the bottom of the wrapper over the filling and roll it into a tight cylinder, folding its sides to secure the fillings. Do the same steps with the remaining fillings and wrappers.

Nutrition Information

- Calories: 293 calories;
- Total Fat: 21
- Saturated Fat: 3
- Cholesterol: 4
- Sugar: 2
- Protein: 8
- Sodium: 263
- Fiber: 5
- Total Carbohydrate: 22

---

22. Spiralized Beet Salad

Serving: 8 | Prep: 15mins | Ready in:

Ingredients

- ⅓ cup minced shallot (1 medium)
- ¼ cup extra-virgin olive oil
- ½ teaspoon freshly grated lemon zest
- 2 tablespoons lemon juice
- ½ teaspoon salt
- ¼ teaspoon ground pepper
- 2 pounds beets (3 to 4 medium)
- ½ cup slivered almonds, toasted
- ½ cup chopped fresh flat-leaf parsley

Direction

- In a small bowl, add the shallot. Whisk in pepper, salt, lemon juice, lemon zest and oil to get them incorporated. Put to one side.
- Rinse beets to clean and peel them. Using a thin blade, spiralize the beets. Chop the spirals into 3-inch lengths. Transfer them to a large bowl. Toss the spiralized beets with dressing until coated well.

- Right before serving, put in parsley and almonds; mix to coat.

Nutrition Information

- Calories: 158 calories;
- Saturated Fat: 1
- Sodium: 237
- Fiber: 4
- Total Carbohydrate: 14
- Sugar: 9
- Protein: 4
- Total Fat: 11
- Cholesterol: 0

23. Strawberry Fields Lettuce Cups

Serving: 12 | Prep: 25mins | Ready in:

Ingredients

- 2 tablespoons seasoned rice vinegar
- 1 tablespoon olive oil
- 1½ teaspoons Dijon-style mustard
- 1 teaspoon poppy seeds
- ½ teaspoon ground black pepper
- 1¼ cups finely chopped seedless cucumber
- 1¼ cups finely chopped celery
- 1 cup finely chopped radishes
- 1½ cups chopped fresh strawberries
- ½ cup chopped pecans, toasted
- ¼ cup snipped fresh basil
- 24 butterhead (Boston or bibb) or green leaf lettuce leaves
- 2 ounces goat cheese (chèvre), crumbled
- Fresh basil sprigs (optional)

Direction

- Combine pepper, oil, poppy seeds, mustard, and vinegar together in a large bowl. Stir in celery, radishes, and cucumber, tossing the ingredients well until coated evenly.

- Add pecans, snipped basil and strawberries into the cucumber mixture just before serving. Scoop about 1/4 cup of the strawberry mixture onto every lettuce leaf. Top each with 1 tsp. of goat cheese. You can garnish it with basil sprigs if you want; serve right away.

Nutrition Information

- Calories: 73 calories;
- Fiber: 1
- Sugar: 2
- Protein: 2
- Total Fat: 6
- Saturated Fat: 1
- Sodium: 79
- Cholesterol: 4
- Total Carbohydrate: 4

24. Sweet Savory Hummus Plate

Serving: 4 | Prep: 10mins | Ready in:

Ingredients

- ¾ cup white bean dip (see Tip)
- 1 cup green beans or sugar snap peas, stem ends trimmed
- 8 mini bell peppers
- 20 Castelvetrano olives
- 8 small watermelon wedges or 2 cups cubed watermelon
- 1 cup red grapes
- 20 gluten-free crackers
- ½ cup salted roasted pepitas
- 8 coconut-date balls

Direction

- Separate the items equally into 4 plates. Serve with hard cider if desired.

Nutrition Information

- Calories: 654 calories;
- Cholesterol: 0
- Protein: 14
- Total Fat: 30
- Fiber: 11
- Sugar: 39
- Saturated Fat: 3
- Sodium: 568
- Total Carbohydrate: 84

25. Tomato, Cucumber White Bean Salad With Basil Vinaigrette

Serving: 4 | Prep: 25mins | Ready in:

Ingredients

- ½ cup packed fresh basil leaves
- ¼ cup extra-virgin olive oil
- 3 tablespoons red-wine vinegar
- 1 tablespoon finely chopped shallot
- 2 teaspoons Dijon mustard
- 1 teaspoon honey
- ¼ teaspoon salt
- ¼ teaspoon ground pepper
- 10 cups mixed salad greens
- 1 (15 ounce) can low-sodium cannellini beans, rinsed
- 1 cup halved cherry or grape tomatoes
- ½ cucumber, halved lengthwise and sliced (1 cup)

Direction

- In a mini food processor, place honey, pepper, salt, oil, basil, shallot, mustard, and vinegar and then process until the contents are mostly smooth. Pour into a large bowl. Add cucumber, tomatoes, greens, and beans. Stir to coat.

Nutrition Information

- Calories: 246 calories;

- Sugar: 5
- Total Fat: 15
- Fiber: 8
- Total Carbohydrate: 22
- Cholesterol: 0
- Protein: 8
- Saturated Fat: 2
- Sodium: 271

26. Tropical Chicken Salad Wraps

Serving: 4 | Prep: 25mins | Ready in:

Ingredients

- 2 cups shredded, cooked chicken breast
- 2 cups finely shredded Napa cabbage
- 1 (8 ounce) can crushed pineapple, drained
- ⅓ cup light mayonnaise
- 2 tablespoons flaked coconut, toasted
- 1 tablespoon lime juice
- 1 tablespoon chopped fresh cilantro
- 1 teaspoon Jamaican jerk seasoning
- 8 leaves Bibb or Boston lettuce
- Lime wedges (optional)

Direction

- Whisk mayonnaise, lime juice, shredded cabbage, Jamaican jerk seasoning, drained pineapple, coconut, cilantro, and chicken in a large bowl.
- Distribute the chicken mixture among the leaves and fold its sides. Roll it up and secure it with toothpicks, if necessary. You can serve it together with lime wedges if you want.

Nutrition Information

- Calories: 243 calories;
- Cholesterol: 66
- Total Carbohydrate: 14
- Sugar: 11
- Protein: 23

- Saturated Fat: 3
- Fiber: 1
- Total Fat: 10
- Sodium: 269

- Sugar: 3
- Protein: 18
- Total Fat: 16
- Saturated Fat: 2
- Fiber: 5
- Cholesterol: 21
- Total Carbohydrate: 25

27. Tuna Salad Pockets

Serving: 4 | Prep: 15mins | Ready in:

Ingredients

- 1 (12 ounce) can solid white tuna (water-pack), drained
- ¼ cup finely chopped onion
- ¼ cup thinly sliced celery
- ¼ cup shredded carrot
- 1 tablespoon capers, rinsed and drained
- 2 tablespoons olive oil
- 2 tablespoons lime juice
- 1 tablespoon Dijon-style mustard
- 1 tablespoon Champagne vinegar or white wine vinegar
- 1½ cups torn mixed salad greens
- ½ cup slivered almonds, toasted
- 2 large whole wheat pita bread rounds, halved crosswise

Direction

- Mix capers, carrot, celery, onion and tuna in a medium bowl; put aside. Vinaigrette: Mix vinegar, Dijon mustard, lime juice and olive oil in small screw-top jar. Cover; shake well to mix. Put vinaigrette on tuna mixture; gently toss to mix. Add almonds and greens; gently toss to mix.
- Halve pita breads; in each of the 4 shallow salad bowls, put pita bread. Put tuna mixture over pita bread halves; creates 4 servings.

Nutrition Information

- Calories: 305 calories;
- Sodium: 447

28. Turkey, Cheese Veggie Plate

Serving: 4 | Prep: 20mins | Ready in:

Ingredients

- 2 teaspoons honey mustard (optional)
- 8 thin slices deli smoked turkey (4 ounces)
- 8 thin slices mild Cheddar cheese (4 ounces)
- 1 cup baby carrots or 4 carrots, cut into sticks
- 1 cup sliced cucumber
- 1 apple, cut into 4 or 8 wedges (see Tips)
- 1 cup hummus (see Tips)
- 32 low-sodium whole-wheat crackers
- 20 whole almonds, preferably salted Marcona almonds
- ½ cup corn nuts
- 4 clementines
- 4 cookies (see Tips)

Direction

- Here's how you can make turkey-cheese roll-ups if you prefer to do so: Put 1/2 teaspoon of honey mustard on each slice of turkey. Put a slice of cheese on each slice of turkey then roll. Put a toothpick to keep the turkey-cheese roll-ups in place.
- Put carrots, apple, cucumber, hummus, turkey and cheese (or the roll-ups) in easy to carry containers and put in a cooler. Add in almonds, clementines, crackers, cookies and corn nuts. Pair it with 100% juice boxes for kids to enjoy and Pinot Noir for grownups.

Nutrition Information

- Calories: 675 calories;
- Total Fat: 38
- Cholesterol: 63
- Total Carbohydrate: 62
- Sugar: 24
- Saturated Fat: 11
- Sodium: 727
- Fiber: 10
- Protein: 22

29. Turkey Cranberry Wrap

Serving: 1 | Prep: 5mins | Ready in:

Ingredients

- 2½ tablespoons whipped reduced-fat cream cheese spread
- 1 Flatout® Light Original Flatbread
- 1 cup torn romaine lettuce
- 3 ounces sliced cooked turkey or chicken breast meat
- 2 tablespoons reduced-sugar or light cranberry sauce

Direction

- Spread cream cheese on one side of the flatbread. Put cranberry sauce, turkey and romaine on top, then roll up the flatbread to enclose the filling.

Nutrition Information

- Calories: 270 calories;
- Sodium: 421
- Fiber: 12
- Protein: 36
- Total Fat: 6
- Saturated Fat: 3
- Cholesterol: 82
- Total Carbohydrate: 34
- Sugar: 12

30. Vegan Creamy Coleslaw

Serving: 6 | Prep: 20mins | Ready in:

Ingredients

- 6 tablespoons vegan or eggless mayonnaise
- 1 tablespoon Dijon mustard
- 1 tablespoon cider vinegar
- 1 teaspoon sugar
- ½ teaspoon caraway seeds or celery seed
- Pinch of salt
- Pinch of ground pepper
- 2 cups thinly sliced red cabbage (about ¼ of a medium head)
- 2 cups thinly sliced green cabbage (about ¼ of a medium head)
- 1 cup shredded carrots (about 2 medium)

Direction

- In a big bowl, mix sugar, vinegar, mustard and mayonnaise. Put in pepper, salt and celery seed or caraway seeds. Finish off by adding carrots, green cabbage and red cabbage then tossing everything together properly.

Nutrition Information

- Calories: 114 calories;
- Cholesterol: 0
- Total Carbohydrate: 6
- Sugar: 3
- Protein: 1
- Total Fat: 10
- Saturated Fat: 1
- Sodium: 160
- Fiber: 2

Chapter 2: Budget Lunch Recipes

***

31. Alphabet Soup

Serving: 12 | Prep: 10mins | Ready in:

Ingredients

- 1 pound ground round
- 3 cubes beef bouillon
- 3 cups hot water
- 1 (46 fluid ounce) bottle spicy vegetable juice cocktail
- 1 pound frozen mixed vegetables, thawed
- 8 ounces uncooked alphabet pasta
- 6 cups water
- salt and pepper to taste

Direction

- Transfer the meat into a large stock pot and then cook with medium-high heat until browned evenly. Drain meat and save about two tablespoons of the juices.
- Combine bouillon cubes with three cups of hot water until the cubes are dissolved. Pour into the stock pot of meat. Mix in 6 cups of water, spicy vegetable juice cocktail, alphabet pasta and mixed vegetables. Let it simmer for 20 minutes or until the pasta becomes tender. Season with pepper and salt to taste. Serve.

Nutrition Information

- Calories: 182 calories;
- Total Fat: 5.1
- Sodium: 580
- Total Carbohydrate: 23.5
- Cholesterol: 23
- Protein: 11.2

32. Amish Broccoli Salad

Serving: 6 | Prep: 20mins | Ready in:

Ingredients

- ¼ cup mayonnaise
- ¼ cup low-fat plain Greek yogurt
- 1 tablespoon lemon juice
- 1 teaspoon sugar
- ¼ teaspoon ground pepper
- 2 cups chopped broccoli (florets and peeled stems)
- 2 cups chopped cauliflower
- ½ cup shredded sharp Cheddar cheese
- 2 slices cooked bacon, chopped
- ¼ cup finely chopped red onion

Direction

- In a large bowl, combine lemon juice, pepper, sugar, mayonnaise, and yogurt. Stir in bacon, onion, broccoli, cheese and cauliflower, tossing them well to coat.

Nutrition Information

- Calories: 144 calories;
- Total Fat: 12
- Sodium: 186
- Protein: 6
- Saturated Fat: 3
- Fiber: 1
- Cholesterol: 0
- Total Carbohydrate: 5
- Sugar: 3

33. Classic House Salad With Chicken

Serving: 1 | Prep: 15mins | Ready in:

Ingredients

- 2 cups Classic House Salad (see associated recipe)
- ¾ cup sliced or diced cooked chicken breast (see associated recipe)
- ¼ cup cherry tomatoes, halved
- ¼ cup sliced cucumber
- ¼ cup whole-wheat croutons (see associated recipe)
- 2 tablespoons fresh parsley leaves
- 2 tablespoons red-wine vinaigrette (see associated recipe)

Direction

- Place salad in an airtight container; put in parsley, chicken, croutons, tomatoes, and cucumber. Arrange vinaigrette separately in a small container. Toss salad with the vinaigrette to coat.

Nutrition Information

- Calories: 488 calories;
- Total Fat: 31
- Saturated Fat: 5
- Sodium: 780
- Cholesterol: 37
- Fiber: 4
- Total Carbohydrate: 28
- Sugar: 4
- Protein: 19

34. Green Machine Salad With Baked Tofu

Serving: 1 | Prep: 15mins | Ready in:

Ingredients

- 2 cups Green Machine Salad (see associated recipe)
- 4 ounces baked tofu, cut into ½-inch-thick slices
- 2 tablespoons chopped fresh parsley
- 2 tablespoons chopped fresh dill
- 2 tablespoons slivered almonds, toasted
- 2 tablespoons grated or shaved Parmesan cheese
- 2 tablespoons Honey-Mustard Vinaigrette (see associated recipe)

Direction

- In a large mason jar or an airtight storage container, pack salad then add dill, parsley and tofu. Place Parmesan and almonds on top. In a small jar, pack vinaigrette separately. Toss the vinaigrette into the salad just before serving.

Nutrition Information

- Calories: 464 calories;
- Protein: 20
- Saturated Fat: 5
- Total Carbohydrate: 22
- Sugar: 9
- Total Fat: 34
- Sodium: 310
- Fiber: 8
- Cholesterol: 9

35. Macaroni Salad With Creamy Avocado Dressing

Serving: 12 | Prep: 25mins | Ready in:

Ingredients

- 8 ounces whole-wheat elbow macaroni (about 2 cups)

- 1 cup chopped red bell pepper
- ½ cup thinly sliced celery
- 2 scallions, chopped
- 2 tablespoons chopped fresh parsley or cilantro
- 1 ripe medium avocado
- ¼ cup mayonnaise
- 2 tablespoons rice vinegar
- ¾ teaspoon salt
- ½ teaspoon dried minced garlic
- ¼ teaspoon ground pepper

Direction

- Follow the package directions to cook macaroni in a big pot of boiling water. Drain and rinse under cold water, then drain well again. Move to a big bowl, then put in parsley (or cilantro), scallions, celery and bell pepper.
- Halve avocado, remove pit and scoop flesh into a mini food processor. Put in pepper, dried garlic, salt, vinegar and mayonnaise, then process until smooth. Put the avocado dressing to a big bowl with the macaroni salad and stir until coated completely.

Nutrition Information

- Calories: 130 calories;
- Sodium: 182
- Fiber: 3
- Cholesterol: 2
- Saturated Fat: 1
- Total Carbohydrate: 17
- Sugar: 1
- Protein: 3
- Total Fat: 6

36. PB Bistro Lunch Box

Serving: 1 | Prep: 5mins | Ready in:

Ingredients

- 1 slice whole-grain bread, halved
- 2 tablespoons natural peanut butter
- 1 tablespoon your favorite fruit jam
- ¾ cup low-fat plain Greek yogurt
- ½ cup diced fresh mango
- Ground cinnamon for sprinkling
- 2 stalks celery, cut into 4-inch lengths
- 1 cup lightly salted popcorn

Direction

- Spread peanut butter over half of a slice of bread, and jam on the other half. Fold the bread together.
- Put the yogurt in a small sealable cup or in a sealable container divided into 4 cups. Put mango on top and sprinkle on cinnamon.
- Put the popcorn, celery, yogurt mixture and sandwich in container. Refrigerate it until you want to eat.

Nutrition Information

- Calories: 552 calories;
- Saturated Fat: 5
- Cholesterol: 17
- Sugar: 32
- Protein: 30
- Total Fat: 21
- Sodium: 331
- Fiber: 8
- Total Carbohydrate: 59

37. Pesto Pasta Salad

Serving: 5 | Prep: 20mins | Ready in:

Ingredients

- 8 ounces whole-wheat fusilli (about 3 cups)
- 1 cup small broccoli florets
- 2 cups packed fresh basil leaves
- ¼ cup pine nuts, toasted
- ¼ cup grated Parmesan cheese

- 2 tablespoons mayonnaise
- 2 tablespoons extra-virgin olive oil
- 2 tablespoons lemon juice
- 1 large clove garlic, quartered
- ¾ teaspoon salt
- ½ teaspoon ground pepper
- 1 cup quartered cherry tomatoes

Direction

- Boil water in a large saucepan. Following instruction on package, add and cook fusilli. Mix in broccoli 1 minute before done cooking pasta. Cook for 1 minute, then drain off and wash in cold running water to stop the cooking process.
- At the same time, in a mini food processor, add pepper, salt, garlic, lemon juice, oil, mayonnaise, Parmesan, pine nuts and basil. Run the processor until nearly smooth in consistency. Put in a big bowl. Add the broccoli and pasta, alongside tomatoes. Coat by tossing.

Nutrition Information

- Calories: 317 calories;
- Total Fat: 16
- Sodium: 474
- Fiber: 5
- Protein: 8
- Saturated Fat: 2
- Cholesterol: 6
- Total Carbohydrate: 38
- Sugar: 1

38. Power Greens Salad With Baked Tofu Honey Mustard Vinaigrette

Serving: 1 | Prep: 10mins | Ready in:

Ingredients

- 2 cups Power Greens Salad (see associated recipe)
- 4 ounces baked tofu, cut into ½-inch-thick slices
- 2 tablespoons slivered almonds, toasted
- 2 tablespoons unsweetened coconut
- 2 tablespoons Honey-Mustard Vinaigrette (see associated recipe)

Direction

- In a big mason jar or an airtight storage container, pack the salad. Put in coconut, almonds and tofu. In a small jar, separately pack the vinaigrette. Drizzle the vinaigrette on the salad then toss to coat prior to eating.

Nutrition Information

- Calories: 545 calories;
- Saturated Fat: 10
- Sodium: 145
- Cholesterol: 0
- Total Carbohydrate: 31
- Sugar: 13
- Protein: 21
- Total Fat: 41
- Fiber: 11

39. Power Greens Salad With Kale Brussels Sprouts

Serving: 4 | Prep: 20mins | Ready in:

Ingredients

- 5 cups chopped kale
- 1 pound Brussels sprouts, trimmed and thinly sliced (3 cups)
- 4 scallions, chopped
- ¼ cup dried sweetened cranberries

Direction

- In a large bowl, combine dried cranberries, scallions, Brussels sprouts and kale. Place between paper towels in layer and store in an airtight storage container.

Nutrition Information

- Calories: 94 calories;
- Saturated Fat: 0
- Fiber: 6
- Sugar: 5
- Sodium: 39
- Cholesterol: 0
- Total Carbohydrate: 21
- Protein: 5
- Total Fat: 1

40. Spring Green Salad With Hard Boiled Eggs

Serving: 1 | Prep: 10mins | Ready in:

Ingredients

- 2 cups Spring Vegetable Salad (see associated recipe)
- 2 hard-boiled eggs, sliced (see Tip)
- 2 tablespoons coarsely chopped fresh dill
- ¼ cup whole-wheat croutons (see associated recipe)
- 2 tablespoons Garlic-Dijon Vinaigrette (see associated recipe)

Direction

- In an airtight container, put in salad, croutons, dill and eggs. Store vinaigrette in another small container or jar. Toss vinaigrette with salad to coat; serve.

Nutrition Information

- Calories: 474 calories;
- Fiber: 6

- Cholesterol: 373
- Total Carbohydrate: 32
- Sugar: 6
- Protein: 19
- Total Fat: 30
- Saturated Fat: 6
- Sodium: 804

41. Vegan Bistro Lunch Box

Serving: 1 | Prep: 5mins | Ready in:

Ingredients

- ¼ cup hummus
- ½ whole-wheat pita bread, cut into 4 wedges
- 2 tablespoons mixed olives
- 1 Persian cucumber or ½ English cucumber, cut into spears
- ¼ large red bell pepper, sliced
- ¼ teaspoon chopped fresh dill

Direction

- In a sealable 4-cup divided container, place pita, hummus, cucumber, bell peppers and olives. Optional: separate hummus and olives by placing them in silicone baking cups before arranging inside the container. Garnish cucumber with dill. Refrigerate until ready to serve.

Nutrition Information

- Calories: 194 calories;
- Saturated Fat: 1
- Total Carbohydrate: 23
- Sugar: 4
- Protein: 8
- Total Fat: 9
- Sodium: 443
- Fiber: 7
- Cholesterol: 0

Chapter 3: Awesome Lunch Recipes

***

42. Almost Authentic Caesar Salad

Serving: 6 | Prep: 20mins | Ready in:

Ingredients

- 3 thick slices French bread, cut into cubes
- 2 tablespoons butter
- 1 clove garlic, minced
- salt and ground black pepper to taste
- 1 1/2 teaspoons dried parsley
- 1/2 lemon, juiced
- 1 tablespoon Dijon mustard
- 1 1/2 teaspoons Worcestershire sauce
- 1 1/2 teaspoons kosher salt
- 1 1/2 teaspoons anchovy paste
- 1 clove garlic, minced
- fresh ground black pepper to taste
- 1/3 cup canola oil
- 1 head romaine lettuce, coarsely chopped
- 1/2 cup freshly grated Parmesan cheese

Direction

- Set oven to 190°C (375°F) and start preheating.
- In a rimmed baking sheet, place French bread cubes in one layer. In a small saucepan, melt butter on medium ; cook, while stirring one clove of garlic for 1-2 minutes until aroma comes out. Add butter mixture onto bread cubes layer, then add parsley, black pepper and salt to season. Mix until coated.
- Bake for 10-15 minutes in the prepared oven until bread turns light brown on the outside and crispy in the center.
- In a bowl, stir together black pepper, 1 clove of garlic, anchovy paste, kosher salt, Worcestershire sauce, Dijon mustard and lemon juice. Sprinkle with canola oil gradually, while use the other hand to mix lemon juice until emulsified.
- In a bowl, incorporate half of the dressing, Parmesan cheese and romaine lettuce; mix until coated. Add the rest of the dressing and croutons; mix to coat.

Nutrition Information

- Calories: 243 calories;
- Total Fat: 18.7
- Sodium: 961
- Total Carbohydrate: 14.6
- Cholesterol: 17
- Protein: 5.8

43. Almost White Castle® Hamburgers

Serving: 24 | Prep: 15mins | Ready in:

Ingredients

- 1 1/2 pounds ground chuck
- 1/3 cup plain bread crumbs
- 1 egg
- 1 (1 ounce) package dry onion soup mix
- 2 tablespoons water
- 1/2 teaspoon ground black pepper
- 24 small square dinner rolls

Direction

- Preheat the oven on 200°C or 400°Fahrenheit.
- In a bowl, mix black pepper, ground chuck, water, bread crumbs, onion soup mix, and egg; press the mixture on a 10-in. by 15-in. jelly roll pan. Puncture holes over the mixture to ventilate as it cooks.

- Bake for 10mins in the 400°Fahrenheit oven until completely cooked and brown. An inserted instant-read thermometer in the middle should register at least 70°C or 160°Fahrenheit. Remove the excess grease.
- Slice the chuck mixture to squares that fit the rolls. Put one chuck patty in every roll.

Nutrition Information

- Calories: 155 calories;
- Total Carbohydrate: 16.4
- Cholesterol: 26
- Protein: 8.3
- Total Fat: 6.2
- Sodium: 283

44. Amazing Gnocchi Soup

Serving: 3 | Prep: 15mins | Ready in:

Ingredients

- 3 cups water
- 1 1/4 cups potato gnocchi
- 1 chopped cooked chicken breast
- 1 small tomato, diced
- 1/3 onion, diced
- 1/2 cup corn
- 1 green onion, chopped
- 2 teaspoons chicken bouillon granules
- 3 broccoli stalks
- 1/4 teaspoon dried thyme
- 1/8 teaspoon ground black pepper
- 1/8 teaspoon salt
- 1 pinch dried basil

Direction

- In a stockpot, mix together basil, salt, pepper, thyme, broccoli, chicken bouillon, green onion, corn, onion, tomato, chicken, gnocchi and water. Bring to a boil. Lower the heat; let it

simmer for 15 minutes to blend the flavor and cook the gnocchi well.

Nutrition Information

- Calories: 275 calories;
- Cholesterol: 42
- Protein: 18.1
- Total Fat: 9.4
- Sodium: 491
- Total Carbohydrate: 33.2

45. Andrea's Broccoli Slaw

Serving: 6 | Prep: 20mins | Ready in:

Ingredients

- 1/3 cup light mayonnaise
- 1/4 cup crumbled blue cheese, or more to taste
- 2 tablespoons white sugar, or more to taste
- 1 tablespoon olive oil
- 1 tablespoon stone-ground mustard
- 2 1/2 teaspoons red wine vinegar
- 1/2 teaspoon red pepper flakes
- 1/2 teaspoon onion powder
- 1/2 teaspoon celery salt
- 1/2 head cabbage, shredded
- 2 carrots, grated
- 1 cup chopped broccoli florets
- 1/2 cup raisins

Direction

- In a big bowl, combine celery salt, mayonnaise, onion powder, blue cheese, red pepper flakes, sugar, vinegar, olive oil, and mustard. Toss in raisins, cabbage, broccoli, and carrots to coat. Refrigerate for at least two hours. Serve.

Nutrition Information

- Calories: 183 calories;

- Total Fat: 8.8
- Sodium: 363
- Total Carbohydrate: 25.5
- Cholesterol: 9
- Protein: 3.8

46. Antipasto Salad II

Serving: 10 | Prep: 30mins | Ready in:

Ingredients

- 8 ounces Genoa salami, cut into bite-size pieces
- 8 ounces sopressata or other hard salami, cut into bite-size pieces
- 8 ounces sharp provolone cheese, cut into bite-size pieces
- 8 ounces fresh mozzarella cheese, cut into bite-size pieces
- 2 large tomatoes, cut into bite-size pieces
- 1 (14 ounce) can artichokes, drained and cut into bite-size pieces
- 1/2 (12 ounce) jar roasted red peppers, drained and sliced
- 1/2 cup pitted and coarsely chopped Kalamata olives
- 1/4 cup pitted and chopped green olives
- 1 tablespoon extra-virgin olive oil
- 3 tablespoons red wine vinegar
- freshly-ground black pepper, to taste
- 1/4 cup shredded fresh basil leaves

Direction

- Mix artichokes, tomatoes, mozzarella, provolone, sopressata salami and Genoa in a bowl. Slice roasted red peppers; add in the bowl with 3 tablespoons of the juice.
- Mix chopped olives in; drizzle olive oil on the whole dish then black pepper and red wine vinegar. You can prepare salad ahead of time then refrigerate till serving.
- Tear fresh basil leaves to bite-sized pieces; add to salad before serving. Mix well; serve.

Nutrition Information

- Calories: 383 calories;
- Sodium: 1783
- Total Carbohydrate: 7.9
- Cholesterol: 74
- Protein: 21.7
- Total Fat: 29.1

47. Authentic German Potato Salad

Serving: 4 | Prep: 30mins | Ready in:

Ingredients

- 3 cups diced peeled potatoes
- 4 slices bacon
- 1 small onion, diced
- 1/4 cup white vinegar
- 2 tablespoons water
- 3 tablespoons white sugar
- 1 teaspoon salt
- 1/8 teaspoon ground black pepper
- 1 tablespoon chopped fresh parsley

Direction

- Put the potatoes in a pot and fill with sufficient amount of water to immerse the potatoes. Allow the water to boil and let the potatoes cook in the boiling water for about 10 minutes until you can prick the potatoes with ease using a fork. Drain the cooked potatoes and put aside to let it cool down.
- In a big and deep skillet placed over medium-high heat setting, put in the bacon and let it cook while flipping the bacon if need be until it becomes crispy and turns brown in color. Take the cooked bacon from the skillet and put it aside.
- Sauté the onion in the bacon drippings over medium heat setting until it turns brown in color. Put in the sugar, vinegar, pepper, water

and salt. Let the mixture boil, then put in the parsley and cooked potatoes. Break 1/2 of the cooked bacon to smaller pieces and add it into the potato mixture. Let the mixture cook until fully heated, then place it in a serving dish. Break the remaining 1/2 of the cooked bacon to smaller pieces directly on top of the potato mixture; serve it while still warm.

Nutrition Information

- Calories: 183 calories;
- Total Carbohydrate: 32.2
- Cholesterol: 10
- Protein: 5.4
- Total Fat: 3.9
- Sodium: 796

---

48. Avocado, Beet And Arugula Salad With Chevre Tartine

Serving: 4 | Prep: 20mins | Ready in:

Ingredients

- 4 ounces goat cheese, softened
- 1 teaspoon dried basil
- 4 (1/2 inch thick) slices crusty bread
- 1 tablespoon Dijon mustard
- 2 tablespoons balsamic vinegar
- salt and pepper to taste
- 1/4 cup olive oil
- 1 (15 ounce) can sliced beets, drained and diced
- 1 (10 ounce) package mixed salad greens with arugula
- 2 avocados - peeled, pitted and diced
- 1/3 cup chopped toasted hazelnuts

Direction

- Set the broiler to high heat for preheating. Use a foil to line the baking sheet.

- In a bowl, mix the basil and goat cheese. Spread the cheese mixture into the 4 slices of bread evenly. Arrange the bread slices into the prepared baking sheet.
- Let them cook under the preheated broiler for 3-5 minutes until the cheese starts to turn golden brown. Remove from the broiler and put them aside.
- For the vinaigrette, mix the vinegar and mustard in a small bowl until well-combined. Season the mixture with salt and pepper to taste. Pour in olive oil gradually while whisking the dressing until smooth.
- In a large bowl, toss in mixed greens and diced beets and drizzle salad with vinaigrette. Toss the salad until well-coated. Divide the salad onto the 4 chilled plates. Place the hazelnuts and avocado on each top. Serve them with goat-cheese tartines.

Nutrition Information

- Calories: 550 calories;
- Sodium: 573
- Total Carbohydrate: 31.3
- Cholesterol: 22
- Protein: 13.6
- Total Fat: 44.1

---

49. Avocado Shrimp Salad

Serving: 4 | Prep: 25mins | Ready in:

Ingredients

- 2 avocados - peeled, pitted, and cubed
- 2 tomatoes, diced
- 1 small sweet onion, chopped
- 1 pound cooked salad shrimp
- 1 pinch salt and pepper to taste
- 2 tablespoons lime juice

Direction

- In a large bowl, stir shrimp, onion, tomatoes and avocadoes together. Add pepper and salt to taste. Add lime juice and stir. Serve cold.

Nutrition Information

- Calories: 319 calories;
- Cholesterol: 196
- Protein: 29.1
- Total Fat: 17.1
- Sodium: 203
- Total Carbohydrate: 14.9

50. Aw Some Coleslaw

Serving: 12 | Prep: 15mins | Ready in:

Ingredients

- 1/2 cup mayonnaise
- 1/3 cup white sugar
- 1/4 cup milk
- 2 1/2 tablespoons lemon juice
- 1 1/2 tablespoons vinegar
- salt and pepper to taste
- 9 1/2 cups shredded cabbage
- 1/2 cup grated carrots
- 1/4 cup minced sweet onion

Direction

- In a big bowl, beat pepper, salt, vinegar, lemon juice, milk, sugar and mayonnaise together.
- Add onion, carrots and cabbage, tossing until thoroughly combined. Before serving, keep it in the fridge for a minimum of 3 hours or all through the night.

Nutrition Information

- Calories: 108 calories;
- Protein: 1.1
- Total Fat: 7.4
- Sodium: 80

- Total Carbohydrate: 10.3
- Cholesterol: 4

51. Awesome Grilled Cheese Sandwiches

Serving: 9 | Prep: 10mins | Ready in:

Ingredients

- 18 slices bread
- 4 tablespoons butter
- 9 slices Cheddar cheese

Direction

- Set the oven to 230°C or 450°F to preheat.
- Coat one side of 9 bread slices with butter and put them on a baking sheet with butter-side facing down. Put on each bread slice with cheese. Spread on 9 leftover slices of bread with butter and put them on top of the cheese with buttered-side facing up.
- In the preheated oven, bake for 6-8 minutes. Flip the sandwiches and bake until they turn golden brown, about 6 to 8 more minutes.

Nutrition Information

- Calories: 293 calories;
- Total Fat: 16.2
- Sodium: 553
- Total Carbohydrate: 25.7
- Cholesterol: 43
- Protein: 10.9

52. Awesome Spicy Beef Kabobs OR Haitian Voodoo Sticks

Serving: 4 | Prep: 20mins | Ready in:

Ingredients

- 2 tablespoons beef bouillon granules
- 2 tablespoons water
- 3 cloves garlic, minced
- 2 teaspoons cayenne pepper
- 1/2 teaspoon salt
- 1 teaspoon black pepper
- 1 1/2 pounds beef sirloin, cut into 1/2-inch cubes
- 10 wooden skewers, soaked in water for 1 hour
- 2 tablespoons vegetable oil

Direction

- Let bouillon dissolve in water. Mix in salt, black pepper, garlic, and cayenne pepper. Toss the meat in, cover the container, and marinate, refrigerated, for at least a couple of hours.
- Pre-heat grill on high.
- Thread 6 to 8 cubes of beef onto a skewer. Roll skewers over a plate of oil, coating all sides.
- Grill until beef is light pink, turning often, for 12 to 15 minutes.

Nutrition Information

- Calories: 327 calories;
- Sodium: 1018
- Total Carbohydrate: 2.5
- Cholesterol: 91
- Protein: 29.3
- Total Fat: 21.6

53. B.L.T. Salad With Basil Mayo Dressing

Serving: 4 | Prep: 15mins | Ready in:

Ingredients

- 1/2 pound bacon
- 1/2 cup mayonnaise
- 2 tablespoons red wine vinegar
- 1/4 cup finely chopped fresh basil
- 4 slices French bread, cut into 1/2 inch pieces
- 1 teaspoon salt
- 1 teaspoon ground black pepper
- 1 tablespoon canola oil
- 1 pound romaine lettuce - rinsed, dried, and torn into bite-size pieces
- 1 pint cherry tomatoes, quartered

Direction

- In a large, deep skillet, place bacon and cook to brown evenly over medium high heat. Let drain then crumble the bacon; put aside. Save 2 tbsp. of drippings.
- Whisk basil, vinegar, mayonnaise and reserved bacon drippings together in a small bowl. Cover and allow the dressing to stand at room temperature.
- Toss pepper and salt with bread pieces over medium heat in a large skillet. Drizzle oil over; keep tossing and cook till it turns golden brown over medium-low heat.
- Mix croutons, bacon, tomatoes and romaine together in a large bowl. Top the salad with dressing and toss well.

Nutrition Information

- Calories: 440 calories;
- Total Carbohydrate: 23.4
- Cholesterol: 31
- Protein: 12.2
- Total Fat: 34.1
- Sodium: 1344

54. BLT Wraps

Serving: 4 | Prep: 15mins | Ready in:

Ingredients

- 1 pound thick sliced bacon, cut into 1 inch pieces
- 4 (12 inch) flour tortillas
- 1 cup shredded Cheddar cheese
- 1/2 head iceberg lettuce, shredded
- 1 tomato, diced

Direction

- Cook bacon till evenly brown in a big, deep skillet on medium high heat. Drain; put aside.
- On microwave-safe plate, put 1 tortilla; sprinkle 1/4 cup cheese on tortilla. Cook for 1-2 minutes till cheese melts in microwave. Put tomato, lettuce and 1/4 bacon over immediately. Fold tortilla sides over; roll up. Repeat using leftover ingredients; before serving, halve each wrap.

Nutrition Information

- Calories: 695 calories;
- Cholesterol: 71
- Protein: 31.4
- Total Fat: 34.1
- Sodium: 1788
- Total Carbohydrate: 64.2

55. Bacon Avocado Salad

Serving: 6 | Prep: 20mins | Ready in:

Ingredients

- 1 pound bacon, chopped
- 1 cucumber, diced
- 1 cup quartered cherry tomatoes
- 1/4 cup seasoned rice vinegar
- salt and ground black pepper to taste
- 5 avocados - peeled, pitted, and diced
- 1/2 cup chopped fresh cilantro
- 4 green onions, chopped

Direction

- In a large skillet, put the bacon and cook for about 10 minutes over medium-high heat, flipping occasionally until equally browned. Use paper towels to drain bacon.
- In a bowl, mix pepper, salt, rice vinegar, tomatoes and cucumber. Lightly mix green onions, cilantro, avocado and bacon into cucumber mixture.

Nutrition Information

- Calories: 427 calories;
- Sodium: 828
- Total Carbohydrate: 20.5
- Cholesterol: 27
- Protein: 13.3
- Total Fat: 35.1

56. Bacon Dijon Egg Salad Sandwich

Serving: 6 | Prep: 10mins | Ready in:

Ingredients

- 10 hard-cooked eggs, chopped
- 6 slices crispy cooked bacon, chopped
- 1/3 cup creamy salad dressing (such as Miracle Whip®), or more to taste
- 1/4 cup chopped red onion
- 2 tablespoons Dijon mustard
- 1 tablespoon honey mustard
- 1 tablespoon chopped fresh chives
- 1 teaspoon lemon juice
- 1/2 teaspoon dill
- 1/2 teaspoon seasoned salt
- 6 Kaiser rolls, split

Direction

- Combine together bacon, eggs, red onion, salad dressing, honey mustard, chives, Dijon mustard, dill, lemon juice and seasoned salt using a bowl. Spread into Kaiser rolls before serving.

Nutrition Information

- Calories: 429 calories;
- Total Fat: 26.9
- Sodium: 888
- Total Carbohydrate: 27
- Cholesterol: 377
- Protein: 17.9

57. Bacon Potato Salad With Ranch

Serving: 8 | Prep: 30mins | Ready in:

Ingredients

- 6 russet potatoes, peeled and cubed
- 4 eggs
- 4 slices bacon, cooked and crumbled
- 1/4 cup finely chopped dill pickles
- 1/4 cup chopped green onion
- 1/4 cup finely shredded Cheddar cheese
- 2 tablespoons chopped fresh parsley
- salt and ground black pepper to taste
- 1/3 cup fat-free ranch dressing
- 2 tablespoons light mayonnaise
- 1 tablespoon prepared mustard

Direction

- In a big pot, add potatoes and salted water to cover, then bring to a boil. Lower heat to moderately low and simmer about 10 minutes, until softened. Drain, then cut potatoes into cubes. Put potato cubes in a big bowl.
- In a saucepan, add eggs and water to cover. Bring to a boil and simmer for 10 minutes. Put eggs under cold running water to cool and peel. Mince eggs into small bits and put into potato cubes.

- Put ground black pepper, salt, parsley, Cheddar cheese, green onion, pickles and bacon into the bowl. Stir to blend.
- In a bowl, whisk together mustard, mayonnaise and ranch dressing. Pour over potato mixture and blend well to coat. Before serving, chill for a minimum of 2 hours.

Nutrition Information

- Calories: 232 calories;
- Total Fat: 7.4
- Sodium: 403
- Total Carbohydrate: 32.7
- Cholesterol: 104
- Protein: 9.4

58. Bacon And Eggs Potato Salad

Serving: 8 | Prep: 10mins | Ready in:

Ingredients

- 2 1/2 pounds red potatoes, quartered
- 1 cup mayonnaise
- 1 cup petite green peas
- 5 hard-boiled eggs, chopped
- 4 slices cooked bacon, chopped
- 1/4 cup minced onion
- 2 tablespoons mustard
- 1/2 teaspoon salt
- 1/4 teaspoon ground black pepper

Direction

- In a large pot, put potatoes, pour in salted water to cover, then bring to a boil. Reduce heat to medium-low then let the pot simmer for about 10 minutes till the potatoes get soft. Drain then set the pot aside to cool down.
- In a bowl, combine salt, black pepper, mustard, onion, bacon, hard-boiled eggs, peas, mayonnaise and potatoes. Keep in the fridge

for about an hour to let bacon soften and flavors blend.

Nutrition Information

- Calories: 381 calories;
- Cholesterol: 146
- Protein: 9.2
- Total Fat: 26.8
- Sodium: 483
- Total Carbohydrate: 27.2

59. Bacon, Potato, And Egg Taco Ole

Serving: 4 | Prep: 15mins | Ready in:

Ingredients

- 8 bacon strips
- 8 eggs
- 1/3 cup milk
- 3 tablespoons water
- salt and pepper to taste
- 1/3 cup diced onion
- 2 large potatoes, peeled and chopped
- 1 tablespoon butter
- 4 corn or flour tortilla

Direction

- Cook bacon in skillet on medium high heat till browned evenly. Remove bacon, keep drippings in skillet, and drain over paper towels then crumble bacon.
- Mix pepper, salt, water, milk and eggs till combined in a bowl as bacon cooks.
- Add potatoes to bacon drippings; cook till semi-soft. Mix onions in; mix and cook for a minute. Put egg mixture in skillet; mix butter and crumbled bacon in. Cook till eggs set to your preferred firmness. Put mixture in tortillas; serve.

Nutrition Information

- Calories: 485 calories;
- Cholesterol: 402
- Protein: 24.9
- Total Fat: 21.9
- Sodium: 615
- Total Carbohydrate: 48.2

60. Baja Fish Tacos From KRAFT®

Serving: 4 | Prep: 20mins | Ready in:

Ingredients

- 1/2 pound fresh tilapia fillets
- 3 tablespoons lime juice, divided
- 1 tablespoon TACO BELL® HOME ORIGINALS® Taco Seasoning Mix
- 1/3 cup KRAFT Mayo Real Mayonnaise
- 3 tablespoons chopped fresh cilantro, divided
- 3 cups coleslaw blend (cabbage slaw mix)
- 8 (6 inch) corn tortillas, warmed
- 1/2 cup KRAFT Mexican Style Shredded Four Cheese

Direction

- Use a brush to glaze fish with 1 tablespoon of lime juice. Sprinkle seasoning mix onto the fillet. Prepare a skillet and spray it with cooking spray. Place in fish fillet and cook over medium heat for 3 to 3-1/2 minutes, turn the fish over and cook an additional 3 to 3-1/2 minutes or until the fish can be shredded easily with a fork. Pour the remaining 1 tablespoon lime juice onto the fish for the last minute. Use fork to shred into bite-size pieces
- In a bowl, add in 1 tablespoon cilantro, remaining lime juice and mayo, mix well. Add the mixture to coleslaw blend, mix gently.
- Put remaining cilantro, cheese, fish and coleslaw over tortillas and served

Nutrition Information

- Calories: 407 calories;
- Total Fat: 23.2
- Sodium: 401
- Total Carbohydrate: 32.4
- Cholesterol: 45
- Protein: 18.7

61. Baja Salad

Serving: 6 | Prep: 20mins | Ready in:

Ingredients

- Salad:
- 1 (12 ounce) package romaine lettuce leaves
- 1 large tomato, diced
- 1 avocado, diced
- 1 pickling cucumber, diced
- 3/4 cup crumbled feta cheese
- 1/4 cup diced red onion
- 1/4 cup white corn kernels
- 1/4 cup cooked black beans
- 1/4 cup crushed tortilla chips, or to taste
- Dressing:
- 2 tablespoons olive oil (optional)
- 2 tablespoons lemon juice (optional)
- 1/4 teaspoon ground cumin (optional)
- salt and ground black pepper to taste (optional)

Direction

- In a large bowl, put the romaine lettuce. Then put in black beans, corn, onion, feta cheese, cucumber, avocado and tomato; then toss well. Sprinkle tortilla chips over salad.
- In a bowl, combine pepper, salt, cumin, lemon juice and olive oil until the dressing turns smooth; drizzle on salad.

Nutrition Information

- Calories: 223 calories;

Cholesterol: 28

- Cholesterol: 28
- Protein: 7.4
- Total Fat: 16.8
- Sodium: 405
- Total Carbohydrate: 13.6

62. Baked Mac And Cheese For One

Serving: 1 | Prep: 10mins | Ready in:

Ingredients

- 3 tablespoons uncooked macaroni pasta
- 1 tablespoon butter
- 1 tablespoon all-purpose flour
- 1/4 teaspoon salt
- 1 pinch pepper
- 1/8 teaspoon onion powder
- 1/2 cup milk
- 1/3 cup shredded Cheddar cheese
- 1/8 teaspoon ground mustard
- 1 dash Worcestershire sauce
- 1 dash hot sauce
- 1 teaspoon bread crumbs
- 1 tablespoon shredded Cheddar cheese

Direction

- Prepare the oven by preheating to 400°F (200°C). Prepare a 1 cup baking dish or an oven-proof soup crock then grease.
- In a small saucepan, add water and let it boil. Add in the macaroni then boil for about 8 minutes until cooked yet still firm to the bite. Strain well and set aside.
- Dissolve butter in the same saucepan over medium high heat. Mix in the milk, onion powder, pepper, salt and flour until smooth. Cook for 2 minutes while whisking. Lower the heat to low and mix in hot sauce, Worcestershire sauce, mustard and 1/3 cup cheese. Mix in the cooked macaroni. Scoop the macaroni and cheese into the prepared dish.

Top with 1 tablespoon cheddar cheese and bread crumbs.

- Place in the preheated oven and bake for about 10 minutes, uncovered, until the cheese is dissolved and the macaroni is heated through.

Nutrition Information

- Calories: 469 calories;
- Sodium: 1046
- Total Carbohydrate: 30
- Cholesterol: 89
- Protein: 19.8
- Total Fat: 30

63. Baked Potato Salad

Serving: 12 | Prep: 30mins | Ready in:

Ingredients

- 4 pounds potatoes, peeled
- 15 slices bacon
- 1 (16 ounce) container reduced-fat sour cream
- 2 tablespoons mayonnaise
- 2 cups shredded Cheddar cheese
- 2 tablespoons dried chives
- 1 teaspoon salt
- 1 teaspoon ground black pepper

Direction

- In a big pot, add potatoes and lightly salted water to cover. Bring to a boil on high heat, then lower heat to moderately low, cover and simmer for about 15 minutes, until just softened. Drain the potatoes and let cool to room temperature. Dice once cooled.
- Cook bacon in a big, deep skillet on moderately high heat for about 10 minutes, while flipping sometimes, until evenly browned. Transfer bacon to a paper towel-lined plate to drain. Let them cool and crumble bacon into a big bowl.

- Put cooled potatoes into the bowl with bacon, then stir in pepper, salt, chives, Cheddar cheese, mayonnaise and sour cream. Before serving, chill overnight.

Nutrition Information

- Calories: 322 calories;
- Total Fat: 17.5
- Sodium: 614
- Total Carbohydrate: 28.6
- Cholesterol: 48
- Protein: 13.2

64. Banh Mi

Serving: 2 | Prep: 30mins | Ready in:

Ingredients

- 1/2 cup rice vinegar
- 1/4 cup water
- 1/4 cup white sugar
- 1/4 cup carrot, cut into 1/16-inch-thick matchsticks
- 1/4 cup white (daikon) radish, cut into 1/16-inch-thick matchsticks
- 1/4 cup thinly sliced white onion
- 1 skinless, boneless chicken breast half
- garlic salt to taste
- ground black pepper to taste
- 1 (12 inch) French baguette
- 4 tablespoons mayonnaise
- 1/4 cup thinly sliced cucumber
- 1 tablespoon fresh cilantro leaves
- 1 small jalapeno pepper - seeded and cut into 1/16-inch-thick matchsticks
- 1 wedge lime

Direction

- In a saucepan over medium heat, add sugar, water and rice vinegar; bring to a boil. Stir for 1 minute to dissolve the sugar. Let it cool.

- In a bowl, add onion, radish and carrot; pour the vinegar mixture over. Let it stand for at least 30 minutes. Remove excess vinegar mixture after marinated.
- When marinating the vegetables, turn on the oven's broiler to preheat. Position the rack 6 inches away from heat. Use oil to lightly grease a slotted broiler pan.
- Use pepper and garlic salt to sprinkle on chicken breast; put on the slotted pan to broil for 6 minutes on each side, flipping once, until the surface turns brown and the center of breast is no longer pink. Take the chicken out; cut into bite-size pieces.
- Cut the baguette in 2 lengthwise; remove the center to make space for filing. Put baguette halves under broiler for 2-3 minutes to toast a bit.
- For banh mi assembling: Use mayonnaise to spread out on each half of the toasted baguette. Use jalapeno pepper, cilantro leaves, radish, onion, pickled carrot, cucumber slices and broiled chicken to fill the cavity of bottom half of the bread. Use a wedge of lime to squeeze over the filling; use the other half of the baguette to top.

Nutrition Information

- Calories: 657 calories;
- Sodium: 990
- Total Carbohydrate: 85.2
- Cholesterol: 43
- Protein: 24
- Total Fat: 25.2

65. Barbeque Chicken Pasta Salad

Serving: 12 | Prep: 30mins | Ready in:

Ingredients

- 3 skinless, boneless chicken breast halves
- 1 cup barbeque sauce
- 1 (16 ounce) package small whole-wheat pasta shells
- 1 cup barbeque sauce
- 1 cup mayonnaise
- 1 teaspoon ground cumin
- 1 cup jicama, peeled and diced
- 2 red bell peppers, seeded and diced
- 2 orange bell peppers, seeded and diced
- 2 (15.25 ounce) cans whole kernel corn, drained
- 3/4 cup minced fresh cilantro
- 2 (15 ounce) cans black beans, rinsed and drained
- 2 jalapeno peppers, seeded and chopped (wear gloves) (optional)
- 1 red onion, chopped (optional)

Direction

- In the saucepan over moderately-low heat, put chicken breasts, and add a cup of the barbeque sauce. Simmer the chicken for 15 minutes till meat is not pink anymore on the inside. Let cool, and chop the chicken meat into cubes.
- Pour slightly salted water in a big pot over high heat, bring to a rolling boil. When boiling, mix in shell pasta, and bring back to a boil. Cook the pasta without a cover for 10 minutes, mixing from time to time, till pasta has cooked through, yet firm to the bite. Drain thoroughly in a colander placed in sink. Wash the pasta in cold water till chilled, and drain well once more.
- Mix mayonnaise and a cup of barbeque sauce in a big salad bowl till well blended. Stir in cumin, then mix in the cooked chicken. In the salad bowl, put red onion, jalapeno peppers, black beans, cilantro, corn, red and orange bell peppers, jicama and cooked pasta, and slowly fold to mix with dressing. Serve chilled or while warm.

Nutrition Information

- Calories: 435 calories;
- Total Fat: 16.4
- Sodium: 808

- Total Carbohydrate: 61.6
- Cholesterol: 24
- Protein: 15

66. Basic Chicken Salad

Serving: 2 | Prep: 5mins | Ready in:

Ingredients

- 1/2 cup mayonnaise
- 1 tablespoon lemon juice
- 1/4 teaspoon ground black pepper
- 2 cups chopped, cooked chicken meat
- 1/2 cup blanched slivered almonds
- 1 stalk celery, chopped

Direction

- In a skillet, put almonds. Toast over medium-high heat, shake regularly. Watch carefully because they're easy to burn.
- Combine pepper, lemon juice, mayonnaise in a medium bowl. Mix with celery, almonds, and chicken.

Nutrition Information

- Calories: 779 calories;
- Cholesterol: 126
- Protein: 44.3
- Total Fat: 63.1
- Sodium: 403
- Total Carbohydrate: 8.4

67. Basil Avocado Chicken Salad Wraps

Serving: 4 | Prep: 20mins | Ready in:

Ingredients

- 2 ripe avocados - peeled, pitted, and mashed
- 1 lime, juiced
- 2 tablespoons chopped fresh basil
- 1/2 teaspoon garlic salt
- 1/2 teaspoon ground black pepper
- 4 cups chopped cooked chicken
- 1/4 cup raisins
- 1/4 cup chopped walnuts
- 2 heads Bibb lettuce, leaves separated

Direction

- In a bowl, combine pepper, garlic salt, basil, lime juice and mashed avocados. Put walnuts, raisins and chicken into the avocado mixture; stir to coat evenly. Scoop chicken mixture into lettuce leaves, then roll leaves around the filling.

Nutrition Information

- Calories: 471 calories;
- Sodium: 311
- Total Carbohydrate: 21.6
- Cholesterol: 105
- Protein: 42.7
- Total Fat: 25.5

68. Beaker's Vegetable Barley Soup

Serving: 8 | Prep: 15mins | Ready in:

Ingredients

- 2 quarts vegetable broth
- 1 cup uncooked barley
- 2 large carrots, chopped
- 2 stalks celery, chopped
- 1 (14.5 ounce) can diced tomatoes with juice
- 1 zucchini, chopped
- 1 (15 ounce) can garbanzo beans, drained
- 1 onion, chopped
- 3 bay leaves
- 1 teaspoon garlic powder

- 1 teaspoon white sugar
- 1 teaspoon salt
- 1/2 teaspoon ground black pepper
- 1 teaspoon dried parsley
- 1 teaspoon curry powder
- 1 teaspoon paprika
- 1 teaspoon Worcestershire sauce

Direction

- Pour out vegetable broth in a big pot. Add in bay leaves, onion, garbanzo beans, zucchini, tomatoes, celery, carrots, and barley. Season the mixture with Worcestershire sauce, paprika, curry powder, parsley, pepper, salt, sugar, and garlic powder, then set to boil. Simmer with a cover upon a medium-low heat for around 90 minutes. It should have a very thick consistency. You can adjust the dish with less amounts of barley or more broth if you prefer. Take out the bay leaves before you serve.

Nutrition Information

- Calories: 188 calories;
- Total Carbohydrate: 37
- Cholesterol: 0
- Protein: 6.9
- Total Fat: 1.6
- Sodium: 969

69. Bean Rarebit

Serving: 6 | Prep: 10mins | Ready in:

Ingredients

- 1/4 cup butter
- 1/4 cup chopped onion
- 1/4 cup all-purpose flour
- 1/2 teaspoon salt
- 2 cups milk
- 1 teaspoon Dijon mustard

- 2 cups shredded Cheddar cheese
- 1 (15.5 ounce) can white beans, drained and rinsed

Direction

- In a saucepan, melt butter over medium heat. Cook and stir onion for 5 minutes, until soft.
- Add salt and flour to onion, mix 1-2 minutes till flour forms a paste.
- Gradually blend Dijon mustard and milk into onion mixture; heat to a simmer, blending constantly for 5-7 minutes until the sauce is thickened.
- Mix white beans and Cheddar cheese into sauce, about 5-7 minutes, until cheese is melted.

Nutrition Information

- Calories: 365 calories;
- Cholesterol: 66
- Protein: 18
- Total Fat: 22
- Sodium: 540
- Total Carbohydrate: 24.4

70. Beans, Greens And Garlic Soup

Serving: 6 | Prep: 20mins | Ready in:

Ingredients

- 2 tablespoons olive oil
- 4 cloves garlic, peeled and chopped
- 1 onion, chopped
- 6 cups chicken broth
- 1 (15.5 ounce) can cannellini beans, drained and rinsed
- 1 cup ditalini or other small pasta
- 1 (10 ounce) bag baby spinach, rinsed and dried
- salt and black pepper to taste

Direction

- In a big stockpot, heat olive oil on medium heat. Mix onions and garlic in. Stir and cook for 8-10 minutes till onions are transparent. Put chicken broth. Bring heat to high. Boil mixture.
- Mix pasta and beans in. Reduce heat to medium. Simmer for 8-10 minutes till pasta is al dente, uncovered. Add spinach. Mix till wilted. Season to taste with pepper and salt.

Nutrition Information

- Calories: 186 calories;
- Cholesterol: 0
- Protein: 6.9
- Total Fat: 5.3
- Sodium: 190
- Total Carbohydrate: 28

71. Becky's Chicken Salad

Serving: 10 | Prep: 20mins | Ready in:

Ingredients

- 2 1/2 cups diced and chilled, cooked chicken meat
- 1 cup chopped celery
- 1 cup sliced, seedless grapes
- 1/2 cup sliced almonds
- 2 tablespoons chopped fresh parsley
- 1 teaspoon salt
- 1 cup mayonnaise
- 1/4 cup heavy whipping cream

Direction

- Whip the cream in a medium bowl to soft peaks.
- Mix the whipped cream together with mayonnaise, salt, parsley, almonds, grapes, celery, and meat. Chill.

Nutrition Information

- Calories: 274 calories;
- Total Fat: 23.6
- Sodium: 388
- Total Carbohydrate: 5
- Cholesterol: 43
- Protein: 11

72. Beet White Bean Salad

Serving: 4 | Prep: 10mins | Ready in:

Ingredients

- Dressing:
- 2 tablespoons cider vinegar
- 1 tablespoon Dijon mustard
- 1/2 teaspoon sugar
- 1/4 cup extra-virgin olive oil
- Salt and ground black pepper to taste
- Salad:
- 1 (16 ounce) can whole beets, well drained, halved
- 1 (15 ounce) can white kidney beans (cannellini), drained
- 1/2 cup reduced-fat crumbled blue cheese
- 1/2 cup coarsely chopped walnuts, toasted
- Baby arugula leaves

Direction

- Dressing: Mix sugar, Dijon mustard and cider vinegar in small bowl. Add olive oil gradually till blended well. Season with pepper and salt.
- Salad: Mix white kidney beans and beets in a big bowl. Toss it with dressing.
- Serving: On platter/serving bowl, put arugula leaves. Put beet mixture on top. Sprinkle walnuts and crumbled blue cheese on.

Nutrition Information

- Calories: 396 calories;
- Total Fat: 27.4

- Sodium: 801
- Total Carbohydrate: 26.8
- Cholesterol: 9
- Protein: 11.6

73. Bellepepper's Orzo And Wild Rice Salad

Serving: 6 | Prep: 30mins | Ready in:

Ingredients

- 2 cups cooked orzo
- 1/2 cup cooked wild rice
- 1/2 cup diced orange bell pepper
- 1/2 cup diced red bell pepper
- 1/2 cup frozen corn, thawed
- 1/2 cup dried currants
- 1/4 cup diced red onion
- Dressing:
- 1/4 cup vegetable oil
- 3 tablespoons white sugar
- 2 tablespoons white wine vinegar
- 2 tablespoons cider vinegar
- 1 teaspoon minced fresh onion
- 1 pinch ground white pepper
- 1 pinch paprika
- 1 pinch garlic powder, or to taste
- salt to taste
- salt and ground black pepper to taste
- 1/4 cup chopped toasted pecans
- 1/4 cup toasted slivered almonds
- 1/4 cup chopped fresh parsley

Direction

- In a big bowl, mix the red onion, currants, corn, red bell pepper, orange bell pepper, wild rice and orzo together.
- In a food processor or blender, blend 1 pinch of salt, garlic powder, paprika, white pepper, minced onion, cider vinegar, white wine vinegar, sugar and vegetable oil together until smooth.

- Stir parsley, almonds and pecans into the orzo mixture; drizzle enough dressing to coat the salad, then toss until coated evenly. Sprinkle black pepper and salt to season.

Nutrition Information

- Calories: 297 calories;
- Total Fat: 15.3
- Sodium: 6
- Total Carbohydrate: 37
- Cholesterol: 0
- Protein: 5.5

74. Berry Fruit Salad

Serving: 6 | Prep: 10mins | Ready in:

Ingredients

- 1 cup fresh strawberries, hulled and quartered lengthwise
- 1 cup fresh blueberries
- 1 cup fresh blackberries
- 1 cup fresh raspberries
- 1 teaspoon white sugar

Direction

- Combine blueberries, raspberries, blackberries, and strawberries together in a mixing bowl. Drizzle with sugar.

Nutrition Information

- Calories: 45 calories;
- Total Fat: 0.4
- Sodium: 1
- Total Carbohydrate: 10.9
- Cholesterol: 0
- Protein: 0.9

75. Best Greek Quinoa Salad

Serving: 10 | Prep: 15mins | Ready in:

Ingredients

- 3 1/2 cups chicken broth
- 2 cups quinoa
- 1 cup halved grape tomatoes
- 3/4 cup chopped fresh parsley
- 1/2 cup sliced pitted kalamata olives
- 1/2 cup minced red onion
- 4 ounces chopped feta cheese, or more to taste
- 3 tablespoons olive oil
- 3 tablespoons red wine vinegar
- 2 cloves garlic, minced
- 1 lemon, halved
- salt and ground black pepper to taste

Direction

- Place quinoa and broth in a saucepan and make it boil. Minimize heat to medium low, and simmer for 15 to 20 minutes, covered, until water has been absorbed and quinoa is soft.
- Move quinoa to a large bowl and reserve to cool for about 10 minutes.
- Mix garlic, vinegar, feta cheese, olive oil, onion, Kalamata olives, parsley and tomatoes into quinoa. Then squeeze lemon juice over quinoa salad, add pepper and salt to taste; coat by tossing. Let it chill inside the refrigerator for 1 to 4 hours.

Nutrition Information

- Calories: 227 calories;
- Cholesterol: 12
- Protein: 7.4
- Total Fat: 10.6
- Sodium: 666
- Total Carbohydrate: 25.8

76. Best Ever Cucumber Dill Salad

Serving: 6 | Prep: 15mins | Ready in:

Ingredients

- 1/2 cucumber, very thinly sliced
- salt and ground black pepper to taste
- 1/4 cup sour cream, or to taste
- 1/4 cup vinegar, or more to taste
- 1/4 cup plain yogurt
- 2 tablespoons mayonnaise
- 1/2 lime, juiced
- 2 teaspoons white sugar
- 1 teaspoon dill
- 1/2 red onion, thinly sliced
- 1/2 stalk celery, thinly sliced

Direction

- In a strainer, put cucumber slices. Use salt to drizzle liberally over the cucumber; let stand for 10 minutes until the water begins to draw out from the slices. Strain the water from the cucumber slices.
- In a big bowl, combine dill, sugar, lime juice, mayonnaise, yogurt, vinegar, and sour cream until the dressing is creamy. Toss celery, onion, and cucumber into the dressing until evenly combined, use pepper and salt to season.

Nutrition Information

- Calories: 75 calories;
- Sodium: 42
- Total Carbohydrate: 5.1
- Cholesterol: 7
- Protein: 1.2
- Total Fat: 5.9

77. Black Bean And Corn Quesadillas

Serving: 8 | Prep: 10mins | Ready in:

Ingredients

- 2 teaspoons olive oil
- 3 tablespoons finely chopped onion
- 1 (15.5 ounce) can black beans, drained and rinsed
- 1 (10 ounce) can whole kernel corn, drained
- 1 tablespoon brown sugar
- 1/4 cup salsa
- 1/4 teaspoon red pepper flakes
- 2 tablespoons butter, divided
- 8 (8 inch) flour tortillas
- 1 1/2 cups shredded Monterey Jack cheese, divided

Direction

- In a big saucepan on medium heat, heat oil. Mix in onion and cook 2 minutes until softened. Mix in corn and beans; add pepper flakes, salsa and sugar, then combine nicely. Cook 3 minutes until heated through.
- In a big skillet on medium heat, melt 2 teaspoons butter. Put tortilla into the skillet and evenly sprinkle with cheese; place a portion of bean mixture atop. Top with another tortilla and cook until golden. Flip to cook on the other side. If necessary, melt more butter; follow the same steps for the rest of tortillas and filling.

Nutrition Information

- Calories: 363 calories;
- Cholesterol: 26
- Protein: 13.9
- Total Fat: 14.5
- Sodium: 732
- Total Carbohydrate: 45.6

78. Black Bean And Couscous Salad

Serving: 8 | Prep: 30mins | Ready in:

Ingredients

- 1 cup uncooked couscous
- 1 1/4 cups chicken broth
- 3 tablespoons extra virgin olive oil
- 2 tablespoons fresh lime juice
- 1 teaspoon red wine vinegar
- 1/2 teaspoon ground cumin
- 8 green onions, chopped
- 1 red bell pepper, seeded and chopped
- 1/4 cup chopped fresh cilantro
- 1 cup frozen corn kernels, thawed
- 2 (15 ounce) cans black beans, drained
- salt and pepper to taste

Direction

- In a 2-quart or a bigger saucepan, boil chicken broth and mix in the couscous. Put a cover on and take away from heat. Let it sit for 5 minutes.
- Mix together cumin, vinegar, lime juice, and olive oil in a big bowl. Add beans, corn, cilantro, red pepper, and green onions and mix to coat.
- Make the couscous by fluffing well, crack up any chunks. Add vegetables to the bowl and toss well. Use pepper and salt to season and serve immediately or put in the fridge before serving.

Nutrition Information

- Calories: 253 calories;
- Total Fat: 5.8
- Sodium: 415
- Total Carbohydrate: 41.1
- Cholesterol: 0
- Protein: 10.3

79. Blue Cheese And Bacon Potato Salad

Serving: 6 | Prep: 15mins | Ready in:

Ingredients

- 5 cups iced water, or as needed
- 1 pound small red potatoes
- 1/2 pound fresh green beans, cut into 1-inch pieces
- 4 slices bacon
- 1/4 cup white wine vinegar
- 1/4 cup olive oil
- 2 tablespoons mayonnaise
- 1 tablespoon stone-ground mustard
- salt and ground black pepper to taste
- 4 ounces crumbled blue cheese
- 4 green onions, thinly sliced

Direction

- Pour iced water to fill a large bowl. Use a dish towel to line a baking sheet.
- In a large pot, put potatoes, pour in enough salted water to cover, bring to a boil. Reduce heat to medium-low and let the pot simmer for about 18-20 minutes till the potatoes get soft. Put green beans in the boiling water; let blanch for only a minute. Drain green beans and potatoes; put them into a bowl filled with iced water for about 5 minutes to stop cooking. Use a slotted spoon to move beans and potatoes out of iced water then put them on a prepared baking sheet to let them dry. Chop potatoes into quarters.
- In a large skillet, add bacon, then cook on medium-high heat for about 10 minutes; remember to turn once in a while till both sides turn brown evenly. Drain and let bacon slices cool on paper towel, then break bacon into pieces.
- Mix mustard, mayonnaise, olive oil and vinegar in a large bowl. Use salt and black pepper to season. Put potatoes and green beans to the bowl, stir to coat. Add green

onions, blue cheese and bacon on top, stir once to combine.

Nutrition Information

- Calories: 282 calories;
- Sodium: 476
- Total Carbohydrate: 16.3
- Cholesterol: 23
- Protein: 8.8
- Total Fat: 20.9

80. Blueberry Spinach Salad

Serving: 6 | Prep: 10mins | Ready in:

Ingredients

- 3 tablespoons red wine vinegar
- 1/2 cup olive oil
- 1 teaspoon Dijon mustard
- 1 teaspoon white sugar
- 1 pound fresh spinach
- 1 pint fresh blueberries
- 4 ounces crumbled blue cheese
- 4 ounces candied pecans

Direction

- In a jar with a tight-fitting lid, combine sugar, mustard, oil and vinegar then shake well.
- In a large salad bowl, toss candied pecans, blue cheese, blueberries and spinach. Drizzle dressing over; gently toss and serve at once.

Nutrition Information

- Calories: 375 calories;
- Total Carbohydrate: 19.2
- Cholesterol: 14
- Protein: 13.2
- Total Fat: 28.6
- Sodium: 439

81. Bob's Sweet Pepper Skillet

Serving: 4 | Prep: 15mins | Ready in:

Ingredients

- 2 teaspoons extra-virgin olive oil
- 2 teaspoons sesame oil
- 3 green bell peppers, thinly sliced
- 1 yellow bell pepper, chopped
- 1 red bell pepper, chopped
- 1 red onion, chopped
- 2 teaspoons minced garlic
- 1/4 teaspoon salt
- 1/4 teaspoon ground black pepper

Direction

- In a large skillet, heat sesame oil and olive oil on medium heat; put in pepper, salt, garlic, red onion, and red, yellow, and green bell peppers. Stir and cook the pepper mixture for 7-10 minutes until the peppers are heated thoroughly and the onion turns translucent.

Nutrition Information

- Calories: 91 calories;
- Total Fat: 5.1
- Sodium: 151
- Total Carbohydrate: 10.9
- Cholesterol: 0
- Protein: 1.8

82. Boozy Birdy

Serving: 5 | Prep: 10mins | Ready in:

Ingredients

- 8 (.18 ounce) packets sazon seasoning with coriander and achiote (such as Goya®)
- 1 tablespoon ground black pepper
- 1 tablespoon garlic powder
- 1 (12 fluid ounce) can or bottle Mexican beer (such as Corona®)
- 10 bone-in chicken thighs with skin
- 1/2 cup barbecue sauce

Direction

- In the large resealable plastic bag with zipper, put in garlic powder, black pepper and sazon seasoning. Add beer, then seal bag. Use your fingers to smush bag around for a few seconds to mix seasonings with beer. Put chicken thighs into the marinade. Reseal bag, squeeze as much air out as you can. Place in the refrigerator for at least 6 hours or up to overnight.
- Start preheating outdoor grill to medium-high heat, oil grate lightly.
- Take away chicken from the marinade, save the marinade. Grill the chicken for 5-8 minutes each side until juices run clear, chicken is no longer pink inside and has good grill marks. An instant-read meat thermometer should register at least 160°F (70°C) when inserted into thickest part of the thigh.
- Transfer reserved marinade to saucepan over medium-high heat. Boil, cook for 10 minutes or until marinade is reduced by half. Mix in barbecue sauce. Slather over the chicken. Enjoy.

Nutrition Information

- Calories: 388 calories;
- Cholesterol: 117
- Protein: 32.3
- Total Fat: 19.6
- Sodium: 1589
- Total Carbohydrate: 13.6

83. Brazilian White Rice

Serving: 8 | Prep: 15mins | Ready in:

Ingredients

- 2 cups long-grain white rice
- 2 tablespoons minced onion
- 2 cloves garlic, minced
- 2 tablespoons vegetable oil
- 1 teaspoon salt
- 4 cups hot water

Direction

- Rinse thoroughly the rice with cold water in a colander; set aside.
- In a saucepan, heat the oil over medium heat. Add the onion, and cook for one minute. Stir the garlic into the pan and cook until the golden brown. Pour in salt and the rice, cook and stir until the rice starts to brown. Add hot water over the rice mixture; stir. Lower the heat, take a cover to the saucepan, and let the mixture simmer for 20 to 25 minutes, until the water has been absorbed.

Nutrition Information

- Calories: 201 calories;
- Total Fat: 3.7
- Sodium: 297
- Total Carbohydrate: 37.5
- Cholesterol: 0
- Protein: 3.4

84. Bread Machine Pumpernickel Bread

Serving: 12 | Prep: 10mins | Ready in:

Ingredients

- 1 1/8 cups warm water
- 1 1/2 tablespoons vegetable oil
- 1/3 cup molasses
- 3 tablespoons cocoa
- 1 tablespoon caraway seed (optional)
- 1 1/2 teaspoons salt
- 1 1/2 cups bread flour
- 1 cup rye flour
- 1 cup whole wheat flour
- 1 1/2 tablespoons vital wheat gluten (optional)
- 2 1/2 teaspoons bread machine yeast

Direction

- Follow the order of putting the ingredients into the bread machine pan suggested by the manufacturer. Choose the Basic cycle on the machine and press the Start button to run the machine.

Nutrition Information

- Calories: 119 calories;
- Total Fat: 2.3
- Sodium: 295
- Total Carbohydrate: 22.4
- Cholesterol: 0
- Protein: 3.4

85. Bread Machine Swedish Coffee Bread

Serving: 8 | Prep: 15mins | Ready in:

Ingredients

- 1 cup milk
- 1/2 teaspoon salt
- 1 egg yolk
- 2 tablespoons softened butter
- 3 cups all-purpose flour
- 1/3 cup sugar
- 1 (.25 ounce) envelope active dry yeast
- 3 teaspoons ground cardamom
- 2 egg whites, slightly beaten
- pearl sugar, or other decorative sugar

Direction

- Follow the order of putting the ingredients into the pan of the bread machine suggested by the manufacturer. Choose the Dough cycle on the machine and press the Start button.
- Once the machine has finished the whole cycle, separate the dough into 3 even sizes. Shape each dough portion into a rope about 12-14 inches in length. Place the 3 dough ropes alongside each other and weave them into a braid. Secure the ends underneath the braided bread and put it on a baking sheet that is greased; place a towel loosely to cover the top and let it rise until it has doubled in size.
- Preheat the oven to 375°F (190°C).
- Use a brush to coat the top of the braided bread with beaten egg white; top it off with a dash of pearl sugar. Put in the preheated oven and bake for 20-25 minutes until it turns golden brown in color.

Nutrition Information

- Calories: 283 calories;
- Sodium: 195
- Total Carbohydrate: 52.8
- Cholesterol: 36
- Protein: 7.5
- Total Fat: 4.6

---

86. Breadsticks

Serving: 18 | Prep: 20mins | Ready in:

Ingredients

- 1/4 cup white sugar, divided
- 1 (.25 ounce) package active dry yeast
- 1 cup warm water, divided
- 2 1/4 cups all-purpose flour, or more if needed
- 3 tablespoons vegetable oil
- 1 egg
- 1/2 teaspoon salt
- 1/2 cup butter, melted
- 1/2 teaspoon garlic salt

- 1/4 cup Parmesan cheese

Direction

- Fill a bowl with 1/2 cup of warm water and dissolve yeast and 1 1/2 teaspoons of sugar. Let the yeast form a creamy foam and soften for around 5 minutes.
- Beat the remaining warm water, remaining sugar, salt, egg, oil, and flour into the yeast mixture until mixture smoothens. Add more flour as needed until dough is soft. Dust a work surface with flour and place the dough on the floured surface. Knead for 6 to 8 minutes, until the dough is elastic and smooth.
- In a greased bowl, place the dough and turn it around once until coated with the oil. Use a damp towel to cover the dough and transfer to a warm area for 40 minutes, until dough has doubled in size.
- Prepare a baking sheet with a coat of grease.
- Punch the dough down and transfer to a floured work surface. Equally divide the dough into 18 pieces. Shape each piece into a rope 6 inches long. Arrange each piece 2 inches apart on the baking sheet. Cover with either a plastic wrap or towel for 25 minutes, and allow to rise until doubled in size.
- Preheat oven to 200°C/400°F. Uncover the dough.
- Bake for 10 to 12 minutes, until golden brown.
- In a bowl, whisk garlic salt and butter. Brush mixture over the breadsticks. Sprinkle each breadstick with Parmesan cheese.

Nutrition Information

- Calories: 143 calories;
- Protein: 2.6
- Total Fat: 8.2
- Sodium: 173
- Total Carbohydrate: 14.9
- Cholesterol: 25

87. Broccoli Cranberry Salad

Serving: 8 | Prep: 15mins | Ready in:

Ingredients

- 6 strips bacon
- 1 cup mayonnaise
- 1/4 cup white sugar
- 2 tablespoons red wine vinegar
- 3 heads broccoli, finely chopped
- 1/2 cup chopped red onion
- 1/3 cup salted sunflower kernels, toasted
- 1/4 cup dried cranberries

Direction

- Cook bacon in a big skillet on medium high heat, occasionally turning, for 10 minutes till evenly browned. On paper towels, drain bacon slices; crumble.
- Whisk sugar, vinegar and mayonnaise in a bowl; refrigerate till ready to mix with salad.
- In a big bowl, mix cranberries, sunflower seeds, bacon, onion and broccoli. Drizzle mayonnaise dressing on broccoli mixture; toss till coated.

Nutrition Information

- Calories: 314 calories;
- Total Carbohydrate: 19
- Cholesterol: 18
- Protein: 6.1
- Total Fat: 25.2
- Sodium: 355

88. Brown Sugar Brats

Serving: 12 | Prep: 15mins | Ready in:

Ingredients

- 3 pounds fresh bratwurst sausages
- 5 large apples - peeled, cored and sliced
- 6 onions, sliced
- 1 (16 ounce) package brown sugar
- 1 cup water

Direction

- At the bottom of a big electric covered roaster like Nesco, put brats. Layer apples then onions. Then brown sugar on brats. Pour water on the ingredients.
- Cover roaster. Cook brats for 3 hours at 165 degrees C/325 degrees F. They'll look candied and dark when finished.

Nutrition Information

- Calories: 611 calories;
- Total Fat: 33.4
- Sodium: 977
- Total Carbohydrate: 62.7
- Cholesterol: 84
- Protein: 17.1

89. Buffalo Chicken Chili

Serving: 10 | Prep: 15mins | Ready in:

Ingredients

- 1 tablespoon extra-virgin olive oil
- 2 tablespoons butter
- 2 pounds ground chicken breast
- 1 large carrot, peeled and finely chopped
- 1 large onion, chopped
- 3 stalks celery, finely chopped
- 5 cloves garlic, chopped
- 5 tablespoons chili powder
- 2 tablespoons ground cumin
- 1 tablespoon ground paprika
- salt and pepper to taste
- 1/2 cup hot buffalo wing sauce (such as Frank's® REDHOT Buffalo Wing Sauce), or to taste
- 2 (15 ounce) cans tomato sauce

- 1 (15 ounce) can crushed tomatoes
- 1 (15 ounce) can white kidney or cannellini beans, drained
- 1 (19 ounce) can red kidney beans, drained

Direction

- In a large pot, warm butter and olive oil over medium-high heat. Cook and stir chicken for 7-10 minutes, until the chicken is no longer pinkish. Mix in celery, salt, pepper, chili powder, carrot, cumin, garlic, paprika, and onion. Allow it to cook for 3-4 minutes until the vegetables start to tender, and the onion is already translucent.
- Add tomato sauce, white and red kidney beans, hot sauce, and crushed tomatoes into the mixture. Allow it to boil. Reduce the heat to medium-low, and bring the mixture to simmer for 1 hour until the flavors are well-blended and the vegetables are tender.

Nutrition Information

- Calories: 301 calories;
- Total Fat: 8.6
- Sodium: 1152
- Total Carbohydrate: 30
- Cholesterol: 61
- Protein: 28.3

90. Buttered Noodles

Serving: 8 | Prep: 5mins | Ready in:

Ingredients

- 1 (16 ounce) package fettuccine noodles
- 6 tablespoons butter
- 1/3 cup grated Parmesan cheese
- salt and ground black pepper to taste

Direction

- Put big pot of lightly salted water on rolling boil. Mix fettuccine in; boil. Cook pasta on medium heat for 8-10 minutes till tender yet firm to chew. Drain; put pasta in pot.
- Mix pepper, salt, parmesan cheese and butter into pasta till combined evenly.

Nutrition Information

- Calories: 294 calories;
- Sodium: 135
- Total Carbohydrate: 41.4
- Cholesterol: 26
- Protein: 8.9
- Total Fat: 10.9

91. California Tacos

Serving: 4 | Prep: 15mins | Ready in:

Ingredients

- 3 tomatoes, seeded and chopped
- 2 avocados, chopped
- 1 small onion, chopped
- 1/4 cup chopped fresh cilantro
- 2 cloves garlic, minced
- 1 lime, juiced
- 2 tablespoons vegetable oil
- 8 corn tortillas
- 1 (15 ounce) can black beans, drained and rinsed
- 1 cup cooked white rice
- 2 tablespoons chopped fresh cilantro
- 1 dash green pepper sauce (such as Tabasco®), or to taste (optional)

Direction

- In a bowl, mix together the garlic, 1/4 cup cilantro, onion, avocados and tomatoes. Drizzle lime juice on top of the tomato mixture, then toss until coated.

- In a frying pan, heat the vegetable oil on medium heat, then layout the tortillas in hot oil, 2 pieces at a time. Let it cook for around 1 minute on each side, until it becomes crisp. Use tongs to take out the tortillas and redo the process with the leftover tortillas.
- Spoon 2 tbsp. of cooked rice and 2 tbsp. of black beans into each crisp tortilla, then put tomato mixture on top. Put green pepper sauce and leftover 2 tbsp. of cilantro on top to garnish the tacos.

Nutrition Information

- Calories: 512 calories;
- Cholesterol: 0
- Protein: 13.7
- Total Fat: 23.7
- Sodium: 448
- Total Carbohydrate: 67.2

92. Campbell's® Slow Cooked Pulled Pork Sandwiches

Serving: 12 | Prep: 15mins | Ready in:

Ingredients

- 1 tablespoon vegetable oil
- 3 1/2 pounds boneless pork shoulder roast, netted or tied
- 1 (10.5 ounce) can Campbell's® Condensed French Onion Soup
- 1 cup ketchup
- 1/4 cup cider vinegar
- 3 tablespoons packed brown sugar
- 12 round sandwich rolls or hamburger rolls, split

Direction

- Heat oil on medium high heat in a 10-in. skillet. Add pork; cook till all sides brown well.
- Mix brown sugar, vinegar, ketchup and soup in a 5-qt. slow cooker. Add pork; turn to coat.
- Cover; cook on low till pork is fork tender for 8-9 hours.
- Transfer pork from cooker onto cutting board; stand for 10 minutes. Shred pork using 2 forks; put pork into cooker.
- Divide sauce mixture and pork to rolls.

Nutrition Information

- Calories: 344 calories;
- Sodium: 684
- Total Carbohydrate: 31.2
- Cholesterol: 53
- Protein: 17.9
- Total Fat: 16.1

93. Caprese On A Stick

Serving: 8 | Prep: 15mins | Ready in:

Ingredients

- 1 pint cherry tomatoes, halved
- 1 (.6 ounce) package fresh basil leaves
- 1 (16 ounce) package small fresh mozzarella balls
- toothpicks
- 3 tablespoons olive oil
- salt and pepper to taste

Direction

- Use toothpicks to thread a mozzarella ball, a small piece of basil leaf and tomato half until all ingredients are used. Sprinkle with olive oil all over the basil, cheese and tomato but leave the toothpick's end clean. Drizzle with pepper and salt. Serve right away.

Nutrition Information

- Calories: 215 calories;

- Total Fat: 17.4
- Sodium: 85
- Total Carbohydrate: 3
- Cholesterol: 45
- Protein: 10.5

94. Caveman Stew

Serving: 4 | Prep: 10mins | Ready in:

Ingredients

- 1 pound ground beef
- 5 carrots, sliced
- 4 potatoes, cut into quarters
- 1 onion, quartered
- 1 (10.75 ounce) can condensed tomato soup
- 1 (10.75 ounce) can water

Direction

- Form 6 meatballs using ground beef.
- In the bottom of a pressure cooker, combine onion, potatoes and carrots. Place meatballs on top of the vegetables then pour water and tomato soup over the vegetables and meatballs.
- Secure the pressure cooker and cook over high heat to raise the pressure. Turn down the heat to medium and cook for 15 minutes. Follow manufacturer's directions to release the pressure from the pot.

Nutrition Information

- Calories: 481 calories;
- Total Fat: 15.3
- Sodium: 567
- Total Carbohydrate: 61.2
- Cholesterol: 71
- Protein: 26.1

95. Celery Salad

Serving: 2 | Prep: 10mins | Ready in:

Ingredients

- 3/4 cup sliced celery
- 1/3 cup dried sweet cherries
- 1/3 cup frozen green peas, thawed
- 3 tablespoons chopped fresh parsley
- 1 tablespoon chopped pecans, toasted
- 1 1/2 tablespoons fat-free mayonnaise
- 1 1/2 tablespoons plain low-fat yogurt
- 1 1/2 teaspoons fresh lemon juice
- 1/8 teaspoon salt
- 1/8 teaspoon ground black pepper

Direction

- Mix together the pecans, parsley, peas, cherries and celery in a medium bowl, then mix in the lemon juice, yogurt and mayonnaise. Sprinkle pepper and salt to season, then chill prior to serving.

Nutrition Information

- Calories: 150 calories;
- Total Fat: 3
- Sodium: 304
- Total Carbohydrate: 26.5
- Cholesterol: 1
- Protein: 4.1

96. Cheesy Potato Pancakes

Serving: 6 | Prep: 15mins | Ready in:

Ingredients

- 4 russet potatoes, peeled and grated
- 2 eggs
- 1/2 cup milk
- 1 cup all-purpose flour
- 1/2 cup grated Parmesan cheese

- 1/2 cup shredded Cheddar cheese
- 1/4 cup real bacon bits (optional)
- 1 teaspoon onion salt
- 1 teaspoon baking powder
- 1 teaspoon salt
- 1/2 teaspoon ground black pepper
- 1/4 cup corn oil
- 2 tablespoons butter

Direction

- In a big bowl, combine the eggs, milk and potatoes together.
- Use a fork to mix the Cheddar cheese, salt, flour, baking powder, black pepper, onion salt, Parmesan cheese and bacon bits together in the potato mixture.
- Put the butter and corn oil in a big skillet and let it heat up on medium heat.
- Put 2 tablespoons of the potato mixture in the skillet and shape it to a patty. Let the patties cook for 4 minutes on every side until it turns golden brown in color.
- Place the cooked pancakes on a plate with paper towels to drain excess oil.

Nutrition Information

- Calories: 427 calories;
- Total Fat: 22.1
- Sodium: 1159
- Total Carbohydrate: 42.6
- Cholesterol: 95
- Protein: 15.3

97. Cheesy Potato Salad

Serving: 6 | Prep: 15mins | Ready in:

Ingredients

- 2 1/2 pounds red potatoes, cubed
- 1 cup sour cream
- 1/2 cup mayonnaise

- 1/4 cup white sugar
- 1/2 bunch green onions, chopped
- 1 cup shredded Cheddar cheese
- 1 tablespoon real bacon bits

Direction

- In a pot, cover potatoes with water and bring to a boil. Cook until easily stabbed with a fork, about 10 minutes. Drain and put to one side to cool.
- Combine half of the cheese, half of the onions, sugar, mayonnaise, and sour cream in a large bowl. Pour over cooled potatoes, stir gradually. Sprinkle with remaining onions and cheese and top with bacon bits.

Nutrition Information

- Calories: 497 calories;
- Cholesterol: 49
- Protein: 11.1
- Total Fat: 30.7
- Sodium: 314
- Total Carbohydrate: 46.5

98. Chef John's Creamy Mushroom Soup

Serving: 6 | Prep: 15mins | Ready in:

Ingredients

- 1/4 cup unsalted butter
- 2 pounds sliced fresh mushrooms
- 1 pinch salt
- 1 yellow onion, diced
- 1 1/2 tablespoons all-purpose flour
- 6 sprigs fresh thyme
- 2 cloves garlic, peeled
- 4 cups chicken broth
- 1 cup water
- 1 cup heavy whipping cream

- 1 pinch salt and freshly ground black pepper to taste
- 1 teaspoon fresh thyme leaves for garnish, or to taste

Direction

- Over medium-high heat, in a big soup pot, melt butter; put mushrooms in butter and cook with 1 pinch of salt until the mushroom gives their juices off; lower heat to low. Keep cooking, stirring often, for 15 minutes approximately until the mushrooms turn golden brown and juices evaporate. If you like, set a few pretty slices of mushroom aside for later decoration. Mix onion into mushrooms and cook for 5 more minutes until onion turns translucent and soft.
- Stir flour into mixture of mushroom and cook for 2 minutes, stirring often, to remove the taste of raw flour. Use kitchen twine to tie a small bundle of thyme sprigs and put in mushroom mixture; include garlic cloves. Pour into mushroom mixture the water and chicken stock. Heat to simmer and cook for an hour. Take the thyme bundle out.
- In small batches, transfer soup to a blender and puree until thick and smooth on high speed.
- Pour soup back into pot and stir in cream. Use salt and black pepper to season. Serve in bowls, decorated with reserved slices of mushroom and some thyme leaves.

Nutrition Information

- Calories: 272 calories;
- Total Carbohydrate: 12.2
- Cholesterol: 78
- Protein: 6.9
- Total Fat: 23.3
- Sodium: 667

99. Chef John's Pita Bread

Serving: 8 | Prep: 30mins | Ready in:

Ingredients

- 1 (.25 ounce) package active dry yeast
- 1 cup warm water (90 to 100 degrees F/32 to 38 degrees C)
- 1 cup all-purpose flour
- 1 1/2 tablespoons olive oil
- 1 3/4 teaspoons salt
- 1 3/4 cups all-purpose flour, or more as needed
- 1 teaspoon olive oil, divided

Direction

- In stand mixer's bowl, combine yeast, a cup of warm water and a cup of flour. Mix together and set aside for 15-20 minutes to rise and forms a loose sponge. The mixture will foam and bubble.
- Add salt, 1 3/4 cup flour, and 1 1/2 tbsp. olive oil in the sponge. Use a dough hook to mix at low speed until the dough is slightly sticky, soft, and flexible. Gradually add up to quarter cup flour in the mixture if it sticks to the corners of the mixing bowl.
- Set the machine on low speed to knead for 5-6 minutes until soft and a little springy. Form dough into a ball on a floured surface.
- Grease bowl with quarter teaspoon olive oil, roll dough ball inside the bowl to grease thinly; cover the bowl with foil. Set aside for 2 hours until the dough rises and doubles.
- Take the dough out of the bowl and flatten to an inch thick on a floured surface. Divide the dough into 8 parts with a knife.
- Make a small ball with a smooth surface from each dough portion. Pull the sides of the dough balls and tuck the ends at the bottom.
- Use a lightly greased plastic wrap to cover the dough balls; set aside for half hour.
- Dust the surface of dough ball and the work surface with a little flour. Flatten the balls slightly with your fingers into quarter inch thick round and flat bread; set aside for 5

minutes. Repeat process with the rest of the balls.

- On medium heat, grease a cast-iron skillet with the rest of the 3/4 tsp olive oil. Place the pita bread in a hot skillet and cook for 3 minutes until it starts to puff up and brown patches appears at the bottom. Turn bread and cook for another 2 minutes. Turn once again and cook for another half minute. The bread will puff up and will be filled with hot air. Place pita bread on top of each other on a dish. Break bread in half once it cools down. Open the inside pocket for stuffing.

Nutrition Information

- Calories: 187 calories;
- Cholesterol: 0
- Protein: 4.8
- Total Fat: 3.6
- Sodium: 511
- Total Carbohydrate: 33.1

---

100.   Chef John's Raw Kale Salad

Serving: 4 | Prep: 15mins | Ready in:

Ingredients

- 1/4 cup rice vinegar
- 1 tablespoon orange juice
- 1 teaspoon Dijon mustard
- 1 teaspoon grated orange zest
- 1 teaspoon ground cumin
- 1/4 teaspoon red pepper flakes
- 1/3 cup olive oil
- salt and ground black pepper to taste
- 1 bunch kale
- 1 persimmon, sliced
- 1 apple, cut into matchsticks
- 2 orange, peeled and cut into segments (see footnote)
- 1/4 cup chopped pistachio nuts

Direction

- Mix red pepper flakes, cumin, orange zest, Dijon mustard, orange juice, and vinegar in a bowl. Gradually pour the olive oil in orange juice mixture, mixing until well combined and thick. Season with black pepper and salt.
- Take stems of every kale leaf. Stack 3-4 kale leaves then roll them together. Slice kale leaves finely, crosswise, to make thin ribbons.
- Mix pistachio nuts, orange, apple, persimmon, and sliced kale in a bowl. Add dressing and mix until coated well.

Nutrition Information

- Calories: 292 calories;
- Total Fat: 22.7
- Sodium: 115
- Total Carbohydrate: 21.3
- Cholesterol: 0
- Protein: 5.7

---

101.   Chef John's Shrimp Cocktail

Serving: 4 | Prep: 15mins | Ready in:

Ingredients

- Poaching Liquid:
- 3 quarts cold water
- 1/4 onion, sliced
- 1/2 lemon
- 2 cloves garlic, peeled and bruised
- 2 sprigs fresh tarragon
- 1 tablespoon seafood seasoning (such as Old Bay®)
- 1 teaspoon whole black peppercorns
- 1 bay leaf
- Cocktail Sauce:
- 1/2 cup ketchup
- 1/4 cup chili sauce
- 1/4 cup prepared horseradish

- 1 teaspoon lemon juice
- 1 teaspoon Worcestershire sauce
- 3 drops hot sauce, or to taste
- 1 pinch salt
- 2 pounds shell-on deveined jumbo shrimp

Direction

- In a big pot, mix together bay leaf, peppercorns, seafood seasoning, tarragon, garlic, lemon, onion and water; simmer and cook for 15 minutes till flavors meld.
- In a bowl, mix together salt, hot sauce, Worcestershire sauce, lemon juice, horseradish, chili sauce and ketchup; put in refrigerator for a minimum of 15 minutes till chilled.
- Let poaching liquid come to a rapid boil. In boiling liquid, let the shrimp cook for about 5 minutes till the outer is bright pink and meat is not clear anymore in the middle. To a bowl with ice water, put the shrimp and immerse in ice water till chilled; drain. On a platter, set cold shrimp and serve along with chilled sauce.

Nutrition Information

- Calories: 306 calories;
- Cholesterol: 345
- Protein: 47.7
- Total Fat: 4.3
- Sodium: 1415
- Total Carbohydrate: 18.9

102. Chef John's Shrimp And Grits

Serving: 4 | Prep: 25mins | Ready in:

Ingredients

- 4 slices bacon, cut into 1/4-inch pieces
- 1/4 cup water
- 2 tablespoons heavy whipping cream
- 2 teaspoons lemon juice
- 1 dash Worcestershire sauce
- 4 cups water
- 2 tablespoons butter
- 1 teaspoon salt
- 1 cup white grits
- 1/2 cup shredded white Cheddar cheese
- 1 pound shrimp, peeled and deveined
- 1/2 teaspoon Cajun seasoning
- 1/2 teaspoon salt, or to taste
- 1/4 teaspoon ground black pepper
- 1 pinch cayenne pepper
- 1 tablespoon minced jalapeno pepper
- 2 tablespoons minced green onion
- 3 cloves garlic, minced
- 1 tablespoon chopped fresh parsley

Direction

- In a large skillet, position bacon and cook over medium-high heat while flipping infrequently for 5 – 7 minutes until almost crisp. Take away from heat and move the bacon to a dish, reserving drippings in the skillet.
- In a bowl, whisk Worcestershire sauce, lemon juice, cream, and a quarter cup of water together.
- In a pot, mix 1 teaspoon of salt, butter, and 4 cups of water together; boil. Whisk the grits into pot, set to a simmer, decrease heat to low, and cook for 20 – 25 minutes until grits become creamy. Take away from heat and mix the white Cheddar cheese into grits.
- In a big bowl, put shrimp and season with a pinch of cayenne pepper, black pepper, a half teaspoon of salt, and Cajun seasoning.
- Over high heat, heat the skillet containing bacon drippings. Cook the shrimp in hot bacon fat in a single layer for about 1 minute. Flip the shrimp and put in jalapeno; cook for 30 seconds until fragrant. Stir garlic, green onion, bacon, and cream mixture into the shrimp mixture; cook and stir, while adding enough water to thin the sauce, for 3 – 4 minutes until shrimp are cooked through. Take away from heat then whisk in parsley.

- Serve the grits in a bowl, top with sauce and shrimp.

Nutrition Information

- Calories: 434 calories;
- Protein: 30.1
- Total Fat: 19.5
- Sodium: 1498
- Total Carbohydrate: 33.2
- Cholesterol: 226

103. Cherry Tomato Sauce With Penne

Serving: 4 | Prep: 15mins | Ready in:

Ingredients

- 2 cups cherry tomatoes (such as Sun Gold)
- 2 tablespoons olive oil
- 2 cloves garlic, sliced
- salt and ground black pepper to taste
- 2 cups chicken broth
- 2 tablespoons fresh oregano leaves
- 1/2 teaspoon red pepper flakes
- 14 ounces penne pasta
- 1/2 cup grated Parmigiano-Reggiano cheese

Direction

- In a saucepan, mix together salt, garlic, oil, and cherry tomatoes over medium-low heat. Cook while stirring for 2-3 minutes until the garlic has barely toasted.
- Pour into the tomato mixture with chicken broth; simmer and cook for 10 minutes until the tomatoes begin to pop and crumble. Mix red pepper flakes and oregano into the tomato mixture.
- Use a stick blender to puree the tomato mixture until the sauce is smooth.
- Boil lightly salted water in a big pot; put in penne and cook for 11 minutes until soft but

not mushy, tossing sometimes. Strain and put back into the pot. Pour over the penne with the tomato sauce and toss for 1-2 minutes until the pasta has absorbed some of the sauce. Mix into the pasta with Parmigiano-Reggiano cheese and use pepper and salt to season to taste.

Nutrition Information

- Calories: 475 calories;
- Total Fat: 12.3
- Sodium: 204
- Total Carbohydrate: 76.2
- Cholesterol: 9
- Protein: 17.7

104. Chicken Club Pasta Salad

Serving: 6 | Prep: 20mins | Ready in:

Ingredients

- 8 ounces corkscrew-shaped pasta
- 3/4 cup Italian-style salad dressing
- 1/4 cup mayonnaise
- 2 cups chopped, cooked rotisserie chicken
- 12 slices crispy cooked bacon, crumbled
- 1 cup cubed Muenster cheese
- 1 cup chopped celery
- 1 cup chopped green bell pepper
- 8 ounces cherry tomatoes, halved
- 1 avocado - peeled, pitted, and chopped

Direction

- Boil lightly salted water in a big pot. In the boiling water, cook the pasta for 10-12 minutes until fully cooked but not mushy, tossing sometimes. Strain and wash under cold water.
- In a big bowl, mix together mayonnaise and Italian-style dressing. Mix avocado, cherry tomatoes, green bell pepper, celery, Muenster

cheese, bacon, chicken, and pasta into the dressing until evenly combined.

Nutrition Information

- Calories: 550 calories;
- Sodium: 1000
- Total Carbohydrate: 37.3
- Cholesterol: 61
- Protein: 23.7
- Total Fat: 35.1

105. Chicken Mango Salsa Salad With Chipotle Lime Vinaigrette

Serving: 6 | Prep: 30mins | Ready in:

Ingredients

- 1 mango - peeled, seeded and diced
- 2 roma (plum) tomatoes, chopped
- 1/2 onion, chopped
- 1 jalapeno pepper, seeded and chopped - or to taste
- 1/4 cup cilantro leaves, chopped
- 1 lime, juiced
- 1/2 cup olive oil
- 1/4 cup lime juice
- 1/4 cup white sugar
- 1/2 teaspoon ground chipotle chile powder
- 1/2 teaspoon ground cumin
- 1/4 teaspoon garlic powder
- 1 (10 ounce) bag baby spinach leaves
- 1 cup broccoli coleslaw mix
- 1 cup diced cooked chicken
- 3 tablespoons diced red bell pepper
- 3 tablespoons diced green bell pepper
- 2 tablespoons diced yellow bell pepper
- 2 tablespoons dried cranberries
- 2 tablespoons chopped pecans
- 2 tablespoons crumbled blue cheese

Direction

- In a large bowl, combine mango, jalapeno pepper, tomatoes, juice of one lime onion, and cilantro. Reserve.
- In a bowl, whisk together chipotle chile powder, olive oil, garlic powder, 1/4 cup lime juice, sugar, and cumin. Reserve.
- In a large bowl, mix together red, green, and yellow bell peppers, spinach leaves, chicken, broccoli coleslaw mix, pecans and cranberries.
- Top with blue cheese and mango salsa.
- Sprinkle lime dressing atop the salad and mix before you serve.

Nutrition Information

- Calories: 317 calories;
- Total Fat: 22.3
- Sodium: 110
- Total Carbohydrate: 25
- Cholesterol: 14
- Protein: 7.6

106. Chicken Noodle Salad With Peanut Ginger Dressing

Serving: 8 | Prep: 45mins | Ready in:

Ingredients

- Dressing
- 1/3 cup smooth peanut butter
- 1/4 cup soy sauce
- 2 tablespoons unseasoned rice vinegar
- 1 tablespoon Asian garlic-chili sauce
- 1 tablespoon brown sugar, packed
- 1 tablespoon finely chopped fresh ginger root
- 1/8 teaspoon red pepper flakes
- 3 tablespoons low-sodium chicken broth
- salt and ground black pepper to taste
- Salad
- 1 (16 ounce) package uncooked linguine pasta
- 3 1/2 cups cooked chicken, cut into strips

- 1 cup julienne-sliced carrot
- 6 green onions, chopped
- 1 red bell pepper, seeded and cut into strips
- 1 celery rib, thinly sliced
- 1/2 cup fresh cilantro leaves, chopped
- 1/2 cup chopped roasted peanuts, for garnish

Direction

- In a blender or a food processor bowl, add 3 tablespoons of chicken broth, red pepper flakes, ginger, brown sugar, chili-garlic sauce, rice vinegar, soy sauce and peanut butter to make dressing. Blend until everything is well-combined and smoothened. Add pepper and salt to season. Add more water or chicken broth if you want the dressing to be thinner.
- Boil lightly salted water in a large pot. Cook linguine for 8-10 minutes until al dente. Drain and transfer to a large mixing bowl. Stir in cilantro, celery, red pepper, green onions, carrots and chicken into the linguine bowl. Stir the dressing into the chicken-noodle mixture and mix well until everything is evenly coated. Prepare 8 plates for serving and evenly divide salad into each plate. Top with a sprinkle of peanuts on each plate.

Nutrition Information

- Calories: 461 calories;
- Sodium: 745
- Total Carbohydrate: 51.6
- Cholesterol: 46
- Protein: 30.2
- Total Fat: 15.8

107.   Chicken Ranch Tacos

Serving: 5 | Prep: 25mins | Ready in:

Ingredients

- 1 (4.7 ounce) box Old El Paso® Stand 'N Stuff® taco shells

- 3 cups cut-up deli rotisserie chicken
- 1 (1 ounce) package Old El Paso® taco seasoning mix
- 1/2 cup ranch dressing
- 1 1/2 cups shredded lettuce
- 1 medium tomato, chopped
- 1 cup shredded Cheddar cheese
- 1/4 cup sliced green onions (optional)
- Old El Paso® Thick 'n Chunky Salsa (optional)
- Additional ranch dressing (optional)

Direction

- Set oven to 325 degrees Fahrenheit. Heat the taco shells in the oven as instructed on the box.
- At the same time, place the chicken into a medium-sized microwavable bowl. Sprinkle with taco seasoning mix, gently tossing to coat. Microwave without a cover on a high setting until hot, 2-3 minutes. Stir in 1/2 cup of dressing.
- Spoon the warm chicken mix into the warm taco shells. Top with onions, cheese, tomato, and lettuce. Drizzle with more dressing and salsa.

Nutrition Information

- Calories: 470 calories;
- Sodium: 1083
- Total Carbohydrate: 23.9
- Cholesterol: 73
- Protein: 23.5
- Total Fat: 30.5

108.   Chicken Salad With Bacon And Red Grapes

Serving: 6 | Prep: 20mins | Ready in:

Ingredients

- 3 slices bacon
- 3 cups diced cooked chicken

- 1 (8 ounce) can water chestnuts, drained and minced
- 1/4 cup thinly sliced celery
- 1 1/2 cups seedless red grapes, halved
- 1 1/2 cups mayonnaise
- 4 teaspoons dried parsley flakes
- 2 1/2 teaspoons lime juice
- 1 1/2 teaspoons onion powder
- 1/2 teaspoon ground ginger
- 1 dash Worcestershire sauce
- salt and ground black pepper to taste

Direction

- Heat a deep pan on medium high heat, fry bacon slices for 10 minutes until crispy. Remove bacon oil using paper towels, and let it cool, break into tiny crumbs.
- In a big salad bowl, mix the crumbled bacon, red grapes, water chestnuts, cooked chicken, and celery.
- To make the dressing, mix together Worcestershire sauce, ground ginger, mayonnaise, salt, onion powder, lime juice, black pepper, and dried parsley until smooth.
- Pour the dressing over the chicken mixture and coat the whole dish evenly.
- Cool for 30 or more minutes, covered.

Nutrition Information

- Calories: 537 calories;
- Total Fat: 48.4
- Sodium: 456
- Total Carbohydrate: 14.5
- Cholesterol: 55
- Protein: 12.8

109. Chicken Salad With Grapes And Apples

Serving: 4 | Prep: 15mins | Ready in:

Ingredients

- 2 tablespoons mayonnaise
- 1 cup cubed cooked chicken
- 1 cup halved grapes
- 1 Gala apple, diced
- 1/3 cup diced red onion
- 1 tablespoon honey mustard
- 1/4 teaspoon garlic powder
- 1/8 teaspoon ground black pepper

Direction

- Combine black pepper, garlic powder, honey mustard, onion, apple, grapes, chicken, and mayonnaise in a bowl.

Nutrition Information

- Calories: 154 calories;
- Total Fat: 7.8
- Sodium: 86
- Total Carbohydrate: 15.3
- Cholesterol: 20
- Protein: 7.2

110. Chicken Sandwiches With Zang

Serving: 4 | Prep: 20mins | Ready in:

Ingredients

- 4 skinless, boneless chicken breast halves
- 3 tablespoons Italian seasoning
- 3 tablespoons grill seasoning (such as Montreal Steak Seasoning)
- 1/2 cup barbeque sauce (such as Big Moe's®)
- 1 teaspoon butter
- 1 onion, thinly sliced
- 1 green bell pepper, sliced
- 4 mushrooms, sliced
- 4 hamburger buns, split and toasted
- 4 slices Swiss cheese

Direction

- Preheat indoor or outdoor grill to low heat; oil grate lightly.
- Generously sprinkle all sides of chicken breasts with grill and Italian seasonings; cook on preheated grill slowly, flipping every 10 minutes. Each time you flip it, brush barbeque sauce on the chicken. Cook till juices are clear and chicken isn't pink in the middle anymore. An inserted instant-read thermometer in the middle should read a minimum of 74°C/165°F when done.
- Melt butter in a skillet on medium low heat as chicken is cooking; cook mushrooms, bell peppers and onions in butter, frequently mixing till veggies are tender.
- Make sandwiches: Onto each hamburger bun half, put a chicken breast; scoop onion and pepper mixture over. Top with a Swiss cheese slice; cover using hamburger bun tops.

Nutrition Information

- Calories: 465 calories;
- Total Carbohydrate: 46.2
- Cholesterol: 93
- Protein: 36.9
- Total Fat: 14.6
- Sodium: 2778

---

111. Chicken Tortilla Soup

Serving: 6 | Prep: 10mins | Ready in:

Ingredients

- 1 cup chopped onion
- 3 cups chicken broth
- 1 (14.5 ounce) can diced tomatoes with green chile peppers
- 1 envelope taco seasoning
- 1 1/2 pounds skinless, boneless chicken breast meat - cubed
- 2 tablespoons cornstarch
- 1/4 cup cold water

- 1/4 cup shredded Mexican cheese blend
- 1 tablespoon chopped fresh cilantro (optional)

Direction

- Boil taco seasoning, tomatoes, chicken broth and onion in big saucepan on medium heat; mix chicken in. Lower heat to low. Cover; simmer for 4-6 minutes till chicken isn't pink. Mix water and cornstarch till smooth in small bowl; mix into soup slowly.
- Boil soup on medium high heat; cook, occasionally mixing, for 1 minute till thick. Put cilantro and Mexican cheese on top.

Nutrition Information

- Calories: 195 calories;
- Total Carbohydrate: 12
- Cholesterol: 66
- Protein: 24.6
- Total Fat: 4.4
- Sodium: 1269

---

112. Chicken Zoodle Soup

Serving: 6 | Prep: 20mins | Ready in:

Ingredients

- 2 tablespoons olive oil
- 1 cup diced onions
- 1 cup diced celery
- 3 cloves garlic, minced
- 5 (14.5 ounce) cans low-sodium chicken broth
- 1 cup sliced carrots
- 3/4 pound cooked chicken breast, cut into bite sized pieces
- 1/2 teaspoon dried basil
- 1/2 teaspoon dried oregano
- 1 pinch dried thyme (optional)
- salt and ground black pepper to taste
- 3 zucchini squash, cut into 'noodles' using a spiral slicer or vegetable peeler

Direction

- In a big pot, heat olive oil on medium-high. Add celery, garlic, and onion to the hot oil and sauté until just tender, 5 minutes.
- Add chicken broth to the pot; then add oregano, pepper, carrots, salt, basil, thyme, and chicken. Heat broth to a boil, put heat down to medium-low, and simmer the mixture for 20 minutes until the veggies are soft.
- Divide between six bowls the zucchini noodles; spoon the broth mixture on top of the noodles.

Nutrition Information

- Calories: 208 calories;
- Total Fat: 9.5
- Sodium: 257
- Total Carbohydrate: 8.9
- Cholesterol: 48
- Protein: 21.6

113. Chopped Cashew Salad

Serving: 8 | Prep: 20mins | Ready in:

Ingredients

- 1 pound seedless red grapes, halved
- 1/2 pint cherry tomatoes, halved
- 1 red bell pepper, diced
- 1 orange bell pepper, diced
- 1 yellow bell pepper, diced
- 1/2 cup edamame (green soybeans)
- 1/2 cup crumbled feta cheese with herbs
- 1 teaspoon dried basil
- 1/2 teaspoon lemon-pepper seasoning
- salt to taste
- 1 avocado, diced
- 3/4 cup cashews
- 1 tablespoon extra-virgin olive oil, or to taste
- 1 tablespoon red wine vinegar, or to taste

Direction

- In a bowl, combine feta cheese, edamame, yellow bell pepper, orange bell pepper, red bell pepper, tomatoes and grapes with herbs. To the vegetable-grape mixture, put the salt, lemon pepper and basil; coat by tossing. To vegetable-grape mixture, put the cashews and avocado just prior to serving. Sprinkle vinegar and olive oil on top of the salad; coat by tossing.

Nutrition Information

- Calories: 235 calories;
- Total Fat: 14.7
- Sodium: 134
- Total Carbohydrate: 23.1
- Cholesterol: 6
- Protein: 7.4

114. Chunky And Creamy Potato Salad

Serving: 12 | Prep: 20mins | Ready in:

Ingredients

- 3 pounds yellow mini potatoes
- 12 slices bacon
- 5 hard-boiled eggs, chopped
- 1 cup chopped broccoli florets
- 1 cup diced Cheddar cheese
- 1 (8 ounce) bottle ranch salad dressing (such as Hidden Valley® Original Ranch®)
- 2 1/2 teaspoons dried dill weed
- 1 teaspoon salt
- 1/2 teaspoon ground black pepper

Direction

- In a saucepan of lightly salted water, put potatoes; boil it, cook for 20 minutes until softened. Put potatoes in a strainer to drain and let it cool.

- Cook bacon in a big, deep frying pan on medium-high until crunchy and browned, about 10 minutes; flip sometimes. Put bacon strips on a dish lined with paper towel to strain. Use a scissor to cut or chop the cooked bacon into pieces.
- Mix pepper, salt, dill weed, ranch salad dressing, Cheddar cheese, broccoli, hard-boiled eggs, chopped bacon, and mini potatoes together in a big bowl until well blended and enjoy.

Nutrition Information

- Calories: 318 calories;
- Total Fat: 20.2
- Sodium: 701
- Total Carbohydrate: 22.5
- Cholesterol: 115
- Protein: 11.6

115.   Cilantro Lime Coleslaw

Serving: 7 | Prep: 25mins | Ready in:

Ingredients

- 3/4 cup mayonnaise
- 1 lime, zested
- 2 teaspoons fresh lime juice
- 1/2 teaspoon rice vinegar
- 2 cloves garlic, minced
- 2 teaspoons sweet chili sauce
- 2 teaspoons white sugar
- 3 tablespoons finely chopped fresh cilantro
- 1/4 red onion, finely diced, or more to taste
- 4 cups shredded green cabbage, or more to taste

Direction

- In a big bowl, stir sugar, mayonnaise, sweet chili sauce, lime zest, garlic, lime juice, and rice vinegar together until the sugar dissolves; mix

in red onion and cilantro. Toss in a cup of cabbage at a time until everything is well coated.

Nutrition Information

- Calories: 189 calories;
- Sodium: 164
- Total Carbohydrate: 5.6
- Cholesterol: 9
- Protein: 0.9
- Total Fat: 18.8

116.   Cinnamon Ants On Sticks

Serving: 3 | Prep: 5mins | Ready in:

Ingredients

- 1 large stalk celery, cut into 3 pieces
- 3 tablespoons peanut butter
- 1 teaspoon ground cinnamon
- 2 tablespoons raisins

Direction

- Put celery pieces on a clean surface with the hollow part facing up. Drizzle evenly with cinnamon. Put peanut butter into the hollow part of the celery and garnish with raisins.

Nutrition Information

- Calories: 121 calories;
- Total Fat: 8.3
- Sodium: 93
- Total Carbohydrate: 9.9
- Cholesterol: 0
- Protein: 4.5

117. Classic American Style Potato Salad

Serving: 6 | Prep: | Ready in:

Ingredients

- 2 pounds red boiling potatoes, scrubbed
- 2 tablespoons red wine vinegar
- 1/2 teaspoon salt
- 1/2 teaspoon freshly ground black pepper
- 3 hard-cooked eggs
- 1 small celery stalk
- 1/4 cup chopped sweet pickle (not relish)
- 3 scallions
- 2 tablespoons chopped fresh parsley
- 1/2 cup mayonnaise
- 2 tablespoons Dijon-style mustard

Direction

- Cover potatoes with water in a pot. Boil, cover then simmer for 25-30 minutes till you can easily remove a metal skewer or a thin-bladed paring knife inserted into a potato, stirring to make sure potatoes are cooked evenly. Drain, let rinse under cold water then drain for the second time. Let cool slightly.
- Use a serrated knife to slice warm potatoes into 3/4-in. dice. Place as a layer in a bowl. Add pepper, salt and vinegar to taste as you go. Slice pickle, celery and eggs into 1/4-in. dice and cut scallions thinly. Place in potatoes together with parsley. Add mustard and mayonnaise; stir till all combined. Cover then let chill before serving.

Nutrition Information

- Calories: 291 calories;
- Cholesterol: 99
- Protein: 6.5
- Total Fat: 17.3
- Sodium: 550
- Total Carbohydrate: 28.8

118. Cobb Sandwich

Serving: 4 | Prep: 25mins | Ready in:

Ingredients

- 1/2 cup mayonnaise
- 1/4 cup blue cheese dressing
- 8 slices multigrain bread
- 2 cooked chicken breasts, sliced
- 1 ripe avocado, sliced
- 8 slices cooked bacon
- 2 hard boiled eggs, chopped
- 4 lettuce leaves

Direction

- Mix bleu cheese dressing and mayonnaise to prep sandwich spread; spread 2 tbsp. on 1 side of every bread slice. Put 1/4 each of lettuce, hard boiled eggs, bacon, avocado and chicken over 4 of prepped bread pieces. Put another bread slice over each sandwich; serve with leftover blue cheese spread alongside.

Nutrition Information

- Calories: 811 calories;
- Total Fat: 56.1
- Sodium: 908
- Total Carbohydrate: 29.6
- Cholesterol: 204
- Protein: 46.3

119. Cold Rice Salad

Serving: 8 | Prep: 30mins | Ready in:

Ingredients

- 2 cups water
- 1 cup uncooked white rice
- 3 eggs

- 1 tablespoon olive oil
- 2 boneless skinless chicken breasts, bite-size pieces
- 3 tablespoons olive oil
- 1 teaspoon vinegar
- 1 teaspoon salt
- 1/4 teaspoon pepper
- 1 cup tomatoes, diced
- 1 bunch raw broccoli, with stalk, chopped
- 1 cup frozen peas, thawed
- 1 cup frozen corn kernels, thawed

Direction

- In a medium-sized saucepan, boil water. Put in rice and mix. Lower heat, keep it covered and let simmer for 20 minutes. Take away from heat, and put aside to let it cool down.
- In a saucepan, add eggs and pour in cold water to cover. Boil and take away from heat instantly. Keep it covered and let eggs rest in hot water for 10 - 12 minutes. Let it cool down, remove egg shells, and chop.
- Over medium-high heat, heat 1 tbsp. of oil in a skillet. Cook chicken, flipping once in a while, till not pink anymore and juices run out clear.
- In a small bowl, mix together pepper, salt, vinegar, leftover oil till emulsified a bit, then put aside. In a big mixing bowl, add corn, peas, broccoli, and tomatoes; mix by tossing. Put in rice, eggs and chicken, and toss again. Keep it covered, and let chill in the refrigerator for no less than 60 minutes prior to serve. Coat by tossing with dressing just prior to serve.

Nutrition Information

- Calories: 300 calories;
- Total Fat: 11.1
- Sodium: 448
- Total Carbohydrate: 30.2
- Cholesterol: 105
- Protein: 20.2

120. Colombian Stewed Flank

Serving: 4 | Prep: 25mins | Ready in:

Ingredients

- 2 tablespoons corn oil
- 1 pound flank steak
- 1 large Spanish onion, thinly sliced
- 4 large cloves garlic, chopped
- 5 Roma tomatoes, chopped
- 1/2 teaspoon salt
- 2 teaspoons black pepper, or to taste
- 1 1/2 teaspoons ground cumin
- 2 1/2 cups water
- 2 cubes beef bouillon, crumbled

Direction

- In a skillet, heat corn oil on moderate heat. Lie in the oil with the steak gently and cook until each side is browned. Transfer steak to a plate. Put into the skillet with cumin, pepper, salt, tomatoes, garlic and onions, then cook and stir until onions are soft. Turn steak back to the skillet. Add to skillet with water, then stir in crumbled bouillon. Bring water to a boil then lower heat to low and place a cover. Let simmer for 2 hours, until it is easy to use a fork to pull meat apart.
- Transfer steak to a cutting board and use 2 forks to shred the meat. Remove to a serving platter. Drizzle over shredded beef with onion and tomato mixture from the skillet.

Nutrition Information

- Calories: 236 calories;
- Sodium: 770
- Total Carbohydrate: 9.2
- Cholesterol: 36
- Protein: 15.4
- Total Fat: 15.6

121. Coney Island Hot Dogs

Serving: 8 | Prep: 15mins | Ready in:

Ingredients

- 1 1/2 pounds lean ground beef
- 2 cups water, or more to taste
- 1/2 cup diced onion
- 1/3 cup ketchup
- 2 tablespoons butter
- 2 cloves garlic, crushed
- 2 tablespoons chili powder, or more to taste
- 1 1/2 teaspoons salt, or to taste
- 1 teaspoon freshly ground black pepper, or to taste
- 1 teaspoon ground cumin, or to taste
- 1/2 teaspoon celery salt, or to taste
- 1 pinch cayenne pepper, or to taste
- 8 all-beef hot dogs
- 8 hot dog buns
- 1/4 cup prepared yellow mustard, or to taste
- 1/4 cup diced onion, or to taste

Direction

- In a pot, mix cayenne pepper, ground beef, celery salt, water, cumin, half cup diced onion, black pepper, ketchup, salt, butter, chili powder, and garlic together. On medium-high heat, stir the mixture using a spatula or potato masher for 10mins until it starts to bubble and has finely ground texture.
- Let the mixture simmer then turn to medium-low heat. Cook while mixing from time to time for an hour until the sauce reduces and thickens. Sprinkle pepper and salt to taste.
- Boil a big pot of water; add hot dogs. Cook for 5-7mins until completely heated.
- Preheat the oven to 175°C or 350°Fahrenheit. Place the hot dog buns on a baking pan.
- Cook buns in the 350°Fahrenheit oven for 2-3mins until warm and soft.
- Put a bun on a dish, arrange one hot dog then add meat sauce on top. Spread diced onion and yellow mustard on top of the sauce. Arrange the rest of the hot dogs.

Nutrition Information

- Calories: 528 calories;
- Total Fat: 32.3
- Sodium: 1684
- Total Carbohydrate: 29.6
- Cholesterol: 99
- Protein: 29

122. Corn Salad With Lime Vinaigrette

Serving: 8 | Prep: 15mins | Ready in:

Ingredients

- 1 (14.5 ounce) can whole kernel corn, drained
- 2 tomatoes, diced
- 1 avocado, diced
- 1/2 white onion, diced
- 1 jalapeno pepper, or more to taste, seeded and diced
- 1/2 cup chopped fresh cilantro
- 1/4 cup olive oil
- 1 lime, juiced
- salt and ground black pepper to taste

Direction

- In a bowl, combine the cilantro, avocado, corn, jalapeño pepper, onion and tomatoes together.
- In a small bowl, mix the lime juice and olive oil together then pour it on top of the corn salad. Put pepper and salt to taste.
- Use a plastic wrap to cover the bowl and keep in the fridge for not less than 30 minutes.

Nutrition Information

- Calories: 154 calories;
- Total Carbohydrate: 14.9
- Cholesterol: 0
- Protein: 2.4

- Total Fat: 11
- Sodium: 157

123. Couscous A La Me!

Serving: 4 | Prep: 10mins | Ready in:

Ingredients

- 2 cups water
- 1 teaspoon chicken bouillon granules (optional)
- 2 teaspoons butter
- 1 (10 ounce) box couscous
- 2 tablespoons olive oil
- 1/2 red bell pepper, chopped
- 1/2 yellow bell pepper, chopped
- 1/2 orange bell pepper, chopped
- 1/2 onion, chopped
- 1/4 teaspoon garlic powder, or to taste
- 1/2 pound boneless chicken tenders, cut into bite sized pieces
- 2 (14.5 ounce) cans diced tomatoes
- 1 (14.5 ounce) can black beans, drained
- 1 splash dry white wine (optional)
- 1/4 cup shredded Cheddar cheese (optional)

Direction

- Boil the water in a saucepan together with butter and chicken bouillon. Pour the mixture all over the couscous in a large bowl. Use a plastic wrap to cover the bowl. Let the couscous absorb the moisture entirely for 5-7 minutes. Use a fork to fluff the couscous; put aside.
- Put olive oil in a large skillet and heat it over high heat. Stir in orange, yellow, and red bell pepper together with onion and cook for 5 minutes until softened. Season the mixture with garlic powder. Add the chicken and cook it for 5 minutes until its juices run clear and the center is no longer pink. Stir in tomatoes, couscous, white wine, and black beans. Let the mixture cook for 2-3 more minutes, stirring

well until heated through. Before serving, top the mixture with cheese.

Nutrition Information

- Calories: 584 calories;
- Sodium: 935
- Total Carbohydrate: 70
- Cholesterol: 66
- Protein: 36.5
- Total Fat: 15.1

124. Cranberry And Cilantro Quinoa Salad

Serving: 6 | Prep: 10mins | Ready in:

Ingredients

- 1 1/2 cups water
- 1 cup uncooked quinoa, rinsed
- 1/4 cup red bell pepper, chopped
- 1/4 cup yellow bell pepper, chopped
- 1 small red onion, finely chopped
- 1 1/2 teaspoons curry powder
- 1/4 cup chopped fresh cilantro
- 1 lime, juiced
- 1/4 cup toasted sliced almonds
- 1/2 cup minced carrots
- 1/2 cup dried cranberries
- salt and ground black pepper to taste

Direction

- Pour the water into a saucepan and cover with a lid. Make it boil over high heat, then place in the quinoa, cover again, and keep simmering over low heat for 15 to 20 minutes until the water has been absorbed. Then scrape it into a mixing bowl, and place inside the refrigerator to chill until cold.
- Once cold, mix in the cranberries, carrots, sliced almonds, lime juice, cilantro, curry powder, red onion, yellow bell pepper, and

red bell pepper. Add pepper and salt to taste. Let it chill before serving.

Nutrition Information

- Calories: 176 calories;
- Total Fat: 3.9
- Sodium: 13
- Total Carbohydrate: 31.6
- Cholesterol: 0
- Protein: 5.4

---

125.   Crawfish Potato Soup

Serving: 12 | Prep: 15mins | Ready in:

Ingredients

- 3 slices bacon
- 1 onion, chopped
- 1 green bell pepper, seeded and chopped
- 1 red bell pepper, seeded and chopped
- 2 stalks celery, finely chopped
- 2 tablespoons minced garlic
- 5 cups diced red potatoes
- 1 cup grated carrot
- 1 pound crawfish tails
- 3 cups chicken broth
- 1 quart half-and-half cream
- salt and pepper to taste
- 1 cup shredded Cheddar cheese

Direction

- Cook bacon in a pot over medium-high heat. Turn and cook until crisp, turn as needed. Crumble it then put it back in the pot.
- Lower heat to medium. Sauté onion, red pepper, green pepper, garlic and celery. Cook until peppers are tender and the onion is translucent. Toss in crawfish. Cook until crawfish is browned, and the liquid has evaporated. Take out the contents from the pot. Set aside.

- Add the chicken broth and potatoes to the pot. Add water if the broth is not enough to cover the potatoes. Let it boil until potatoes are tender, for 8-10 minutes. Toss in carrots and cook for another 8 minutes.
- Turn heat to low. Put the crawfish and veggies back in the pot. Add half-and-half and stir until it is heated through. Don't let it boil. Sprinkle with salt and pepper to taste. Serve in bowls. Top with cheddar cheese.

Nutrition Information

- Calories: 250 calories;
- Total Carbohydrate: 17.2
- Cholesterol: 85
- Protein: 13.4
- Total Fat: 14.5
- Sodium: 198

---

126.   Creamy Carolina Potato Salad

Serving: 8 | Prep: 30mins | Ready in:

Ingredients

- 2 pounds red potatoes
- 3 hard-cooked eggs, chopped
- 1/2 cup sour cream
- 1/2 cup mayonnaise
- 1/2 (4 ounce) jar chopped pimento peppers
- 2 green onions, chopped
- 2 slices cooked bacon, chopped
- 2 tablespoons yellow mustard
- 1 tablespoon white sugar
- 1 tablespoon red wine vinegar
- 1/2 teaspoon salt
- 1/2 teaspoon ground black pepper
- 1/2 teaspoon celery seed
- 1/4 teaspoon garlic powder
- 1 pinch paprika, or as desired

Direction

- In a large pot, pour salted water to cover potatoes, then boil. Lower the heat to medium-low and simmer for 20 - 25 minutes until tender. Drain off water, allow to cool, and cut potatoes into 1-in. cubes. Mix eggs and potato cubes together in a large bowl.
- In another bowl, combine garlic powder, celery seed, black pepper, salt, vinegar, sugar, mustard, bacon, green onions, pimento peppers, mayonnaise, and sour cream. Pour the dressing mixture over eggs and potatoes, stir gradually until evenly coated. Top the salad with paprika to finish.

Nutrition Information

- Calories: 260 calories;
- Total Fat: 16.9
- Sodium: 341
- Total Carbohydrate: 22.1
- Cholesterol: 93
- Protein: 6

127. Creamy Chicken Tortellini Soup

Serving: 4 | Prep: 10mins | Ready in:

Ingredients

- 1/2 pound chicken breast, cut into bite-sized pieces
- 1 (14.5 ounce) can chicken broth
- 1 (9 ounce) package refrigerated cheese tortellini
- 2 (10.5 ounce) cans cream of chicken soup
- 2 cups half-and-half
- 1 (10 ounce) package frozen chopped spinach, thawed and drained
- 1/2 teaspoon thyme
- 1/4 teaspoon ground black pepper

Direction

- Boil water in a saucepan. Cook the chicken in boiling water for about 7 to 10 minutes until it is no longer pink in the center and drain.
- Boil the chicken broth in a soup pot and add the cheese tortellini. Lower the heat to medium-low and cook for about 8 minutes until the tortellini are cooked through and still firm to the bite. Stir black pepper, thyme, spinach, half-and-half, cream of chicken soup and chicken with the tortellini. Bring the mixture to a simmer and continue cooking for 7 to 10 minutes until hot. Serve hot.

Nutrition Information

- Calories: 529 calories;
- Total Fat: 29
- Sodium: 1645
- Total Carbohydrate: 39.9
- Cholesterol: 113
- Protein: 28.4

128. Creamy Summer Squash Soup

Serving: 6 | Prep: 15mins | Ready in:

Ingredients

- 6 small yellow summer squash, trimmed and coarsely chopped
- 1 large zucchini, trimmed and coarsely chopped
- 2 cups vegetable stock
- 1 cup half-and-half cream
- 2 tablespoons chopped fresh tarragon
- 1 cup shredded Cheddar cheese
- ground white pepper to taste
- coarse sea salt to taste
- 2 tablespoons lemon juice, or more to taste
- 1 teaspoon chopped fresh tarragon

Direction

- Boil tarragon, half and half, vegetable stock, zucchini and summer squash in a big soup pot; lower the heat to a simmer. Cook for 10 minutes till veggies are tender.
- No more than halfway full, fill the pitcher, pour the soup into a blender. Use a folded kitchen towel to hold blender lid down; start the blender carefully, with a few quick pulses to move soup then leave on to puree. In batches, puree till almost smooth; put into a clean pot. Or, puree the soup right in the cooking pot with a stick blender.
- Sprinkle cheddar cheese into the hot soup; let melt. Mix till mixed thoroughly. Mix lemon juice in; sprinkle tarragon on top. Serve.

Nutrition Information

- Calories: 163 calories;
- Sodium: 286
- Total Carbohydrate: 8.8
- Cholesterol: 35
- Protein: 8.2
- Total Fat: 11.4

129. Creamy Tomato Tuna Penne Pasta

Serving: 2 | Prep: 15mins | Ready in:

Ingredients

- 6 2/3 ounces tuna packed in olive oil
- 3 cloves garlic, crushed
- 1 teaspoon anchovy paste
- 1 pinch dried oregano
- 1 pinch red pepper flakes, or more as needed
- 3 cups cream of tomato soup, not from concentrate
- 1/2 cup water
- 14 1/2 ounces dry penne pasta
- 2/3 cup finely grated Parmigiano-Reggiano cheese
- 1 tablespoon minced fresh tarragon

- salt and freshly ground black pepper to taste
- 1 pinch red pepper flakes, for garnish
- 1/4 cup finely grated Parmigiano-Reggiano cheese

Direction

- On medium-low heat, cook and stir red pepper flakes, olive oil, oregano, garlic, and anchovy paste together in a big pot for a minute until the oil starts to sizzle.
- Mix in water and cream of tomato soup. Turn to medium heat and let it simmer for 10 mins.
- Boil a big pot of lightly salted water; add in penne and boil again. Cook and stir for 11 mins, uncovered, until a bit undercooked; drain.
- Mix in cooked penne into the soup mixture. Toss in tarragon and two-third cup of Parmigiano-Reggiano cheese; cover. Cook for two minutes.
- Sprinkle black pepper, and salt to taste; cover. Cook for another minute.
- Sprinkle red pepper flakes and more Parmigiano-Reggiano cheese on top.

Nutrition Information

- Calories: 1269 calories;
- Total Carbohydrate: 202.3
- Cholesterol: 62
- Protein: 72.4
- Total Fat: 22.1
- Sodium: 3019

130. Creamy Tomato Basil Soup

Serving: 8 | Prep: 10mins | Ready in:

Ingredients

- 1/4 cup butter
- 1/4 cup olive oil

- 1 1/2 cups chopped onions
- 3 pounds tomatoes - cored, peeled, and quartered
- 1/2 cup chopped fresh basil leaves
- salt to taste
- ground black pepper to taste
- 1 quart chicken broth
- 1 cup heavy cream
- 8 sprigs fresh basil for garnish

Direction

- Place a large pot on medium heat; heat in olive oil and butter. Cook in onions while stirring until tender. Stir in chopped basil and tomatoes. Season with pepper and salt. Transfer in chicken broth; turn the heat down to low; keep cooking for 15 minutes.
- Pour the soup into a blender (or an immersible hand blender instead); blend until perfectly smooth.
- Turn back to the pot; bring the mixture to a boil. Turn the heat down to low; slowly stir in heavy cream. Strain through a strainer. Top a sprig of basil on each serving.

Nutrition Information

- Calories: 258 calories;
- Sodium: 62
- Total Carbohydrate: 10.7
- Cholesterol: 56
- Protein: 2.8
- Total Fat: 23.9

131. Crescent Dogs

Serving: 8 | Prep: 10mins | Ready in:

Ingredients

- 8 hot dogs
- 4 slices American cheese, each cut into 6 strips

- 1 (8 ounce) can Pillsbury® refrigerated crescent dinner rolls

Direction

- Heat an oven to 375°F. Within 1/2-in. of ends, slit hotdogs; in each slit, insert 3 cheese strips.
- Separate dough to triangles; around each hotdog, wrap dough triangle. Put, cheese side up, onto ungreased cookie sheet.
- Bake till golden brown for 12-15 minutes.

Nutrition Information

- Calories: 313 calories;
- Sodium: 947
- Total Carbohydrate: 13.2
- Cholesterol: 37
- Protein: 10.2
- Total Fat: 23.8

132. Croque Monsieur

Serving: 3 | Prep: 15mins | Ready in:

Ingredients

- 1 tablespoon Dijon mustard
- 2 tablespoons mayonnaise
- 4 tablespoons butter or margarine, softened
- 6 slices white bread
- 6 slices Swiss cheese
- 12 slices thinly sliced deli ham
- 4 tablespoons all-purpose flour
- 1/2 teaspoon baking powder
- 1/4 teaspoon salt
- 2 eggs
- 1/4 cup water
- 1 tablespoon vegetable oil

Direction

- Slather 2 tbsps. butter on one portion of each sliced bread. Spread Dijon butter on top of the butter on 3 of the bread slices; add four ham slices on top of each. Spread mayonnaise on the other 3 bread slices; add two Swiss cheese slices on top of each. Press both sides together to make a sandwich.

- Mix water, flour, eggs, baking powder, and salt together in a flat-bottomed dish until well combined; set aside.
- On medium heat, heat vegetable oil and leftover butter in a big pan. Submerge each sandwich side in the egg mixture. Fry sandwich until both sides are brown.

Nutrition Information

- Calories: 960 calories;
- Sodium: 2492
- Total Carbohydrate: 38.1
- Cholesterol: 284
- Protein: 45.6
- Total Fat: 69

133.   Crunchy Ranch Chicken Tenders

Serving: 6 | Prep: 15mins | Ready in:

Ingredients

- 2/3 cup corn flake cereal crumbs*
- 1/2 cup all-purpose flour
- 2 Land O'Lakes® Eggs, slightly beaten
- 1 (1 ounce) package dry ranch-flavored dressing mix
- 1 pound boneless skinless chicken tenders
- 3 squares Land O'Lakes® Garlic Herb Saute Express®
- Ranch dressing

Direction

- Place eggs, flour, and cornflake crumbs each into individual shallow bowls. Add ranch dressing mix to flour; mix until blended.

- Put chicken tender into the flour mixture to coat, shaking off excess. Put into the beaten egg to dip. Press into the cornflake crumbs.
- In a 12-in. nonstick skillet, melt Sauté Express® squares over medium-low heat until bubbles just starts to appear.
- Into the skillet, put the coated chicken tenders. Cook until the chicken is not pink anymore, about 10-12 minutes, flipping sometimes.
- Enjoy with ranch dressing.

Nutrition Information

- Calories: 346 calories;
- Sodium: 793
- Total Carbohydrate: 21.9
- Cholesterol: 146
- Protein: 30.1
- Total Fat: 13.7

134.   Crusty Herb Potato Wedges

Serving: 2 | Prep: 10mins | Ready in:

Ingredients

- 2 Russet potatoes, each cut into 6 equal wedges
- olive oil
- 1 tablespoon herbes de Provence
- 1 pinch paprika, or to taste
- salt and ground black pepper to taste

Direction

- Set an oven to preheat to 220°C (425°F). Use a silicone baking mat to line a baking tray.
- In a bowl, toss together the black pepper, salt, paprika, herbes de Provence, olive oil and potato wedges, until the potatoes are coated evenly. Put the wedges on their sides onto the prepped baking tray.

- Let it bake for 15 minutes in the preheated oven, then turn the potatoes onto the other sides. Put it back into the oven and let it cook for about 20 more minutes, until it turns golden brown in color and crusty.

Nutrition Information

- Calories: 225 calories;
- Protein: 4.4
- Total Fat: 7
- Sodium: 13
- Total Carbohydrate: 37.5
- Cholesterol: 0

---

135. Cucumber Honeydew Salad

Serving: 6 | Prep: 20mins | Ready in:

Ingredients

- 1 honeydew melon - peeled, seeded and cubed
- 2 cucumbers, peeled and sliced
- 1/2 red onion, minced
- 1 bunch fresh mint, minced
- 1/3 cup extra-virgin olive oil
- 1/2 lemon, juiced, or to taste
- salt and ground black pepper to taste

Direction

- In a large bowl, mix mint, red onion, cucumbers and honeydew melon together. Toss in olive oil till coated. Add pepper, salt and lemon juice to taste then stir. Cover and keep for 40 minutes in the fridge to chill.

Nutrition Information

- Calories: 208 calories;
- Cholesterol: 0
- Protein: 2
- Total Fat: 12.9

- Sodium: 40
- Total Carbohydrate: 23.8

---

136. Cucumber Sandwich

Serving: 1 | Prep: 10mins | Ready in:

Ingredients

- 2 thick slices whole wheat bread
- 2 tablespoons cream cheese, softened
- 6 slices cucumber
- 2 tablespoons alfalfa sprouts
- 1 teaspoon olive oil
- 1 teaspoon red wine vinegar
- 1 tomato, sliced
- 1 leaf lettuce
- 1 ounce pepperoncini, sliced
- 1/2 avocado, mashed

Direction

- Put a tablespoon of cream cheese on each slice of bread. On a single bread, put a single layer of cucumber slices. Add sprouts then drizzle with vinegar and oil. Add a layer of tomato slices, pepperoncini and lettuce. Spread mashed avocado on the other slice of bread. Close the two slices together then serve right away.

Nutrition Information

- Calories: 496 calories;
- Total Fat: 32.5
- Sodium: 1024
- Total Carbohydrate: 46.3
- Cholesterol: 32
- Protein: 11.4

137. Cucumber Tomato Salad With Zucchini And Black Olives In Lemon Balsamic Vinaigrette

Serving: 6 | Prep: 30mins | Ready in:

Ingredients

- 2 large cucumbers, diced
- 1 zucchini, diced
- 1/2 red onion, thinly sliced
- 3 large tomatoes, diced
- 1 cup chopped black olives
- 2 tablespoons chopped fresh basil
- 2 teaspoons fresh thyme leaves
- 3 tablespoons red wine vinegar
- 1 tablespoon balsamic vinegar
- 1 1/2 teaspoons lemon zest
- 1/2 lemon, juiced
- 1 1/4 teaspoons kosher salt, or to taste
- 1/2 teaspoon white sugar
- 1/4 teaspoon freshly ground black pepper
- 1/2 cup extra-virgin olive oil

Direction

- Combine thyme, cucumbers, basil, zucchini, black olives, red onion, and tomatoes in a big salad bowl. Combine white pepper, red wine vinegar, sugar, balsamic vinegar, kosher salt, lemon juice, and lemon zest in another bowl until well blended. Gradually pour in olive oil on the dressing mixture while whisking. Drizzle dressing over salad. Serve.

Nutrition Information

- Calories: 242 calories;
- Protein: 2.2
- Total Fat: 21.6
- Sodium: 618
- Total Carbohydrate: 12.2
- Cholesterol: 0

138. Curried Butternut Squash And Pear Soup

Serving: 8 | Prep: 15mins | Ready in:

Ingredients

- 1 (2 pound) butternut squash
- 3 tablespoons unsalted butter
- 1 onion, diced
- 2 cloves garlic, minced
- 2 teaspoons minced fresh ginger root
- 1 tablespoon curry powder
- 1 teaspoon salt
- 4 cups reduced sodium chicken broth
- 2 firm ripe Bartlett pears, peeled, cored, and cut into 1 inch dice
- 1/2 cup half and half

Direction

- Set the oven to 375°F (190°C) for preheating. Use a parchment paper to line the rimmed baking sheet.
- Slice the squash in half lengthwise, discarding the membrane and seeds. Arrange the squash halves onto the prepared baking sheet, cut sides down. Roast the squash inside the preheated oven for 45 minutes until very soft. Scoop the pulp from the peel then set aside.
- Put butter in a large pot and melt it over medium heat. Stir in curry powder, salt, ginger, onion, and garlic. Cook and stir for 10 minutes, or until the onion is soft. Pour in chicken broth. Bring the mixture to a boil. Stir in pears and the reserved squash. Simmer for 30 minutes until the pears are very soft.
- Transfer the soup into the blender, about no more than halfway full of the pitcher. Use a folded kitchen towel to hold the lid of the blender. Puree the mixture in batches until smooth. Bring the mixture back into the pot. Mix in half-and-half; reheat.

Nutrition Information

- Calories: 167 calories;

- Total Fat: 6.6
- Sodium: 786
- Total Carbohydrate: 27.5
- Cholesterol: 20
- Protein: 3

---

139. Curried Chicken Tea Sandwiches

Serving: 6 | Prep: 20mins | Ready in:

Ingredients

- 2 cups cubed, cooked chicken
- 1 unpeeled red apple, chopped
- 3/4 cup dried cranberries
- 1/2 cup thinly sliced celery
- 1/4 cup chopped pecans
- 2 tablespoons thinly sliced green onions
- 3/4 cup mayonnaise
- 2 teaspoons lime juice
- 1/2 teaspoon curry powder
- 12 slices bread
- 12 lettuce leaves

Direction

- In a bowl, mix green onions, pecans, celery, cranberries, apple and chicken. In a small bowl, mix curry powder, lime juice and mayonnaise. Fold the mayonnaise mixture in the chicken mixture. Mix to coat. Refrigerate, covered, until serving time.
- Cut every slice of bread using a 3-in. heart-shaped cookie cutter. Put a lettuce leaf and the chicken salad on top.

Nutrition Information

- Calories: 528 calories;
- Total Fat: 32.7
- Sodium: 540
- Total Carbohydrate: 43.9
- Cholesterol: 47

- Protein: 16.5

---

140. Curried Coconut Carrot Soup

Serving: 4 | Prep: | Ready in:

Ingredients

- 1 pound carrots, peeled and cut in chunks
- 1 small onion, quartered
- 1/3 cup raw cashews
- 1 (14 ounce) can unsweetened light coconut milk
- 1 teaspoon curry powder
- 1/2 teaspoon ground ginger
- 1/2 teaspoon kosher salt (optional)
- 1 cup vegetable stock

Direction

- Preheat the oven to 350°F.
- Put an onion and carrots in a baking pan, ungreased. Roast them until tender, or for 30 to 35 minutes.
- Move the roasted vegetables to Oster(R) Versa(R) Performance Blender. Put in coconut milk, cashews, and your seasonings to the blender. Pulse blend on High twice or thrice.
- Blend for another 1 to 2 minutes or until creamy on High.
- Transfer to a saucepan. Add stock.
- Cook the mixture for 5 minutes or until heated through over medium heat.

Nutrition Information

- Calories: 317 calories;
- Protein: 5.2
- Total Fat: 26.7
- Sodium: 473
- Total Carbohydrate: 19.8
- Cholesterol: 0

141. Curried Pumpkin Soup With Chives

Serving: 4 | Prep: 5mins | Ready in:

Ingredients

- 1 (15 ounce) can pure pumpkin puree
- 2 cups Swanson® Chicken Broth
- 1/2 cup fat free half-and-half
- 1/2 teaspoon curry powder
- 1/8 teaspoon ground nutmeg
- Salt and freshly ground black pepper to taste
- 1/4 cup reduced-fat sour cream
- 1 tablespoon chopped fresh chives

Direction

- In a medium saucepan, beat Swanson® Chicken Broth and pureed pumpkin together. Stir in half-and-half, nutmeg, pepper, curry powder and salt.
- Steam over medium heat for about 10 minutes, ensuring it does not to boil. If necessary, adjust seasoning. Until it is ready for serving, keep warm on low heat.
- Divide into small bowls. Use a dollop of sour cream and chopped chives to garnish each bowl.

Nutrition Information

- Calories: 81 calories;
- Total Fat: 2.9
- Sodium: 1368
- Total Carbohydrate: 12.7
- Cholesterol: 10
- Protein: 3

142. Curried Sweet Potato And Carrot Soup

Serving: 5 | Prep: 15mins | Ready in:

Ingredients

- 2 teaspoons canola oil
- 1/2 cup chopped shallots
- 3 cups 1/2-inch cubes peeled sweet potato
- 1 1/2 cups 1/4-inch slices peeled carrot
- 1 tablespoon grated fresh ginger root
- 2 teaspoons curry powder
- 3 cups fat free, low-sodium chicken broth
- 1/2 teaspoon salt

Direction

- Pour some oil in a saucepan and put over medium-high heat. Sauté shallots in the hot oil for 3 minutes or until tender.
- Add carrot, curry powder, ginger, and sweet potato to the saucepan. Stir and cook for 3 to 4 minutes or until they start to soften.
- Add chicken broth to the mixture. Let it boil and place a lid on the saucepan. Reduce to low heat and let the vegetables simmer for 25 to 30 minutes or until they are tender. Add salt to taste.
- Transfer half of the soup into a blender. Make sure the blender is not more than half full. Put the lid on and pulse blender the mixture a few times, then leave it on to puree. Finally, serve the soup in a bowl and enjoy.
- Pour about half the soup into a blender do not fill over half full. Hold lid in place and pulse the blender a few times before leaving to puree. Pour pureed soup into a serving bowl and repeat with the rest of the soup.

Nutrition Information

- Calories: 131 calories;
- Sodium: 539
- Total Carbohydrate: 23.1
- Cholesterol: 0
- Protein: 5.7

- Total Fat: 2.1

143.   Dan's Favorite Chicken Sandwich

Serving: 2 | Prep: 15mins | Ready in:

Ingredients

- 2 skinless, boneless chicken breast halves
- 2 tablespoons barbeque sauce
- 4 slices bacon
- 2 hoagie rolls, split lengthwise
- 2 tablespoons Ranch dressing
- 4 slices Swiss cheese
- 1 small avocado - peeled, pitted and diced

Direction

- Set oven to 190°C or 375°F. Apply cooking spray to a baking dish. For the chicken breasts, brush each side with barbeque sauce then place them in baking dish. Place two bacon slices on each chicken breast.
- Let the chicken bake for 25 minutes until juices are clear. Remove excess oil from the bacon strips with paper towels. Cut the breasts lengthwise in two.
- Prepare and heat oven's broiler. Spread Ranch dressing to both halves of every hoagie roll. On one side of every roll, put two breast halves. Put two strips bacon on each left roll half. Place 1 slice of Swiss cheese on every half.
- Place halves on cookie sheet. Broil them for 2-5 minutes until the cheese melts and is bubbling. Put avocado slices on chicken hoagie halves and put bacon halves on top; then serve.

Nutrition Information

- Calories: 1063 calories;
- Total Carbohydrate: 84.8
- Cholesterol: 143
- Protein: 59.8

- Total Fat: 53.3
- Sodium: 1663

144.   Darra's Famous Tuna Waldorf Salad Sandwich Filling

Serving: 4 | Prep: 15mins | Ready in:

Ingredients

- 1/2 cup mayonnaise
- 1 tablespoon prepared Dijon-style mustard
- 1/4 teaspoon curry powder
- salt and pepper to taste
- 1 (5 ounce) can tuna, drained
- 1 shallot, finely chopped
- 1 Granny Smith apple, cored and diced
- 1/4 cup chopped walnuts
- 1/2 cup diced celery
- 1 teaspoon sweet pickle relish
- 4 large croissants
- 4 leaves lettuce
- 4 slices Swiss cheese

Direction

- Combine pepper, salt, curry powder, mustard, and mayonnaise in a medium-sized bowl. Add pickle relish, celery, walnuts, apple, shallot, and tuna and mix until all ingredients are covered with dressing.
- Toast the croissants lightly. Divide in half, on the bottom half of the croissant put a lettuce leaf and fill with tuna salad. Put a slice of Swiss cheese and the top half of croissant on top. Eat with potato chips and a dill pickle. Enjoy!

Nutrition Information

- Calories: 695 calories;
- Cholesterol: 91
- Protein: 23.1
- Total Fat: 48.9

- Sodium: 844
- Total Carbohydrate: 42.4

---

145.   Day After Thanksgiving Turkey Pho

Serving: 4 | Prep: 15mins | Ready in:

Ingredients

- 1 whole cardamom pod
- 2 whole cloves
- 1 star anise pod
- 1 teaspoon fennel seeds
- 2 teaspoons coriander seed
- 1 (2 inch) piece fresh ginger, peeled and smashed
- 1/2 onion, peeled
- 1 turkey carcass
- 8 cups water, or more as needed
- 1 (16 ounce) package dried flat rice noodles
- 1/4 cup fish sauce
- salt to taste
- 1 cup shredded leftover cooked turkey
- 1 tablespoon shredded fresh basil leaves (optional)
- 1 tablespoon chopped fresh cilantro (optional)
- 1/4 onion, thinly sliced (optional)
- 1 lime, cut into wedges (optional)
- 1 tablespoon chile-garlic sauce (such as Sriracha®), or to taste (optional)

Direction

- Toast coriander, fennel, star anise, cloves, and cardamom pod in a small skillet on medium-low heat for 5-7 minutes until fragrant. Put spices onto the middle of an 8-inch square cheesecloth. Bring edges of cheesecloth together then tie using kitchen twine to make it secure. Sear ginger on both sides and half the onion for about 3 minutes per side in the same skillet until charred slightly.
- Put onion, ginger, sachet, water, and turkey carcass in a big pot on medium-high heat. Boil

then bring down to simmer. Simmer it for 2 hours.
- Put a big pot full of lightly salted water to a rolling boil on high heat. When water is boiling, mix in rice noodles then boil again. Cook noodles, occasionally stirring and uncovered, for 4-5 minutes until noodles are cooked through yet firm to chew. Drain it well inside a colander in the sink.
- Take out onion, ginger, sachet, and carcass from soup. Strain soup to get rid of meat that fell of the bones if needed. Season with salt and fish sauce. Distribute turkey meat and rice noodles into 4 big bowls evenly. Scatter sliced onion, cilantro, and basil on the top. Pour soup on top. Eat with hot sauce and a lime wedge.

Nutrition Information

- Calories: 755 calories;
- Protein: 24
- Total Fat: 27.3
- Sodium: 1524
- Total Carbohydrate: 99.7
- Cholesterol: 87

---

146.   Delicious Avocado Egg Salad

Serving: 2 | Prep: 10mins | Ready in:

Ingredients

- 4 eggs
- 1/2 avocado - peeled, pitted and diced
- 2 stalks celery, finely chopped
- 2 tablespoons prepared mustard
- 1 teaspoon salt
- 1 teaspoon ground black pepper
- 1 teaspoon garlic powder

Direction

- Cover eggs in water in a saucepan; boil for 10 minutes. Put eggs into bowl of warm water; rest eggs for 10 minutes in warm water.
- Peel eggs; rinse to cool under cold water. Cube eggs.
- Mash mustard, celery, avocado and eggs with a fork till mixed well yet chunky in a bowl; season with garlic powder, black pepper and salt.

Nutrition Information

- Calories: 230 calories;
- Cholesterol: 327
- Protein: 13.4
- Total Fat: 16.8
- Sodium: 1497
- Total Carbohydrate: 8.7

147. Delicious Beef Tongue Tacos

Serving: 20 | Prep: 15mins | Ready in:

Ingredients

- 1 beef tongue
- 1/2 white onion, sliced
- 5 cloves garlic, crushed
- 1 bay leaf
- salt to taste
- 3 tablespoons vegetable oil
- 5 Roma tomatoes
- 5 serrano peppers
- salt to taste
- 1/2 onion, diced
- 2 (10 ounce) packages corn tortillas

Direction

- In a slow cooker, put the beef tongue and pour water to cover. Add the bay leaf, garlic and slices of onion, then add salt to season. Put cover on and cook for 8 hours or overnight on low. Take out the tongue and shred the meat into strands.
- In a skillet, heat the oil on medium heat. Cook the peppers and tomatoes in the hot oil until all sides become soft. Transfer the peppers and tomatoes in a blender and keep the oil on the heat, then add salt to season. Briefly blend until still a bit chunky. In the skillet, cook the diced onion until it becomes translucent; mix in the tomato mixture. Cook for an additional 5-6 minutes. Assemble the tacos by putting the shredded tongue meat into a tortilla and scooping the salsa on top of the meat.

Nutrition Information

- Calories: 227 calories;
- Total Fat: 14
- Sodium: 46
- Total Carbohydrate: 14
- Cholesterol: 66
- Protein: 11.4

148. Dijon Chicken Salad

Serving: 6 | Prep: 20mins | Ready in:

Ingredients

- 2 (10 ounce) cans chunk chicken
- 1 cup sliced celery
- 1 cup halved seedless green grapes
- 1 cup halved seedless red grapes
- 1/4 cup dried cranberries
- 2 teaspoons dried chives
- 2 tablespoons honey
- 1 tablespoon Dijon mustard
- 3/4 cup mayonnaise
- 1/2 teaspoon salt
- 1/8 teaspoon ground black pepper

Direction

- In a bowl, combine chives, cranberries, red grapes, green grapes, celery, and chicken. In another bowl, stir together pepper, salt, mayonnaise, mustard, and honey. Combine chicken mixture and mustard mixture until evenly coated.

Nutrition Information

- Calories: 432 calories;
- Cholesterol: 68
- Protein: 21.1
- Total Fat: 29.6
- Sodium: 900
- Total Carbohydrate: 21.4

149.	Donna's Nest Eggs

Serving: 6 | Prep: 20mins | Ready in:

Ingredients

- 1/2 cup milk
- 1 (3 ounce) package seasoned coating mix (such as SHAKE-N-BAKE®)
- 1 pound bulk pork sausage
- 6 hard-boiled eggs, peeled

Direction

- Start preheating the oven to 400°F (200°C).
- In a shallow dish, add milk; empty the seasoned coating packet into the large plastic zipper bag. Equally portion pork sausage into six parts. Completely wrap every egg using 1 sausage layer. Roll egg and sausage balls in milk and put inside the plastic bag. Then seal the bag, shake gently until the balls are coated with the seasoned coating. Put coated egg and sausage balls on a rack over the baking dish.
- Bake in prepared oven for half an hour or until crisp slightly and golden brown.

Nutrition Information

- Calories: 337 calories;
- Cholesterol: 257
- Protein: 18.6
- Total Fat: 23.4
- Sodium: 1057
- Total Carbohydrate: 12

150.	Easiest Corn On The Cob

Serving: 1 | Prep: 5mins | Ready in:

Ingredients

- 1 ear fresh corn in the husk
- 1 teaspoon butter, or more to taste
- salt to taste

Direction

- Cook corn in the microwave for 3 1/2 minutes or until it becomes tender and cooked through.
- Using a towel, hold the tapered end of the corn and transfer to a cutting board. Cut off the bottom end of the cob, about 1 inch in length. Remove corn cob from the husk and silk.
- Put butter on the corn then season with salt.

Nutrition Information

- Calories: 113 calories;
- Total Fat: 5.1
- Sodium: 42
- Total Carbohydrate: 17.1
- Cholesterol: 11
- Protein: 2.9

151.	Easy Broccoli Bacon Salad

Serving: 8 | Prep: 20mins | Ready in:

Ingredients

- 1 large head broccoli, cut into florets
- 1 small red onion, chopped
- 12 slices cooked bacon, crumbled
- 1 cup raisins
- 1/4 cup sunflower seeds
- Dressing:
- 1/2 cup mayonnaise
- 1/3 cup white sugar
- 3 tablespoons red wine vinegar

Direction

- In a bowl, mix sunflower seeds, raisins, bacon, onion and broccoli.
- In a bowl, mix red wine vinegar, sugar and mayonnaise till the dressing is smooth in texture then add on top of broccoli mixture and coat by mixing.

Nutrition Information

- Calories: 280 calories;
- Total Fat: 17.2
- Sodium: 303
- Total Carbohydrate: 28.2
- Cholesterol: 15
- Protein: 6.2

152.   Easy Mini Bagel Pizzas

Serving: 4 | Prep: 10mins | Ready in:

Ingredients

- 8 mini bagels, split
- 1/4 cup pizza sauce
- 1/3 cup shredded pizza cheese blend
- 16 slices turkey pepperoni (such as Hormel®)

Direction

- Set the oven to 220°C or 425°F. Use aluminum foil to line a baking sheet.
- On prepared baking sheet, add bagels, with cut sides up. Scoop over each bagel half with a thin payer of pizza sauce, then sprinkle with pizza cheese. Put on each bagel with 2 pepperoni slices.
- In the preheated oven, bake for 6 minutes, until pepperoni is browned a little bit and cheese is melted.

Nutrition Information

- Calories: 232 calories;
- Cholesterol: 33
- Protein: 13.9
- Total Fat: 5.8
- Sodium: 788
- Total Carbohydrate: 30.3

153.   Easy Tortellini Soup

Serving: 8 | Prep: 15mins | Ready in:

Ingredients

- 1 tablespoon olive oil
- 1 small red onion, chopped
- 1 zucchini, chopped
- 1 tablespoon minced garlic
- 1 (28 ounce) can crushed tomatoes
- 2 (14.5 ounce) cans chicken broth
- 1 tablespoon white sugar
- 1 tablespoon Italian seasoning
- 1/4 cup red wine
- 1 dash hot pepper sauce
- 1 (11 ounce) can white corn, undrained
- 1/2 cup freshly grated Parmesan cheese
- 8 ounces cheese tortellini

Direction

- Cook garlic, zucchini, and onion in oil in a big pot over medium heat until the onion is translucent, about 3 minutes. Mix in pepper

sauce, wine, Italian seasoning, sugar, broth, and crushed tomatoes and boil.
- Lower the heat and mix in Parmesan and corn. Simmer for 30 minutes.
- Mix in tortellini and simmer until the pasta is soft, about another 10 minutes.

Nutrition Information

- Calories: 218 calories;
- Cholesterol: 16
- Protein: 8.7
- Total Fat: 6.2
- Sodium: 423
- Total Carbohydrate: 32.5

154.   Edamame Fresca

Serving: 8 | Prep: 15mins | Ready in:

Ingredients

- 1 small red onion, chopped
- 2 (12 ounce) packages frozen shelled edamame (green soybeans), thawed
- 2 (14 ounce) cans black beans, drained and rinsed
- 1 (14 ounce) can garbanzo beans, drained and rinsed
- 2 cups seasoned rice vinegar
- 1 red bell pepper, chopped
- 1 yellow bell pepper, chopped
- 3 tablespoons chopped fresh Italian parsley
- 3 tablespoons grated fresh ginger root
- 2 tablespoons extra-virgin olive oil
- salt and ground black pepper to taste

Direction

- In a bowl, add red onion and water to cover sufficiently, then soak for 5 minutes. Drain.
- In a big glass bowl, mix together extra-virgin olive oil, ginger root, parsley, yellow bell pepper, red bell pepper, rice vinegar, garbanzo

beans, black beans, edamame and soaked red onion, then folding carefully to prevent smashing the beans. Season to taste with salt and black pepper.
- Chill for 8 hours or overnight.

Nutrition Information

- Calories: 319 calories;
- Sodium: 545
- Total Carbohydrate: 40.2
- Cholesterol: 0
- Protein: 19.9
- Total Fat: 10.1

155.   Egg Drop Soup (Better Than Restaurant Quality!)

Serving: 1 | Prep: 5mins | Ready in:

Ingredients

- 1 cup chicken broth
- 1/4 teaspoon soy sauce
- 1/4 teaspoon sesame oil
- 1 teaspoon cornstarch (optional)
- 2 teaspoons water (optional)
- 1 egg, beaten
- 1 drop yellow food coloring (optional)
- 1 teaspoon chopped fresh chives
- 1/8 teaspoon salt (optional)
- 1/2 teaspoon ground white pepper (optional)

Direction

- Mix sesame oil, chicken broth, and soy sauce in a small pot. Allow the mixture to come to a boil. Meanwhile, mix water and cornstarch until dissolved. Pour the mixture into the pot. Pour in an egg (and yellow food coloring if desired) into the soup while stirring.

Nutrition Information

- Calories: 112 calories;
- Sodium: 1396
- Total Carbohydrate: 4.8
- Cholesterol: 191
- Protein: 7.5
- Total Fat: 6.7

156. Egg Pesto Breakfast Wrap

Serving: 1 | Prep: 10mins | Ready in:

Ingredients

- 2 eggs
- 1 1/2 teaspoons reduced-fat sour cream
- 1/4 cup shredded reduced-fat Cheddar cheese
- 2 tablespoons finely chopped onion
- 1 1/2 teaspoons prepared pesto sauce
- 3 grape tomatoes, sliced
- 1 slice turkey bacon
- 1/2 ounce marinated artichoke hearts, drained and thinly sliced
- 1 10-inch flour tortilla
- salt and pepper to taste

Direction

- In a bowl with the sour cream, beat the eggs until blended. Stir in cheddar cheese.
- In a skillet sprayed with cooking spray, cook and stir pesto sauce and onion for about 6 minutes over medium heat until the onion is translucent. Stir tomatoes in and put egg mixture in skillet. Cook and stir egg mixture for about 3 minutes and until eggs are cooked but not dry. Move eggs out from skillet. Set aside.
- In the skillet, put the turkey bacon and fry for about 3 minutes per side until the bacon is starting to crisp and thoroughly cooked, flipping once. Once bacon is cooked, heat the artichokes in the skillet for about a minute. Take the artichokes and bacon from the pan.

- Use cooking spray to spray the skillet then put the tortilla in the hot skillet. Heat until flexible and warm and put into a plate.
- In the center of the tortilla, spoon artichokes, turkey bacon and eggs. Use pepper and salt to season. To enclose filling, fold 2 inches of the bottom of the tortilla up and tightly wrap.

Nutrition Information

- Calories: 533 calories;
- Total Fat: 26.8
- Sodium: 1015
- Total Carbohydrate: 44.9
- Cholesterol: 333
- Protein: 27.6

157. Eggplant Caponata (Sicilian Version)

Serving: 16 | Prep: 30mins | Ready in:

Ingredients

- 1 eggplant, peeled and cut into 1/2-inch cubes
- salt to taste
- 1/4 cup olive oil, divided
- 1 cup finely chopped celery
- 1 onion, finely chopped
- 1 clove garlic, minced
- 1 1/2 cups canned plum tomatoes, drained and coarsely chopped
- 12 green olives, pitted and coarsely chopped
- 1 1/2 tablespoons drained capers
- 1 tablespoon tomato paste
- 1 teaspoon minced oregano
- 2 tablespoons red wine vinegar
- 2 teaspoons white sugar
- 1 teaspoon salt
- ground black pepper to taste
- 2 teaspoons minced fresh parsley, or to taste

Direction

- Sprinkle eggplant with salt then put in a colander set over a bowl. Let it stand for about 30 minutes then rinse and pat dry eggplant.
- In a big pan set over medium temperature, heat 2 tablespoons olive oil. Add celery and cook for about 4 minutes or until tender. Stir often as it cooks. Toss in onion and garlic. Continue to cook and stir for about 5 minutes until onion is tender and lightly golden. Use a slotted spoon to scoop the mixture and transfer to a bowl.
- In the same pan, heat 2 tablespoons olive oil that remains. Toss in eggplant and cook for 5-7 minutes or until lightly browned. Stir constantly as it cooks. Mix in tomatoes, capers, tomato paste, olives, oregano and the celery mixture. Cook to a boil then turn down heat to low. Remove cover and let it simmer for about 15 minutes until caponata is thickened.
- Season with salt, pepper, sugar and vinegar to taste. Serve in a bowl garnished with parsley.

Nutrition Information

- Calories: 56 calories;
- Cholesterol: 0
- Protein: 0.9
- Total Fat: 3.9
- Sodium: 297
- Total Carbohydrate: 5.5

---

158. Everyone's Favorite Spinach Salad With Poppy Seed Dressing

Serving: 4 | Prep: 20mins | Ready in:

Ingredients

- 1/4 cup white vinegar
- 1/2 cup vegetable oil
- 1/3 cup white sugar
- 1 tablespoon poppy seeds
- 2 teaspoons finely minced onion

- 1/2 teaspoon Worcestershire sauce
- 1/4 teaspoon paprika
- 1 (10 ounce) bag baby spinach
- 1 cup sliced fresh strawberries, or as needed
- 1 (4 ounce) package crumbled blue cheese, or as needed
- 1/2 cup roasted pecan halves, or as needed

Direction

- In a bowl, whisk paprika, Worcestershire sauce, onion, poppy seeds, sugar, vegetable oil and vinegar together to dissolve the sugar completely.
- In individual bowls, make layers of spinach, strawberries, blue cheese and pecans. Generously drizzle each salad with dressing.

Nutrition Information

- Calories: 542 calories;
- Sodium: 458
- Total Carbohydrate: 25.9
- Cholesterol: 21
- Protein: 10
- Total Fat: 46.5

---

159. Fancy Chicken Salad

Serving: 5 | Prep: | Ready in:

Ingredients

- 1/2 cup light mayonnaise
- 2 tablespoons cider vinegar
- 2 cloves crushed garlic
- 3 tablespoons chopped fresh dill
- 1 pound skinless, boneless chicken breast halves - cooked
- 1/4 cup crumbled feta cheese
- 1/2 cup red bell pepper, chopped

Direction

- Combine dill, garlic, vinegar and mayonnaise. Let refrigerate for several hours or overnight.
- Mix cheese, peppers and, chicken together then blend with the chilled dressing. Serve!

Nutrition Information

- Calories: 166 calories;
- Total Carbohydrate: 1.8
- Cholesterol: 77
- Protein: 27.7
- Total Fat: 4.4
- Sodium: 143

---

160.   Festival Style Grilled Italian Sausage Sandwiches

Serving: 4 | Prep: 20mins | Ready in:

Ingredients

- 4 (4 ounce) links hot Italian sausage
- 1 red bell pepper, halved and seeded
- 1 small onion, peeled and cut in half crosswise
- 2 teaspoons olive oil
- salt and pepper to taste
- 1 tablespoon olive oil
- 4 (6 inch) sandwich rolls, split and toasted

Direction

- Set an outdoor grill for medium heat and start preheating. Coat the grate lightly with oil and place 4 inches from the heat source.
- Use a fork to pierce in several places of the sausages, then put aside. Cut the bottoms off the onion halves to let them sit flat on the grill. Brush 2 teaspoons of olive oil over onion halves and bell pepper.
- On the prepared grill, arrange peppers, onions, and sausages. Turn and cook the sausages until juices from them run clear and the sausages are browned nicely. Cook the vegetables until they become tender and the

peppers are charred slightly. Take the sausages and vegetables out of the grill.
- Fill a paper bag with the peppers, seal, and let it slightly cool. Then remove the charred skin from the peppers and throw away; cut the peppers into strips. Cut the onion halves into slices. Put pepper and salt to taste, and a tablespoon of olive oil into a bowl. Add onions and peppers, then toss them until coated evenly. In the sandwich rolls, arrange the sausages, then place the onion and pepper mixture on top to serve.

Nutrition Information

- Calories: 631 calories;
- Total Fat: 33.7
- Sodium: 1258
- Total Carbohydrate: 56.2
- Cholesterol: 61
- Protein: 27

---

161.   Feta Chicken Salad

Serving: 4 | Prep: 30mins | Ready in:

Ingredients

- 3 cups diced cooked chicken
- 2 large stalks celery, diced
- 1 red bell pepper, seeded and diced
- 1/2 red onion, diced
- 6 tablespoons mayonnaise
- 6 tablespoons sour cream
- 1 (4 ounce) package feta cheese, crumbled
- 2 teaspoons dried dill weed
- 1 pinch salt and pepper to taste

Direction

- Combine red onion, celery, and chicken together in a serving bowl. Combine dill, feta cheese, sour cream, and mayonnaise in another bowl. Put on the chicken mixture and mix to combine. Taste, and use pepper and salt to season if necessary. Chill until serving or enjoy immediately.

Nutrition Information

- Calories: 599 calories;
- Protein: 40.8
- Total Fat: 44.8
- Sodium: 1061
- Total Carbohydrate: 7.2
- Cholesterol: 163

---

162. Fresh Fruit Salad With Honey Lime Dressing

Serving: 14 | Prep: 10mins | Ready in:

Ingredients

- 1 cup fresh pineapple chunks
- 1 cup orange segments
- 1 cup halved fresh strawberries
- 1 cup cantaloupe chunks
- 1 cup watermelon chunks
- 1 cup grapefruit chunks
- 1 cup halved seedless grapes
- Dressing:
- 6 tablespoons salad oil
- 3 tablespoons lime juice
- 3 tablespoons honey
- 1/4 teaspoon vinegar, or to taste
- 1 pinch ground ginger

Direction

- In a bowl, mix grapes, grapefruit, watermelon, cantaloupe, strawberries, oranges and pineapple together then store in the fridge for at least 30 minutes to chill.
- In a bottle with a lid, combine ginger, vinegar, honey, lime juice and oil then cover and shake to mix the dressing. Store for at least 30 minutes in the fridge to chill. Shake again and

drizzle the dressing over fruit and toss till coated.

Nutrition Information

- Calories: 103 calories;
- Total Fat: 6
- Sodium: 3
- Total Carbohydrate: 13.1
- Cholesterol: 0
- Protein: 0.6

---

163. Fresh Mint And Cilantro Melon Salad

Serving: 10 | Prep: 15mins | Ready in:

Ingredients

- 4 cups 1-inch chunks honeydew
- 1 tablespoon fresh lime juice
- 3 tablespoons chopped cilantro leaves and stems
- 1/3 cup chopped fresh mint leaves
- white sugar to taste

Direction

- In a bowl, combine sugar, mint, cilantro, lime juice and honeydew; toss till combined. Before serving, store for at least 2 hours in the fridge.

Nutrition Information

- Calories: 27 calories;
- Total Fat: 0.1
- Sodium: 13
- Total Carbohydrate: 6.7
- Cholesterol: 0
- Protein: 0.4

164. Fresh Salsa

Serving: 36 | Prep: 45mins | Ready in:

Ingredients

- 6 roma tomatoes, diced
- 3 fresh jalapeno peppers, seeded and chopped
- 1/4 red onion, chopped
- 3 green onions, chopped
- 2 cloves cloves garlic, crushed
- 2 tablespoons chopped fresh cilantro
- 2 tablespoons fresh lime juice
- 2 tablespoons fresh lemon juice
- 1 1/2 teaspoons ground cumin
- 1 small jicama, peeled and chopped
- 1 (10 ounce) can diced tomatoes with green chilies, drained
- salt and ground black pepper to taste

Direction

- In a bowl, combine together chilies, diced tomatoes, jicama, cumin, lemon juice, lime juice, cilantro, garlic, green onion, red onion, jalapeno pepper and tomato , then season to taste with pepper and salt. Let the mixture sit for a minimum of an hour before serving.

Nutrition Information

- Calories: 9 calories;
- Protein: 0.3
- Total Fat: 0.1
- Sodium: 17
- Total Carbohydrate: 2.1
- Cholesterol: 0

165. Fruit, Veggie, And Tuna Salad Wrap

Serving: 4 | Prep: 20mins | Ready in:

Ingredients

- 1 (5 ounce) can tuna, drained
- 2 tablespoons mayonnaise
- 4 cups chopped fresh spinach
- 1 large carrot, shredded
- 1 apple, cored and diced
- 1/2 cup shredded mozzarella cheese
- 1/4 cup fresh blueberries
- 4 (10 inch) flour tortillas

Direction

- In a bowl, mix the tuna and mayonnaise until well-combined.
- In a separate bowl, mix the carrot, blueberries, apple, spinach, and mozzarella cheese. Fold in tuna salad gently and mix, careful not to crush the blueberries.
- Place the flour tortillas inside the microwave for 10 seconds until pliable and warmed slightly. Fill the center of each tortilla with 1 1/2 cups of the spinach and tuna mixture. Fold the tortilla up the bottom, about 2 inches, to enclose the filling. Wrap up and serve!

Nutrition Information

- Calories: 382 calories;
- Total Fat: 13.7
- Sodium: 640
- Total Carbohydrate: 46.2
- Cholesterol: 21
- Protein: 19.1

166. Fruited Curry Chicken Salad

Serving: 8 | Prep: | Ready in:

Ingredients

- 4 skinless, boneless chicken breast halves - cooked and diced
- 1 stalk celery, chopped
- 1/2 onion, chopped

- 1 small apple - peeled, cored and chopped
- 1/3 cup golden raisins
- 1/3 cup seedless green grapes, halved
- 1/2 cup chopped toasted pecans
- 1/8 teaspoon ground black pepper
- 1/2 teaspoon curry powder
- 3/4 cup mayonnaise

Direction

- Mix mayonnaise, curry powder, pepper, pecans, grapes, raisins, apple, onion, celery, and chicken in a big salad bowl. Mix all together, stirring to coat. Enjoy!

Nutrition Information

- Calories: 306 calories;
- Sodium: 153
- Total Carbohydrate: 11.5
- Cholesterol: 44
- Protein: 15
- Total Fat: 23

167.   Garbanzo Bean Salad

Serving: 4 | Prep: 10mins | Ready in:

Ingredients

- 1 (15 ounce) can garbanzo beans, drained
- 1/2 cup chopped celery
- 1 tablespoon diced onion
- 1 apple, cored and chopped
- 1/4 cup chopped walnuts
- 1/4 cup mayonnaise
- 1 tablespoon honey
- 1/2 teaspoon prepared mustard
- 1/4 teaspoon lemon juice
- 1/2 head iceberg lettuce - rinsed, dried, and shredded

Direction

- Mix together the chopped nuts, grapes, apple, onion, celery and chickpeas in a salad bowl.
- Whisk lemon juice, mustard, honey and mayonnaise together to make dressing.
- Mix the dressing and salad mixture together, then toss and serve on shredded lettuce.

Nutrition Information

- Calories: 277 calories;
- Protein: 5.6
- Total Fat: 16.7
- Sodium: 314
- Total Carbohydrate: 29.1
- Cholesterol: 5

168.   Garden Fresh Tomato Soup

Serving: 4 | Prep: 20mins | Ready in:

Ingredients

- 7 cups chopped fresh tomatoes (with seeds and juice)
- 1 onion, finely chopped
- 1 cup finely chopped carrots
- 3 cloves garlic, crushed
- 1 teaspoon extra-virgin olive oil, or more to taste
- 2 cups chicken broth
- 2 teaspoons salt, or to taste
- 3/4 teaspoon white sugar
- 3/4 teaspoon dried dill weed
- 1/2 teaspoon ground black pepper
- 1/4 teaspoon celery salt
- 1/4 teaspoon ground cloves
- 1 cup skim milk
- 1 tablespoon cornstarch
- 1 1/2 teaspoons butter (optional)
- 5 large fresh basil leaves, or more to taste
- 1/4 cup grated Parmesan cheese, or to taste
- 2 tablespoons shredded fresh basil, or to taste

Direction

- In a big pot, combine garlic, carrots, onion, and tomatoes. Drizzle tomato mixture with olive oil; stir and cook on medium heat. Put on cover and allow to simmer 25 minutes until vegetables are tender, mixing from time to time.
- Into tomato mixture, mix cloves, celery salt, black pepper, dill, sugar, salt, and chicken broth. Put cover on the pot, let simmer about 20 minutes, mixing from time to time, until soup flavors blend.
- In a bowl, beat cornstarch together with milk until dissolved.
- In a saucepan, heat butter on medium-low heat. Into melted butter, beat cornstarch mixture for 3-5 minutes until thick and smooth.
- Gradually transfer cornstarch mixture to tomato soup, mixing until combined.
- In a blender, place basil leaves and 1/2 of the soup, no more than half-full. Put on cover and hold lid down; pulse several time before letting blend by itself. In batches, puree soup until smooth. Bring blended soup back to the pot; heat 3-5 minutes on low. Transfer soup into serving bowls with a spoon. Put shredded basil and Parmesan cheese over top.

Nutrition Information

- Calories: 163 calories;
- Protein: 7.7
- Total Fat: 5
- Sodium: 1409
- Total Carbohydrate: 25
- Cholesterol: 10

---

169.   Garlic Bread Spread

Serving: 10 | Prep: 10mins | Ready in:

Ingredients

- 1/2 cup butter, softened
- 1/4 cup grated Parmesan cheese
- 2 cloves garlic, minced
- 1/4 teaspoon dried marjoram
- 1/4 teaspoon dried basil
- 1/4 teaspoon fines herbs
- 1/4 teaspoon dried oregano
- ground black pepper to taste
- 1/4 teaspoon dried parsley, or to taste
- 1 loaf unsliced Italian bread

Direction

- Turn on the oven to 350°F (175°C) to preheat.
- Combine parsley, black pepper, oregano, fines herbs mix, basil, marjoram, garlic, Parmesan cheese and butter in a bowl until combined thoroughly. Cut Italian bread loaf into half lengthwise; use butter mixture to spread generously on each half.
- Put the garlic bread into oven to bake on the top rack for 10-15 minutes until the butter mixture bubbles and melts. Turn on the broiler; broil for another 1-2 minutes until the bread turns golden brown shade as you desired.

Nutrition Information

- Calories: 274 calories;
- Sodium: 489
- Total Carbohydrate: 34
- Cholesterol: 26
- Protein: 6.8
- Total Fat: 12.1

---

170.   Garlic, Basil, And Bacon Deviled Eggs

Serving: 24 | Prep: 15mins | Ready in:

Ingredients

- 12 eggs

- 2 large cloves garlic, pressed
- 5 slices bacon
- 1/2 cup finely chopped fresh basil
- 1/3 cup mayonnaise
- 1/4 teaspoon crushed red pepper flakes
- salt and pepper to taste
- 1/4 teaspoon paprika for garnish

Direction

- In a saucepan, lay eggs in a single layer and add water till eggs get covered by 1 inch. Cover the saucepan and bring to a boil over high heat. Remove from the heat and allow the eggs to stand for 15 minutes in the hot water. Strain. Run cold water over eggs for cooling down. When eggs cool, peel eggs. Halve lengthways and remove the yolks to a bowl. Use a fork to mash the yolks and pressed garlic together.
- In a deep and large skillet, cook the bacon for about 10 minutes over medium-high heat till turns browned evenly. Place on a plate lined with paper towel to drain; chop when bacon cools down. Mix into the mashed egg yolks. Stir into the mixture with pepper, salt, red pepper flakes, mayonnaise, and basil till mixed well. Fill the mixture in egg white halves; use a bit of paprika to dredge over each of stuffed eggs.

Nutrition Information

- Calories: 69 calories;
- Protein: 3.9
- Total Fat: 5.7
- Sodium: 136
- Total Carbohydrate: 0.5
- Cholesterol: 96

171. Gisela's Butternut Squash Soup

Serving: 4 | Prep: 25mins | Ready in:

Ingredients

- 2 tablespoons butter
- 1 onion, finely chopped
- 1 (14.5 ounce) can chicken broth
- 1 (2 pound) butternut squash - peeled, seeded, and cut into 1-inch cubes
- 1 orange, juiced
- 1 orange, juiced and zested
- 3 tablespoons sour cream
- salt and pepper to taste

Direction

- Melt butter in a soup pot/big saucepan on medium heat; mix and cook onion for 5 minutes till translucent. Add chicken broth; mix orange zest, orange juice and butternut squash cubes in. Boil; lower heat. Simmer for 15-20 minutes till squash cubes are tender.
- Filling pitcher no more than halfway full, put soup into a blender. Use a folded kitchen towel to hold the blender lid down; start blender carefully, using several quick pulses to move soup then leave on to puree. In batches, puree till smooth; put back into pot. Or puree soup in the cooking pot with a stick blender. Whisk sour cream in till smooth; season with pepper and salt to taste. Heat on medium-low heat till nearly simmering; serve hot.

Nutrition Information

- Calories: 245 calories;
- Total Fat: 8.6
- Sodium: 493
- Total Carbohydrate: 42.6
- Cholesterol: 22
- Protein: 4.5

172. Gluten Free Elbows With Mixed Mushrooms And Italian Sausage Soup

Serving: 6 | Prep: 15mins | Ready in:

Ingredients

- 1 (12 ounce) box Barilla® Gluten Free Elbows
- 3 quarts chicken stock
- 3 cloves garlic, minced
- 4 tablespoons extra-virgin olive oil
- 1 sprig rosemary
- 4 (6 ounce) packages mixed mushrooms
- 1 pound Italian sausage, boiled for 10 minutes and cut into 1/3 inch slices
- 1 (15 ounce) can cannellini beans, drained
- 1 pint cherry tomatoes, halved
- Salt and black pepper to taste
- 1 tablespoon parsley, chopped

Direction

- Bring chicken stock to a simmer in a big soup pot.
- In the meantime, sauté garlic with rosemary and olive oil in a saucepan until turning light yellow, about 1 minute. Add mushrooms and sauté until turning light brown. Add sausage and sauté for 2 minutes.
- Add sausage and mushrooms to the broth, mix in Barilla® Gluten Free Elbows, tomatoes, and beans. Cook for 1/2 of the time the box recommends.
- Allow the soup to sit for 10 minutes before eating. Use pepper and salt to season. Use parsley to garnish and use olive oil to drizzle on top.

Nutrition Information

- Calories: 818 calories;
- Sodium: 2094
- Total Carbohydrate: 99.2
- Cholesterol: 59
- Protein: 24

- Total Fat: 36.6

173. Gourmet Chicken Sandwich

Serving: 4 | Prep: 10mins | Ready in:

Ingredients

- 4 skinless, boneless chicken breast halves - pounded to 1/4 inch thickness
- ground black pepper to taste
- 1 tablespoon olive oil
- 1 teaspoon minced garlic
- 2 tablespoons mayonnaise
- 2 teaspoons prepared Dijon-style mustard
- 1 teaspoon chopped fresh rosemary
- 8 slices garlic and rosemary focaccia bread

Direction

- Add pepper on 1 side of each chicken cutlet. In a big skillet, heat the oil and cook the garlic in oil until it becomes brown, then add the chicken pepper-side facing down. Sauté the chicken for about 12-15 minutes, until the juices run clear and cooked through.
- Mix together the rosemary, mustard and mayonnaise in a small bowl. Mix together and spread the mixture on four focaccia bread slices. Put one chicken cutlet on each of the slices, then put on another slice of bread.

Nutrition Information

- Calories: 522 calories;
- Total Fat: 15.7
- Sodium: 826
- Total Carbohydrate: 58
- Cholesterol: 70
- Protein: 34.6

174.   Grandma's Easy Turkey Taco Salad

Serving: 6 | Prep: 20mins | Ready in:

Ingredients

- 1 pound ground turkey
- 1 (1.25 ounce) package taco seasoning mix
- 1 (15 ounce) can black beans, rinsed and drained
- 1 head iceberg lettuce, shredded
- 2 tomatoes, diced
- 1 (10 ounce) bag tortilla chips, coarsely crumbled
- 1 (8 fluid ounce) bottle thousand island dressing

Direction

- Heat the large skillet over medium-high heat. Add the ground turkey and let it cook and stir, until the turkey is browned evenly, crumbly and no longer pinkish. Follow the package directions on mixing the taco seasoning mix. Remove the mixture from heat.
- In a large bowl, mix the lettuce, tortilla chips, black beans, turkey, and tomatoes. Toss the mixture with the salad dressing. You can refrigerate it for an hour before serving or you can serve it immediately.

Nutrition Information

- Calories: 553 calories;
- Total Fat: 32.7
- Sodium: 1130
- Total Carbohydrate: 48.5
- Cholesterol: 69
- Protein: 19.8

175.   Great Chicken Salad

Serving: 2 | Prep: 10mins | Ready in:

Ingredients

- 2 cooked, boneless chicken breast halves, chopped
- 1/4 cup mayonnaise
- 4 tablespoons cole slaw dressing
- 1/2 lemon, juiced
- 1 stalk celery, chopped
- salt and pepper to taste

Direction

- Mix celery, lemon juice, coleslaw dressing, mayonnaise, and chicken together in a food processor.
- Process until completely combined. Use pepper and salt to season to taste and chill until cold.

Nutrition Information

- Calories: 518 calories;
- Total Fat: 39.1
- Sodium: 471
- Total Carbohydrate: 11.4
- Cholesterol: 103
- Protein: 30.8

176.   Greek Grilled Cheese

Serving: 1 | Prep: 5mins | Ready in:

Ingredients

- 1 1/2 teaspoons butter, softened
- 2 slices whole wheat bread, or your favorite bread
- 2 tablespoons crumbled feta cheese
- 2 slices Cheddar cheese
- 1 tablespoon chopped red onion
- 1/4 tomato, thinly sliced

Direction

- Place a skillet over medium heat. Spread butter on 1 side of each bread slice. Layer feta cheese, Cheddar cheese, red onion, and tomato on the unbuttered side of 1 bread slice. Place the other bread slice atop the filling, buttered side out.
- Fry sandwich, approximately 2 minutes on each side, until golden brown. (The second side takes a shorter time to cook).

Nutrition Information

- Calories: 482 calories;
- Sodium: 876
- Total Carbohydrate: 27.1
- Cholesterol: 92
- Protein: 24.6
- Total Fat: 30.9

177.   Greek Zoodle Salad

Serving: 4 | Prep: 15mins | Ready in:

Ingredients

- 2 zucchini
- 1/4 English cucumber, chopped
- 10 cherry tomatoes, halved, or more to taste
- 10 pitted kalamata olives, halved, or more to taste
- 1/4 cup thinly sliced red onion
- 2 ounces crumbled reduced-fat feta cheese
- 2 tablespoons extra-virgin olive oil
- 2 tablespoons fresh lemon juice
- 1 teaspoon dried oregano
- salt and ground black pepper to taste

Direction

- Use a spiralizer to cut zucchini into noodle threads. Put zoodles in a big bowl with olives, cucumber, red onion, tomatoes and feta cheese on top.

- To make dressing, stir lemon juice, pepper, olive oil, salt, and oregano in a bowl until smooth; dump over the zoodle mixture and mix to coat. Put salad in refrigerator to marinate for 10-15 minutes.

Nutrition Information

- Calories: 147 calories;
- Sodium: 391
- Total Carbohydrate: 9.1
- Cholesterol: 5
- Protein: 5
- Total Fat: 11.1

178.   Green Salad With Cranberry Vinaigrette

Serving: 8 | Prep: 15mins | Ready in:

Ingredients

- 1 cup sliced almonds
- 3 tablespoons red wine vinegar
- 1/3 cup olive oil
- 1/4 cup fresh cranberries
- 1 tablespoon Dijon mustard
- 1/2 teaspoon minced garlic
- 1/2 teaspoon salt
- 1/2 teaspoon ground black pepper
- 2 tablespoons water
- 1/2 red onion, thinly sliced
- 4 ounces crumbled blue cheese
- 1 pound mixed salad greens

Direction

- Preheat the oven to 190°C or 375°Fahrenheit. In a single layer, place almonds on a baking sheet. Toast almonds in the oven for five minutes until it starts to brown.
- Process water, vinegar, pepper, oil, salt, cranberries, garlic, and mustard in a food processor or blender until smooth.

- Mix greens, almonds, blue cheese, onion, and the vinegar mixture together in a large bowl until well coated.

Nutrition Information

- Calories: 218 calories;
- Total Carbohydrate: 6.2
- Cholesterol: 11
- Protein: 6.5
- Total Fat: 19.2
- Sodium: 405

179.	Grilled Bacon Apple Sandwich

Serving: 2 | Prep: 5mins | Ready in:

Ingredients

- 6 slices maple-cured bacon
- 5 tablespoons peanut butter
- 4 slices whole wheat bread
- 5 tablespoons apricot jelly
- cayenne pepper to taste
- 1 Granny Smith apple, cored and thinly sliced
- 3 tablespoons softened butter

Direction

- Cook bacon over medium-high heat in a large, deep skillet for about 10 minutes, flipping sometimes, until browned on all sides. Transfer bacon slices to a plate lined with paper towel to drain.
- Smear peanut butter onto 2 slices of bread; put to one side. Spread the remaining 2 slices of bread with apricot jelly; sprinkle with cayenne pepper to season. Place half of each of cooked bacon and sliced apple atop each bread slice covered with apricot jam. Place the peanut butter-spread bread slices on top.
- Bring a large skillet to medium heat on the stove. Spread the outside of the sandwiches

with butter; set into the heated skillet. Cook until crispy and golden browned; flip over; keep cooking until the other side turns golden brown, approximately 4 minutes on each side.

Nutrition Information

- Calories: 832 calories;
- Protein: 28.5
- Total Fat: 51.3
- Sodium: 1233
- Total Carbohydrate: 72.6
- Cholesterol: 76

180.	Grilled Cheese De Mayo

Serving: 1 | Prep: 10mins | Ready in:

Ingredients

- 1 tablespoon mayonnaise, divided
- 2 slices white bread
- 2 slices American cheese
- 1 slice pepperjack cheese

Direction

- Spread 1 side of a bread slice with a half of the mayonnaise and put in a skillet with mayonnaise-side facing down. Put on top of the bread the American and pepperjack cheeses. Spread 1 side of leftover bread with leftover mayonnaise and put on top of the cheese, mayonnaise-side facing up.
- In the skillet, cook sandwich on medium heat for 2 1/2 minutes each side, until bread turn golden brown and cheese has melted.

Nutrition Information

- Calories: 500 calories;
- Total Fat: 34.9
- Sodium: 1349
- Total Carbohydrate: 27.2

- Cholesterol: 74
- Protein: 19.5

Serving: 6 | Prep: 35mins | Ready in:

Ingredients

- Marinade
- 1/4 cup extra virgin olive oil
- 2 tablespoons distilled white vinegar
- 2 tablespoons fresh lime juice
- 2 teaspoons lime zest
- 1 1/2 teaspoons honey
- 2 cloves garlic, minced
- 1/2 teaspoon cumin
- 1/2 teaspoon chili powder
- 1 teaspoon seafood seasoning, such as Old Bay™
- 1/2 teaspoon ground black pepper
- 1 teaspoon hot pepper sauce, or to taste
- 1 pound tilapia fillets, cut into chunks
- Dressing
- 1 (8 ounce) container light sour cream
- 1/2 cup adobo sauce from chipotle peppers
- 2 tablespoons fresh lime juice
- 2 teaspoons lime zest
- 1/4 teaspoon cumin
- 1/4 teaspoon chili powder
- 1/2 teaspoon seafood seasoning, such as Old Bay™
- salt and pepper to taste
- Toppings
- 1 (10 ounce) package tortillas
- 3 ripe tomatoes, seeded and diced
- 1 bunch cilantro, chopped
- 1 small head cabbage, cored and shredded
- 2 limes, cut in wedges

Direction

- For making the marinade, in a bowl, whisk hot sauce, black pepper, seafood seasoning, chili powder, cumin, garlic, honey, lime zest, lime juice, vinegar, and olive oil together till blended. In a shallow dish, lay the tilapia, then

181.   Grilled Corn Salad

Serving: 6 | Prep: 15mins | Ready in:

Ingredients

- 6 ears freshly shucked corn
- 1 green pepper, diced
- 2 Roma (plum) tomatoes, diced
- 1/4 cup diced red onion
- 1/2 bunch fresh cilantro, chopped, or more to taste
- 2 teaspoons olive oil, or to taste
- salt and ground black pepper to taste

Direction

- Preheat the outdoor grill to medium heat and slightly grease the grill grate with oil.
- Put the corn onto the preheated grill and let it grill for about 10 minutes until the corn is soft and slightly charred, turn the corn from time to time; let it cool down until cool enough to the touch. Take the kernels off from the corn cob and put it in a bowl.
- Mix the grilled corn kernels together with the cilantro, diced tomato, olive oil, green pepper and onion. Put pepper and salt to taste then mix until well-combined. Put it aside for a minimum of 30 minutes and let the flavors seep through the salad right before serving.

Nutrition Information

- Calories: 103 calories;
- Sodium: 43
- Total Carbohydrate: 19.7
- Cholesterol: 0
- Protein: 3.4
- Total Fat: 2.8

use the marinade to pour over the fish. Cover, and let sit in the fridge for 6 to 8 hours.

- For making the dressing, in a bowl, mix adobo sauce and sour cream together. Add in seafood seasoning, chili powder, cumin, lime zest, and lime juice and stir well. Add pepper, and salt in desired amounts. Cover, and let sit in the fridge till needed.
- Heat an outdoor grill for high heat beforehand and oil grate lightly. Set grate 4 inches apart from the heat.
- Remove fish from marinade, drain and discard any excess marinade. Grill fish pieces for about 9 minutes till easily flakes with a fork, flipping once.
- To assemble tacos, in the center of tortillas, lay fish pieces together with desired amounts of cabbage, cilantro, and tomatoes; drizzle using dressing. Roll up tortillas around fillings, and use lime wedges for garnish when serving.

Nutrition Information

- Calories: 416 calories;
- Sodium: 644
- Total Carbohydrate: 38.5
- Cholesterol: 43
- Protein: 22.6
- Total Fat: 19.2

183. Grilled Hot Turkey Sandwiches

Serving: 4 | Prep: 10mins | Ready in:

Ingredients

- 4 tablespoons mayonnaise
- 2 tablespoons salsa
- 2 green onions, chopped
- 8 slices sourdough bread
- 1/2 pound deli-sliced turkey
- 4 slices pepperjack cheese
- 4 tablespoons butter

Direction

- In a small bowl, combine green onions, salsa and mayonnaise together. Spread evenly on each bread slice with seasoned mayonnaise. Layer on four slices with turkey and cheese, then place leftover bread on top to form 4 sandwiches.
- In a big skillet, melt 2 tbsp. of butter on moderate heat. Fry in butter with sandwiches until toasted slightly. Put into the skillet with leftover butter and flip sandwiches over. Cook until bread turn brown and cheese has melted.

Nutrition Information

- Calories: 515 calories;
- Cholesterol: 89
- Protein: 21.7
- Total Fat: 33.5
- Sodium: 1373
- Total Carbohydrate: 32.7

184. Grilled Italian Sausage With Marinated Tomatoes

Serving: 6 | Prep: 20mins | Ready in:

Ingredients

- 1 1/2 tablespoons red wine vinegar
- 1 tablespoon balsamic vinegar
- 1/4 teaspoon salt
- 1/8 teaspoon fresh-ground black pepper
- 1 teaspoon dried oregano
- 1 teaspoon dried basil
- 1 1/2 tablespoons olive oil
- 3 vine-ripened tomatoes, each cut into 6 slices
- 1/3 red onion, thinly sliced
- 6 (4 ounce) mild Italian sausage links
- 6 French rolls, halved lengthwise

Direction

- Set the outdoor grill to medium heat for preheating.
- In a small bowl, mix the balsamic vinegar, pepper, salt, olive oil, red wine vinegar, oregano and basil. On a serving platter, arrange the slices of onion and tomato. Spread over with the dressing. Let them marinate at room temperature. In the meantime, cook the sausages.
- Use the tip of the sharp knife to pierce the sausages several times. Arrange the sausages onto the grill. Cook for a total of 15 minutes, flipping them often until evenly cooked and lightly browned and the center is no longer pink. Serve on French rolls together with the marinated onions and tomatoes.

Nutrition Information

- Calories: 447 calories;
- Sodium: 1325
- Total Carbohydrate: 32.2
- Cholesterol: 45
- Protein: 19.6
- Total Fat: 26.4

185. Grilled Pizza Wraps

Serving: 8 | Prep: 10mins | Ready in:

Ingredients

- 2 tablespoons margarine, softened
- 8 (10 inch) flour tortillas
- 1 (16 ounce) package shredded Cheddar-Monterey Jack cheese blend
- 1/2 cup pizza sauce
- 4 ounces sliced pepperoni

Direction

- Over medium-low heat, heat a big skillet. On 1 side of a tortilla, scatter margarine, and put it in skillet, margarine-side facing down. Onto 1/2 of tortilla, scoop 1 tablespoon of pizza

sauce. On top of the sauce, scatter half cup of shredded cheese, and place several pepperoni slices on top. On top of filling, fold clean half of tortilla, and let cook till golden on every side. Redo with the rest of tortillas.

Nutrition Information

- Calories: 543 calories;
- Sodium: 1174
- Total Carbohydrate: 40.6
- Cholesterol: 69
- Protein: 22.5
- Total Fat: 31.9

186. Grilled Portobello With Basil Mayonnaise Sandwich

Serving: 6 | Prep: 10mins | Ready in:

Ingredients

- 1/3 cup balsamic vinegar
- 1/4 cup olive oil
- 1 tablespoon minced garlic
- 6 portobello mushroom caps
- 1/2 cup mayonnaise
- 1 tablespoon Dijon mustard
- 1 teaspoon lemon juice
- 2 tablespoons chopped fresh basil
- 6 kaiser rolls, split, toasted
- 1 tablespoon butter
- 6 leaves lettuce
- 6 tomato slices

Direction

- Set the outdoor grill over medium heat for preheating. Put oil onto the grate lightly. In a small bowl, mix the balsamic vinegar, garlic, and olive oil.
- Place the Portobello mushrooms onto the baking sheet or tray, arranging them gill-side up. Coat the mushrooms with some of the

vinegar mixture. Let them marinate for 3-5 minutes.

- Arrange the marinated mushrooms onto the preheated grill gill-side down. Grill each side of the mushrooms for 4 minutes, coating both sides with the remaining marinade until tender.
- In a small bowl, mix the Dijon mustard, basil, lemon juice, and mayonnaise. Spread butter onto the toasted Kaiser rolls. Spread the rolls with the mayonnaise mixture. Distribute the mushrooms, slices of tomato, and lettuce evenly until you have a total of 6 sandwiches.

Nutrition Information

- Calories: 412 calories;
- Total Carbohydrate: 35.6
- Cholesterol: 12
- Protein: 8.3
- Total Fat: 27.7
- Sodium: 417

187.   Grilled Potato Salad

Serving: 8 | Prep: 15mins | Ready in:

Ingredients

- 2 pounds red potatoes
- 2 tablespoons extra-virgin olive oil
- Dressing:
- 1/2 cup extra-virgin olive oil
- 1 tablespoon apple cider vinegar
- 1 teaspoon kosher salt
- 1 teaspoon ground black pepper
- 1 clove garlic, chopped
- 1/2 teaspoon white sugar
- 6 slices cooked bacon, chopped
- 4 green onions, chopped
- 2 tablespoons minced fresh parsley

Direction

- Set grill to medium heat to preheat, and lightly grease the grate.
- In a bowl, mix potatoes with 2 tablespoons olive oil, shake gently to coat.
- Put potatoes onto the heated grill and cook for about 30 minutes until tender. Allow to cool for 10 - 15 minutes then divide into quarters.
- Combine sugar, garlic, black pepper, salt, vinegar, and 1/2 cup olive oil in a bowl, mix until smooth to make the dressing. In a bowl, toss parsley, green onions, bacon and potatoes until coated evenly.

Nutrition Information

- Calories: 266 calories;
- Total Fat: 19.4
- Sodium: 353
- Total Carbohydrate: 19.3
- Cholesterol: 5
- Protein: 4

188.   Guaco Tacos

Serving: 6 | Prep: 15mins | Ready in:

Ingredients

- 1 (14.5 ounce) can whole tomatoes, drained, rinsed, patted dry
- 2 roma tomatoes, quartered
- 1 onion, chopped, divided
- 1 clove garlic, coarsely chopped
- 1/4 cup fresh cilantro
- 1/2 jalapeno pepper
- salt and pepper to taste
- 4 avocados, halved with pits removed
- 12 (6 inch) whole wheat tortillas
- 1 (15 ounce) can kidney beans, rinsed and drained
- 2 cups torn romaine lettuce

Direction

- Preheat an oven to 350 degrees F (175 degrees C).
- Add fresh and canned tomatoes, 1/2 an onion, cilantro, garlic, and jalapeno to a food processor. Chop roughly and do not puree
- Combine the pulp of the avocados and the rest of the onion in a large bowl. Mash until almost smooth. Season with salt and pepper.
- Arrange tortillas in a single layer on baking sheet. Place in oven for about 5 minutes until warm. Spread guacamole onto tortillas. Top with lettuce, beans and salsa.

Nutrition Information

- Calories: 455 calories;
- Total Fat: 21.1
- Sodium: 604
- Total Carbohydrate: 70.1
- Cholesterol: 0
- Protein: 13.8

---

189.   Ham Salad II

Serving: 16 | Prep: 15mins | Ready in:

Ingredients

- 2 cups mayonnaise
- 1 cup sweet pickle relish
- 1/2 teaspoon freshly ground black pepper
- 2 teaspoons salt
- 2 pounds smoked boneless ham, diced
- 1 onion, diced
- 1 small green bell pepper, diced
- 2 stalks celery, diced

Direction

- Mix salt, pepper, relish, and mayonnaise in a big bowl till blended. Put in celery, green pepper, onion, and ham and mix till coated. Keep the salad chilled in the refrigerator while covered.

Nutrition Information

- Calories: 278 calories;
- Total Fat: 24
- Sodium: 1264
- Total Carbohydrate: 7.3
- Cholesterol: 38
- Protein: 9.9

---

190.   Hawaiian Style Sausage And Rice

Serving: 6 | Prep: 20mins | Ready in:

Ingredients

- 2 cups white rice
- 4 cups water
- 12 ounces country-style smoked link sausage
- 1/2 cup water
- 1 large onion, sliced
- 1 large green bell pepper, cut into 1-inch pieces
- 1 cup diagonally sliced celery, 1 inch thick
- 1 (14 ounce) can whole peeled tomatoes, quartered
- 1 cup beef broth
- 1 (8 ounce) can pineapple rings in juice, cubed and juice reserved
- 1/4 teaspoon garlic powder
- 1/4 teaspoon ground black pepper
- 1 tablespoon brown sugar
- 2 tablespoons cornstarch

Direction

- Place 2 cups of water and rice in a saucepan then make it simmer. Minimize heat to medium-low, cover, and boil for 20-25 minutes until the liquid has been absorbed and the rice is tender,
- In a skillet, put sausages with 1/cup of water on medium heat, then cook, covered for

approximately 5 minutes until heated well. Cut sausages, thinly. In a big skillet set on medium heat, mix celery, green pepper, sausages, and onion; stir and cook for approximately 5 minutes until vegetables begin to soften. Mix brown sugar, black pepper, garlic powder, pineapple, beef broth, and tomatoes to sausage mixture. Stir and cook until brown sugar melts and mixture simmers. In a small bowl, mix leftover pineapple juice with the cornstarch until smooth. Mix cornstarch mixture in sausage mixture then cook for approximately 2 minutes until sauce becomes thick and becomes clear. Pour sausage mixture on cooked rice to serve.

Nutrition Information

- Calories: 527 calories;
- Sodium: 1108
- Total Carbohydrate: 69.5
- Cholesterol: 39
- Protein: 18.7
- Total Fat: 18.7

---

191. Hearty Ranch And Bacon Potato Soup

Serving: 8 | Prep: 25mins | Ready in:

Ingredients

- 6 slices smoked bacon
- 1 onion, diced
- 1 stalk celery, diced
- 1 (32 ounce) carton low-sodium chicken broth
- 10 potatoes, peeled and cubed
- 4 teaspoons all-purpose flour
- 1 (1 ounce) package ranch dressing mix
- 2 cups half-and-half cream
- 1 cup sour cream
- salt and pepper to taste
- 2 cups shredded Cheddar cheese

- 1/4 cup chopped green onion

Direction

- In a Dutch oven, cook the bacon on medium high heat for 10 minutes. Turn the bacon from time to time until it's evenly cooked and brown. Drain the bacon oil using a paper towel. Crush it. Keep for topping.
- In pan with bacon drippings, stir and sauté the onions and celery for 5-10 minutes until soft. Pour in the chicken broth and add potatoes. Turn the heat to high and boil. Decrease to medium-low heat and let simmer until potatoes become fork-tender. Take off heat and smash 1/3 of potatoes.
- In a bowl, pour in the dry ranch mix and flour. Pour the sour cream and half and half while whisking well to mix well. Gradually add sour cream mixture in soup. Heat the soup gently on medium heat but don't boil. Add a pinch of salt and pepper to taste. Serve the soup with crumbled bacon, green onions, and cheddar cheese on top.

Nutrition Information

- Calories: 552 calories;
- Sodium: 732
- Total Carbohydrate: 55.7
- Cholesterol: 81
- Protein: 21.1
- Total Fat: 27.8

---

192. Hearty Vegan Slow Cooker Chili

Serving: 15 | Prep: 45mins | Ready in:

Ingredients

- 1 tablespoon olive oil
- 1 green bell pepper, chopped
- 1 red bell pepper, chopped

- 1 yellow bell pepper, chopped
- 2 onions, chopped
- 4 cloves garlic, minced
- 1 (10 ounce) package frozen chopped spinach, thawed and drained
- 1 cup frozen corn kernels, thawed
- 1 zucchini, chopped
- 1 yellow squash, chopped
- 6 tablespoons chili powder
- 1 tablespoon ground cumin
- 1 tablespoon dried oregano
- 1 tablespoon dried parsley
- 1/2 teaspoon salt
- 1/2 teaspoon ground black pepper
- 2 (14.5 ounce) cans diced tomatoes with juice
- 1 (15 ounce) can black beans, rinsed and drained
- 1 (15 ounce) can garbanzo beans, drained
- 1 (15 ounce) can kidney beans, rinsed and drained
- 2 (6 ounce) cans tomato paste
- 1 (8 ounce) can tomato sauce, or more if needed
- 1 cup vegetable broth, or more if needed

Direction

- In a big skillet, put olive oil and cook in medium fire; mix in onions and garlics for 8 to 10 minutes until brown. Add red, yellow and green bell peppers. In a slow cooker, transfer the mixture. Combine corn, yellow squash, cumin, parsley, black pepper, black beans, kidney beans, spinach, zucchini, chili powder, oregano, salt, tomatoes, tomato paste, tomatoes and garbanzo beans until thoroughly mixed. Put vegetable broth and tomato sauce over the mixture.
- Let vegetables cook in the cooker in low heat for 4 to 5 hours until vegetables are tender. Adjust the seasoning; add more tomato sauce and vegetable broth if chili is too thick to achieve preferred thickness. Continue to cook for another 1 to 2 hours until flavors are completely blended.

Nutrition Information

- Calories: 134 calories;
- Total Fat: 2.4
- Sodium: 617
- Total Carbohydrate: 24.8
- Cholesterol: 0
- Protein: 6.3

193. Heather's Updated Potato Salad

Serving: 10 | Prep: 15mins | Ready in:

Ingredients

- 5 pounds red potatoes, peeled and diced
- 1/2 cup mayonnaise
- 1/4 cup buttermilk
- 2 tablespoons Dijon mustard
- 2 tablespoons dried dill weed
- 1/2 cup diced red onion
- 1/2 cup diced celery
- salt and ground black pepper to taste

Direction

- In a large pot, put potatoes, pour salted water to cover, then bring to a boil. Reduce heat to medium-low and let the pot simmer for about 20 minutes till the potatoes get soft. Drain and allow to cool.
- In a large salad bowl, combine celery, red onion, dill, Dijon mustard, buttermilk and mayonnaise; fold the mixture gently in the potatoes. Use salt and black pepper to season. Allow the mixture to chill for 4 hours before serving.

Nutrition Information

- Calories: 249 calories;
- Sodium: 164
- Total Carbohydrate: 38.7

- Cholesterol: 4
- Protein: 4.9
- Total Fat: 9.2

194. Herbed Rice And Spicy Black Bean Salad

Serving: 8 | Prep: 45mins | Ready in:

Ingredients

- 1 tablespoon chopped fresh basil
- 1 tablespoon chopped fresh thyme
- 1 tablespoon chopped fresh parsley
- 1 tablespoon chopped fresh cilantro
- 1/2 teaspoon salt
- 1/2 teaspoon ground black pepper
- 1/2 teaspoon cayenne pepper
- 1/4 teaspoon garlic powder
- 2 cups cold, cooked white rice
- 1 (14 ounce) can black beans, rinsed and drained
- 2 celery stalks, finely chopped
- 1 (4 ounce) can chopped black olives
- 3 green onions, chopped
- 1/4 cup red wine vinegar
- 1/4 cup extra-virgin olive oil

Direction

- In a bowl, mix together the garlic powder, cayenne pepper, pepper, salt, cilantro, parsley, thyme and basil to make the seasoning.
- In a big bowl, gently mix the green onions, olives, celery, black beans and rice together, then sprinkle 1 tsp of the seasoning on the rice mixture to season.
- Make the dressing by whisking the olive oil and vinegar with the seasoning, then let it rest for 10 minutes. Pour the dressing on top of the rice mixture, then stir to blend.

Nutrition Information

- Calories: 185 calories;
- Total Fat: 8.8
- Sodium: 477
- Total Carbohydrate: 22.1
- Cholesterol: 0
- Protein: 4.5

195. Holiday Chicken Salad

Serving: 12 | Prep: 15mins | Ready in:

Ingredients

- 4 cups cubed, cooked chicken meat
- 1 cup mayonnaise
- 1 teaspoon paprika
- 1 1/2 cups dried cranberries
- 1 cup chopped celery
- 2 green onions, chopped
- 1/2 cup minced green bell pepper
- 1 cup chopped pecans
- 1 teaspoon seasoning salt
- ground black pepper to taste

Direction

- Combine seasoned salt and paprika together with mayonnaise in a medium bowl. Mix in nuts, onion, bell pepper, celery, and the dried cranberries. Put in the chopped chicken and combine thoroughly. Flavor to taste with black pepper. Chill for an hour.

Nutrition Information

- Calories: 315 calories;
- Total Fat: 23.1
- Sodium: 213
- Total Carbohydrate: 15.2
- Cholesterol: 42
- Protein: 13.9

196. Homemade Deviled Ham Sandwiches

Serving: 6 | Prep: 15mins | Ready in:

Ingredients

- 1/2 pound cooked ham, cut into chunks
- 1/4 onion, sliced
- 3 tablespoons low-fat creamy salad dressing (such as Miracle Whip Light®)
- 2 teaspoons honey
- 1 teaspoon prepared mustard
- 1 teaspoon Worcestershire sauce
- 1 teaspoon dry mustard powder
- 1 dash hot pepper sauce (such as Tabasco®), or to taste
- 1/2 teaspoon paprika
- 1/8 teaspoon salt
- 1/8 teaspoon ground white pepper

Direction

- In a food processor, add onion and ham, then process until they are chopped finely.
- Remove ham mixture to a bowl, and then mix in thoroughly with white pepper, salt, paprika, hot pepper sauce, dry mustard powder, Worcestershire sauce, prepared mustard, honey and salad dressing.
- Chill the ham spread with a cover until using.

Nutrition Information

- Calories: 128 calories;
- Total Fat: 8.7
- Sodium: 624
- Total Carbohydrate: 4.6
- Cholesterol: 23
- Protein: 7.4

197. Homemade Turkey Soup

Serving: 6 | Prep: 15mins | Ready in:

Ingredients

- 1 tablespoon olive oil
- 1 1/2 cups diced celery
- 1 1/2 cups diced carrots
- 1 cup diced onion
- 1 tablespoon dried parsley
- 1 bay leaf
- 3 cups beef stock
- 3 cups chicken stock
- 2 cups roasted white turkey meat
- 1 teaspoon salt
- 1 teaspoon ground black pepper
- 3/4 cup rotini pasta

Direction

- In a big pot, heat oil on medium heat and sauté bay leaf, parsley, onion, carrots, and celery for about 10 minutes until vegetables become tender. Add in pepper, salt, turkey, chicken stock, and beef stock into the vegetable mixture, then, boil. Lower heat, cover with a lid, and simmer for about 15 minutes until the soup heats through.
- Stir in rotini and cook for about 15 minutes until the pasta is tender but still firm to bite.

Nutrition Information

- Calories: 196 calories;
- Protein: 18.3
- Total Fat: 5.7
- Sodium: 857
- Total Carbohydrate: 17
- Cholesterol: 36

198. Honey Wheat Sandwich Rolls

Serving: 14 | Prep: 30mins | Ready in:

Ingredients

- 1 1/4 cups warm milk
- 1 egg, beaten
- 2 tablespoons butter, softened
- 1/4 cup honey
- 3/4 teaspoon salt
- 2 3/4 cups bread flour
- 1 cup whole wheat flour
- 1 1/4 teaspoons bread machine yeast
- 2 tablespoons butter, melted

Direction

- Put all of the ingredients into the bread machine pan following the order suggested by the manufacturer. Choose the Dough cycle on the machine and press the Start button.
- Once the machine has finished the whole cycle, place the dough on a clean surface that is covered with a little bit of flour and roll it out to 3/4-inch thickness. Use a 3- to 4-inch biscuit cutter to cut rolls from the dough. Put it on cookie sheets that are a little bit greased then cover the dough and allow it to rise for about an hour until it doubles in size. While the dough is rising, preheat the oven to 350°F (175°C).
- Put in the preheated oven and bake for 10-15 minutes. Use a brush to coat the freshly baked rolls with melted butter.

Nutrition Information

- Calories: 191 calories;
- Total Fat: 4.7
- Sodium: 163
- Total Carbohydrate: 31.9
- Cholesterol: 24
- Protein: 5.8

Ingredients

- 1 (16 ounce) package elbow macaroni
- 6 hard-cooked eggs, diced
- 1/2 cup diced onion
- 1/2 cup diced celery
- 1/2 cup diced green bell pepper
- 2 cups mayonnaise
- 1 cup milk
- 1/2 cup sweet pickle relish
- 1/3 cup prepared honey mustard
- 1/2 teaspoon sea salt
- 1/4 teaspoon ground black pepper

Direction

- Place lightly salted water in a big pot and make it boil. Put in the elbow macaroni in simmering water and cook for 8 minutes, stirring occasionally until cooked through but firm. Strain and wash macaroni under cold water until chilled. Place macaroni to a big salad bowl.
- Then toss pasta with green bell pepper, celery, onion and hard-cooked eggs. In a bowl, mix honey mustard, pickle relish, milk and mayonnaise and put the dressing on the salad; combine well and add ground black pepper and sea salt to taste.

Nutrition Information

- Calories: 484 calories;
- Total Carbohydrate: 38.1
- Cholesterol: 122
- Protein: 9.5
- Total Fat: 33.3
- Sodium: 465

---

199.   Honey Mustard Macaroni Salad

Serving: 12 | Prep: 20mins | Ready in:

200.   Hot Curried Tuna Sandwiches

Serving: 4 | Prep: 10mins | Ready in:

Ingredients

- 1 (5 ounce) can tuna, drained
- 1/4 cup finely chopped celery
- 1/4 cup chopped green onion
- 2 tablespoons mayonnaise
- 1 tablespoon lemon juice
- 1/2 teaspoon curry powder, or to taste
- 2 English muffins, split, toasted and buttered
- 4 thin slices Cheddar cheese

Direction

- Preheat the oven's broiler.
- Stir curry powder, lemon juice, mayonnaise, green onion, celery and tuna together in a moderate-sized bowl. Scoop onto each English muffin half an even amount of the mix, then put a cheese slice on top of each. Put the sandwiches on a baking sheet.
- Broil until toasty and cheese has melted, or 2-3 minutes. Serve hot.

Nutrition Information

- Calories: 213 calories;
- Total Carbohydrate: 14.5
- Cholesterol: 27
- Protein: 14
- Total Fat: 10.9
- Sodium: 246

201.   How To Make Cheese Sticks

Serving: 9 | Prep: 25mins | Ready in:

Ingredients

- 1/2 (17.5 ounce) package frozen puff pastry
- 2 teaspoons olive oil (preferably drained from a tin of anchovies)
- 1 pinch salt and freshly ground black pepper to taste
- 1 pinch cayenne pepper, or to taste
- 1/4 cup shredded sharp white Cheddar cheese
- 5 tablespoons freshly shredded Parmigiano-Reggiano cheese, divided

Direction

- Preheat an oven to 200 °C or 400 °F. Line parchment paper or a silicone baking mat on a baking sheet.
- Onto a floured work area, put 1 sheet of frozen puff pastry dough and let the dough thaw just till it can be unfolded. Into a flat sheet, roll dough out; with olive oil, glaze puff pastry dough top. Put cayenne pepper, black pepper and salt to season.
- Onto the dough, scatter 1/4 cup Parmigiano-Reggiano cheese and white Cheddar cheese, coating the top. Put a piece of plastic wrap on top; firmly push seasonings and cheese into dough using fingers or by putting a sheet pan onto dough on top of plastic and forcing it down.
- Take off the plastic and cut dough down to the seam lines into 3 pieces with a sharp knife or pizza cutter; slice every third lengthwise into 3 for 9 breadsticks total.
- Get a dough strip, put on the work surface, it seasoned side facing down and to create a dough rolled tube with seasoned side out, twirl from each end 8 or 9 times. Onto prepped baking sheet, put the breadsticks.
- On top of the sticks scatter leftover 1 tablespoon Parmigiano-Reggiano cheese. Gently roll the sticks to even up their forms and collect and push any dropped cheese onto surfaces.
- In the prepped oven, bake for approximately 10 minutes; turn over and keep baking for 10 to 20 minutes longer till breadsticks are crisp and browned. Once a picked-up stick ends droops, bake for few minutes more. Allow to cool on a wire rack prior serving.

Nutrition Information

- Calories: 184 calories;

- Cholesterol: 5
- Protein: 3.8
- Total Fat: 13.2
- Sodium: 134
- Total Carbohydrate: 12.4

202.   Huli Huli Pineapple Chicken

Serving: 12 | Prep: 15mins | Ready in:

Ingredients

- 1 (20 ounce) can crushed pineapple in juice
- 3/4 cup brown sugar
- 1/2 cup shoyu (Japanese soy sauce)
- 1/3 cup ketchup
- 1/3 cup red wine
- 1/4 cup Worcestershire sauce
- 1 (1 inch) piece fresh ginger, minced
- 1 clove garlic, minced
- 4 drops liquid smoke, or more to taste (optional)
- 3 (3 1/2) pound fryer chickens, quartered

Direction

- In a pot, mix liquid smoke, garlic, ginger, Worcestershire sauce, red wine, ketchup, shoyu, brown sugar, and pineapple; make it boil, minimize heat to medium-low, and simmer for approximately 30 minutes, occasionally stirring, until sauce is thickened and lessened. Let it fully cool. Place 1 1/2 cups sauce in a bowl and keep in the refrigerator.
- In a big bowl, put the chicken pieces and drop the rest of the sauce on the top; equally, coat by tossing. Use plastic wrap to cover the bowl and refrigerate for 4 hours up to overnight to marinate.
- Prepare an outdoor grill by preheating to medium-high and oil the grate lightly. Take the chicken from marinade; get rid of the used marinade.

- Place the chicken on the preheated grill then cook for approximately 5 minutes on each side, until caramelized. Lower heat then cook for 10-15 more minutes, flipping and frequently basting with leftover 1 1/2 cups of pineapple juice, until it is not pink at the bone and juices are clear. An instant-read thermometer poked into the biggest part near the bone should register 165°F (74°C).

Nutrition Information

- Calories: 611 calories;
- Total Fat: 30.1
- Sodium: 911
- Total Carbohydrate: 20.3
- Cholesterol: 239
- Protein: 60.9

203.   Ima's Potato Salad

Serving: 6 | Prep: 10mins | Ready in:

Ingredients

- 2 pounds russet potatoes, peeled
- 3/4 cup mayonnaise
- 1 cup frozen peas and carrots, thawed
- 6 hard-cooked eggs, chopped
- 6 Israeli-style pickles, chopped
- 1/2 cup spicy mustard
- salt and pepper to taste

Direction

- Cover potatoes with salted water in a large pot. Boil over high heat then lower to medium-low. Cover then simmer for 20 minutes till tender. Drain and let steam dry for 1-2 minutes.
- Finely chop the pickles and hard-cooked eggs.
- Once the potatoes are cool enough to handle, cube and move them to a 9x13-inch dish. Add in carrots, peas, mustard, mayonnaise, pickles

and chopped eggs then stir gently till combined. Add pepper and salt to taste. Store the salad in the fridge before serving or immediately serve.

Nutrition Information

- Calories: 424 calories;
- Total Fat: 28.7
- Sodium: 596
- Total Carbohydrate: 32
- Cholesterol: 222
- Protein: 11.7

| 204. | **Inside Out Grilled Cheese Sandwich** |

Serving: 1 | Prep: 5mins | Ready in:

Ingredients

- 2 tablespoons butter, divided
- 2 slices white bread
- 1/2 cup shredded extra sharp Cheddar cheese, divided

Direction

- In a nonstick frying pan, melt 1 1/2 tbsp butter on medium low heat. In the frying pan, put the slices of bread over the melted butter.
- On 1 slice of bread, spread approximately 1/4 cup of cheddar cheese, then put the other bread slice, butter side up, over the cheese. Spread approximately 2 tbsp of cheese over the sandwich.
- In the frying pan next to the sandwich, melt the leftover 1/2 tbsp butter. Turn over the sandwich onto the melted butter so that the cheese side faces down. Spread the leftover cheese over the sandwich. Cook the sandwich for 3-4 minutes, until the cheese on the bottom becomes caramelized and crispy. Turn over the sandwich and let it cook for additional 3-4

minutes, until the cheese becomes caramelized and crispy on the other side.

Nutrition Information

- Calories: 564 calories;
- Total Fat: 43.4
- Sodium: 855
- Total Carbohydrate: 26
- Cholesterol: 120
- Protein: 18.1

| 205. | **Italian Grilled Cheese Sandwiches** |

Serving: 6 | Prep: 8mins | Ready in:

Ingredients

- 1/4 cup unsalted butter
- 1/8 teaspoon garlic powder (optional)
- 12 slices white bread
- 1 teaspoon dried oregano
- 1 (8 ounce) package shredded mozzarella cheese
- 1 (24 ounce) jar vodka marinara sauce

Direction

- Set an oven's broiler to preheat.
- On a baking tray, put 6 bread slices. Scatter a little handful of mozzarella cheese on top of each slice, then put the leftover 6 bread slices on top. Combine the garlic powder and butter, then brush some on top of the sandwiches or spread using the back of a tablespoon. Sprinkle dried oregano on top.
- Put the baking tray under the broiler for 2-3 minutes, until they turn golden brown in color. Take the pan out of the oven, turn the sandwiches and use butter to brush the other sides, then sprinkle oregano on top. Put sandwiches back into the broiler and cook for around 2 minutes, until they turn golden.

- Halve each of the sandwiches diagonally and serve right away alongside vodka sauce for dipping.

Nutrition Information

- Calories: 394 calories;
- Sodium: 1032
- Total Carbohydrate: 42
- Cholesterol: 46
- Protein: 15
- Total Fat: 18.3

---

206. Italian Heroes

Serving: 4 | Prep: 10mins | Ready in:

Ingredients

- 1 (14 ounce) can marinated artichoke hearts, drained
- 2 cloves garlic, peeled
- 1/4 cup extra-virgin olive oil
- 4 (6 inch) French sandwich rolls
- 3/4 cup sliced roasted red peppers
- 2 cups arugula leaves or spring mix
- 8 ounces thinly sliced hard salami
- 8 ounces thinly sliced provolone cheese
- 4 pepperoncini peppers, drained and chopped (optional)
- 1/2 cup sliced black olives (optional)
- 1/2 red onion, thinly sliced (optional)

Direction

- Process olive oil, garlic and artichoke hearts till smooth in a food processor/blender. Season to taste with pepper and salt.
- Lengthwise, slice sandwich rolls in halve; pull most of soft bread out from bottom and top. On each side of every roll, spread artichoke paste. Put layers of onion, olives, pepperoncini, provolone cheese, salami, arugula and red peppers on rolls. Press the

sandwiches together; tightly wrap with aluminum foil.
- Put sandwiches in the fridge; put something heavy over like a plate with cans on top or weighted containers over it (i.e, cottage cheese). Chill for a maximum of 3 hours then unwrap; halve and serve.

Nutrition Information

- Calories: 1068 calories;
- Sodium: 3762
- Total Carbohydrate: 96.3
- Cholesterol: 95
- Protein: 48.3
- Total Fat: 56

---

207. Italian Vegetable Soup With Beans, Spinach Pesto

Serving: 10 | Prep: | Ready in:

Ingredients

- 1 1/2 tablespoons olive oil
- 1 large onion, cut into small dice
- 3 medium carrots, peeled and sliced 1/4-inch thick
- 3 medium celery stalks, sliced 1/4-inch thick
- 1 medium bell pepper (red or yellow), stemmed, seeded and cut into medium dice
- 1 pound all-purpose potatoes, unpeeled and cut into medium dice
- 1 (16 ounce) can petite diced tomatoes
- 2 (15.5 ounce) cans cannellini or other white beans, undrained
- 6 cups low-sodium chicken broth in can or carton
- 7 ounces loosely packed baby spinach
- 1 cup frozen green peas
- Salt and ground black pepper
- Prepared pesto (found in grocer's refrigerated section)

Direction

- In a soup kettle, heat oil over medium-high flame. Put in onions, and sauté for 5 minutes until tender. Put in chicken broth, bean, tomatoes, potatoes, peppers, celery, and carrots; bring it to the boil. Turn to low heat and simmer for 15 minutes just until vegetables are tender. Put in peas and spinach; keep simmering for 3-4 more minutes until spinach wilts. Sprinkle with pepper and salt to season. Ladle into bowls, putting a spoonful of pesto into each serving of soup.
- For lunch, pack soup in another leakproof containers. Heat soup in microwave and add pesto on top.

Nutrition Information

- Calories: 214 calories;
- Total Carbohydrate: 31.2
- Cholesterol: 5
- Protein: 11.8
- Total Fat: 7.2
- Sodium: 586

---

208.   Italian Vegetarian Patties

Serving: 16 | Prep: 20mins | Ready in:

Ingredients

- 2 tablespoons vegetable oil
- 3/4 cup uncooked brown rice
- 1 1/2 cups red lentils
- 6 cups water
- 1 teaspoon salt
- 2 eggs
- 2 1/2 cups dry bread crumbs
- 1 1/2 cups grated Parmesan cheese
- 2 teaspoons dried basil
- 1 1/2 teaspoons garlic powder
- 3 tablespoons vegetable oil

Direction

- In a big saucepan, heat 2 tablespoons of oil and stir in brown rice, then cook until it becomes golden brown. Add salt, water, and lentils, then set to boil. Bring heat down to low and cook while covered for 40 minutes until rice gets tender and absorbs the water. If needed, add more water. The mixture should be really thick. Take off the heat and allow to slightly cool.
- Place the rice mixture into food processor with garlic powder, basil, Parmesan cheese, breadcrumbs, and eggs, then process until combined well to make the texture like ground meat. Use 3 tablespoons of the mixture to form each of 1/4 - 1/2-inch thick patties.
- Heat 3 tablespoons of oil in a big pan and fry the patties in batches for 2-3 minutes on each side until brown. Drain onto paper towels and cool. Fry the remaining patties in the same way. Store the patties in airtight containers, keeping them in the freezer or refrigerator.

Nutrition Information

- Calories: 242 calories;
- Total Carbohydrate: 30.3
- Cholesterol: 27
- Protein: 11.2
- Total Fat: 8.3
- Sodium: 395

---

209.   Jen's Heavenly Egg Salad

Serving: 4 | Prep: 5mins | Ready in:

Ingredients

- 6 eggs
- 1/4 cup mayonnaise
- 1 teaspoon Dijon mustard
- 1/2 teaspoon prepared yellow mustard
- 1/2 lemon, juiced

- 1/4 cup chopped green onions
- salt and pepper to taste

Direction

- In a saucepan, add egg and cold water to cover. Bring the water to a boil and take away from the heat promptly. Cover and allow eggs to stand in the hot water for 10-12 minutes. Take eggs out of hot water, then allow to cool and peel. Put the eggs in an ice bath before peeling if you want it to quickly cool.
- Stir green onions, lemon juice, yellow mustard, Dijon mustard and mayonnaise together in a medium bowl. Chop eggs into big chunks and combine with the dressing gently. Season to taste with pepper and salt.

Nutrition Information

- Calories: 212 calories;
- Protein: 9.9
- Total Fat: 18.4
- Sodium: 223
- Total Carbohydrate: 3.2
- Cholesterol: 284

210.   Jerre's Black Bean And Pork Tenderloin Slow Cooker Chili

Serving: 8 | Prep: 10mins | Ready in:

Ingredients

- 1 1/2 pounds pork tenderloin, cut into 2 inch strips
- 1 small onion, coarsely chopped
- 1 small red bell pepper, coarsely chopped
- 3 (15 ounce) cans black beans
- 1 (16 ounce) jar salsa
- 1/2 cup chicken broth
- 1 teaspoon dried oregano
- 1 teaspoon ground cumin

- 2 teaspoons chili powder

Direction

- Mix together chili powder, cumin, oregano, chicken broth, salsa, black beans, red pepper, onion and pork tenderloin in a slow cooker. Set cooker to low setting and cook for about 8-10 hours.
- Before serving, break up pieces of cooked pork to thicken the chili.

Nutrition Information

- Calories: 245 calories;
- Total Fat: 2.8
- Sodium: 1045
- Total Carbohydrate: 31.9
- Cholesterol: 37
- Protein: 24

211.   Kentucky Tomato Soup

Serving: 6 | Prep: 10mins | Ready in:

Ingredients

- 3 tablespoons butter
- 1 cup chopped onion
- 1/2 cup chopped carrots
- 2 stalks celery, chopped
- 2 cloves garlic, minced
- 1/4 cup chopped fresh flat-leaf parsley
- 2 1/2 cups chopped fresh tomatoes
- 1 (8 ounce) can tomato sauce
- 3/4 cup strong brewed coffee
- 1/4 cup water
- 1 teaspoon white sugar
- 1 teaspoon salt
- ground black pepper to taste
- 1/3 cup heavy cream

Direction

- Put the butter in a stock pot and let it melt on medium heat. Add in the celery, onion, parsley, carrots and garlic and let it cook while stirring for 5 minutes until the onion is soft and translucent. Mix in the water, pepper, salt, tomato sauce, sugar, tomatoes and coffee. Allow the mixture to boil and let it simmer for 20-25 minutes.
- Fill half of a blender pitcher with the hot soup mixture. Use a folded kitchen towel to hold the blender lid in place and run the blender starting with a few short pulses just to let the soup mixture move around the blender before running the blender continuously to let it puree. Blend the soup mixture in batches until the consistency is smooth; pour the puree in a clean pot. Mix in the cream and let it heat up until warmed through. Don't boil.

Nutrition Information

- Calories: 142 calories;
- Total Fat: 11
- Sodium: 654
- Total Carbohydrate: 10.5
- Cholesterol: 33
- Protein: 2.2

212.   Killer Bacon Cheese Dogs

Serving: 8 | Prep: 10mins | Ready in:

Ingredients

- 8 slices bacon
- 8 all-beef hot dogs
- 8 hot dog buns
- 8 slices Swiss cheese
- 1/2 cup barbeque sauce, or amount to taste
- 1 small red onion, diced

Direction

- Preheat outdoor grill to medium high heat; oil grate lightly then put it 4-in. away from heat.

- Cook bacon in big deep skillet on medium high heat till browned evenly; on paper towels, drain.
- Cook hot dogs on grill for 5-8 minutes till done to preference, turning once. Grill hotdog buns lightly.
- Assemble sandwiches: Put 1 slice of bacon and cheese on every roll; add hot dog. Put 1 tbsp. or desired amount of barbecue sauce and red onion over each.

Nutrition Information

- Calories: 493 calories;
- Total Fat: 30.5
- Sodium: 1299
- Total Carbohydrate: 31.7
- Cholesterol: 66
- Protein: 21.6

213.   Lawn Mower Salad

Serving: 6 | Prep: 20mins | Ready in:

Ingredients

- 1/2 cup canola oil
- 1/2 cup white sugar
- 1/4 cup water
- 1/4 cup balsamic vinegar
- 2 (3 ounce) packages chicken-flavored ramen noodles, crushed, seasoning packets reserved
- 1 (12 ounce) package broccoli coleslaw mix
- 1 bunch green onions, sliced
- 1 cup roasted cashews
- 1/4 cup roasted sunflower seed kernels

Direction

- In a bowl, whisk ramen noodle seasoning packets, balsamic vinegar, water, sugar and canola oil till combined thoroughly and seasoning packets and sugar melt.

- In a big salad bowl, toss ramen noodles, green onions and broccoli slaw mix. Put dressing on salad. Let stand for 1/2-4 hours, longer for soft noodles, shorter for crunchy noodles. Prior to serving, toss salad again with sunflower seeds and cashews.

Nutrition Information

- Calories: 527 calories;
- Sodium: 491
- Total Carbohydrate: 51.3
- Cholesterol: 0
- Protein: 10.3
- Total Fat: 33

214.   Lebanese Style Red Lentil Soup

Serving: 8 | Prep: 20mins | Ready in:

Ingredients

- 6 cups chicken stock
- 1 pound red lentils
- 3 tablespoons olive oil
- 1 tablespoon minced garlic
- 1 large onion, chopped
- 1 tablespoon ground cumin
- 1/2 teaspoon cayenne pepper
- 1/2 cup chopped cilantro
- 3/4 cup fresh lemon juice

Direction

- Boil lentils and chicken stock in a big saucepan on high heat; lower the heat to medium low and cover, simmer for 20 minutes.
- Meanwhile, in a skillet, heat olive oil on medium heat. Mix in onion and garlic; cook for 3 minutes till onion is translucent and soft.
- Mix onions into the lentils; season with cayenne and cumin. Keep simmering for 10 minutes till the lentils are tender.

- Puree soup with a stick blender or in a standing blender till smooth carefully; before serving, mix in lemon juice and cilantro.

Nutrition Information

- Calories: 276 calories;
- Sodium: 524
- Total Carbohydrate: 39.1
- Cholesterol: 1
- Protein: 16.7
- Total Fat: 7

215.   Lemon Chicken Orzo Soup

Serving: 12 | Prep: 20mins | Ready in:

Ingredients

- 8 ounces orzo pasta
- 1 teaspoon olive oil
- 3 carrots, chopped, or more to taste
- 3 ribs celery, chopped
- 1 onion, chopped
- 2 cloves garlic, minced
- 1/2 teaspoon dried thyme
- 1/2 teaspoon dried oregano
- salt and ground black pepper to taste
- 1 bay leaf
- 3 (32 ounce) cartons fat-free, low-sodium chicken broth
- 1/2 cup fresh lemon juice
- 1 lemon, zested
- 8 ounces cooked chicken breast, chopped
- 1 (8 ounce) package baby spinach leaves
- 1 lemon, sliced for garnish (optional)
- 1/4 cup grated Parmesan cheese (optional)

Direction

- Boil a big pot of lightly salted water. Let the orzo cook in the boiling water for about 5 minutes, until partly cooked through but not

112

yet soft; drain. Rinse it in cold water until completely cooled.

- Heat the oil in a big pot on medium heat. Cook and stir the onion, celery and carrots in the hot oil for 5-7 minutes, until the onion is translucent, and the veggies start to soften. Add the garlic and cook and stir for about 1 more minute until aromatic. Sprinkle bay leaf, black pepper, salt, oregano and thyme to season the mixture. Keep on cooking for additional 30 seconds prior to pouring the chicken broth into the pot.
- Boil the broth, then partly cover the pot. Lower the heat to medium-low. Let it simmer for about 10 minutes, until the veggies are just tender.
- Mix lemon zest, lemon juice and orzo into the broth, then add chicken. Cook for around 5 minutes, until the orzo and chicken are thoroughly heated. Add the baby spinach and cook for 2-3 minutes, until the orzo is tender and the spinach wilts into the broth. Ladle the soup into the bowls and put Parmesan cheese and slices of lemon on top to garnish.

Nutrition Information

- Calories: 167 calories;
- Cholesterol: 20
- Protein: 12.1
- Total Fat: 4.1
- Sodium: 187
- Total Carbohydrate: 21.7

---

216. Lemon Thyme Chicken Tenders

Serving: 4 | Prep: 10mins | Ready in:

Ingredients

- 2 tablespoons olive oil
- 1 clove garlic, minced
- 6 sprigs fresh thyme, leaves stripped and chopped
- 1 tablespoon lemon zest
- 1/4 cup lemon juice
- salt and pepper to taste
- 1 pound chicken breast tenders
- olive oil-flavored cooking spray

Direction

- In a large mixing bowl, mix lemon juice, lemon zest, chopped thyme, garlic, and olive oil. Season the chicken tenders with pepper and salt. Toss olive oil mixture and chicken together; let it marinate for 5 minutes.
- Use a cooking spray to coat a nonstick skillet and set over medium-high heat. Add chicken tenders in the hot pan and cook each side for about 4 minutes until cooked through and lightly browned.

Nutrition Information

- Calories: 192 calories;
- Total Carbohydrate: 2
- Cholesterol: 65 ·
- Protein: 23.7
- Total Fat: 9.5
- Sodium: 57

---

217. Lemony Lentils With Kale

Serving: 4 | Prep: 10mins | Ready in:

Ingredients

- 2 tablespoons olive oil
- 1 onion, diced
- 1 carrot, diced
- 3 cloves garlic, minced
- 4 thyme sprigs
- 1/2 teaspoon kosher salt
- ground black pepper to taste

- 1/2 teaspoon crushed red pepper flakes, or to taste
- 1/2 pound green lentils
- 1 (14.5 ounce) can diced tomatoes, undrained
- 3 cups chicken broth
- 1 bunch dinosaur kale, stems removed and leaves roughly chopped
- 1 lemon, zested and juiced

Direction

- In a skillet placed over medium heat, heat olive oil. Add carrot and onion and cook in hot oil for about 4 minutes until tender, stir while cooking. Add red pepper flakes, black pepper, kosher salt, thyme sprigs and garlic; cook for 1 minute, stirring until well coated.
- Stir in chicken stock, tomatoes and their juice and lentils. Simmer, covered, for about 40 minutes until lentils are softened. Add lemon juice, lemon zest and kale; cook for about 5 minutes until kale is wilted. Add salt and black pepper to season.

Nutrition Information

- Calories: 368 calories;
- Total Carbohydrate: 55.4
- Cholesterol: 4
- Protein: 20.6
- Total Fat: 8.8
- Sodium: 1169

218.   Lentil Tacos

Serving: 4 | Prep: 15mins | Ready in:

Ingredients

- Spice Mix:
- 2 teaspoons ground ancho chile powder
- 1 teaspoon ground cumin
- 1/2 teaspoon ground coriander
- 1/2 teaspoon dried oregano
- 1/2 teaspoon salt
- 1/4 teaspoon ground fennel seed
- Filling:
- 2 teaspoons olive oil
- 1 small onion, minced
- 2 cloves garlic, minced
- 2 1/2 cups cooked brown or green lentils
- 3 tablespoons tomato paste
- 2 tablespoons water, or as needed
- 2 canned chipotle chiles in adobo sauce, seeded and minced
- adobo or hot sauce (optional)
- Tacos:
- 8 (6 inch) vegan corn or flour tortillas
- 1 cup shredded lettuce
- 1 cup chopped tomatoes
- 1/4 cup chopped fresh cilantro
- 1 cup guacamole
- 1 lime, cut into 8 wedges

Direction

- In a small bowl, combine fennel, salt, oregano, coriander, cumin, and ancho chile powder.
- In a large skillet, heat oil over medium-high heat. Cook garlic and onion for 3 minutes, or until lightly browned, stirring occasionally. Stir in the spice mixture and cook while stirring for 30 seconds, until toasted.
- Lower heat to medium and add chipotle peppers, tomato paste, lentils, and a few splashes of water. Cook while lightly mashing with a fork and adding water if necessary, for 5 minutes until lentils are heated through and hold together. Season to taste with more salt if necessary and adobo or hot sauce.
- In a cast-iron skillet over medium heat, toast tortillas lightly. Spread 1/3 cup of filling in the center of each tortilla and top with cilantro, tomatoes, and lettuce. Serve with lime wedges and guacamole.

Nutrition Information

- Calories: 389 calories;
- Total Fat: 11

- Sodium: 477
- Total Carbohydrate: 61.8
- Cholesterol: 0
- Protein: 16.8

219. Light Spaghetti Salad

Serving: 12 | Prep: 20mins | Ready in:

Ingredients

- 2 (12 ounce) packages spaghetti
- 1 small red onion, finely chopped
- 1 red bell pepper, seeded and finely chopped
- 1 cucumber, chopped
- 1 tomato, chopped
- 1 (16 ounce) bottle fat-free Italian salad dressing
- 1 (.7 ounce) package dry Italian salad dressing mix (such as Good Seasons®)
- 1 teaspoon salt

Direction

- Boil a large pot filled with lightly salted water. Place the spaghetti in and cook for 12 minutes, stirring occasionally until the pasta is firm to the bite and cooked through. Let it drain and rinse in cold water.
- Toss spaghetti into the large salad bowl together with cucumber, Italian salad dressing, salt, tomato, red onion, salad dressing mix, and red bell pepper. Let it chill before serving. Take note that the longer it chills, the better the salad is.

Nutrition Information

- Calories: 268 calories;
- Protein: 7.2
- Total Fat: 1
- Sodium: 814
- Total Carbohydrate: 56.2
- Cholesterol: 0

220. Low Carb Fauxtato Salad

Serving: 4 | Prep: 15mins | Ready in:

Ingredients

- 1 head cauliflower, cut into bite-size pieces
- 4 hard-boiled eggs, chopped
- 1/2 cup mayonnaise, or more to taste
- 2 tablespoons dill pickle relish
- 2 tablespoons diced green onion
- 1 tablespoon prepared yellow mustard
- salt and ground black pepper to taste

Direction

- In a saucepan, position a steamer insert and fill with water to just below the bottom of the steamer. Bring water to a boil, then put in cauliflower, cover and steam for about 5 minutes, until tender.
- In a bowl, combine pepper, salt, mustard, green onion, dill pickle relish, mayonnaise, eggs and cauliflower.

Nutrition Information

- Calories: 315 calories;
- Cholesterol: 222
- Protein: 9.7
- Total Fat: 27.5
- Sodium: 410
- Total Carbohydrate: 9.7

221. Lunch Box Hot Hot Dogs

Serving: 1 | Prep: 5mins | Ready in:

Ingredients

- 1 all-beef hot dog
- 1 hot dog bun
- 1 packet ketchup
- 1 packet prepared yellow mustard
- 2 tablespoons shredded Cheddar cheese

Direction

- Assemble your child's lunch box by packing the Cheddar cheese, ketchup, hotdog bun and mustard.
- Preheat your kid's insulated water bottle by pouring in boiling water. Let it sit, 15-20 minutes. Let the kettle heat while your kids get ready for school. Before they leave, throw out the water and pour more boiling water. The preheating makes the water bottle stay hot longer. Put hotdog into the water and seal the lid.
- When your child takes their lunch, they can get the hotdog out of the bottle and put it on the bun. Drizzle with mustard, cheese and ketchup for a hot lunch.

Nutrition Information

- Calories: 384 calories;
- Total Fat: 24.4
- Sodium: 1083
- Total Carbohydrate: 25.6
- Cholesterol: 48
- Protein: 15

222. Macaroni Salad With A Twist

Serving: 8 | Prep: 20mins | Ready in:

Ingredients

- 1 (16 ounce) package small seashell pasta
- 1 cup mayonnaise
- 1/4 cup distilled white vinegar
- 2/3 cup white sugar

- 2 1/2 tablespoons prepared yellow mustard
- 1 1/2 teaspoons salt
- 1/2 teaspoon ground black pepper
- 1 large Vidalia or sweet onion, chopped
- 2 stalks celery, chopped
- 1 green bell pepper, seeded and chopped
- 1/4 cup grated carrots
- 1 pound diced cooked ham

Direction

- Bring a big pot of slightly salted water to the boil. Add and cook pasta for 8 to 10 minutes until al dente. Drain pasta off, but don't rinse. Let it rest for 5 minutes.
- To make the dressing, in a bowl, mix the pepper, salt, mustard, sugar, vinegar, and mayonnaise. Put aside.
- In a big bowl, mix the ham, carrots, bell pepper, celery and onion. Mix in the dressing. Put in the pasta and blend all ingredients by tossing gently. Keep it chilled for at least 4 hours prior to serving.

Nutrition Information

- Calories: 582 calories;
- Total Fat: 29.2
- Sodium: 1416
- Total Carbohydrate: 64.1
- Cholesterol: 44
- Protein: 17.7

223. Magical Egg Salad

Serving: 2 | Prep: 15mins | Ready in:

Ingredients

- 5 eggs
- 3 tablespoons mayonnaise
- 2 tablespoons Dijon mustard
- 2 tablespoons sweet pickle relish
- 1 teaspoon steak sauce

- 1/4 teaspoon paprika
- 1/4 teaspoon dried dill weed
- salt and ground black pepper to taste
- 1 pinch cayenne pepper

Direction

- In a saucepan, add eggs and water to cover. Bring to a boil then take away from the heat to allow eggs stand about 15 minutes in the hot water. Take the eggs out of hot water and cool under cold running water then peel. Chop eggs and turn to a big bowl.
- Mix into eggs the dill, paprika, steak sauce, sweet pickle relish, Dijon mustard and mayonnaise until well combined, then season with black pepper and salt. Place in the fridge, covered, until chilled if you want. Before serving, sprinkle with cayenne pepper.

Nutrition Information

- Calories: 366 calories;
- Total Carbohydrate: 10.7
- Cholesterol: 473
- Protein: 16.1
- Total Fat: 29
- Sodium: 828

---

224.   Marinated Black Eyed Pea Salad

Serving: 14 | Prep: 30mins | Ready in:

Ingredients

- 1 yellow bell pepper, finely chopped
- 1 red bell pepper, finely chopped
- 1/2 onion, finely chopped
- 2 jalapeno chiles, seeded and finely chopped
- 4 (15 ounce) cans black-eyed peas, rinsed and drained
- 2 tablespoons chopped fresh parsley
- 1 clove garlic, minced

- 1/2 cup red wine vinegar
- 2 tablespoons balsamic vinegar
- 1/4 cup olive oil
- 1/2 teaspoon ground cumin
- 1 teaspoon salt
- 1 teaspoon ground black pepper
- 4 slices cooked bacon, crumbled

Direction

- In a big bowl, mix together the garlic, parsley, black-eyed peas, jalapeno chiles, onion and red and yellow peppers.
- In a small bowl, whisk together the balsamic vinegar and red wine vinegar, then slowly add the olive oil, whisking continuously to blend thoroughly with vinegars. Mix in black pepper, salt and cumin. Pour the dressing on top of the vegetable mixture, then toss until evenly coated. Put cover and let it chill in the fridge for 3-4 hours. Mix in the crumbled bacon, just prior to serving.

Nutrition Information

- Calories: 143 calories;
- Total Fat: 4.8
- Sodium: 540
- Total Carbohydrate: 19.5
- Cholesterol: 1
- Protein: 6.3

---

225.   Marinated Cucumber, Onion, And Tomato Salad

Serving: 6 | Prep: 15mins | Ready in:

Ingredients

- 1 cup water
- 1/2 cup distilled white vinegar
- 1/4 cup vegetable oil
- 1/4 cup sugar
- 2 teaspoons salt

- 1 tablespoon fresh, coarsely ground black pepper
- 3 cucumbers, peeled and sliced 1/4-inch thick
- 3 tomatoes, cut into wedges
- 1 onion, sliced and separated into rings

Direction

- In a large bowl, combine pepper, salt, sugar, oil, vinegar and water; whisk until smoothened. Mix in onion, tomatoes and cucumbers and stir until everything is coated.
- Use plastic wrap to cover the bowl. Put it into the refrigerator in 2 hours at least.

Nutrition Information

- Calories: 156 calories;
- Total Carbohydrate: 18
- Cholesterol: 0
- Protein: 1.8
- Total Fat: 9.5
- Sodium: 784

226.   Marinated Green Beans With Olives, Tomatoes, And Feta

Serving: 10 | Prep: 30mins | Ready in:

Ingredients

- 2 pounds fresh green beans, trimmed
- 1/4 cup olive oil
- 2 cloves garlic, minced
- 1 cup kalamata olives, pitted and sliced
- 2 tomatoes, seeded and chopped
- 2 tablespoons red wine vinegar
- 1 tablespoon chopped fresh oregano
- 1/2 teaspoon salt
- 1/4 teaspoon ground black pepper
- 1 (8 ounce) package crumbled feta
- 1 bunch fresh oregano sprigs

Direction

- Bring salted water in a big pot to a boil on medium heat and put in green beans. Cook for 8-10 minutes, until softened a little bit yet still crisp. Drain the green beans promptly and put into ice water to prevent beans from cooking further. Drain the beans and transfer into a shallow serving dish.
- In a skillet, heat the olive oil on medium heat. Cook garlic about a half minute in the oil, then take the skillet away from the heat. Stir in pepper, salt, oregano, vinegar, tomatoes and olives. Drizzle over green beans with the dressing mixture, then toss together until beans are coated evenly. Sprinkle over top with feta cheese and decorate with oregano sprigs. Refrigerate for a minimum of 3 hours before serving.

Nutrition Information

- Calories: 183 calories;
- Total Fat: 14
- Sodium: 597
- Total Carbohydrate: 10.6
- Cholesterol: 20
- Protein: 5.5

227.   Mayo Free Tuna Sandwich Filling

Serving: 2 | Prep: 5mins | Ready in:

Ingredients

- 1 (5 ounce) can albacore tuna in water, drained and flaked
- 1 tablespoon red onion, diced
- 1 teaspoon fresh oregano, minced
- 1 teaspoon fresh rosemary, minced
- 1 tablespoon diced green chile pepper
- black pepper to taste
- 2 tablespoons red pepper hummus

Direction

- Combine onion, oregano, pepper, rosemary, green chile pepper, tuna and hummus in a mixing bowl.

Nutrition Information

- Calories: 119 calories;
- Total Fat: 3.5
- Sodium: 318
- Total Carbohydrate: 3.4
- Cholesterol: 29
- Protein: 17.9

---

228.   Mediterranean Quinoa Salad

Serving: 8 | Prep: 15mins | Ready in:

Ingredients

- 2 cups water
- 2 cubes chicken bouillon
- 1 clove garlic, smashed
- 1 cup uncooked quinoa
- 2 large cooked chicken breasts - cut into bite size pieces
- 1 large red onion, diced
- 1 large green bell pepper, diced
- 1/2 cup chopped kalamata olives
- 1/2 cup crumbled feta cheese
- 1/4 cup chopped fresh parsley
- 1/4 cup chopped fresh chives
- 1/2 teaspoon salt
- 2/3 cup fresh lemon juice
- 1 tablespoon balsamic vinegar
- 1/4 cup olive oil

Direction

- Place together in a sauce pan the garlic, bouillon cubes and water then bring to a boil. Mix in the quinoa, minimize the heat to medium low, and simmer for 15 to 20 minutes, covered, until the water has been absorbed and the quinoa is softened. Get rid of the garlic clove and into a large bowl, scrape the quinoa
- Gently mix the salt, chives, parsley, feta cheese, olives, bell pepper, onion and the chicken into the quinoa. Trickle with olive oil, balsamic vinegar, and lemon juice. Mix until equally combined. Place inside the refrigerator and serve cold or warm.

Nutrition Information

- Calories: 278 calories;
- Total Fat: 13.9
- Sodium: 713
- Total Carbohydrate: 20.1
- Cholesterol: 45
- Protein: 18.4

---

229.   Mediterranean Three Bean Salad

Serving: 8 | Prep: 15mins | Ready in:

Ingredients

- 1 (15 ounce) can cannellini (white kidney) beans, rinsed and drained
- 1 (15 ounce) can garbanzo beans, rinsed and drained
- 1 (15 ounce) can dark red kidney beans, rinsed and drained
- 1/2 onion, minced
- 2 cloves garlic, minced
- 2 tablespoons minced fresh parsley, or to taste
- 1/4 cup olive oil
- 1 lemon, juiced
- salt and ground black pepper to taste

Direction

- Mix garbanzo beans, kidney beans, and cannellini beans in a mixing bowl. Stir in garlic, lemon juice, black pepper, salt, parsley, onion, and olive oil. Mix well.

Nutrition Information

- Calories: 193 calories;
- Protein: 6.8
- Total Fat: 7.6
- Sodium: 328
- Total Carbohydrate: 24.9
- Cholesterol: 0

230. Mediterranean Zucchini And Chickpea Salad

Serving: 6 | Prep: 25mins | Ready in:

Ingredients

- 2 cups diced zucchini
- 1 (15 ounce) can chickpeas, drained and rinsed
- 1 cup halved grape tomatoes
- 3/4 cup chopped red bell pepper
- 1/2 cup chopped sweet onion (such as Vidalia®)
- 1/2 cup crumbled feta cheese
- 1/2 cup chopped Kalamata olives
- 1/3 cup olive oil
- 1/3 cup packed fresh basil leaves, roughly chopped
- 1/4 cup white balsamic vinegar
- 1 tablespoon chopped fresh rosemary
- 1 tablespoon capers, drained and chopped
- 1 clove garlic, minced
- 1/2 teaspoon dried Greek oregano
- 1 pinch crushed red pepper flakes (optional)
- salt and ground black pepper to taste

Direction

- In a big bowl, mix together black pepper, salt, red pepper flakes, oregano, garlic, capers, rosemary, vinegar, basil, olive oil, Kalamata

olives, feta, onion, red bell pepper, tomatoes, chickpeas and zucchini.

Nutrition Information

- Calories: 258 calories;
- Total Fat: 18.5
- Sodium: 515
- Total Carbohydrate: 19
- Cholesterol: 11
- Protein: 5.6

231. Mendocino Chicken Salad

Serving: 6 | Prep: 15mins | Ready in:

Ingredients

- 1 (6 ounce) package smoked chicken breast, skin removed, cubed
- 1 cup seedless grapes, halved
- 1/2 cup diced red onion
- 3 stalks celery, diced
- 1/4 cup fresh basil leaves, cut into thin strips
- 1 cup blanched slivered almonds
- 3/4 cup mayonnaise

Direction

- Whisk mayonnaise, almonds, basil, celery, red onion, grapes, and smoked chicken in a big bowl. Toss thoroughly, let chill and serve.

Nutrition Information

- Calories: 365 calories;
- Cholesterol: 25
- Protein: 9.5
- Total Fat: 32.2
- Sodium: 535
- Total Carbohydrate: 12

232.   Mexi Chicken Avocado Cups

Serving: 3 | Prep: 10mins | Ready in:

Ingredients

- 3 (6 ounce) cans canned chicken, drained
- 1 tablespoon cilantro, finely chopped
- 1/2 teaspoon chili powder, or more to taste
- 3 avocados, halved lengthwise and pitted
- 1 teaspoon lime juice, or to taste

Direction

- In a bowl, mix chili powder, cilantro and chicken together.
- Onto a serving dish, spread avocado halves and drizzle with lime juice. Scoop the mixture of chicken into halves of avocado.

Nutrition Information

- Calories: 601 calories;
- Cholesterol: 104
- Protein: 40.7
- Total Fat: 42.9
- Sodium: 864
- Total Carbohydrate: 17.6

233.   Mexican Ceviche

Serving: 8 | Prep: 30mins | Ready in:

Ingredients

- 5 large lemons, juiced
- 1 pound jumbo shrimp, peeled and deveined
- 1/4 cup chopped fresh cilantro, or to taste
- tomato and clam juice cocktail
- 2 white onions, finely chopped
- 1 cucumber, peeled and finely chopped
- 1 large tomatoes, seeded and chopped

- 3 fresh jalapeno peppers, seeded and minced
- 1 bunch radishes, finely diced
- 2 cloves fresh garlic, minced
- tortilla chips

Direction

- Put the shrimp in a bowl. You may leave the shrimp whole or chop it coarsely; it depends on your preference. Add the lemon and cover the shrimp totally. Put cover and let it chill in the fridge for 30 minutes or until it becomes a bit firm and turns opaque.
- Add garlic, radishes, cucumber, onions and tomatoes, then toss to blend. Slowly add jalapenos and cilantro to your preferred taste (jalapeno's taste will be stronger as it marinates). Stir in the clam juices and tomato to your preferred consistency. Put cover and let it chill in the fridge for an hour, then serve chilled alongside tortilla chips.

Nutrition Information

- Calories: 387 calories;
- Total Fat: 12.4
- Sodium: 733
- Total Carbohydrate: 57.6
- Cholesterol: 86
- Protein: 17.7

234.   Mexican Chicken And Black Bean Salad

Serving: 2 | Prep: 10mins | Ready in:

Ingredients

- 2 (4 ounce) frozen skinless, boneless chicken breast halves
- 1 (8 ounce) can low sodium tomato sauce
- 1/4 cup water
- 1 (1 ounce) packet taco seasoning
- 1 (15.5 ounce) can black beans

- 4 cups baby spinach leaves
- 2 tablespoons fat-free sour cream
- 1/2 cup shredded Mexican cheese blend
- 1/2 cup salsa

Direction

- Set the oven to 190°C or 375°F, then grease a baking dish lightly.
- In the prepared dish, position chicken breasts. In a small bowl, combine taco seasoning, water and tomato sauce together, then drizzle over chicken with the sauce.
- Bake in preheated oven for a half hour, until chicken isn't pink in the center anymore.
- Split spinach between 2 plates, then put the chicken breasts on the beds of spinach and scoop half of the black beans on top of each piece. Split salsa, shredded cheese and sour cream to place on top of each salad.

Nutrition Information

- Calories: 580 calories;
- Total Carbohydrate: 63.3
- Cholesterol: 99
- Protein: 49.5
- Total Fat: 14.7
- Sodium: 2665

235.   Mexican Orzo Salad

Serving: 8 | Prep: 24mins | Ready in:

Ingredients

- 1 (16 ounce) package orzo pasta
- 1 small red bell pepper, chopped
- 1 small yellow bell pepper, chopped
- 1 bunch green onions, chopped
- 1 small red onion, finely chopped
- 1 (15 ounce) can chickpeas, rinsed and drained
- 1 (15 ounce) can kidney beans, rinsed and drained

- 1 (15 ounce) can black beans, rinsed and drained
- 1 (8.75 ounce) can whole kernel corn, drained
- 1 cup chopped cilantro leaves
- salt to taste
- pepper to taste
- 5 limes, juiced
- 6 tablespoons canola oil

Direction

- Pour lightly salted water to fill a big pot, then boil on high heat. Mix in orzo, then boil once again. Cook the pasta for about 10 minutes without cover while mixing from time to time, until the pasta is completely cooked but firm to chew; drain.
- In a big salad bowl, put the drained orzo and fold in the pepper and salt to taste, cilantro, corn, black beans, kidney beans, chickpeas, red onion, green onions, yellow pepper and red pepper. Pour the oil and lime juice on top of the salad, then toss until coated. Place in the refrigerator to chill for at least 2 hours prior to serving.

Nutrition Information

- Calories: 457 calories;
- Sodium: 319
- Total Carbohydrate: 73.7
- Cholesterol: 0
- Protein: 14.7
- Total Fat: 12.9

236.   Midnight Snack Avocado Sandwich

Serving: 1 | Prep: 15mins | Ready in:

Ingredients

- 2 slices bacon, cut into 1-inch pieces
- 2 green onions, chopped

- 1 tablespoon mayonnaise
- 2 slices whole wheat bread, toasted
- 1/2 avocado, mashed
- 3 slices tomato
- 1/3 cup alfalfa sprouts
- salt and ground black pepper to taste

Direction

- In a large skillet, place the bacon and cook over medium-high heat, flipping from time to time, until nearly brown, for 2 to 3 minutes. Put green onion to bacon; cook and stir until onion is tender and bacon is crisp, for extra 3 to 5 minutes.
- Spread mayonnaise on a side of each slice of toast. Spread onto a side of one piece of toast with mashed avocado. Place bacon mixture, sprouts, and tomato slices on top of avocado; sprinkle with black pepper and salt. Place the remaining slice of toast on top.

Nutrition Information

- Calories: 532 calories;
- Total Carbohydrate: 39.4
- Cholesterol: 25
- Protein: 18.8
- Total Fat: 35.5
- Sodium: 780

237.   Mom's Dill Potato Salad

Serving: 12 | Prep: 15mins | Ready in:

Ingredients

- 3 pounds new red potatoes
- 1 cup mayonnaise
- 3/4 cup sour cream
- 2 tablespoons dried dill weed
- 4 green onions, chopped
- salt and ground black pepper to taste (optional)

Direction

- In a large pot, pour water to cover potatoes, and boil over high heat; bring the heat to medium-low, and cook while covered for about 15 minutes until tender but still firm. Drain off water and soak in an ice water bath for about 5 minutes to cool. Leave the potato skins on and chop into cubes, then transfer to a mixing bowl.
- In another bowl, mix green onions, dill weed, sour cream, and mayonnaise together until well incorporated. Add pepper and salt for seasoning. Pour the mayo dressing over potatoes and stir until evenly coated. Adjust seasonings if desired. Chill while covered for at least 2 hours, or overnight before serving.

Nutrition Information

- Calories: 245 calories;
- Protein: 3
- Total Fat: 17.8
- Sodium: 133
- Total Carbohydrate: 19.9
- Cholesterol: 13

238.   Mom's Gourmet Grilled Cheese Sandwich

Serving: 1 | Prep: 5mins | Ready in:

Ingredients

- 2 slices sourdough bread
- 1 tablespoon butter
- 1 tablespoon grated Parmesan cheese
- 1 slice American cheese
- 1 slice Cheddar cheese

Direction

- On moderate heat, heat a skillet. Coat on 1 side of each bread slice with butter. Sprinkle on the buttered sides with Parmesan cheese. Put in the skillet with 1 slice, buttered side facing down, then put on top of it an American cheese slice and a slice of Cheddar cheese. Place the leftover bread slice on top with butter side facing up. Fry until each side is golden.

Nutrition Information

- Calories: 488 calories;
- Protein: 21.3
- Total Fat: 32.1
- Sodium: 1081
- Total Carbohydrate: 29.2
- Cholesterol: 91

239. Mom's Mashed Potato Salad

Serving: 8 | Prep: 20mins | Ready in:

Ingredients

- 6 Yukon Gold potatoes
- 1 small sweet onion, diced
- 3 hard-cooked eggs, chopped
- 1/2 cup diced celery
- 1/4 cup chopped sweet pickles
- salt and ground black pepper to taste
- 1 cup mayonnaise
- 1/3 cup sweet pickle juice
- 1 teaspoon prepared yellow mustard

Direction

- Cover potatoes with salted water in a large pot and boil. Lower heat to medium-low and simmer for 20 minutes till tender. Let drain and move to a large bowl.
- Use a potato masher to mash potatoes. Add in black pepper, salt, pickles, celery, eggs and onion then stir. In a separate bowl, mix mustard, pickle juice and mayonnaise. Spread over the potatoes then mix well. Store in the

fridge, covered, for at least 60 minutes then serve.

Nutrition Information

- Calories: 308 calories;
- Sodium: 222
- Total Carbohydrate: 19.7
- Cholesterol: 90
- Protein: 4.7
- Total Fat: 24

240. Mom's Sushi Rice

Serving: 10 | Prep: 10mins | Ready in:

Ingredients

- 2 1/4 cups Japanese sushi-style rice
- 1 (4 inch) piece konbu dried kelp (optional)
- 3 cups water
- 1/4 cup rice vinegar
- 1/4 cup white sugar
- 1 1/4 teaspoons salt

Direction

- In a big and deep bowl, put rice then pour in cold water to fill. With your hands, rub the rice together until the water is milky white. Drain the cloudy water carefully avoid pouring out the rice. Repeat for 3 or 4 more times until the rice is visible through 3-in water.
- Using a fine strainer, drain rice then put in a saucepan; add three cups water and konbu. Set aside for half an hour to sit. In a small bowl, mix salt, sugar, and rice vinegar until dissolved; set aside.
- On high heat, boil rice white with a cover. Turn to low heat then simmer for 15 mins Take off heat then let it sit for 5mins while covering.
- Scrape rice to a bowl; get rid of the konbu. Mix in vinegar mixture until there is no remaining rice lumps and well blended. Cool at room

temperature. You can cool it rapidly with an electric fan for a shinier presentation.

Nutrition Information

- Calories: 181 calories;
- Total Carbohydrate: 40.7
- Cholesterol: 0
- Protein: 2.9
- Total Fat: 0.2
- Sodium: 296

241.   Monte Cristo Sandwich

Serving: 1 | Prep: 5mins | Ready in:

Ingredients

- 2 slices bread
- 1 teaspoon mayonnaise
- 1 teaspoon prepared mustard
- 2 slices cooked ham
- 2 slices cooked turkey meat
- 1 slice Swiss cheese
- 1 egg
- 1/2 cup milk

Direction

- Spread mustard and mayonnaise on bread; alternate turkey, swiss and ham slices on bread.
- Beat milk and egg in small bowl; coat sandwich in milk and egg mixture. Heat greased skillet on medium heat then brown sandwich on both sides and serve hot.

Nutrition Information

- Calories: 641 calories;
- Total Carbohydrate: 33.1
- Cholesterol: 298
- Protein: 48.7
- Total Fat: 33.8

- Sodium: 1308

242.   Morgan's Waldorf Salad

Serving: 8 | Prep: 20mins | Ready in:

Ingredients

- 1 Granny Smith apple, cubed
- 1 Golden Delicious apple, cubed
- 1 Gala apple, cubed
- 1 Bosc pear, cubed
- 3 ribs celery, chopped
- 3/4 cup sweetened dried cranberries
- 1/2 cup chopped walnuts
- 1/4 cup chopped pecans
- 1 cup sour cream
- 3/4 cup mayonnaise
- 1 tablespoon granulated cane sugar
- 2 teaspoons fresh lemon juice (optional)

Direction

- In a big bowl, mix together pecans, walnuts, cranberries, celery, Bosc pear, Gala apple, Golden Delicious apple, and Granny Smith apple.
- To make the dressing, combine lemon juice, sugar, mayonnaise, and sour cream in another bowl.
- Put the dressing on the apple mixture, mix until evenly combined. Put into the fridge to chill for a minimum of 15 minutes before eating.

Nutrition Information

- Calories: 364 calories;
- Sodium: 153
- Total Carbohydrate: 25
- Cholesterol: 20
- Protein: 2.9
- Total Fat: 29.7

243.   Mountain Mama's Potato Pancakes

Serving: 8 | Prep: 10mins | Ready in:

Ingredients

- 2/3 cup instant mashed potato flakes
- 1/3 cup complete dry pancake mix
- 1/2 cup chopped onion
- 1 cup shredded Cheddar cheese
- 1 cup skim milk
- 1 egg, beaten
- 1 tablespoon extra-virgin olive oil
- 1/2 teaspoon garlic powder
- salt and pepper to taste
- 1 pinch cayenne pepper (optional)

Direction

- In a mixing bowl, combine cayenne pepper, pepper, salt, garlic powder, olive oil, egg, milk, Cheddar cheese, onion, pancake mix, and potato flakes until well mixed.
- Lightly oil a large skillet or a griddle, and place over medium heat. To make pancakes, drop 1/4 cup of cake mixture at a time onto the hot griddle, cook until edges turn dry and the center shows 1 bubble, about 3 minutes. Turn over the pancakes, and cook for about 3 more minutes until the other side is browned.

Nutrition Information

- Calories: 131 calories;
- Total Fat: 7.3
- Sodium: 180
- Total Carbohydrate: 10.1
- Cholesterol: 39
- Protein: 6.3

244.   Natasha's Chicken Burgers

Serving: 4 | Prep: 10mins | Ready in:

Ingredients

- 1 pound extra-lean ground chicken
- 1/2 cup Italian-seasoned bread crumbs, divided
- 1/2 small onion, finely grated
- 1 egg
- 2 cloves garlic, minced
- salt and ground black pepper to taste
- 2 teaspoons olive oil

Direction

- In a bowl, combine together black pepper, salt, garlic, egg, onion, 1/4 cup of bread crumbs and ground chicken. Wet your hands and form the chicken mixture into flat, oval-shaped patties with 2 tbsp. at a time.
- In a shallow dish, spread leftover 1/4 cup of bread crumbs, then roll into bread crumbs with patties to coat well.
- In a big skillet, heat olive oil on moderately high heat.
- In the hot oil, cook patties for 5-6 minutes, until deep brown in color on the bottom. Turn patties and cook for 3-4 minutes longer, until the other side is browned.

Nutrition Information

- Calories: 238 calories;
- Total Carbohydrate: 11.5
- Cholesterol: 110
- Protein: 28.8
- Total Fat: 7.8
- Sodium: 175

245. New Wife Tuna Salad

Serving: 12 | Prep: 15mins | Ready in:

Ingredients

- 4 (5 ounce) cans tuna, drained
- 5 hard-boiled eggs, chopped
- 1/2 cup chopped sweet onion
- 1 stalk celery, chopped
- 3/4 cup mayonnaise
- 1 1/2 tablespoons dill pickle relish
- 2 teaspoons honey mustard
- 1/2 teaspoon celery seed
- 1/2 teaspoon seasoned salt
- 1/2 teaspoon ground black pepper

Direction

- In a big bowl, mix celery, onion, eggs and tuna.
- Mix pepper, seasoned salt, celery seed, honey mustard, relish and mayonnaise in a small bowl. Add on top of the ingredients in another bowl, and coat by lightly mixing. Serve it at room temperature or keep chilled till ready to serve.

Nutrition Information

- Calories: 186 calories;
- Total Carbohydrate: 2
- Cholesterol: 106
- Protein: 13.6
- Total Fat: 13.6
- Sodium: 189

246. New Year Black Eyed Peas

Serving: 10 | Prep: 20mins | Ready in:

Ingredients

- 1 pound dry black-eyed peas

- 2 tablespoons olive oil
- 1 large yellow onion, diced
- 2 cloves garlic, minced
- 2 (32 ounce) cartons chicken broth
- 8 cups water
- 1 pound smoked ham hocks
- 1 (14.5 ounce) can diced tomatoes
- 5 pepperoncini peppers
- 1 bay leaf
- 1/2 teaspoon garlic powder
- 1/4 teaspoon ground thyme
- salt and pepper to taste

Direction

- In a large container, place the black-eyed peas and cover with a few inches of cool water; let stand for 8 hours to overnight. Before using, rinse and drain.
- In a large stock pot, cook and stir onion and garlic in olive oil over medium heat for about 5 minutes until onion becomes translucent. Pour 8 cups of water and chicken broth, bring to a boil and decrease heat to a simmer. Stir in ham hocks, soaked black-eyed peas, pepperoncini, tomatoes, bay leaf, pepper, salt, thyme, and garlic powder. Cover and simmer for about 3 hours until the broth gets thickened, ham meat separates from the bones, and peas are tender.

Nutrition Information

- Calories: 307 calories;
- Total Carbohydrate: 27.9
- Cholesterol: 35
- Protein: 18.1
- Total Fat: 13.4
- Sodium: 1281

247. Nonie's Best BBQ

Serving: 12 | Prep: 10mins | Ready in:

Ingredients

- 1 (14 ounce) bottle ketchup
- 1/2 cup water
- 1/4 cup white sugar
- 1 tablespoon brown sugar
- 1 tablespoon red wine vinegar
- 1 tablespoon prepared yellow mustard
- 1 teaspoon salt
- 1/4 teaspoon ground black pepper
- 1/4 teaspoon paprika
- 2 pounds ground beef
- 2 teaspoons minced onion
- 12 hamburger buns, split

Direction

- Whisk paprika, pepper, salt, mustard, vinegar, brown sugar, white sugar, water and ketchup in a big saucepan; simmer on medium high heat. Lower heat to medium low; simmer for 15 minutes.
- Meanwhile, heat big skillet on medium high heat; mix and cook onion and ground beef in hot skillet till not pink, evenly browned and beef is crumbly. Drain extra grease; discard. Mix beef into simmering barbeque sauce; simmer for 10 minutes. Put onto buns; serve.

Nutrition Information

- Calories: 314 calories;
- Total Carbohydrate: 35.5
- Cholesterol: 47
- Protein: 17
- Total Fat: 11.5
- Sodium: 863

248.   Noodle Kugel (Dairy)

Serving: 8 | Prep: 15mins | Ready in:

Ingredients

- 8 ounces wide egg noodles

- 2 extra large eggs
- 1/4 cup white sugar
- 3 tablespoons butter, melted
- 1 cup lowfat whipped cottage cheese
- 8 ounces sour cream
- 1 pinch salt and ground black pepper to taste
- 2 tablespoons brown sugar, or to taste

Direction

- Put lightly salted water in a big pot and bring it to a rolling boil over high heat. Mix in the egg noodles when the water is boiling. Boil again. Cook the pasta without a cover for about 5 minutes, occasionally stirring it until the pasta is cooked through but still firm to bite. Drain well in a colander in the sink.
- Heat the oven beforehand to 175 °C or 350 °F. Use nonstick cooking spray to spray a one quart baking dish.
- Combine white sugar with the eggs until thoroughly mixed in a bowl. Mix in the pepper, salt, sour cream, whipped cottage cheese and melted butter. Mix in the noodles lightly then put the kugel in the baking sheet that was prepared. Sprinkle brown sugar on top.
- Bake for about 40 minutes until the top becomes brown in the preheated oven. Before serving, allow to cool for 10 minutes.

Nutrition Information

- Calories: 287 calories;
- Total Fat: 13.2
- Sodium: 163
- Total Carbohydrate: 31.6
- Cholesterol: 103
- Protein: 10.7

249.   Not Your Everyday Green Beans

Serving: 4 | Prep: 10mins | Ready in:

Ingredients

- 1/2 pound fresh green beans, trimmed
- 2 tablespoons butter
- 1/2 pound crimini mushrooms, chopped
- salt and pepper to taste
- 1/4 cup seasoned almond slices

Direction

- In a big frying pan, melt butter over medium heat. Stir and cook green beans in the butter, about 5 minutes. Mix in mushrooms. Use pepper and salt to season; keep cooking for 5 minutes until the beans are soft. Mix in almonds right before eating.

Nutrition Information

- Calories: 123 calories;
- Total Fat: 8.8
- Sodium: 66
- Total Carbohydrate: 7
- Cholesterol: 15
- Protein: 4.8

250. Okra With Tomatoes

Serving: 6 | Prep: 15mins | Ready in:

Ingredients

- 1 teaspoon olive oil
- 3 cloves garlic, minced
- 1 small onion, minced
- 1 teaspoon cayenne pepper
- 1/2 green bell pepper, minced
- 1 pound frozen sliced okra
- 1 (8 ounce) can canned diced tomatoes
- 1 (15 ounce) can stewed tomatoes
- salt and ground black pepper to taste

Direction

- Over medium heat, put the skillet with the olive oil, enough to cover the bottom of the skillet. Put the cayenne pepper, onion and the garlic. Stir until it is fragrant. Mix the green pepper. For about 5 minutes, stir and cook until it is tender. Mix the frozen okra. Wait for 5 more minutes to allow to cook. Mix the stewed and the diced tomatoes and season with pepper and salt. Turn the heat to medium low. Let it simmer for 5-7 minutes until all the vegetables are tender.

Nutrition Information

- Calories: 66 calories;
- Cholesterol: 0
- Protein: 2.8
- Total Fat: 1.1
- Sodium: 312
- Total Carbohydrate: 13.1

251. Omuraisu (Japanese Rice Omelet)

Serving: 1 | Prep: 5mins | Ready in:

Ingredients

- 1 cup cooked white or brown rice
- 2 thin slices cooked ham, cubed
- 2 tablespoons ketchup
- 1 slice processed cheese food (such as Velveeta ®) (optional)
- 2 eggs
- salt and pepper to taste
- 1 tablespoon ketchup
- 1/4 teaspoon chopped fresh parsley

Direction

- Heat skillet on medium heat. Coat using cooking spray. Add cheese (optional), ham, 2 tbsp. ketchup and cooked rice. Cook and mix for 8 minutes till heated through and ingredients are combined well. Put mixture on serving bowl; form an oval shape.

- Beat pepper, salt and eggs in bowl. Heat small skillet coated in cooking spray on medium heat then add egg mixture; cook on medium heat. Lift edges as eggs set, letting uncooked egg flow under it. Gently fold eggs with a spatula into cocoon shape. Take off heat when eggs set completely.
- Put omelet over the rice. Run knife laterally through omelet's top layer. It should open up like a butterfly. Drape over rice. Top with the final tbsp. ketchup and sprinkle with parsley.

Nutrition Information

- Calories: 521 calories;
- Sodium: 1300
- Total Carbohydrate: 59.3
- Cholesterol: 403
- Protein: 26.7
- Total Fat: 20.2

252. Open Faced Egg Sandwiches With Arugula Salad

Serving: 2 | Prep: 15mins | Ready in:

Ingredients

- 1 clove garlic, minced
- 1/4 cup mayonnaise
- 4 3/4-inch thick slices of crusty bread
- 2 cups arugula
- 2 teaspoons olive oil
- 1/2 teaspoon fresh lemon juice
- 1 pinch salt
- 1 pinch freshly ground black pepper
- cooking spray
- 4 eggs

Direction

- In a small bowl, mix together mayonnaise and garlic. On one side of the slices of bread, spread the mayonnaise mixture. In a bowl, mix arugula with black pepper, salt, lemon juice and olive oil. Split the arugula by fours then put them on top of mayonnaise side of the bread.
- Apply cooking spray to a frying pan and put over medium high heat. Crack eggs into frying pan one by one. Cook for 2-3 minutes on one side only until whites are firm but yolks are still slightly runny. Sprinkle eggs with black pepper and salt. Carefully put an egg on each open-face sandwich.

Nutrition Information

- Calories: 501 calories;
- Sodium: 536
- Total Carbohydrate: 23.3
- Cholesterol: 382
- Protein: 17
- Total Fat: 38.2

253. Oriental Shrimp Noodle Soup

Serving: 6 | Prep: 15mins | Ready in:

Ingredients

- 2 teaspoons vegetable oil
- 1 onion, chopped
- 2 cloves garlic, minced
- 1 tablespoon minced fresh ginger root
- 1 pinch crushed red pepper
- 2 quarts chicken broth
- 1 cup peeled, diagonally sliced carrots
- 1 cup diagonally sliced celery
- 2 cups snow peas
- 12 ounces fresh shrimp, peeled and deveined
- 4 ounces rice vermicelli
- 2 tablespoons soy sauce
- 1/4 teaspoon ground black pepper

Direction

- On medium heat, cook crushed red pepper, ginger, garlic, and onion in oil inside a big saucepan for 2 minutes. Place in celery, carrots, and broth and boil. Reduce the heat, simmer for 5 minutes, covered. Mix in shrimp and snow peas, cook for 3 minutes, covered. Break noodles to 2-inch pieces and mix in soup. Cook for another 3 minutes, covered, until shrimp is pink and veggies are tender. Mix in pepper and soy sauce then serve.

Nutrition Information

- Calories: 139 calories;
- Cholesterol: 85
- Protein: 11.2
- Total Fat: 2.3
- Sodium: 436
- Total Carbohydrate: 18.2

254.   Paleo Chorizo Sweet Potato And Kale Stew

Serving: 8 | Prep: 40mins | Ready in:

Ingredients

- 1 large onion, diced
- 2 tablespoons olive oil
- 8 ounces Spanish chorizo, cut into 1/2 inch pieces
- 3 stalks celery, diced
- 3 carrots, diced
- 2 teaspoons ground cumin
- 1 tablespoon paprika
- 1/2 teaspoon ground turmeric
- 2 teaspoons kosher salt
- 1 teaspoon freshly ground black pepper
- 1 pinch saffron threads
- 5 garlic cloves, minced
- 2 sweet potatoes, peeled and cut into 1-inch pieces

- 8 cups chicken broth
- 4 cups lacinato (dinosaur) kale - washed, stemmed, and torn into pieces
- 1 lemon, juiced
- salt and pepper to taste
- 1 pinch harissa, or to taste (optional)
- 1 tablespoon chopped fresh flat-leaf parsley, or to taste (optional)

Direction

- Mix and cook onion in olive oil in soup pot for 5 minutes on medium high heat. Add chorizo; cook for 3 minutes more, frequently mixing.
- Add carrots and celery; mix and cook for 3 minutes till veggies slightly soften. Add garlic, saffron threads, ground black pepper, kosher salt, turmeric, paprika and cumin. Mix and cook for 3 minutes more till garlic is slightly soft and fragrant.
- Add chicken broth and sweet potatoes. Boil, lower heat to medium low; cook for 20 minutes till sweet potatoes are tender. Add kale; cook for 10 minutes longer till kale cooks through and wilted and veggies are soft.
- Mix lemon juice in; adjust ground black pepper and salt to taste. Garnish with parsley and harissa.

Nutrition Information

- Calories: 234 calories;
- Total Carbohydrate: 17.8
- Cholesterol: 25
- Protein: 9.4
- Total Fat: 14.9
- Sodium: 925

255.   Pammy's Slow Cooker Beans

Serving: 10 | Prep: 15mins | Ready in:

Ingredients

- 2 pounds dried pinto beans
- 8 cups water, or more if needed
- 1 small onion, chopped
- 2 teaspoons garlic powder
- 1/2 teaspoon onion powder
- 1 teaspoon ground black pepper
- 2 bay leaves
- 1 smoked turkey leg
- 1/3 cup olive oil

Direction

- Rinse and pick on the beans, then put in a big bowl. With cold water, fill the bowl, and let the beans submerge for 6 to 8 hours.
- Let drain and wash the beans, then put into slow cooker. Add in 8 cups water. Mix in bay leaves, black pepper, onion powder, garlic powder and onion. Into the cooker, put the turkey leg, place the cover, and allow to cook for 6 hours on Low setting. Mix in olive oil, and put additional water in case beans are starting to dry out; let cook for 2 hours longer till beans are really soft.

Nutrition Information

- Calories: 415 calories;
- Sodium: 728
- Total Carbohydrate: 56
- Cholesterol: 19
- Protein: 25.3
- Total Fat: 10.8

256. Pea, Jicama, And Cashew Salad

Serving: 10 | Prep: 30mins | Ready in:

Ingredients

- 2 (3 ounce) packages ramen noodles (flavor packets saved for another use) broken into pieces
- 1/2 cup rice vinegar
- 1/4 cup reduced-sodium soy sauce
- 1 clove garlic, minced
- 1 teaspoon ground ginger
- 1/4 teaspoon crushed red pepper flakes
- black pepper to taste
- 1 tablespoon peanut oil
- 3 tablespoons toasted sesame oil
- 2 (10 ounce) packages frozen petite peas, thawed
- 1 jicama, peeled and diced
- 2 (8 ounce) cans water chestnuts, drained and diced
- 3 stalks celery, diced
- 3 green onions, chopped
- 1 cup cashew pieces

Direction

- In a skillet, toast dry ramen noodles on medium heat for 10 minutes, frequently stirring, until golden brown. Spread noodles in a big mixing bowl. Let cool and put aside. Create dressing by mixing black pepper, red pepper flakes, ginger, garlic, soy sauce, and vinegar in a small bowl. Mix in sesame oil and peanut oil until thick and blended.
- Combine cashews, green onions, celery, water chestnuts, jicama, and peas in a bowl with the toasted noodles. Pour dressing on top then toss to mix immediately prior to serving.

Nutrition Information

- Calories: 239 calories;
- Protein: 6.4
- Total Fat: 12.4
- Sodium: 376
- Total Carbohydrate: 26.7
- Cholesterol: 1

257. Peanut Butter, Mayonnaise, And Lettuce Sandwich

Serving: 1 | Prep: 5mins | Ready in:

Ingredients

- 2 slices bread
- 1 tablespoon mayonnaise
- 2 tablespoons peanut butter
- 2 lettuce leaves

Direction

- Spread mayonnaise over 1 slice of the bread. Spread peanut butter over another slice. Top peanut butter with the lettuce leaves, add mayonnaise-side of the other bread piece over the top to make sandwich.

Nutrition Information

- Calories: 428 calories;
- Protein: 12.4
- Total Fat: 29
- Sodium: 571
- Total Carbohydrate: 33
- Cholesterol: 5

258. Perfect Lobster Bisque

Serving: 6 | Prep: 10mins | Ready in:

Ingredients

- 3 tablespoons butter
- 1/4 cup chopped fresh mushrooms
- 2 tablespoons chopped onion
- 2 tablespoons chopped celery
- 2 tablespoons chopped carrot
- 1 (14.5 ounce) can chicken broth
- 1/8 teaspoon salt
- 1/8 teaspoon cayenne pepper

- 1 1/2 cups half-and-half
- 1/2 cup dry white wine
- 1/2 pound cooked lump lobster meat

Direction

- Melt butter in a big saucepan on medium low heat; add carrot, celery, onion and mushrooms. Mix and cook for 10 minutes till tender. Mix chicken broth in; season with cayenne pepper and salt. Boil; simmer for 10 minutes.
- Put broth and vegetable mixture in a blender's container; add 1/4 cup of lobster meat. Process, covered, till smooth. Put in a saucepan; mix leftover lobster meat, white wine and half-and-half in. Cook on low heat for 30 minutes, frequently mixing till thick.

Nutrition Information

- Calories: 186 calories;
- Total Fat: 13
- Sodium: 264
- Total Carbohydrate: 4.4
- Cholesterol: 65
- Protein: 9.7

259. Pesto Tuna Salad With Sun Dried Tomatoes

Serving: 2 | Prep: 15mins | Ready in:

Ingredients

- 1 (5 ounce) can canned tuna
- 1/4 cup prepared basil pesto sauce
- 6 oil-packed sun-dried tomatoes, drained and diced
- 2 tablespoons mayonnaise
- 2 tablespoons grated Parmesan cheese

Direction

- Combine Parmesan cheese, mayonnaise, sun-dried tomatoes, pesto, and tuna in a bowl. Put a cover on and put in the fridge to chill until serving.

Nutrition Information

- Calories: 368 calories;
- Total Carbohydrate: 4.8
- Cholesterol: 39
- Protein: 24.2
- Total Fat: 28.4
- Sodium: 448

260. Philly Cheesesteak Sandwich With Garlic Mayo

Serving: 4 | Prep: 10mins | Ready in:

Ingredients

- 1 cup mayonnaise
- 2 cloves garlic, minced
- 1 tablespoon olive oil
- 1 pound beef round steak, cut into thin strips
- 2 green bell peppers, cut into 1/4 inch strips
- 2 onions, sliced into rings
- salt and pepper to taste
- 4 hoagie rolls, split lengthwise and toasted
- 1 (8 ounce) package shredded mozzarella cheese
- 1 teaspoon dried oregano

Direction

- Mix the minced garlic and mayonnaise in a small bowl. Put cover and let it chill in the fridge. Set an oven to preheat at 260°C (500°F).
- In a big pan, heat the oil on medium heat. Sauté the beef until it browns lightly. Stir in the onion and green pepper, then sprinkle with pepper and salt to season. Sauté until the veggies become soft, then take it off from heat.

- Spread garlic mayonnaise liberally on each bun. Distribute the beef mixture in the buns. Put shredded cheese on top and sprinkle with oregano. Lay sandwiches on a baking pan.
- Heat the sandwiches in the preheated oven until it turns slightly brown, or cheese has melted.

Nutrition Information

- Calories: 935 calories;
- Total Fat: 66.4
- Sodium: 1405
- Total Carbohydrate: 49.6
- Cholesterol: 96
- Protein: 35.3

261. Picnic Marinated Summer Slaw

Serving: 8 | Prep: 20mins | Ready in:

Ingredients

- 1 (10 ounce) package shredded cabbage
- 1 cucumber, peeled and chopped
- 1 green bell pepper, chopped (optional)
- 1 large tomato, peeled and chopped
- 1 bunch green onions, chopped
- 1/2 cup white sugar
- 1/2 cup vegetable oil
- 1/4 cup white vinegar
- salt and ground black pepper to taste

Direction

- In a large bowl, mix green onions, green bell pepper, cucumber, tomato, and cabbage.
- Cook the vegetable oil, pepper, salt, vinegar and sugar in a saucepan over moderate heat for about 5 minutes, stirring, until the sugar dissolves. Remove from heat. Let the mixture cool before pouring it over the vegetables.

Toss to coat and place it inside the refrigerator for at least 2 hours to marinate.

Nutrition Information

- Calories: 189 calories;
- Cholesterol: 0
- Protein: 1
- Total Fat: 13.8
- Sodium: 7
- Total Carbohydrate: 17

---

262. Pittsburgh Sandwich

Serving: 4 | Prep: 30mins | Ready in:

Ingredients

- 3 cups shredded cabbage
- 2 tablespoons vegetable oil
- 2 tablespoons apple cider vinegar
- 2 tablespoons white sugar
- 1 teaspoon adobo seasoning (such as Goya®)
- 1 teaspoon ground black pepper
- 4 cups vegetable oil for frying
- 3 whole russet potatoes
- 8 thick slices Italian bread
- 1 pound sliced pastrami (divided)
- 4 slices provolone cheese
- 8 slices tomato

Direction

- Prepare the slaw by combining together black pepper, cabbage, adobo seasoning, 2 tablespoons of vegetable oil, sugar and the vinegar until mixed thoroughly. Cover and then chill refrigerate.
- Into a large saucepan or deep-fryer, heat oil to 190 degrees C (375 degrees F).
- Chop potatoes into 1/4-inch thick fries and then fry for 4 to 5 minutes until they turn golden brown and are floating. Reserve the fries.

- Preheat the oven to 110 degrees C (225 degrees F).
- Put bread onto a baking sheet and then toast for 3 to 5 minutes until light brown in the oven. Take out half of the bread slices. Put 1/4 of pastrami on top of remaining four bread slices and then add provolone cheese on top. Place back into the oven for about 5 minutes until the cheese has melted and pastrami becomes hot.
- To assemble, add 2 tomato slices, coleslaw, and French fries on top of the melted cheese of each sandwich. Then top bread pieces.

Nutrition Information

- Calories: 892 calories;
- Protein: 42.7
- Total Fat: 45.3
- Sodium: 1604
- Total Carbohydrate: 79.5
- Cholesterol: 97

---

263. Polish Link Sausage And Cabbage

Serving: 4 | Prep: 10mins | Ready in:

Ingredients

- 3 tablespoons butter
- 1/2 medium head cabbage, cut into chunks
- 1 (16 ounce) package kielbasa sausage, sliced into rounds
- 1 (12 fluid ounce) can beer
- ground black pepper to taste

Direction

- In a pot, melt butter over medium heat. Cook cabbage while stirring in butter for 5 minutes or until tender. Put beer and sausage into cabbage; then stir. Add pepper to season the cabbage mixture. Simmer for 20 minutes or until sausage casings start to shrink. Drain the liquid from the mixture. Then serve.

Nutrition Information

- Calories: 529 calories;
- Total Fat: 43.2
- Sodium: 1018
- Total Carbohydrate: 11.9
- Cholesterol: 104
- Protein: 16.2

264.   Poor Man's Caviar

Serving: 8 | Prep: 15mins | Ready in:

Ingredients

- 2 large avocados - peeled, pitted, and chopped
- 3 plum tomatoes, chopped
- 1 bunch green onions, chopped
- 1 (14.5 ounce) can black beans, rinsed and drained
- 1 (11 ounce) can Mexicorn, drained
- 1/4 cup red wine vinegar
- 1/4 cup canola oil
- hot pepper sauce to taste

Direction

- Stir the Mexicorn, black beans, green onions, tomatoes and avocados together and mix in the hot pepper sauce, canola oil and red wine vinegar. Put cover and let it chill in the fridge for an hour.

Nutrition Information

- Calories: 267 calories;
- Total Carbohydrate: 25.1
- Cholesterol: 0
- Protein: 6.1
- Total Fat: 17.9
- Sodium: 345

265.   Prosciutto Parmesan Pasta

Serving: 4 | Prep: 10mins | Ready in:

Ingredients

- 1 (8 ounce) package bow tie pasta
- 1/2 pound prosciutto, sliced
- 2 cups heavy cream
- 1 1/2 cups freshly grated Parmesan cheese
- 1 (10 ounce) can peas, drained
- salt to taste
- 1/2 cup freshly grated Parmesan cheese

Direction

- Boil a big pot of slightly salty water, then add the pasta, cook for 8-10 minutes until cooked through but still firm to the bite, then drain.
- Grease skillet slightly with some cooking spray and cook the prosciutto over medium heat for 3-5 minutes until browned lightly. Take away from the heat and drain off the excess fat, then set aside the prosciutto on paper towels.
- At the same time, heat a saucepan with cream over medium-low heat, then gradually blend in 1 1/2 cup Parmesan cheese, placing in small portions. Once the cheese melts completely, stir in prosciutto and peas, then heat for another 2 minutes. Pour over the drained pasta and gently toss. Season to taste with salt then garnish with a sprinkle of 1/2 cup Parmesan cheese.

Nutrition Information

- Calories: 1029 calories;
- Total Carbohydrate: 52.3
- Cholesterol: 248
- Protein: 38.6
- Total Fat: 74.9

- Sodium: 1889

266.   Quick Chicken And Corn Chowder

Serving: 6 | Prep: 15mins | Ready in:

Ingredients

- 1 tablespoon olive oil
- 8 ounces skinless, boneless chicken breast halves, cut into bite-size pieces
- 1/2 cup chopped onion
- 1/2 cup chopped red bell pepper
- 1 clove garlic, minced
- 4 cups low-sodium chicken broth
- 1 1/2 cups frozen corn
- 1 cup skim milk
- 1 tablespoon cornstarch, or more as needed
- 1 cup white beans, drained and rinsed
- 1 cup shredded Cheddar cheese
- 1/2 teaspoon salt (optional)
- 1/4 teaspoon ground black pepper

Direction

- In a cooking pan, heat the olive oil on medium heat. Put the chicken, red bell pepper, onion, and garlic in the oil and sauté for 3-5 minutes until the onion is tender and the chicken is not pink at the center.
- Pour into the chicken mixture the chicken broth and corn.
- Mix the cornstarch and milk in a bowl and beat them together until dissolved then pour this mixture into the soup. Boil, lower the heat, and let it simmer for 15 minutes until the soup has thickened. Add the Cheddar cheese, white beans, salt, and pepper, stirring them into the soup and let it simmer for 5 minutes until the cheese has melted.

Nutrition Information

- Calories: 263 calories;
- Cholesterol: 43
- Protein: 20.3
- Total Fat: 10.1
- Sodium: 424
- Total Carbohydrate: 24.1

267.   Quick Tuna Salad

Serving: 3 | Prep: 5mins | Ready in:

Ingredients

- 1 (7 ounce) can solid white tuna packed in water, drained
- 1/4 cup creamy salad dressing (such as Miracle Whip™)
- 1 tablespoon sweet pickle relish, or to taste

Direction

- Mash salad dressing and tuna and use a fork to relish in a small bowl then serve.

Nutrition Information

- Calories: 142 calories;
- Protein: 16.7
- Total Fat: 5.9
- Sodium: 240
- Total Carbohydrate: 4.4
- Cholesterol: 26

268.   Quinoa Tabbouleh Salad

Serving: 12 | Prep: 25mins | Ready in:

Ingredients

- 2 cups vegetable broth
- 1 cup quinoa
- 1 cucumber, chopped

- 2 tomatoes, chopped
- 1/2 cup fresh parsley, chopped
- 2 green onions, chopped
- 2 tablespoons chopped fresh mint
- 2 cloves garlic, minced
- 1/4 cup olive oil
- 1/4 cup lemon juice
- 1/2 teaspoon salt, or to taste

Direction

- Please quinoa and broth in a sauce pan then make it boil. Minimize heat to medium low, and simmer for about 15 minutes, covered, until the water has been absorbed and quinoa is soft.
- In a large bowl, mix together the garlic, mint, green onions, parsley, tomatoes and cucumber. Then add salt, lemon juice, olive oil and quinoa to cucumber mixture; then combine well by tossing.
- Use plastic wrap to cover the bowl and place inside the refrigerator for at least one hour until flavors are combined.

Nutrition Information

- Calories: 107 calories;
- Total Carbohydrate: 12.3
- Cholesterol: 0
- Protein: 2.6
- Total Fat: 5.5
- Sodium: 178

269.   Quinoa Vegetable Salad

Serving: 12 | Prep: 20mins | Ready in:

Ingredients

- 1 teaspoon canola oil
- 1 tablespoon minced garlic
- 1/4 cup diced (yellow or purple) onion
- 2 1/2 cups water

- 2 teaspoons salt, or to taste
- 1/4 teaspoon ground black pepper
- 2 cups quinoa
- 3/4 cup diced fresh tomato
- 3/4 cup diced carrots
- 1/2 cup diced yellow bell pepper
- 1/2 cup diced cucumber
- 1/2 cup frozen corn kernels, thawed
- 1/4 cup diced red onion
- 1 1/2 tablespoons chopped fresh cilantro
- 1 tablespoon chopped fresh mint
- 1 teaspoon salt
- 1/4 teaspoon ground black pepper
- 2 tablespoons olive oil
- 3 tablespoons balsamic vinegar

Direction

- In a sauce pan on medium heat, heat the canola oil. Stir and cook 1/4 cup onion and garlic in the hot oil for about five minutes until onion turned translucent and has softened. Add in 1/4 teaspoon black pepper, 2 teaspoons salt and water then make it boil; add the quinoa into the mixture, minimize the heat to medium low, covered. Simmer for about 20 minutes until the quinoa is soft. Drain any left water from the quinoa using a mesh strainer then move to a large mixing bowl
- Place inside the refrigerator until cold.
- Mix 1/4 cup red onion, corn, cucumber, bell pepper, carrots and tomato into the chilled quinoa. Add 1/4 teaspoon black pepper, 1 teaspoon salt, mint and cilantro to season.
- Drizzle the balsamic vinegar and olive oil over the salad; slowly stir until equally combined.

Nutrition Information

- Calories: 148 calories;
- Cholesterol: 0
- Protein: 4.6
- Total Fat: 4.5
- Sodium: 592
- Total Carbohydrate: 22.9

270. Real German Potato Salad (No Mayo)

Serving: 8 | Prep: 15mins | Ready in:

Ingredients

- 10 red potatoes, peeled and roughly chopped, or more to taste
- 1/2 cup chicken broth, or more as needed
- 1/4 cup white vinegar
- 1/4 cup oil
- 1 large onion, diced
- 6 slices cooked bacon, chopped (optional)
- 1/4 cup chopped fresh dill
- salt and ground black pepper to taste

Direction

- In a big pot, put potatoes and fill with salted water, boil it. Decrease the heat to medium-low and simmer for 15-20 minutes until softened. Strain.
- In a big pot, mix together oil, vinegar, and chicken broth and boil it. Put the onion in the broth mixture, cook for 2-6 minutes until the onion reaches the preferred softness. Take away from heat and add dill, bacon, and potatoes, mix gently. To moisten the salad, add more chicken broth as necessary. Use pepper and salt to season the potato salad.

Nutrition Information

- Calories: 127 calories;
- Total Fat: 8.8
- Sodium: 168
- Total Carbohydrate: 9.5
- Cholesterol: 5
- Protein: 2.9

271. Red, White And Blue Burgers

Serving: 6 | Prep: 5mins | Ready in:

Ingredients

- 2 pounds ground beef sirloin
- 1 red onion, diced
- 1/2 (1 ounce) package dry ranch salad dressing mix
- 4 ounces crumbled blue cheese

Direction

- Preheat outdoor grill to medium high heat; oil grate lightly.
- Mix blue cheese, ranch salad dressing mix, onion and ground sirloin lightly in a bowl; shape to 6 patties.
- Grill burgers on prepped grill till well done or 5 minutes per side.

Nutrition Information

- Calories: 372 calories;
- Sodium: 521
- Total Carbohydrate: 3.3
- Cholesterol: 120
- Protein: 33.7
- Total Fat: 23.9

272. Refreshing Watermelon Salad

Serving: 15 | Prep: 20mins | Ready in:

Ingredients

- 3 tablespoons lime juice
- 1 cup sliced red onion, cut lengthwise
- 15 cups cubed watermelon
- 3 cups cubed English cucumber
- 1 (8 ounce) package feta cheese, crumbled

- 1/2 cup chopped fresh cilantro
- cracked black pepper
- sea salt

Direction

- Pour lime juice in a small bowl of red onions. Assemble the salad while the onions are marinating. In a large bowl, gently combine cilantro, feta cheese, cucumber and watermelon. Add black pepper to taste. Just before serving, toss marinated onions with watermelon salad and add sea salt to taste.

Nutrition Information

- Calories: 94 calories;
- Total Fat: 3.5
- Sodium: 182
- Total Carbohydrate: 14.2
- Cholesterol: 13
- Protein: 3.4

273.   Rhubarb Salsa

Serving: 6 | Prep: 15mins | Ready in:

Ingredients

- 2 cups rhubarb, diced small
- 1 cup chopped apple
- 3 green onions, chopped
- 2 limes, juiced
- 2 tablespoons honey
- 1 jalapeno pepper, seeded and chopped

Direction

- In a pot, boil water over medium heat, and mix in rhubarb; simmer to blanch, about 2 minutes. Put into a colander set over a sink to strain. Cool.
- Combine jalapeno pepper, honey, lime juice, green onions, apple, and the cooled rhubarb until fully blended.

Nutrition Information

- Calories: 47 calories;
- Total Fat: 0.2
- Sodium: 4
- Total Carbohydrate: 12.2
- Cholesterol: 0
- Protein: 0.7

274.   Richard And Suzanne's Famous Red Beans And Sausage

Serving: 8 | Prep: 35mins | Ready in:

Ingredients

- 3 bacon slices
- 2 tablespoons extra-virgin olive oil
- 3 bay leaves
- 2 tablespoons red pepper flakes
- 1 large green bell pepper, chopped
- 1 large red bell pepper, chopped
- 1 large yellow onion, chopped
- 1 bunch green onions, chopped
- 3 cloves garlic, chopped
- 4 (15.5 ounce) cans light red kidney beans
- 2 quarts water
- 1/4 cup salted butter
- 2 pounds andouille sausage, sliced
- salt and pepper to taste

Direction

- In a large, deep skillet add the bacon. Cook over medium-high heat until evenly browned. Keeping the drippings, take out the bacon, remove any excess grease with paper towel; crumble and keep to the side. Into the pan with the bacon drippings add olive oil, bay leaves and red pepper flakes and reheat. Add red, yellow and green bell peppers, yellow and green onion and garlic in the olive oil mixture until soft.

- Over a medium heat place the kidney beans into a heavy pot. Cover beans with water; add vegetable mixture from skillet and the cooked bacon; stir. Stir occasionally while simmering for 30 minutes. Add the butter.
- As the butter is melting into the bean mixture, place the skillet back on the heat and cook the sausage until lightly browned; add the sausage to the beans. Add a little water to the bottom of the skillet and pour into the bean mixture. Cook beans for another 15 minutes. Season to taste with salt and pepper.

Nutrition Information

- Calories: 689 calories;
- Total Carbohydrate: 45
- Cholesterol: 85
- Protein: 28.5
- Total Fat: 44.6
- Sodium: 1653

---

275.   Roast Beef Burritos

Serving: 6 | Prep: 20mins | Ready in:

Ingredients

- 1 tablespoon vegetable oil
- 1 onion, chopped
- 1 clove garlic, minced
- 4 tomatoes, chopped
- 2 cups chopped cooked roast beef
- 1 (8 ounce) jar prepared taco sauce
- 1 (4 ounce) can diced green chile peppers
- 1/2 teaspoon cumin
- 1/8 teaspoon red pepper flakes, or to taste (optional)
- 6 (7 inch) flour tortillas, warmed
- 1 1/2 cups shredded Cheddar cheese
- 2 cups shredded lettuce

Direction

- Heat oil in a skillet on medium high heat. Mix garlic and onion in; cook for 5 minutes till transparent and tender. Mix red pepper flakes (optional), cumin, chile peppers, taco sauce, roast beef and tomatoes in; boil. Lower heat to medium; simmer for 25 minutes, uncovered, till thick.
- Put tortillas on a flat and clean work surface. Spread 2/3 cup of beef mixture in middle of each warm tortilla. Evenly sprinkle lettuce and cheese. Fold sides and ends over to create a package.

Nutrition Information

- Calories: 405 calories;
- Cholesterol: 54
- Protein: 21.9
- Total Fat: 18.5
- Sodium: 1267
- Total Carbohydrate: 38.2

---

276.   Roasted Asparagus Salad With Feta Cheese

Serving: 4 | Prep: 15mins | Ready in:

Ingredients

- 1 bunch fresh asparagus, trimmed and cut into bite-size pieces
- 2 tablespoons olive oil
- 1 pinch garlic powder, or to taste
- 4 cups lettuce leaves, cut into bite-size pieces
- 1 cup grape tomatoes, halved
- 1/2 cup crumbled feta cheese

Direction

- Preheat the oven to 200°C or 400°F.
- In a big bowl, add asparagus, then pour over asparagus with olive oil and season with garlic

powder. Toss well together, then turn to a baking sheet.

- Bake in the preheated oven about 20 minutes, until asparagus are softened.
- In the same bowl used for asparagus, add lettuce and place on top with asparagus, feta cheese and tomatoes.

Nutrition Information

- Calories: 183 calories;
- Sodium: 372
- Total Carbohydrate: 9.2
- Cholesterol: 28
- Protein: 8.2
- Total Fat: 13.8

---

277. Roasted Beets With Goat Cheese And Walnuts

Serving: 2 | Prep: 15mins | Ready in:

Ingredients

- 1/2 cup chopped walnuts
- 1 large beet, top and bottom trimmed and beet greens retained
- 1 tablespoon walnut oil, or more to taste
- 2 ounces soft goat cheese
- kosher salt and freshly ground black pepper to taste
- 2 tablespoons champagne vinegar
- 1 cup reserved beet greens, cut into very thin slivers
- 2 teaspoons chopped fresh chives

Direction

- Set an oven to 135°C (275°F) and start preheating.
- On a baking sheet, arrange walnuts and toast in the prepared oven for around 45 minutes until the nuts release fragrance and turn golden brown. Observe the nuts to prevent

them from burning. To chill to room temperature, put walnuts aside.

- Increase oven heat to 190°C (375°F). Put a crinkled piece of aluminum foil in an oven-safe dish (ex: a pie dish) as a disposable rack. Arrange beet on the foil.
- Place in the prepared oven and bake for around 45 minutes until the beet just begins to become tender. Use aluminum foil to wrap beet and allow to chill to room temperature.
- Increase oven temperature to 205°C (400°F).
- Use a sharp paring knife to remove the skin from beet. Slice beet in half, slice the halves to form thick half-moon-shaped pieces.
- In a baking dish, lightly pour walnut oil, then brush over the bottom of the dish; place beet slices from the dish in a single layer. Crumble goat cheese over beets and into the empty spaces. Use black pepper and kosher salt to dust.
- Bake cheese and beet in the oven for around 15 minutes until the edges of the cheese slightly turn brown and the beet pieces sizzle. Allow to slightly cool for around 10 minutes.
- Lightly sprinkle vinegar over the cheese and warm beet and put chives, beet greens, and roasted walnuts on top. Eventually, serve warm.

Nutrition Information

- Calories: 422 calories;
- Total Carbohydrate: 19
- Cholesterol: 22
- Protein: 13.1
- Total Fat: 35.1
- Sodium: 487

---

278. Roasted Cauliflower And Leek Soup

Serving: 6 | Prep: 10mins | Ready in:

Ingredients

- 2 cloves garlic, minced
- 2 tablespoons vegetable oil
- 1 head cauliflower, broken into florets
- 3 tablespoons butter
- 2 leeks, white part only, chopped
- 1/4 cup all-purpose flour
- 1 quart chicken stock
- 1/3 cup heavy whipping cream
- 1 teaspoon dried chervil
- 1 teaspoon kosher salt
- 1 tablespoon cracked black pepper

Direction

- Preheat oven to 275° F (135° C).
- In a small bowl, mix vegetable oil and garlic together. Line cauliflower florets on a baking sheet; splash the cauliflower with oil mixture. Flip to coat.
- Bake cauliflower in the preheated oven for about 30 minutes, until lightly browned and softened.
- In a 4-quart stockpot, melt butter over medium heat; cook and mix flour and leeks in the melted butter for 5 - 10 minutes until properly blended and fragrant. Add cream, chicken stock, and cauliflower; simmer for around 20 - 25 minutes until flavors are combined. Stir pepper, salt, and chervil into the soup; simmer for 10 - 15 minutes more until thicken as wanted.

Nutrition Information

- Calories: 209 calories;
- Sodium: 856
- Total Carbohydrate: 15.4
- Cholesterol: 34
- Protein: 3.8
- Total Fat: 15.9

279.   Roasted Pork Banh Mi (Vietnamese Sandwich)

Serving: 1 | Prep: 25mins | Ready in:

Ingredients

- 1/4 cup julienned (2-inch matchsticks) daikon radish
- 1/4 cup julienned (2-inch matchsticks) carrots
- 1 tablespoon seasoned rice vinegar
- 1/4 cup mayonnaise
- 1 teaspoon hoisin sauce, or to taste
- 1 teaspoon sriracha hot sauce, or more to taste
- 1 crusty French sandwich roll
- 4 ounces cooked pork roast, thinly sliced
- 2 ounces smooth pate, thinly sliced
- 6 thin spears English cucumber, diced
- 6 thin slices jalapeno pepper, or more to taste
- 1/4 cup cilantro leaves

Direction

- Set the oven for preheating to 400°F. Prepare a baking sheet lined with aluminum foil.
- Mix together the carrot and julienned daikon with seasoned rice vinegar and toss to coat well. Let the mixture stand for 15 to 20 minutes until the vegetables are a bit wilted. Drain. Place inside the fridge or just set aside.
- Combine together the sriracha, hoisin sauce and mayonnaise in a small bowl.
- Slice the French roll on the side just enough to open it like a book. To accommodate the filling better, scoop out some of the bread from the top half if preferred.
- Scoop a mayo mixture and spread the interior surfaces of the roll generously. Arrange the roll placing cut side up in the prepared baking sheet. Bake inside the preheated oven for about 7 minutes until edges begins to get brown, crisp, and heated through.
- Assemble sliced pork, jalapeno, cucumber, picked daikon and carrots, pate and cilantro leaves in the roll. Cut evenly into 2 portions and serve.

Nutrition Information

- Calories: 1263 calories;
- Sodium: 1994
- Total Carbohydrate: 91.3
- Cholesterol: 188
- Protein: 54.2
- Total Fat: 75.9

280. Roasted Potato Salad With Balsamic Dressing

Serving: 8 | Prep: 45mins | Ready in:

Ingredients

- 10 red potatoes, scrubbed and dried with paper towels
- 3 tablespoons canola oil
- 1 tablespoon dried thyme
- 1 tablespoon chili powder
- 1 tablespoon kosher salt
- 1 tablespoon cracked black pepper
- 1 bunch green onions, sliced
- 3/4 cup roasted red peppers, drained and diced
- 1/2 cup kalamata olives, pitted and sliced
- 1 (10 ounce) can artichoke hearts, drained and chopped
- 1/4 cup chopped fresh parsley
- 1/2 cup crumbled Gorgonzola cheese
- 1/4 cup balsamic vinegar
- 1/4 cup extra-virgin olive oil
- 1 tablespoon Dijon mustard
- 1 teaspoon minced garlic
- 1 teaspoon dried oregano
- 1 teaspoon dried basil
- salt and pepper to taste

Direction

- Set oven to 450°F (230°C) to preheat.
- Slice potatoes into 3/4 inch pieces, put into a bowl. Lightly grease a baking sheet with canola oil. Place the potatoes skin side down to the baking sheet. Season potatoes with pepper, kosher salt, chili powder, and thyme.
- Put the potato dish into the preheated oven and bake for about 45 minutes until golden brown. Take out and let it cool.
- Gently toss cooled potatoes with Gorgonzola cheese, parsley, artichoke hearts, olives, roasted red peppers, and green onions in a large salad bowl until completely incorporated.
- Put basil, oregano, garlic, Dijon mustard, olive oil, and balsamic vinegar into a blender, blend a couple of times until the dressing becomes thick and creamy. Add pepper and salt to taste, drizzle over potato salad, stir gently. Freeze in the fridge for 4 hours then enjoy.

Nutrition Information

- Calories: 254 calories;
- Cholesterol: 11
- Protein: 5.7
- Total Fat: 18
- Sodium: 1319
- Total Carbohydrate: 18.7

281. Roasted Raspberry Chipotle Grilled Cheese Sandwich On Sourdough

Serving: 2 | Prep: 5mins | Ready in:

Ingredients

- 4 tablespoons butter, softened
- 4 slices sourdough bread
- 8 Borden® Mild Cheddar Slices
- 4 tablespoons roasted raspberry chipotle sauce

Direction

- Over medium heat, put a skillet.

144

- Butter 4 bread slices, a tablespoon each. Onto skillet, put 2 bread slices, butter side facing down. Put 2 cheese slices on each.
- Onto every sandwich, scatter 2 tablespoons of roasted raspberry chipotle sauce and put 2 additional cheese slices on top of each.
- Put the leftover bread on top of each, butter side facing up. Allow to grill till bottom is browned lightly; turn sandwiches over. Grill the other side till browned and cheese has melted.

Nutrition Information

- Calories: 708 calories;
- Total Fat: 44
- Sodium: 1049
- Total Carbohydrate: 48.2
- Cholesterol: 121
- Protein: 22.1

282.   Russian Carrot Salad

Serving: 6 | Prep: 15mins | Ready in:

Ingredients

- 6 large carrots, shredded
- 3 cloves garlic, minced
- 1/4 cup finely chopped walnuts
- 1/4 cup light mayonnaise

Direction

- Stir the mayonnaise, walnuts, garlic and carrots together until evenly combined, then serve.

Nutrition Information

- Calories: 80 calories;
- Sodium: 143
- Total Carbohydrate: 10.7
- Cholesterol: 0

- Protein: 1.5
- Total Fat: 4

283.   Salmon Salad

Serving: 4 | Prep: 5mins | Ready in:

Ingredients

- 2 (7 ounce) cans salmon, drained
- 2 tablespoons fat-free mayonnaise
- 2 tablespoons plain low-fat yogurt
- 1 cup chopped celery
- 2 tablespoons capers
- 1/8 teaspoon ground black pepper
- 8 leaves lettuce

Direction

- In a 1 quart bowl, crumble the salmon and remove any bones or skin.
- Mix the capers, celery, pepper, mayonnaise, and yogurt in a small bowl. Combine thoroughly and transfer to bowl of salmon and mix. You can serve atop a bed of lettuce leaves.

Nutrition Information

- Calories: 182 calories;
- Total Fat: 7.4
- Sodium: 568
- Total Carbohydrate: 3.7
- Cholesterol: 44
- Protein: 23.9

284.   Sardines With Sun Dried Tomato And Capers

Serving: 1 | Prep: 10mins | Ready in:

Ingredients

- 1 (3.75 ounce) can sardines packed in olive oil, drained (such as King Oscar®)
- 1/2 fresh lemon
- 1 pinch salt and ground black pepper to taste
- 1/4 teaspoon cayenne pepper
- 1/2 teaspoon dried oregano
- 1/2 teaspoon dried thyme
- 1 pinch crushed red pepper flakes, or to taste
- 2 garlic cloves, chopped
- 2 tablespoons chopped sun-dried tomatoes
- 1 tablespoon capers

Direction

- Bring sardines onto a small dish. Pour 1/2 of a lemon juice onto the sardines, then add crushed red pepper flakes, thyme, oregano, cayenne pepper, black pepper and salt to season. Top with capers, sun-dried tomatoes and garlic over the mixture.

Nutrition Information

- Calories: 234 calories;
- Total Fat: 11.2
- Sodium: 864
- Total Carbohydrate: 9.9
- Cholesterol: 131
- Protein: 24.6

285. Savory Couscous Tabbouleh

Serving: 4 | Prep: 25mins | Ready in:

Ingredients

- 1 cup low-sodium chicken broth
- 1/2 cup water
- 1 cup couscous
- 1 cucumber, seeded and diced
- 3 green onions, chopped
- 1 carrot, grated
- 1 cup chopped fresh parsley

- 1/4 cup extra-virgin olive oil
- 1/4 cup lemon juice
- 1/4 teaspoon ground cumin
- 1/2 teaspoon salt
- 1/2 teaspoon ground black pepper
- 1/4 cup crumbled feta cheese

Direction

- Boil water and chicken broth in a saucepan. Remove it from the heat. Mix in couscous. Cover the pan and let the couscous stand for 5-10 minutes until it absorbs the liquid and it is tender. Use a fork to fluff the couscous.
- In a large salad bowl, combine the carrot, parsley, cucumber, couscous, and green onions. In a small bowl, mix the lemon juice and olive oil and pour the mixture all over the vegetables. Mix the salt, black pepper, and cumin into the tabbouleh. Stir in feta cheese before serving.

Nutrition Information

- Calories: 309 calories;
- Total Carbohydrate: 33.3
- Cholesterol: 9
- Protein: 7.6
- Total Fat: 16.6
- Sodium: 454

286. Savory Halibut Enchiladas

Serving: 8 | Prep: 25mins | Ready in:

Ingredients

- 2 pounds skinless halibut fillets, cut into large pieces
- 1 pinch garlic powder
- salt and ground black pepper to taste
- 1 bunch green onions, chopped
- 1 green bell pepper, finely chopped

- 1/4 cup coarsely chopped fresh cilantro
- 1/2 cup sour cream
- 1/4 cup mayonnaise
- 1 cup shredded Cheddar cheese
- 2 (10 ounce) cans enchilada sauce
- 8 flour tortillas
- 1 cup shredded Cheddar cheese
- 2 avocados - peeled, pitted, and sliced

Direction

- Preheat an oven to 190°C/375°F.
- Use pepper, salt and garlic powder to season halibut. Cook in microwave for 2 minutes till slightly cooked. In a bowl, mix 1 cup cheddar cheese, mayonnaise, sour cream, cilantro, bell pepper and green onion. Fold halibut into mixture gently.
- Use cooking spray to prep a 9x13-in. baking dish. Put 1/2 can of enchilada sauce on baking dish's bottom.
- In a bowl, put 1 can enchilada sauce. One at a time, dip tortillas into sauce to coat lightly. In the middle of every tortilla, spoon halibut in even portions. Create enchiladas by rolling tortillas tightly. Put in baking dish, seam-side down. Put leftover enchilada sauce over enchiladas. Sprinkle 1 cup cheddar cheese on top. Use aluminum foil to cover dish.
- In preheated oven, bake for 45 minutes. Put avocado slices on top then serve.

Nutrition Information

- Calories: 605 calories;
- Protein: 38.2
- Total Fat: 32.8
- Sodium: 707
- Total Carbohydrate: 40.3
- Cholesterol: 75

287. Savory Pumpkin Hummus

Serving: 16 | Prep: 15mins | Ready in:

Ingredients

- 2 tablespoons lemon juice
- 2 tablespoons tahini
- 3 cloves garlic
- 3/4 teaspoon salt
- 2 (15 ounce) cans garbanzo beans, drained
- 2 teaspoons extra-virgin olive oil
- 1 (15 ounce) can pumpkin puree
- 1 teaspoon ground cumin
- 1/2 teaspoon cayenne pepper
- 1/4 cup toasted pumpkin seed kernels, or more to taste
- 1 pinch paprika

Direction

- Mix well the salt, garlic, tahini and lemon juice in a blender or food processor until becomes smooth. Add in the olive oil and garbanzo beans then mix until smoothed. Stir in the cayenne pepper, cumin and pumpkin; mix well until well combined. Place the hummus in a container with a lid to cover the place inside the refrigerator for 2 hours.
- Add in pumpkin seeds into hummus; then put paprika to garnish.

Nutrition Information

- Calories: 81 calories;
- Sodium: 281
- Total Carbohydrate: 11.3
- Cholesterol: 0
- Protein: 3
- Total Fat: 3.1

288.   Savory Spanish Potato Salad

Serving: 4 | Prep: 15mins | Ready in:

Ingredients

- 1 pound small red potatoes
- 3 tablespoons olive oil
- 1 tablespoon red wine vinegar
- 2 garlic cloves, crushed
- 1 small red bell pepper, chopped
- 2 tablespoons pimento-stuffed green olives, sliced
- 1 tablespoon minced shallot
- 1 tablespoon chopped fresh parsley
- salt and ground black pepper to taste
- 1 lemon, cut into wedges (optional)

Direction

- Transfer potatoes into a pot and then add salted water to cover. Heat to boil. Decrease the heat to medium-low and let to simmer for about 10 minutes until tender. Drain off water and let to cool until easy to handle. Chop the potatoes about 1/2-inch thick and put in a bowl.
- In a bowl, whisk vinegar and olive oil together. Mix in garlic. Spread the dressing atop potatoes and mix lightly to coat.
- Combine pepper, salt, shallot, red bell pepper, parsley, and green olives into the potatoes. Serve the salad together with lemon wedges to squeeze atop each serving.

Nutrition Information

- Calories: 193 calories;
- Total Fat: 11.2
- Sodium: 193
- Total Carbohydrate: 23.5
- Cholesterol: 0
- Protein: 2.9

289.   Scottie's Chicken Tortilla Soup

Serving: 8 | Prep: 20mins | Ready in:

Ingredients

- 1 (49.5 fluid ounce) can chicken broth
- 1 (14 ounce) can whole kernel corn, drained
- 1 (14 ounce) can black beans, drained
- 1 cube beef bouillon
- 3/4 cup chopped broccoli
- 1 (28 ounce) can stewed tomatoes (crushed)
- 2 tablespoons olive oil
- 8 corn tortillas, cut into 1-inch strips
- 2 tablespoons olive oil
- 2 boneless skinless chicken breasts, cut into 1/2 inch cubes
- 2 tablespoons lime juice
- 1 tablespoon tequila
- 1 tablespoon onion powder
- 1 tablespoon garlic salt
- 1 tablespoon cayenne pepper
- 2 tablespoons Cajun seasoning
- 1 cup shredded white Cheddar cheese

Direction

- In a big pot, combine tomatoes, broccoli, beef bouillon, black beans, corn, and chicken broth over medium heat.
- While simmering broth mixture, in a skillet, heat 2 tablespoons olive oil. In the hot oil, fry tortilla strips until crisp. Take out from skillet and place on paper towels to drain. Into the skillet, pour 2 tablespoons olive oil. Add in chicken when the oil is hot; stir and cook for 5 minutes until cooked through. Mix in Cajun seasoning, cayenne pepper, garlic salt, onion powder, tequila, and lime juice; cook for 2 more minutes.
- Pour chicken mixture into the pot together with broth mixture. Cook for 45 minutes on medium. Decrease to low heat and allow to simmer 45 more minutes. Use a ladle to transfer soup to bowls, put cheese and tortilla strips on top to serve.

Nutrition Information

- Calories: 347 calories;
- Total Carbohydrate: 39.4
- Cholesterol: 35
- Protein: 17.5
- Total Fat: 14.3
- Sodium: 2637

---

290. Seeduction Bread

Serving: 15 | Prep: 20mins | Ready in:

Ingredients

- 1 1/4 cups warm water (105 degrees to 115 degrees)
- 2 tablespoons molasses
- 2 tablespoons honey
- 1 (.25 ounce) envelope active dry yeast
- 2 tablespoons canola oil
- 2 cups unbleached all-purpose flour
- 1 cup whole wheat flour
- 1 1/2 teaspoons sea salt
- 3 tablespoons raw pumpkin seeds
- 2 tablespoons raw sunflower seeds
- 1 tablespoon poppy seeds
- 2 tablespoons millet seed
- 3 tablespoons malted barley flour
- 1 tablespoon wheat gluten
- 1 egg white, beaten
- 1 teaspoon millet seed

Direction

- In a big bowl, stir together yeast, honey, molasses and warm water gently. Let stand for about 5 minutes until foamy. Pour oil into yeast mixture.
- In another bowl, mix vital wheaten gluten, barley flour, 2 tbsp. millet, poppy seeds, sunflower seeds, pumpkin seeds, salt, whole wheat flour and all-purpose flour together.

Mix seed mixture and flour into yeast mixture until it pulls together. On a lightly floured surface, turn the dough out of the bowl. Knead for 7-8 minutes; add extra flour if needed. Put dough into a big oiled bowl. Cover. Let it stand for about an hour, placed in a warm area until it doubles in size. Grease a baking sheet that's 9x13-in.

- Punch the risen dough down. On a lightly floured surface, turn the dough out of the bowl. Shape to an oval/round loaf shape. Put on prepped baking sheet. Cover dough. Let rise for about 40 minutes until it doubles in size again.
- Preheat an oven to 190°C/375°F towards the end of the 2nd rise. With a serrated knife/sharp razor blade, slash top of loaf diagonally. Brush beaten egg white on carefully. Sprinkle leftover millet seeds on top.
- Bake in a preheated oven for 40-45 minutes until you thump on the side and the bread sounds hollow.

Nutrition Information

- Calories: 151 calories;
- Total Fat: 3.4
- Sodium: 183
- Total Carbohydrate: 26.5
- Cholesterol: 0
- Protein: 4.5

---

291. Shish Tawook Grilled Chicken

Serving: 6 | Prep: 30mins | Ready in:

Ingredients

- 1/4 cup lemon juice
- 1/4 cup vegetable oil
- 3/4 cup plain yogurt
- 4 cloves garlic, minced
- 2 teaspoons tomato paste

- 1 1/2 teaspoons salt
- 1 teaspoon dried oregano
- 1/4 teaspoon ground black pepper
- 1/4 teaspoon ground allspice
- 1/4 teaspoon ground cinnamon
- 1/8 teaspoon ground cardamom
- 2 pounds skinless, boneless chicken breast halves - cut into 2 inch pieces
- 2 onions, cut into large chunks
- 1 large green bell pepper, cut into large chunks
- 1 cup chopped fresh flat-leaf parsley

Direction

- In a large bowl, whisk together the vegetable oil, lemon juice, plain yogurt, tomato paste, garlic, oregano, salt, pepper, cinnamon, allspice, and cardamom. Toss in the chicken to coat. Transfer the contents of the bowl into a large plastic bag, seal the bag, and marinate in the refrigerator for at least 4 hours.
- Set an outdoor grill to pre-heat at medium-high. Oil the grates lightly. Cue the chicken, peppers, and onions onto metal skewers. Grill until chicken is golden and cooked through, 5 minutes per side. Scatter the parsley over the skewers before serving.

Nutrition Information

- Calories: 299 calories;
- Cholesterol: 88
- Protein: 34.3
- Total Fat: 13.4
- Sodium: 702
- Total Carbohydrate: 9.8

292. Shredded Apple Carrot Salad

Serving: 6 | Prep: 15mins | Ready in:

Ingredients

- 2 tablespoons sesame seeds
- 2 cups shredded carrots
- 1 Granny Smith apple, cored and shredded
- 1/2 cup chopped fresh parsley
- 1/4 cup lemon juice
- 2 tablespoons apple cider vinegar
- 1 tablespoon white sugar (optional)
- 1 clove garlic, minced
- 1 teaspoon salt
- 1/2 teaspoon ground black pepper
- 2 tablespoons safflower oil

Direction

- Place a skillet on medium heat; add sesame seeds to the hot skillet. Cook for 3-5 minutes until the sesame seeds are aromatic and light brown, tossing frequently. Take away from the heat.
- In a bowl, combine parsley, toasted sesame seeds, apple and carrots.
- In another bowl, mix together pepper, salt, garlic, sugar, vinegar and lemon juice; gradually drizzle into lemon juice mixture with safflower oil while maintaining to stir. Pour over the carrot mixture with the dressing; mix to coat.

Nutrition Information

- Calories: 97 calories;
- Cholesterol: 0
- Protein: 1.2
- Total Fat: 6.2
- Sodium: 417
- Total Carbohydrate: 10.7

293. Shrimp Deviled Eggs

Serving: 24 | Prep: 15mins | Ready in:

Ingredients

- 12 eggs

- 2 teaspoons butter
- 1 cup small salad shrimp
- 1 green onion, chopped
- 1 pinch garlic powder
- 1/2 cup mayonnaise, or to taste
- 1 teaspoon mustard
- 1/4 cup sweet pickle relish, drained
- 1 dash hot pepper sauce (optional)
- 1 tablespoon chopped fresh parsley, or as needed

Direction

- In a saucepan, put the eggs in 1 layer and pour in water to cover them by 1 inch. Bring to boil, while covered over high heat. Take away from the heat and allow the eggs to stay for 15 minutes in hot water. Strain. Put the eggs under cold running water to cool down. Remove shells when cold. Cut the eggs in half lengthwise and put the yolks in a bowl. Use a fork to lightly smash the yolks.
- In a skillet, melt butter on medium heat; cook and stir garlic powder, green onion and shrimp in the melted butter for 4 minutes. Move the shrimp to a cutting board, mince. Mix any leftover liquid from the skillet and 3/4 cup minced shrimp into the egg yolks; keep leftover shrimp for garnish. Put in hot sauce, pickle relish, mustard, and mayonnaise; stir well. Put mixture into a resealable plastic bag, seal, and use scissors to snip a corner off the bag to create a piping bag.
- Lightly squeeze about 1 1/2 tbsp. filling into each egg white half. Use a pinch of the chopped parsley and a few pieces of the reserved chopped shrimp to garnish each; refrigerate for a minimum of half an hour prior to serving.

Nutrition Information

- Calories: 79 calories;
- Total Carbohydrate: 1.3
- Cholesterol: 103
- Protein: 4.1
- Total Fat: 6.5

- Sodium: 134

294. Shrimp And Vegetable Couscous

Serving: 6 | Prep: 15mins | Ready in:

Ingredients

- 1 pound medium shrimp, shelled and deveined, shells reserved
- 2 1/3 cups cold water
- 1/3 cup olive oil
- 2 zucchinis, diced
- 1 eggplant, diced
- salt and ground black pepper to taste
- 1/2 cup diced tomato
- 2 teaspoons olive oil, or as needed
- 2 cups couscous
- 1/2 bunch fresh tarragon, chopped
- 1/2 bunch fresh dill, chopped
- 1 pinch cayenne, or to taste

Direction

- On medium high heat, put on a saucepan and melt butter. Add shrimp shells; sauté for 3 to 4 minutes until they turn fragrant and pink. Pour in water, simmer; lower the heat to low and continue simmering for 20 minutes until flavors all combine.
- On medium-high heat, put on a large skillet and heat 1/3 cup of olive oil. Add eggplant and zucchini; sauté for 6 to 7 minutes in hot oil with a pinch of pepper and salt until softened. Form a space in the center of the skillet. Pour in tomato; caramelize it slightly in 3 to 4 minutes. Stir in garlic and mix it well with all vegetables; cook in 1 minute until the garlic gets fragrant.
- On medium-high heat, put on a skillet and heat 2 teaspoons of oil. Add shrimps and sauté all side, 1 minute per side until the shrimps turn pink.

- In a bowl, mix together dill, tarragon, couscous, shrimps and vegetable mixture. Use cayenne pepper, black pepper and salt to season. Scrape down the sides of the bowl. Form the mixture to a flat shape.
- Strain the hot shrimp sauce through a strainer to separate shells into couscous mixture, throw away the shells. Use aluminum foil to cover and set aside in 5 minutes until the couscous is fluffy and tender. Stir well.

Nutrition Information

- Calories: 450 calories;
- Total Fat: 15.6
- Sodium: 155
- Total Carbohydrate: 52.8
- Cholesterol: 115
- Protein: 24.4

295.   Simple Stromboli

Serving: 3 | Prep: 10mins | Ready in:

Ingredients

- 1/2 pound bulk pork sausage (optional)
- 1 (1 pound) loaf frozen bread dough, thawed
- 4 slices hard salami
- 4 slices thinly sliced ham
- 4 slices American cheese
- 1 cup shredded mozzarella cheese
- salt and ground black pepper to taste
- 1 egg white, lightly beaten

Direction

- Preheat the oven to 220°Celcius or 425°F
- On medium-high heat, heat a big pan; add sausage. Cook and stir for about 10 minutes until evenly brown, crumbly, and the sausage is not pink anymore; drain. Get rid of the excess grease.

- In a baking sheet, ungreased, flatten the bread dough to 3/4 -in thick. Layer the middle of the dough with ham, salami, and slices of American cheese. Top with cooked sausage, mozzarella cheese, pepper, and salt. Wrap the dough up to enclose the ingredients, seal by pressing the edges together to avoid leaks. Slather the surface with egg white.
- Bake in the 425°F preheated oven for 17-20 minutes until the dough is light brown and cooked.

Nutrition Information

- Calories: 1065 calories;
- Total Fat: 54.6
- Sodium: 3633
- Total Carbohydrate: 77.8
- Cholesterol: 162
- Protein: 59

296.   Simple Sweet And Spicy Chicken Wraps

Serving: 8 | Prep: 20mins | Ready in:

Ingredients

- 1/2 cup mayonnaise
- 1/4 cup finely chopped seedless cucumber
- 1 tablespoon honey
- 1/2 teaspoon cayenne pepper
- ground black pepper to taste
- 2 tablespoons olive oil
- 1 1/2 pounds skinless, boneless chicken breast halves - cut into thin strips
- 1 cup thick and chunky salsa
- 1 tablespoon honey
- 1/2 teaspoon cayenne pepper
- 8 (10 inch) flour tortillas
- 1 (10 ounce) bag baby spinach leaves

Direction

- In a bowl, blend black pepper, half teaspoon of cayenne pepper, 1 tablespoon of honey, cucumber, and mayonnaise together until smooth. Refrigerate, covered, until needed.
- In a frying pan on medium-high heat, heat the olive oil; cook the chicken breast strips while stirring for about 8 minutes until about to turn golden and not pink anymore in the center. Whisk in a half teaspoon of cayenne pepper, 1 tablespoon of honey, and salsa. Lower the heat to medium-low and simmer while stirring from time to time for 5 minutes until the flavors have blended.
- In a microwave oven, pile the tortillas, 4 at a time, and heat each batch for 20 – 30 seconds until pliable and warm.
- Pour 1 tablespoon of the mayonnaise-cucumber mixture onto each tortilla, put a layer of baby spinach leaves on top, then pour approximately half cup of chicken mixture atop spinach leaves.
- Fold the ends of each tortilla up approximately 2 inches, then begin rolling the burrito from the right side. Once the burrito is rolled halfway, fold the top of the tortilla down to enclose the filling, then go on rolling to create a tight and compact cylinder.

Nutrition Information

- Calories: 488 calories;
- Total Carbohydrate: 44.7
- Cholesterol: 57
- Protein: 26.6
- Total Fat: 22.6
- Sodium: 791

---

297. Slimmed Down Potato Salad

Serving: 8 | Prep: 25mins | Ready in:

Ingredients

- 3 pounds red new potatoes
- 1 (12 ounce) package silken tofu
- 3 tablespoons fresh lemon juice
- 1 tablespoon prepared yellow mustard
- 1 clove garlic, minced
- 1 teaspoon salt
- 2 tablespoons olive oil
- 1 cup chopped celery
- 1 red bell pepper, seeded and cubed
- 3 eggs, hard-boiled, shelled, and chopped
- 1/2 cup chopped green onions
- 1/2 cup chopped dill pickles
- salt and ground black pepper to taste
- 2 tablespoons whole milk

Direction

- Put potatoes in a Dutch oven, add water in until submerged. Boil, decrease the heat to medium-low. Put the lid on and simmer for about 20 minutes until potatoes are softened and can be pierced and taken out easily with a fork. Strain and let cool slightly. Take the skin off, slice into cubes, and put in a big bowl.
- Mix 1 teaspoon of salt, garlic, mustard, lemon juice, and tofu together in a food processor or a bowl to make the dressing. Process until smooth. While the food processor is running, add a steady, thin stream of olive oil, processing until the mixture is thickened. Put aside.
- Mix pickles, green onions, eggs, red bell pepper, and celery together with the potatoes in a bowl. Put the dressing on the potato mixture, mix gently to make all the ingredients coat evenly. Use pepper and salt to season. Put a cover on and refrigerate for at least 4 hours.
- To reach the wanted consistency, mix together 1 tablespoon of milk at a time and the salad before serving.

Nutrition Information

- Calories: 240 calories;
- Total Fat: 8.1
- Sodium: 483

- Total Carbohydrate: 34
- Cholesterol: 52
- Protein: 9.6

298.   Sloppy Joe Pockets

Serving: 12 | Prep: 30mins | Ready in:

Ingredients

- 1 pound ground beef
- 1/4 cup chopped onion
- 1/4 cup sour cream
- 1/2 cup ketchup
- 1/2 teaspoon salt
- 1/4 teaspoon garlic powder
- 1 (12 ounce) can refrigerated flaky biscuit dough
- 2 tablespoons butter, melted

Direction

- In a skillet, stir and cook onion and ground beef on medium heat, breaking meat to crumbles while cooking, for about 10 minutes until meat browns well. Drain fat from beef inside a colander. Put beef back in skillet. Mix in garlic powder, salt, ketchup and sour cream. Simmer. Lower heat. Simmer while you make the pockets.
- Preheat the oven to 190 degrees C/375 degrees F/
- On a floured work surface, unroll biscuits. Roll every biscuit lightly to about 4-in. (on a side) square. On a baking sheet, put squares. Spoon 2-3 tbsp. beef mixture into the middle of every square. Fold a corner over to meet the opposite corner, creating a triangle. Use a fork to seal edges. At the top of every pocket, slice 3 small slits.
- Bake in preheated oven for 15-20 minutes until golden brown. Brush melted butter on each pocket.

Nutrition Information

- Calories: 197 calories;
- Cholesterol: 30
- Protein: 8.6
- Total Fat: 11.3
- Sodium: 530
- Total Carbohydrate: 15.4

299.   Sloppy Sams

Serving: 4 | Prep: 15mins | Ready in:

Ingredients

- 3 cups water
- 1 cup lentils, rinsed
- salt to taste (optional)
- 1 cup chopped onion
- 3 tablespoons olive oil
- 2 cups chopped tomato
- 2 cloves garlic, minced
- 1/2 (6 ounce) can tomato paste
- 1/2 cup ketchup
- 1 teaspoon mustard powder
- 1 tablespoon chili powder
- 3 tablespoons molasses
- 1 dash Worcestershire sauce
- salt and ground black pepper to taste
- 4 hamburger buns, split

Direction

- In a saucepan, combine lentils and water; if wanted, season with salt to taste. Heat to a boil on high heat; decrease to medium-low heat, put on cover and allow to simmer 30 minutes, mixing occasionally, until tender.
- At the same time, in a big skillet on medium heat, cook olive oil together with onions for 4 minutes, till onions have become translucent and softened. Add in garlic and tomatoes and cook 5 minutes. Mix in Worcestershire sauce, molasses, chili powder, mustard powder,

ketchup, and tomato paste; allow to simmer until thickened, about 5-10 minutes.

- Drain lentils and save the cooking liquid. Mix lentils into the sauce mixture; if necessary, pouring in water or cooking liquid to have your wished "sloppy joe" consistency. Arrange on buns and serve.

Nutrition Information

- Calories: 517 calories;
- Cholesterol: 0
- Protein: 19.3
- Total Fat: 13.9
- Sodium: 782
- Total Carbohydrate: 82.2

| 300. | **Slow Cooked Corned Beef For Sandwiches** |

Serving: 15 | Prep: 15mins | Ready in:

Ingredients

- 2 (3 pound) corned beef briskets with spice packets
- 2 (12 fluid ounce) bottles beer
- 2 bay leaves
- 1/4 cup peppercorns
- 1 bulb garlic cloves, separated and peeled

Direction

- In a large pot, put the corned beef briskets. Add in one of spice packets, keep for future use or discard the other one. Add in the beer, then pour water in the pot, sufficient to cover the briskets by an inch. Put garlic cloves, peppercorns and bay leaves. Put cover, boil.
- When liquid boils, lower heat to medium-low, let simmer, checking hourly, for 4 to 5 hours, to keep the meat covered, add extra water if needed.

- Gently take meat out of the pot, as it will be extremely tender. Place on a cutting board, and let it rest for 10 minutes till it firms up a little. Shred or cut, then serve. Cooking liquid can be kept and use to cook other vegetables like cabbage or thrown away.

Nutrition Information

- Calories: 229 calories;
- Total Carbohydrate: 4.2
- Cholesterol: 78
- Protein: 15
- Total Fat: 15.1
- Sodium: 904

| 301. | **Slow Cooker BBQ Chicken** |

Serving: 8 | Prep: 5mins | Ready in:

Ingredients

- 4 large skinless, boneless chicken breast halves
- 1 cup ketchup
- 2 tablespoons mustard
- 2 teaspoons lemon juice
- 1/4 teaspoon garlic powder
- 1/2 cup maple syrup
- 2 tablespoons Worcestershire sauce
- 1/2 teaspoon chili powder
- 1/8 teaspoon cayenne pepper
- 2 dashes hot pepper sauce, or to taste (optional)
- 8 sandwich rolls, split

Direction

- In the bottom of a slow cooker, place chicken breasts. Mix together hot sauce, cayenne pepper, chili powder, Worcestershire sauce, maple syrup, garlic powder, lemon juice, mustard, and ketchup in a bowl until the mixture is fully combined.

- Spread the sauce over the chicken, turn the cooker to Low, and cook for 6 hours. Use two forks to shred the chicken and cook, 30 more minutes. Spoon sauce and chicken into the sandwich rolls, serve right away.

Nutrition Information

- Calories: 589 calories;
- Total Carbohydrate: 90
- Cholesterol: 59
- Protein: 34.2
- Total Fat: 9.5
- Sodium: 1234

302.   Slow Cooker Ground Beef Barbecue

Serving: 20 | Prep: 10mins | Ready in:

Ingredients

- 3 pounds lean ground beef
- 1 large onion, chopped
- 2 cloves garlic, minced
- 5 stalks celery, finely chopped
- 1 1/2 teaspoons salt
- 1/2 teaspoon ground black pepper
- 1 tablespoon cider vinegar
- 2 tablespoons prepared mustard
- 1/4 cup firmly packed brown sugar
- 3 1/2 cups ketchup

Direction

- In a big skillet, add ground beef on moderate heat then cook for 15 minutes while breaking up meat as it cooks, until browned. Get rid of excess grease.
- In a slow cooker, add ketchup, brown sugar, mustard, cider vinegar, black pepper, salt, celery, garlic, onion and cooked meat, then stir to mix together. Set the cooker on low setting and cook for about 6-8 hours.

Nutrition Information

- Calories: 188 calories;
- Total Fat: 8.5
- Sodium: 710
- Total Carbohydrate: 14.5
- Cholesterol: 45
- Protein: 13.9

303.   Slow And Easy Beef Stock

Serving: 4 | Prep: | Ready in:

Ingredients

- 10 pounds beef soup bones, cut into pieces
- water to cover

Direction

- In a large stockpot, combine water and bones; bring to a boil. Keep a low boil for 24 hours; pour water to maintain the bones submerged. Discard the bones. Keep simmering the mixture for 21-22 hours longer. Use a fine-mesh strainer to drain the liquid; move back to the stockpot. Bring to a boil; keep cooking until the liquid marked down to about 2 quarts.
- Place the stock into heat-safe containers; start freezing. There would be 3 easily-discernable layers when frozen. Discard the top-most of those layers. For using, lightly thaw the remaining portion.

Nutrition Information

- Calories: 0 calories;
- Protein: 0
- Total Fat: 0
- Sodium: 28
- Total Carbohydrate: 0

- Cholesterol: 0

304. Southern Dill Potato Salad

Serving: 8 | Prep: 20mins | Ready in:

Ingredients

- 10 unpeeled red potatoes
- 5 hard boiled eggs, roughly chopped
- 3/4 cup sour cream
- 3/4 cup mayonnaise
- 1 tablespoon apple cider vinegar, or to taste
- 1 tablespoon Dijon mustard, or to taste
- 1/2 white onion, finely chopped
- 1 stalk celery, finely chopped
- 1 teaspoon celery salt
- salt and black pepper to taste
- 1 tablespoon dried dill weed

Direction

- In a large pot, pour water to cover potatoes, and boil over high heat. Lower the heat to medium-low, and simmer the potatoes for about 20 minutes until thoroughly cooked, but still firm. Drain off the water, allow to cool, and chop the potatoes into chunks. Put the chopped potatoes to one side.
- Combine pepper, salt, celery salt, celery, onion, Dijon mustard, apple cider vinegar, mayonnaise, and sour cream in a bowl until well incorporated.
- In a large salad bowl, put eggs and potatoes, sprinkle with some dried dill. Pour the dressing mixture over the eggs and potatoes, toss gently. Chilled while covered for 30 minutes or more, and serve cold.

Nutrition Information

- Calories: 279 calories;
- Cholesterol: 134

- Protein: 5.9
- Total Fat: 24.1
- Sodium: 413
- Total Carbohydrate: 10.8

305. Special Lobster Bisque

Serving: 8 | Prep: 10mins | Ready in:

Ingredients

- 6 tablespoons butter
- 6 tablespoons all-purpose flour
- 1 teaspoon salt
- 1/4 teaspoon ground black pepper
- 1/2 teaspoon celery salt
- 4 1/2 cups milk
- 1 1/2 cups chicken stock
- 3 tablespoons minced onion
- 3 cups cooked lobster meat, shredded
- 1 tablespoon paprika
- 1/2 cup light cream

Direction

- Over medium heat, melt butter in a large pot. Mix in flour, celery salt, pepper and salt until blended well. Slowly mix in milk to prevent formation of lumps. Mix in chicken stock. Let cook over low heat while stirring continuously until soup starts to thicken. Add lobster and onion. Add paprika to taste. Cook while stirring for ten more minutes. Mix in cream, then heat through before serving.

Nutrition Information

- Calories: 279 calories;
- Total Carbohydrate: 13.7
- Cholesterol: 94
- Protein: 16.7
- Total Fat: 17.3
- Sodium: 842

306. Spiced Slow Cooker Applesauce

Serving: 8 | Prep: 10mins | Ready in:

Ingredients

- 8 apples - peeled, cored, and thinly sliced
- 1/2 cup water
- 3/4 cup packed brown sugar
- 1/2 teaspoon pumpkin pie spice

Direction

- Put the apples in a slow cooker with water. Turn heat on Low. Cook for 6-8 hours. Add pumpkin pie spice and brown sugar, stirring occasionally. Cook for another half hour.

Nutrition Information

- Calories: 150 calories;
- Sodium: 8
- Total Carbohydrate: 39.4
- Cholesterol: 0
- Protein: 0.4
- Total Fat: 0.2

307. Spicy Lentil Soup

Serving: 6 | Prep: 10mins | Ready in:

Ingredients

- 1 tablespoon olive oil
- 1/4 cup chopped onion
- 4 cloves garlic, chopped
- 1 large carrot, chopped
- 1 large stalk celery, chopped
- 2 tablespoons tomato paste
- 1/8 teaspoon crushed red pepper flakes, or more to taste
- 1/8 teaspoon cayenne pepper, or more to taste
- salt and ground black pepper to taste
- 6 cups chicken stock
- 1 1/2 cups dry lentils

Direction

- In a big saucepan over medium heat, heat the olive oil; cook and stir the garlic and onion for roughly 5 minutes or till onion becomes translucent.
- Mix in the celery and carrot; cook, mixing frequently, for roughly 8 minutes longer or till the veggies soften.
- Mix in the black pepper, salt, cayenne pepper, crushed red pepper, and tomato paste; stir in the lentils and chicken stock.
- Boil the soup and lower the heat to low; simmer for roughly 20 minutes or till lentils soften.

Nutrition Information

- Calories: 217 calories;
- Total Carbohydrate: 33.7
- Cholesterol: 1
- Protein: 13.6
- Total Fat: 3.5
- Sodium: 711

308. Spicy Pecan Soup

Serving: 8 | Prep: 20mins | Ready in:

Ingredients

- 2 tablespoons butter
- 1/2 cup minced onion
- 3 tablespoons minced garlic
- 6 cups chicken stock
- 1 (6 ounce) can tomato paste
- 2 cups heavy cream
- 2 tablespoons lemon juice
- 3 cups pecan pieces

- 3 tablespoons finely chopped canned chipotle chile in adobo sauce
- salt to taste
- 1/4 cup chopped pecans for garnish

Direction

- Melt butter on medium heat in the big sauce pan. Cook and stir garlic and onion in butter for roughly 5 minutes or till becoming softened yet not brown.
- Add chicken stock to the pot and mix in lemon juice, heavy cream and tomato paste. Switch heat to high and boil the soup. Switch heat down to medium low, put in chopped chipotle peppers and 3 cups of the pecan pieces, and simmer the soup for roughly half an hour or till pecans are tender.
- Put aside 2 cups of the soup. Add the remaining soup to the blender, filling the pitcher up to half-way full. Hold down the blender's lid using the folded kitchen towel, and gently start the blender, with the several quick pulses to have the contents moved prior to leaving it on to puree. Blend in batches till becoming smooth and add into the clean pot. Alternately, you should use the stick blender and puree soup right in the cooking pot.
- Stir reserved 2 cups of the soup back into the pot and simmer and use salt to season to taste. Serve, while hot, with the drizzle of the chopped pecans to decorate.

Nutrition Information

- Calories: 603 calories;
- Sodium: 750
- Total Carbohydrate: 15.8
- Cholesterol: 90
- Protein: 7.4
- Total Fat: 60.4

309.   Spicy Shrimp Tacos

Serving: 4 | Prep: 30mins | Ready in:

Ingredients

- 8 Mission® Small/Fajita Super Soft Flour Tortillas
- 1 pound medium shrimp, peeled and deveined
- 1 teaspoon salt
- 1/4 teaspoon ground black pepper
- 1/4 teaspoon crushed red pepper flakes
- 2 tablespoons fresh lime juice
- 1 tablespoon olive oil
- 1/2 cup diced fresh mango
- 1/2 cup diced red onion
- 1/2 cup fresh cilantro, coarsely chopped
- 1 tablespoon Sriracha sauce
- 1/2 cup Ranch dressing
- Fresh lime wedges, as needed

Direction

- Mix Sriracha and ranch dressing in a small mixing bowl then put aside in refrigerator.
- Mix lime juice, red pepper flakes, black pepper, salt and shrimp in another mixing bowl. Toss until combined.
- On moderately-high heat, heat the sauté pan till hot. Put in the olive oil, next is shrimp, and sauté for 2 to 3 minutes till cooked completely and pink, flipping frequently to cook equally.
- To put tacos together, into every tortilla, put approximately 4 warm shrimp and place a tablespoon of diced onions and a tablespoon of diced mango on top. Sprinkle Sriracha ranch dressing on top and scatter chopped cilantro over. Serve along with wedges of lime to squeeze on top.

Nutrition Information

- Calories: 826 calories;
- Sodium: 2750
- Total Carbohydrate: 43.2
- Cholesterol: 361

- Protein: 46.5
- Total Fat: 44.1

310. Spicy Tomato Bisque With Grilled Brie Toast

Serving: 4 | Prep: 10mins | Ready in:

Ingredients

- 4 ounces Brie cheese
- 4 slices rye bread
- 1 (28 ounce) can tomato puree
- 1/2 teaspoon red pepper flakes
- 1/8 teaspoon freshly ground black pepper
- 3/4 teaspoon dried basil
- 1/2 teaspoon white sugar
- 1/4 cup milk
- 4 ounces cream cheese, cubed
- 2 tablespoons chopped fresh basil leaves (optional)

Direction

- Preheat a toaster oven/oven to 200°C/400°F. On 2 bread slices, spread Brie cheese. Top with leftover slices. Put on a baking sheet; toast for 8 minutes in the oven, turning one time halfway through. Slice in half; put aside.
- Mix sugar, basil, black pepper, red pepper flakes and tomato puree in a saucepan on medium heat; simmer then cook for 10 minutes.
- Whisk cream cheese in till blended well; mix milk in. Without boiling, heat through. Mix fresh basil in; take off heat.
- Serving: In a separate bowl, put each sandwich half. Put soup on each one in bowl. Immediately serve.

Nutrition Information

- Calories: 363 calories;
- Cholesterol: 61

- Protein: 14.6
- Total Fat: 19.6
- Sodium: 1262
- Total Carbohydrate: 35.5

311. Spinach Basil Pasta Salad

Serving: 10 | Prep: 15mins | Ready in:

Ingredients

- 1 (16 ounce) package bow tie pasta
- 1 (6 ounce) package spinach leaves
- 2 cups fresh basil leaves
- 1/2 cup extra virgin olive oil
- 3 cloves garlic, minced
- 4 ounces prosciutto, diced
- salt and ground black pepper to taste
- 3/4 cup freshly grated Parmesan cheese
- 1/2 cup toasted pine nuts

Direction

- With lightly salted water, fill a big pot and over high heat, bring to a rolling boil. When the water is boiling, mix in the bow tie pasta and bring back to a boil. Without cover, cook the pasta for about 12 minutes, mixing from time to time, till cooked through yet still firm to the bite. Wash with cold water to cool. Drain thoroughly in a colander set in the sink.
- In a big bowl, toss the basil and spinach together.
- In a skillet over medium heat, heat the olive oil; in the hot oil, cook and mix the garlic for a minute; mix in the prosciutto and cook 2 to 3 minutes more. Take off heat. Put to the bowl with the basil and spinach mixture; combine by tossing. Add in the drained pasta and toss once more. Put pepper and salt to season. Scatter the pine nuts and Parmesan cheese over, serve.

Nutrition Information

- Calories: 372 calories;
- Protein: 13.6
- Total Fat: 20.7
- Sodium: 329
- Total Carbohydrate: 36.4
- Cholesterol: 15

312. Spinach Watermelon Mint Salad

Serving: 6 | Prep: 20mins | Ready in:

Ingredients

- 1 cup apple cider vinegar
- 1/4 cup Worcestershire sauce
- 1/2 cup vegetable oil
- 1 tablespoon sesame seeds
- 1 tablespoon poppy seeds
- 1/4 cup white sugar
- 1 (10 ounce) bag baby spinach leaves
- 2 cups cubed seeded watermelon
- 1 small red onion, thinly sliced
- 1 cup chopped pecans, toasted
- 1 cup mint leaves, finely chopped

Direction

- Whisk sugar, poppy seeds, sesame seeds, vegetable oil, Worcestershire sauce and apple cider vinegar together in a small bowl, then set aside.
- Mix together mint, pecans, onion, watermelon and spinach in a big serving bowl. Toss together with the dressing right before serving.

Nutrition Information

- Calories: 395 calories;
- Protein: 4.3
- Total Fat: 34.1
- Sodium: 152
- Total Carbohydrate: 21.2

- Cholesterol: 0

313. Spinach And Cauliflower Bhaji

Serving: 4 | Prep: 20mins | Ready in:

Ingredients

- 1/4 cup vegetable oil
- 2 large onions, coarsely chopped
- 1 head cauliflower, cut into florets
- 2 cloves garlic, crushed
- 1 (1 inch) piece fresh ginger, peeled and chopped
- 2 teaspoons ground coriander
- 1 teaspoon ground cumin
- 1 teaspoon ground turmeric
- 1 1/4 teaspoons cayenne pepper
- 1 (14.5 ounce) can diced tomatoes
- 1 1/4 cups vegetable broth
- salt and ground black pepper to taste
- 1 pound fresh spinach, chopped and stems removed

Direction

- Heat vegetable oil on medium heat in a big saucepan; mix and cook cauliflower and onions for 3 minutes till slightly soft. Add cayenne pepper, turmeric, cumin, coriander, ginger and garlic; mix to coat.
- Mix vegetable broth and tomatoes in cauliflower mixture; season with black pepper and salt. Boil it; cover. Lower heat; simmer for 8 minutes till flavors blend. Mix spinach into mixture till it starts to wilt. Cover; simmer for 8-10 minutes till cauliflower is tender and spinach is fully wilted.

Nutrition Information

- Calories: 253 calories;
- Sodium: 427

- Total Carbohydrate: 26.6
- Cholesterol: 0
- Protein: 8.5
- Total Fat: 15

314. Spring Strawberry Salad With Chicken

Serving: 8 | Prep: 25mins | Ready in:

Ingredients

- 2 large boneless, skinless chicken breasts, cubed
- 2 tablespoons olive oil
- 2 tablespoons balsamic vinaigrette salad dressing
- 1 bunch fresh spinach, rinsed and dried
- 1 pint strawberries, sliced
- 4 ounces crumbled goat cheese
- 1 (5 ounce) package candied pecans (such as Emerald® Pecan Pie Glazed Pecans)
- 2 tablespoons olive oil
- 2 tablespoons balsamic vinaigrette salad dressing

Direction

- Place a skillet onto medium heat then put that chicken breast meat with 2 tablespoons of balsamic vinaigrette and 2 tablespoons of olive oil; stir and cook for about 10 minutes until the chicken is brown in color, the pink color in the middle faded, and the juice has almost evaporated. Send the chicken to a bowl and let it cool.
- Into a salad bowl, place the spinach; then spread the candied pecans, goat cheese and strawberries over the spinach. Sprinkle 2 tablespoons of balsamic vinaigrette and 2 tablespoons of olive oil over the salad and the chicken on top. You can serve it slightly warm or chill.

Nutrition Information

- Calories: 317 calories;
- Total Fat: 19.7
- Sodium: 313
- Total Carbohydrate: 12.5
- Cholesterol: 46
- Protein: 23.5

315. Steak Soup

Serving: 8 | Prep: 45mins | Ready in:

Ingredients

- 2 tablespoons butter
- 2 tablespoons vegetable oil
- 1 1/2 pounds lean boneless beef round steak, cut into cubes
- 1/2 cup chopped onion
- 3 tablespoons all-purpose flour
- 1 tablespoon paprika
- 1 teaspoon salt
- 1/4 teaspoon ground black pepper
- 4 cups beef broth
- 2 cups water
- 4 sprigs fresh parsley, chopped
- 2 tablespoons chopped celery leaves
- 1 bay leaf
- 1/2 teaspoon dried marjoram
- 1 1/2 cups peeled, diced Yukon Gold potatoes
- 1 1/2 cups sliced carrots
- 1 1/2 cups chopped celery
- 1 (6 ounce) can tomato paste
- 1 (15.25 ounce) can whole kernel corn, drained

Direction

- In a big frying pan, render the oil and butter together atop a medium heat just until the butter loses its foam, and mix in the onion and steak cubes. Cook them as you stir until brown, around 10 minutes. At the same time, mix flour in a bowl with pepper, salt, and paprika, then sprinkle upon the cooked meat, tossing to coat.

- In a big soup pot, pour in water and beef broth, and stir in marjoram, bay leaf, celery leaves, and parsley. Blend in the beef mixture and allow it to boil. Turn heat down to a medium-low and simmer, keeping it covered and stirring it now and then, until the meat has tenderized, roughly 45 minutes.
- Mix in corn, tomato paste, celery, carrots, and potatoes, then return to a simmer. Continue to cook without covering it and occasionally stirring the soup until it becomes denser and the vegetables are soft, 15-20 minutes. Get rid of the bay leave and serve the soup hot.

Nutrition Information

- Calories: 361 calories;
- Cholesterol: 84
- Protein: 36
- Total Fat: 12.9
- Sodium: 1118
- Total Carbohydrate: 26.9

---

316.   Stir Fried Bok Choy

Serving: 4 | Prep: 15mins | Ready in:

Ingredients

- 1 large head bok choy
- 1 tablespoon grapeseed oil
- 1 tablespoon butter
- 1 onion, sliced
- 1/3 cup cashews
- 3 cloves garlic, minced
- 1/2 teaspoon Chinese five-spice powder, or more to taste
- 1 pinch white sugar

Direction

- Slice up the root side of the bok choy into 1/2 to 1-inch pieces and get rid of the stem. Diagonally slice the stalks into 1/8 inch slices or tear them into bite sized chunks.
- In a skillet on medium heat, heat up butter and oil; place in cashews, bok choy, onion, Chinese five-spice, sugar, and garlic. Stir and cook mixture for about 8-10 minutes or until it is tender.

Nutrition Information

- Calories: 164 calories;
- Total Fat: 11.9
- Sodium: 99
- Total Carbohydrate: 12.8
- Cholesterol: 8
- Protein: 4.3

---

317.   Summer Anytime Crisp Corn Salad

Serving: 4 | Prep: 20mins | Ready in:

Ingredients

- 3 tablespoons apple cider vinegar
- 2 tablespoons white sugar
- 1 tablespoon olive oil
- 1 tablespoon water
- 1 pinch salt and ground black pepper
- 1 (15.25 ounce) can sweet corn, drained
- 1/2 cup chopped green bell pepper
- 1/2 cup chopped red bell pepper
- 1/3 cup chopped sweet onion
- 1 small tomato, chopped

Direction

- In a large bowl, beat pepper, salt, water, olive oil, sugar, and apple cider vinegar together. Put in tomato, onion, red and green bell peppers and corn, then toss lightly together.

Put a cover and put in the fridge until ready to serve.

Nutrition Information

- Calories: 162 calories;
- Sodium: 322
- Total Carbohydrate: 30.5
- Cholesterol: 0
- Protein: 3.5
- Total Fat: 4.5

318.   Summer Corn Salad

Serving: 4 | Prep: 25mins | Ready in:

Ingredients

- 6 ears corn, husked and cleaned
- 3 large tomatoes, diced
- 1 large onion, diced
- 1/4 cup chopped fresh basil
- 1/4 cup olive oil
- 2 tablespoons white vinegar
- salt and pepper to taste

Direction

- Boil a big pot of lightly salt water. Add corn in to boiling water and cook until reaching the wanted tenderness, about 7-10 minutes. Strain and let cool. Use a sharp knife to chop the kernels off the cob.
- Mix pepper, salt, vinegar, oil, basil, onion, tomatoes, and corn together in a big bowl. Let chill until eating.

Nutrition Information

- Calories: 305 calories;
- Total Fat: 15.6
- Sodium: 9
- Total Carbohydrate: 42.8
- Cholesterol: 0

- Protein: 6.2

319.   Summer Grilled Cabbage

Serving: 8 | Prep: 10mins | Ready in:

Ingredients

- 1 large head cabbage, cored and cut into 8 wedges
- 8 teaspoons butter
- 1/4 cup water
- 1/2 teaspoon garlic powder, or to taste
- 1/2 teaspoon seasoned salt, or to taste
- ground black pepper to taste

Direction

- Preheat outdoor grill to medium high heat; oil grate lightly.
- In big metal baking dish's bottom, put cabbage wedges. Put water in dish. On each cabbage wedge, put 1 tbsp. butter. Liberally season with pepper, seasoned salt and garlic powder. Use aluminum foil to cover dish.
- Put dish on preheated grill. Cook for 30 minutes or till cabbage is tender.

Nutrition Information

- Calories: 76 calories;
- Sodium: 115
- Total Carbohydrate: 9.3
- Cholesterol: 11
- Protein: 2.1
- Total Fat: 4.2

320.   Summer Squash Soup

Serving: 6 | Prep: 15mins | Ready in:

Ingredients

- 2 tablespoons butter
- 2 onions, chopped
- 5 cups chicken broth
- 2 potatoes, peeled and chopped
- 2 carrots, peeled and thinly sliced
- 8 cups chopped zucchini
- 2 tablespoons chopped fresh basil
- salt and ground black pepper to taste

Direction

- In a heavy pot, heat butter over medium heat; stir and cook the onion for 10 minutes till opaque. Add potatoes and chicken broth; boil it. Lower the heat to medium-low, put a cover on the pot and simmer for 5 minutes. Put in carrots and simmer for 10 minutes. Add zucchini and simmer for 15 minutes until all of the vegetables are soft.
- In a food processor or blender, mix together pepper, salt, basil, and soup, filling the machine no more than halfway. Put the lid on and hold down, then pulse several times and allow to process. Working in batches, puree until reaching the consistency you want.

Nutrition Information

- Calories: 166 calories;
- Protein: 5.4
- Total Fat: 4.7
- Sodium: 891
- Total Carbohydrate: 27.8
- Cholesterol: 14

---

321. Sunday Afternoon Slow Cooked Spare Ribs

Serving: 8 | Prep: 10mins | Ready in:

Ingredients

- 8 meaty pork loin spareribs
- 1 tablespoon light olive oil

- 1 (14 ounce) can beef broth
- 1/2 cup ketchup
- 1/4 cup brown sugar
- 1/4 cup lemon juice
- 2 tablespoons vinegar
- 2 tablespoons Worcestershire sauce
- 2 tablespoons soy sauce
- 1/2 teaspoon crushed red pepper flakes
- 1 tablespoon seafood seasoning (such as Old Bay®)
- 1/4 cup dried minced onion
- 1/2 teaspoon ground nutmeg
- salt and black pepper to taste

Direction

- In a big pot, cover ribs with lightly salted water. Boil ribs for 45 minutes; drain water off. Put ribs aside.
- In a Dutch oven/big heavy pot, heat olive oil on medium heat until oil shimmers. Brown all sides of ribs, about 10 minutes per side. Take out ribs. Pour in pepper, salt, nutmeg, dried onion, seafood seasoning, red pepper flakes, soy sauce, Worcestershire sauce, vinegar, lemon juice, brown sugar, ketchup and beef broth. Mix ingredients until sauce dissolves. Scrape brown flavor bits from the pan's bottom. Simmer sauce on medium low heat. Put ribs back into the sauce.
- Coat ribs in sauce. Cover pan. Simmer on low heat for about 3 hours until meat falls off the bones and is very tender.

Nutrition Information

- Calories: 323 calories;
- Total Fat: 20.9
- Sodium: 861
- Total Carbohydrate: 14.2
- Cholesterol: 75
- Protein: 19.4

322. Sunflower Chicken Salad

Serving: 4 | Prep: | Ready in:

Ingredients

- 2 cups cubed cooked chicken breast meat
- 1 cup cubed Cheddar cheese
- 1/4 cup sunflower seeds
- 1/4 cup thinly sliced celery
- 1/2 cup seedless green grapes, halved
- 1/2 cup mayonnaise
- salt and pepper to taste

Direction

- Mix mayonnaise, grapes, celery, sunflower seeds, cheese and chicken together in a big bowl and season with pepper and salt. Combine everything together and, if needed, serve on lettuce leaves or on rolls.

Nutrition Information

- Calories: 481 calories;
- Total Fat: 38.6
- Sodium: 420
- Total Carbohydrate: 5.1
- Cholesterol: 99
- Protein: 28.2

323. Super BLT

Serving: 4 | Prep: 10mins | Ready in:

Ingredients

- 8 slices bacon
- 8 slices bread, toasted
- 1/4 cup guacamole
- 1/4 cup cream cheese
- 4 lettuce leaves
- 4 slices tomato

Direction

- In a large, deep skillet put the bacon, and cook over medium-high heat, turn from time to time for about 10 minutes until evenly brown. Transfer the bacon slices in a plate with lined paper towel.
- Place the guacamole on 4 pieces of toasted bread; put the cream cheese on the remaining 4 pieces. Add tomato slice, lettuce leaf and two pieces of bacon above the 4 slices of bread and top with remaining slices.

Nutrition Information

- Calories: 306 calories;
- Total Fat: 15.9
- Sodium: 809
- Total Carbohydrate: 28.5
- Cholesterol: 36
- Protein: 12.3

324. Super Delicious Zuppa Toscana

Serving: 6 | Prep: 25mins | Ready in:

Ingredients

- 1 pound bulk mild Italian sausage
- 1 1/4 teaspoons crushed red pepper flakes
- 4 slices bacon, cut into 1/2 inch pieces
- 1 large onion, diced
- 1 tablespoon minced garlic
- 5 (13.75 ounce) cans chicken broth
- 6 potatoes, thinly sliced
- 1 cup heavy cream
- 1/4 bunch fresh spinach, tough stems removed

Direction

- Place a Dutch oven over medium-high heat and cook red pepper flakes and Italian sausage for 10 to 15 minutes, or until crumbly, browned and not pink anymore. Drain, then set aside.

- In the same Dutch oven, cook bacon over medium heat for 10 minutes, or until crisp. Drain but leave a few tablespoons of the bacon fat with the bacon in the Dutch oven. Stir in garlic and onions and cook for 5 minutes, or until the onions are translucent and tender.
- Pour in chicken broth and bring to a boil over high heat. Add potatoes and boil for 20 minutes, or until the potatoes are soft enough to easily pierce with a fork. Reduce to medium heat and stir in the cooked sausage and heavy cream until heated through. Before serving, mix in spinach.

Nutrition Information

- Calories: 554 calories;
- Cholesterol: 99
- Protein: 19.8
- Total Fat: 32.6
- Sodium: 2386
- Total Carbohydrate: 45.8

---

325. Swabian Meatballs (Fleischkuechle)

Serving: 8 | Prep: 15mins | Ready in:

Ingredients

- 1/2 cup milk
- 2 hard rolls, day-old
- 1/2 pound ground beef
- 1/2 pound ground pork
- 2 eggs
- 1 onion, minced
- 4 tablespoons chopped fresh parsley
- 1 teaspoon dried marjoram
- 1 tablespoon minced garlic
- salt and ground black pepper to taste
- 2 tablespoons butter

Direction

- Put the milk into a bowl; soak the rolls in the milk for around 15 minutes.
- Put pepper, salt, garlic, marjoram, parsley, onion, eggs, pork, beef, and milk-soaked rolls in a large bowl; use your hands to stir until evenly-combined. Split the mixture into eight portions and roll to shape them into balls. Flatten the balls to 1-inch thick patties.
- In a large skillet, melt the butter. Fry 1 patty per time in the melted butter until meat achieves an internal temperature of 160°F (72°C), for around 6 minutes per side. Serve hot or cold.

Nutrition Information

- Calories: 195 calories;
- Protein: 13
- Total Fat: 13
- Sodium: 123
- Total Carbohydrate: 6.2
- Cholesterol: 95

---

326. Tackee David's Split Pea With Ham

Serving: 8 | Prep: 15mins | Ready in:

Ingredients

- 1 pound dried split peas
- 8 cups water
- 1 meaty ham bone
- 1 cup chopped onion
- 1/4 teaspoon dried marjoram leaves, crushed
- 1/4 teaspoon dried thyme leaves, crushed
- 1/4 teaspoon garlic powder
- 1/2 teaspoon ground black pepper, or to taste
- 1 cup chopped celery
- 1/2 teaspoon salt, or to taste

Direction

- Pour the water and peas into a big soup pot on medium heat, then boil. Let it boil for 2 minutes and put aside away from the heat to let it cool for an hour.
- In the pot, put the ham bone and stir in the salt, garlic powder, thyme, marjoram and onion, then boil on medium heat. Lower the heat to a simmer, cover the pot and let it simmer for 2 hours, stirring from time to time. Take out the ham bone and slice as much ham as possible from the bone. Chop the ham and put it back into the soup. Mix in celery. Get rid of the ham bone. Return the soup to a simmer and let it cook for 45 minutes more, mixing from time to time, then season with salt to taste.

Nutrition Information

- Calories: 205 calories;
- Protein: 14.3
- Total Fat: 0.7
- Sodium: 174
- Total Carbohydrate: 36.8
- Cholesterol: 0

---

327. Taco Slaw

Serving: 6 | Prep: 20mins | Ready in:

Ingredients

- 1/2 small head cabbage, chopped
- 1 jalapeno pepper, seeded and minced
- 1/2 red onion, minced
- 1 carrot, chopped
- 1 tablespoon chopped fresh cilantro
- 1 lime, juiced

Direction

- Combine carrot, lime juice, cabbage, red onion, cilantro, and jalapeno pepper in a bowl.

Nutrition Information

- Calories: 27 calories;
- Sodium: 19
- Total Carbohydrate: 6.6
- Cholesterol: 0
- Protein: 1.1
- Total Fat: 0.1

---

328. Tangy Buffalo Chicken Pasta Salad

Serving: 6 | Prep: 20mins | Ready in:

Ingredients

- 1 (8 ounce) package rotini pasta
- 2 cups cubed cooked chicken
- 2 stalks celery, diced
- 1/3 cup jarred roasted red pepper, drained (reserve juice) and chopped
- 1 green onion, thinly sliced
- 1/2 cup mayonnaise (such as Hellmann's®/Best Foods®)
- 2 tablespoons hot pepper sauce (such as Frank's RedHot®), or to taste
- 2 tablespoons crumbled Gorgonzola cheese
- 1 teaspoon Worcestershire sauce

Direction

- Boil the big pot of lightly-salted water; cook rotini at a boil for roughly 8 minutes or till becoming soft but firm to bite; drain off and let cool down.
- In the salad bowl, combine 1 tbsp. of the reserved roasted red pepper juice, roasted red pepper, celery, chicken and pasta. In another bowl, whisk together Worcestershire sauce, Gorgonzola cheese, hot sauce and mayonnaise till combined completely. Add the dressing on the pasta mixture and coat by tossing gently. Keep chilled prior to serving.

Nutrition Information

- Calories: 329 calories;
- Total Carbohydrate: 28.9
- Cholesterol: 30
- Protein: 12.3
- Total Fat: 18
- Sodium: 347

---

329. Tangy Turkey And Swiss Sandwiches

Serving: 4 | Prep: 15mins | Ready in:

Ingredients

- 3/4 cup chopped red onion
- 1 tablespoon dried thyme
- 1/2 cup mayonnaise
- 1/4 cup coarse-grain brown mustard
- 8 slices country style French Bread
- 6 tablespoons butter, softened
- 1 pound thinly sliced roast turkey
- 8 slices tomato
- 8 slices Swiss cheese

Direction

- Mix mustard, red onion, mayonnaise, and thyme together in a small bowl. Spread one side of each bread slice with some of the mixtures. On the other side of each bread slice, spread butter over.
- Set a large skillet over medium heat. Arrange 4 bread slices into the skillet, butter-side down. Layer each slice of the bread with 1/4 of the turkey slices, and then 2 tomato slices. Top them with 2 Swiss cheese slices. Arrange the remaining bread slices on top, butter-side up. Once the bottoms of the sandwiches turn golden brown, flip them over and cook the other side until golden.

Nutrition Information

- Calories: 856 calories;
- Cholesterol: 154
- Protein: 41.9
- Total Fat: 58.9
- Sodium: 2243
- Total Carbohydrate: 42.6

---

330. Tarragon Dill Grilled Chicken Salad

Serving: 6 | Prep: 35mins | Ready in:

Ingredients

- 1/2 cup lemon juice
- 1/4 cup olive oil
- 4 cloves garlic, minced
- 1 tablespoon crushed red pepper flakes, or to taste
- 3 (6 ounce) skinless boneless chicken breasts
- 1/2 cup sour cream
- 1/2 cup reduced-fat mayonnaise
- 1/4 cup rice vinegar or cider vinegar
- 1/4 cup fresh lemon juice
- 1 cup seedless red grapes, halved
- 1 large Granny Smith apple, cored and chopped
- 1/2 cup celery, diced
- 1/2 onion, finely chopped
- 1/2 cup fresh tarragon, finely chopped
- 2 teaspoons finely chopped fresh dill
- salt and pepper to taste

Direction

- For making the marinade, in a bowl, mix red pepper flakes, garlic, olive oil and half cup of lemon juice.
- Add the chicken breasts onto a flat surface, and chop from one side through the center of the breasts to within 1/2-in. of the other side. Open the two sides and spread them out flat in a book-shaped. Add into a shallow plate, and add the olive oil mixture on top of the chicken,

flipping one time to coat equally with marinade. Keep chilled in the refrigerator for no less than half an hour.

- For making the dressing, in a bowl, whisk thoroughly a quarter cup of lemon juice, vinegar, mayonnaise and sour cream. Put aside.
- Preheat an outdoor grill to medium-high heat. Oil the grate a bit, and set about 4 in. away from heat source.
- Take chicken out of marinade, and get rid of marinade. Cook chicken for roughly 4-5 minutes on each side on preheated grill till meat becomes firm and juices run out clear, flipping one time. Take the chicken out of grill, and let it cool. Finely chop chicken, and add into a big bowl.
- Place dill, tarragon, celery, apples and grapes into the bowl with the chicken. Mix in the mayonnaise dressing, and toss until ingredients are equally coated. Use pepper and salt to season to taste. Serve right away, or let chill in the refrigerator overnight to allow flavors to blend further.

Nutrition Information

- Calories: 338 calories;
- Total Fat: 22.1
- Sodium: 221
- Total Carbohydrate: 17.2
- Cholesterol: 64
- Protein: 19.5

331. Tarte A L'Oignon (French Onion Pie)

Serving: 10 | Prep: 30mins | Ready in:

Ingredients

- 10 slices bacon, cut into 1 inch pieces
- 5 onions, thinly sliced
- 1 teaspoon salt

- 1/8 teaspoon freshly ground black pepper
- 1/2 cup milk
- 1/2 cup heavy cream
- 1 tablespoon all-purpose flour
- 4 eggs
- 1 pinch ground nutmeg
- 1 (9 inch) unbaked pie crust

Direction

- To preheat: Set oven to 200°C (400°F).
- Add bacon to a skillet then cook on medium heat till bacon turns brown. Get bacon out of skillet, keep four tablespoons of bacon fat, drain bacon on paper towels.
- Add onion to the same skillet with the bacon fat then cook on medium-high heat for around 8 minutes till onions turn to brown evenly. Use salt and pepper to season. Mix cream and milk in a bowl. Use the flour to sprinkle on top of onions then stir to blend. Pour in the milk mixture. Cook and stir on medium heat till the mixture becomes thick. Take skillet off the heat, add bacon then stir and set aside to cool down for 10 minutes.
- Put eggs in a mixing bowl then beat till they get light color and become frothy. Put a spoonful of the onion mixture into the eggs then stir. Put in another spoonful of the onion mixture, and keep stirring. Repeat till there aren't any onions left (all onion have been stirred into the eggs) and everything is well blended. Transfer the mixture into the prepared pie shell. Use nutmeg to sprinkle.
- Put the pie shell in the preheated oven and bake for approximately 20 minutes till the crust gets slightly brown. Get the pie shell out of the oven and let it cool down for 5 minutes before serving.

Nutrition Information

- Calories: 344 calories;
- Total Fat: 25.4
- Sodium: 601
- Total Carbohydrate: 20.7
- Cholesterol: 111

- Protein: 8.9

332. Teriyaki Pineapple Turkey Burgers

Serving: 4 | Prep: | Ready in:

Ingredients

- 1/4 cup Kikkoman Teriyaki Baste Glaze, divided
- 1 (8 ounce) can pineapple slices, drained, reserve 1/4 cup juice
- 1 pound ground turkey or chicken
- 1 teaspoon grated fresh ginger
- 1/4 cup Kikkoman Panko Bread Crumbs
- 4 whole grain hamburger buns
- 4 slices Cheddar or Monterey Jack cheese

Direction

- Mix pineapple juice and Kikkoman Teriyaki Base Glaze in a bowl. Set 2 tablespoons aside for burgers.
- Combine turkey, 2 tablespoons of the teriyaki mix, ginger, and Kikkoman Panko Bread Crumbs. Mold into 4 patties.
- Grill the patties while brushing with the remaining teriyaki mix until done as desired. Grill pineapple slices until golden brown.
- Serve burgers with pineapple and cheese, on buns.

Nutrition Information

- Calories: 486 calories;
- Protein: 34
- Total Fat: 20.2
- Sodium: 896
- Total Carbohydrate: 41.6
- Cholesterol: 113

333. Thai Ginger Soup

Serving: 4 | Prep: 15mins | Ready in:

Ingredients

- 3 cups coconut milk
- 2 cups water
- 1/2 pound skinless, boneless chicken breast halves - cut into thin strips
- 3 tablespoons minced fresh ginger root
- 2 tablespoons fish sauce, or to taste
- 1/4 cup fresh lime juice
- 2 tablespoons sliced green onions
- 1 tablespoon chopped fresh cilantro

Direction

- Bring a saucepan of water and coconut milk to a boil. Add chicken strips, lower the heat to medium and simmer for about 3 minutes just until chicken is cooked through. Stir in lime juice, fish sauce and ginger. Add cilantro and green onions. Serve.

Nutrition Information

- Calories: 415 calories;
- Cholesterol: 29
- Protein: 14.4
- Total Fat: 39
- Sodium: 598
- Total Carbohydrate: 7.3

334. Thai Inspired Confetti Salad

Serving: 4 | Prep: 35mins | Ready in:

Ingredients

- 1 Roma tomato, chopped
- 1 1/2 cups fresh green beans, cut into 1/2 inch pieces
- 1 cucumber, cut into 1/2 inch cubes

- 1 1/2 cups cubed papaya
- 2 cloves cloves garlic, minced
- 1 fresh Thai or Serrano chile, finely minced
- 1 lemon, juiced
- 2 limes, juiced
- 2 tablespoons fish sauce
- 1 tablespoon white sugar
- 1/2 cup roasted peanuts, chopped
- 1/4 cup cilantro leaves, chopped

Direction

- In a big bowl, mix papaya, tomato, cucumber, beans, chilli pepper, and garlic together.
- In a small bowl, whisk sugar, lemon juice, fish sauce, and lime juice together; combine with the papaya mixture. Top with cilantro and peanuts to serve.

Nutrition Information

- Calories: 181 calories;
- Cholesterol: 0
- Protein: 6.9
- Total Fat: 9.4
- Sodium: 704
- Total Carbohydrate: 24.5

---

335. Thai Style Cucumber Salad

Serving: 2 | Prep: 15mins | Ready in:

Ingredients

- 1/4 cup tamarind juice
- 1 tablespoon chopped fresh cilantro
- 1 tablespoon chopped peanuts
- 1 tablespoon rice vinegar
- 1 1/2 teaspoons brown sugar
- 1 teaspoon fish sauce
- 3/4 teaspoon red pepper flakes
- 1 teaspoon toasted Asian sesame oil
- 3/4 teaspoon minced fresh ginger root

- 1 cucumber, thinly sliced

Direction

- In a large bowl, whisk fish sauce, ginger, rice vinegar, sesame oil, peanuts, cilantro, brown sugar, tamarind juice, and red pepper flakes. Mix in the cucumber. Before serving, cover and allow to chill for 10 minutes in the fridge.

Nutrition Information

- Calories: 113 calories;
- Cholesterol: 0
- Protein: 2.1
- Total Fat: 4.8
- Sodium: 223
- Total Carbohydrate: 17.6

---

336. The Best Veggie Sandwich

Serving: 4 | Prep: 20mins | Ready in:

Ingredients

- 4 English muffins, split and toasted
- 1 avocado, mashed
- 1 cup alfalfa sprouts
- 1 small tomato, chopped
- 1 small sweet onion, chopped
- 4 tablespoons Ranch-style salad dressing
- 4 tablespoons toasted sesame seeds
- 1 cup shredded smoked Cheddar cheese

Direction

- Prepare the oven by preheating it to broil.
- Get a cookie sheet and put each of the muffin open-faced on it. Spread each half of the muffin with mashed avocado and put the halves close to each other. Spread the ingredients evenly then cover each half with tomatoes, sprouts, dressing, onion, cheese and sesame seeds.

- Put it under the broiler until the cheese is melted and bubbly, about 5 minutes.

Nutrition Information

- Calories: 470 calories;
- Sodium: 521
- Total Carbohydrate: 37.1
- Cholesterol: 34
- Protein: 15.8
- Total Fat: 30.2

337. The Last Caesar Salad Recipe You'll Ever Need

Serving: 32 | Prep: 20mins | Ready in:

Ingredients

- 2 anchovy fillets
- 2 cloves garlic, chopped, or to taste
- 1 cup mayonnaise
- 1/3 cup grated Parmesan cheese
- 1/4 cup half-and-half
- 2 tablespoons fresh lemon juice
- 1 tablespoon Dijon mustard
- 2 teaspoons Worcestershire sauce

Direction

- Pulse the garlic and the anchovy fillets in a food processor for a few times until you get a pasty mixture. Put in the half-and-half, mayonnaise, Worcestershire sauce, Parmesan cheese, Dijon mustard, and lemon juice in the mixture; let it blend until the dressing has a creamy texture. Keep in the fridge for 1 hour or could be more prior to serving.

Nutrition Information

- Calories: 57 calories;
- Total Fat: 5.9
- Sodium: 77

- Total Carbohydrate: 0.6
- Cholesterol: 4
- Protein: 0.5

338. The Talk Of The Potluck Kale And Apple Salad

Serving: 10 | Prep: 20mins | Ready in:

Ingredients

- 1 teaspoon salt, or to taste
- 1 bunch kale, stems removed and leaves chopped
- 2 apples, diced
- 1/4 cup olive oil
- 1/3 cup sweetened dried cranberries (such as Ocean Spray® Craisins®)
- 1/3 cup toasted unsalted sunflower seeds
- 2 tablespoons raw apple cider vinegar
- 1/3 cup crumbled Gorgonzola cheese

Direction

- In a large bowl, massage kale with salt for 2 minutes till kale is slightly soft. Gently stir vinegar, sunflower seeds, cranberries, olive oil and apples into the kale to mix the salad evenly. Add Gorgonzola cheese into the salad and fold gently.

Nutrition Information

- Calories: 142 calories;
- Sodium: 308
- Total Carbohydrate: 12.7
- Cholesterol: 6
- Protein: 3.6
- Total Fat: 9.5

339.   Tomato Fennel Soup

Serving: 4 | Prep: 15mins | Ready in:

Ingredients

- 2 tablespoons olive oil
- 1 bulb fennel, chopped
- 1/2 onion, chopped
- 1 celery stalk, chopped
- 1 clove garlic, minced
- 1 (14.5 ounce) can diced tomatoes
- 1 cup low-sodium chicken broth
- 2 tablespoons chopped fresh basil
- 2 tablespoons chopped fresh parsley
- salt and ground black pepper to taste

Direction

- Put olive oil in a large saucepan and heat it over medium-high heat. Stir in celery, garlic, fennel, and onion and then cook in hot oil for approximately 10 minutes until tender.
- Pour chicken broth and tomatoes into the vegetable mixture. Simmer the mixture for 4 minutes. Take the saucepan away from the heat. Add the parsley and basil. Let the soup cool slightly.
- Fill a blender with the soup, no more than half-full. Cover the blender. Holding the lid down, pulse it a couple of times before blending it completely. Make sure to puree the soup in batches until smooth.

Nutrition Information

- Calories: 115 calories;
- Sodium: 275
- Total Carbohydrate: 10.1
- Cholesterol: 1
- Protein: 2.8
- Total Fat: 7

340.   Tomato And Avocado Salad

Serving: 4 | Prep: 15mins | Ready in:

Ingredients

- 1 teaspoon Dijon mustard
- 1/4 cup extra-virgin olive oil
- 1/2 cup balsamic vinegar
- 1 pinch ground black pepper
- 1 avocado - peeled, pitted and sliced
- 2 small tomatoes, each cut into 8 wedges

Direction

- Combine in a small bowl the pepper, balsamic vinegar, olive oil, and mustard. Alternately lay out avocado slices and tomato like the spokes of a wheel on one big serving plate or individual plates. Then drizzle lightly with the dressing and serve right away.

Nutrition Information

- Calories: 236 calories;
- Total Fat: 21.5
- Sodium: 45
- Total Carbohydrate: 11.1
- Cholesterol: 0
- Protein: 1.5

341.   Tonya's Terrific Sloppy Joes

Serving: 8 | Prep: 10mins | Ready in:

Ingredients

- 2 pounds ground beef
- 1/2 cup chopped onion
- 1/4 cup chopped celery
- 7 ounces ketchup
- 1 tablespoon brown sugar

- 1 1/2 teaspoons Worcestershire sauce
- 1 teaspoon vinegar
- 1/4 teaspoon dry mustard powder
- 1/8 teaspoon lemon juice
- 8 white or wheat hamburger buns

Direction

- Put a big skillet on medium-high heat. Crumble the ground beef in the skillet. Put celery and onion. Stir and cook the beef mixture for 7-10 minutes until beef is browned completely.
- Mix Worcestershire sauce, brown sugar, mustard, vinegar, lemon juice, and ketchup through the beef mixture. Lower the heat to medium-low. Cook the mixture at a simmer for around 20 minutes until the mixture gets hot and the sauce thickens.

Nutrition Information

- Calories: 362 calories;
- Total Fat: 15.3
- Sodium: 573
- Total Carbohydrate: 31.2
- Cholesterol: 71
- Protein: 23.7

342.   Top Ramen® Salad

Serving: 6 | Prep: 15mins | Ready in:

Ingredients

- Salad:
- 2 (3 ounce) packages chicken-flavored ramen noodles, broken into pieces, seasoning packets reserved
- 1/2 cup raw sunflower seeds
- 1/2 cup slivered almonds
- 1 (16 ounce) package coleslaw mix
- 3 green onions, chopped
- Dressing:

- 1/2 cup olive oil
- 3 tablespoons white vinegar
- 1 tablespoon white sugar
- 1/2 teaspoon ground black pepper

Direction

- Preheat the oven to 175°C or 350°Fahrenheit. On a baking dish, spread almonds, sunflower seeds, and ramen noodles.
- Bake for 10-15mins until toasted and aromatic. Let it cool down to room temp.
- In a big bowl, mix green onions and coleslaw mix together. Add the cooled noodle mix on top.
- In a bowl, combine black pepper, olive oil, sugar, reserved ramen seasoning packets, and vinegar until smooth. Toss the coleslaw with dressing until well coated.

Nutrition Information

- Calories: 450 calories;
- Sodium: 324
- Total Carbohydrate: 34.9
- Cholesterol: 6
- Protein: 9.9
- Total Fat: 31.1

343.   Triple Decker Grilled Shrimp BLT With Avocado And Chipotle Mayo

Serving: 2 | Prep: 20mins | Ready in:

Ingredients

- 1 cup mayonnaise
- 1 chipotle pepper in adobo sauce
- 1/2 lime, juiced
- 1 pinch salt
- 1 pinch ground black pepper
- 4 slices bacon

- 8 extra-large shrimp - peeled, deveined, and tails removed
- 1 tablespoon olive oil
- salt and ground black pepper to taste
- 1 avocado, peeled, pitted and sliced
- 2 leaves romaine lettuce
- 4 slices ripe red tomato
- 6 slices sourdough bread, toasted

Direction

- In a bowl, mix mayonnaise, lime juice, pepper, a dash of salt and chipotle pepper. Then puree with a stick blender until smooth. You can also puree the ingredients with a food processor if you don't have a blender. Cover the ingredients and then chill until when you are ready to prepare the sandwiches.
- Over medium-high heat, cook bacon in a deep skillet while turning frequently for about 10 minutes until browned evenly. Use a plate lined with paper towel to drain the slices of bacon.
- Medium-high heat, preheat the outdoor grill and then coat the grate lightly with oil. Toss shrimp in a bowl of olive oil, pepper and salt to taste.
- Let the shrimp to cook on the grill preheated for about 3 minutes per side until the center of the meat is no longer transparent and the outside is bright pink.
- To prepare the sandwiches: Onto one slice of bread, generously spread the mayonnaise dressing prepared. Spread avocado slices and half of the shrimp at the top. On top of the avocado, put another slice of bread and then spread a layer of the dressing. Add on top two slices of tomato and a lettuce leaf and lastly a third slice of bread. To make the second sandwich, repeat this step with the remaining ingredients.

Nutrition Information

- Calories: 1433 calories;
- Total Fat: 119
- Sodium: 1769

- Total Carbohydrate: 59.6
- Cholesterol: 234
- Protein: 37.8

344. Tuna Fish Pea Salad

Serving: 6 | Prep: 5mins | Ready in:

Ingredients

- 1 (12 ounce) can chunk light tuna in water, drained
- 1 (15 ounce) can peas, drained
- 1/4 cup reduced-fat mayonnaise, or as needed
- 1 teaspoon garlic powder
- 1 teaspoon ground black pepper

Direction

- In a bowl, add the peas with tuna, and mix gently to break up the tuna then mix with the peas. Put in pepper, garlic powder and mayonnaise, and mix thoroughly by stirring.

Nutrition Information

- Calories: 103 calories;
- Protein: 16.7
- Total Fat: 0.7
- Sodium: 160
- Total Carbohydrate: 7.1
- Cholesterol: 17

345. Turkey Avocado Panini

Serving: 2 | Prep: 17mins | Ready in:

Ingredients

- 1/2 ripe avocado
- 1/4 cup mayonnaise
- 2 ciabatta rolls

- 1 tablespoon olive oil, divided
- 2 slices provolone cheese
- 1 cup whole fresh spinach leaves, divided
- 1/4 pound thinly sliced mesquite smoked turkey breast
- 2 roasted red peppers, sliced into strips

Direction

- In a bowl, mash the mayonnaise and the avocado together until mixed thoroughly.
- Preheat the panini sandwich press.
- To prepare the sandwiches, divide in half the flat way the ciabatta rolls and then use olive oil to polish the bottom of every roll. Onto the panini press, put the bottoms of the rolls with the olive oil side facing down. On each sandwich, put a sliced roasted red pepper, a provolone cheese slice, half the chopped turkey breast, and half spinach leaves. On the cut surface of each top, lay half of the mixture of avocado and then put top of the roll onto the sandwich. Use olive oil to polish the top of the roll.
- Cover the panini press and then cook for about 5 to 8 minutes until bun is crisp and toasted, cheese has melted and has golden brown grill marks.

Nutrition Information

- Calories: 723 calories;
- Total Fat: 51.3
- Sodium: 1720
- Total Carbohydrate: 42.1
- Cholesterol: 62
- Protein: 25.3

---

346. Turkey Bone Soup

Serving: 12 | Prep: 20mins | Ready in:

Ingredients

- 1 turkey carcass, cooked
- 4 (14 ounce) cans low-sodium chicken broth
- 1 onion, quartered
- 1 stalk celery, cut into 2 inch pieces
- 4 cloves garlic, crushed
- 2 cups chopped cooked turkey breast
- 1 (16 ounce) package frozen mixed vegetables
- 1 cup uncooked white rice
- 1 (15 ounce) can kidney beans, rinsed and drained
- salt and pepper to taste
- 1 tablespoon dried oregano
- 1 tablespoon dried basil
- 1 teaspoon paprika

Direction

- In a big stockpot that has a lid, place in the turkey carcass and pour in chicken broth to mostly cover. Drop in garlic, celery, and onion, then boil on medium heat. Simmer while covered, occasionally turning the carcass, for 2 hours.
- Remove the carcass and cool. Take out the garlic, celery, and onion, then blend into a blender with 1/2 cup stock to fill a pitcher halfway. Place a folded kitchen towel on the blender lid and start to pulse the vegetable mixture with several quick pulses then leave to puree, then pour back into the stock.
- Pick out as much turkey meat from the carcass as you can and add into the stock. Stir in paprika, basil, oregano, pepper, salt, canned kidney beans, rice, frozen mixed vegetables, and chopped turkey breast, then boil. Simmer, covered, until rice becomes tender, about 20 - 30 minutes.

Nutrition Information

- Calories: 1164 calories;
- Sodium: 295
- Total Carbohydrate: 25.1
- Cholesterol: 274
- Protein: 57.5
- Total Fat: 91.1

347. Turkey Garbanzo Bean And Kale Soup With Pasta

Serving: 8 | Prep: 10mins | Ready in:

Ingredients

- 16 ounces whole-wheat pasta shells
- 1 tablespoon extra-virgin olive oil
- 1 pound ground turkey
- 1 cup chopped onion
- 3 cloves garlic, minced
- 2 tablespoons chopped fresh sage
- 2 tablespoons chopped fresh rosemary
- 3 (14 ounce) cans chicken broth
- 3/4 cup water
- 1 (15 ounce) can garbanzo beans, drained and rinsed
- 1/3 cup tomato paste
- 2 cups roughly chopped kale
- salt and pepper to taste

Direction

- Boil a big pot of salted water and stir in the pasta, then bring back to boiling. Boil while occasionally stirring for 12 - 15 minutes until the pasta is cooked but still firm to chew, then drain.
- In a big soup pot, heat olive oil and add in garlic, onion, and turkey, then cook on a medium heat until onion becomes soft and the meat is brown, 5 minutes. Stir in the rosemary and sage, then cook for 1 minute without allowing them to brown. Pour in the water and broth with the tomato paste and garbanzo beans, then set to boil. Add in the kale and simmer for 5 minutes until the kale is soft. Season with pepper and salt.
- Place a serving cooked pasta on the bottom of a soup bowl and ladle over with the hot soup to serve.

Nutrition Information

- Calories: 374 calories;
- Cholesterol: 45
- Protein: 23.2
- Total Fat: 7.7
- Sodium: 940
- Total Carbohydrate: 56.8

348. Turkey Wild Rice Soup II

Serving: 8 | Prep: 20mins | Ready in:

Ingredients

- 2/3 cup uncooked wild rice
- 2 cups water
- 6 tablespoons butter
- 1/4 cup finely chopped onion
- 1/4 cup finely chopped celery
- 1/3 cup all-purpose flour
- 4 cups turkey broth
- 1/3 cup shredded carrot
- 2 cups chopped cooked turkey
- 1/2 teaspoon kosher salt, or to taste
- 1/2 teaspoon ground black pepper, or to taste
- 1/4 cup chopped slivered almonds
- 1/2 teaspoon lemon juice
- 3/4 cup half-and-half cream

Direction

- In a saucepan, bring water and wild rice to a boil. Lower heat to medium-low, cover it and simmer for 40 to 45 minutes until the rice is soft yet not mushy. Drain excess liquid, fluff rice with fork, cook for 5 minutes more while uncovered. Put cooked rice aside.
- In a soup pot over medium heat, melt butter. Cook and mix the celery and onion for about 5 minutes until the onions turn translucent. Mix in flour and cook for 3-5 minutes until it turns to a pale yellowish-brown color. Gradually whisk in the turkey stock until you get rid of all the lumps of flour. Mix in the carrot. Bring

mixture to simmer and cook while whisking often for about 2 more minutes until the carrot is soft and the stock is smooth and thick.

- Mix in almonds, pepper, salt, turkey and wild rice. Return to simmer and cook for 2 minutes more to heat the ingredients. Mix in the lemon juice and half-and-half. When soup is almost to a boil, serve.

Nutrition Information

- Calories: 252 calories;
- Sodium: 795
- Total Carbohydrate: 14.4
- Cholesterol: 61
- Protein: 14.3
- Total Fat: 15.2

---

349.   Turkey And Provolone Sandwiches

Serving: 6 | Prep: 15mins | Ready in:

Ingredients

- 1 tablespoon butter
- 6 large mushrooms, sliced
- 1 small onion, chopped
- 6 hoagie rolls, split lengthwise
- 1 pound sliced deli turkey meat
- 1 pound sliced provolone cheese
- 1/4 cup sliced black olives
- 6 slices tomato
- 6 leaves iceberg lettuce

Direction

- Preheat an oven to 200°C/400°F.
- Melt butter in a small skillet on medium heat. Sauté onion and mushrooms till tender; put aside. Put bottom bread halves on a lined cookie sheet; put 1-2 cheese slices, mushroom/onion mixture and 1-2 turkey slices on each.

- In the preheated oven, bake till cheese melts for 5 minutes. Take out of oven; top each with lettuce, tomato and olives. Put top bread half on every sandwich; serve.

Nutrition Information

- Calories: 576 calories;
- Total Fat: 29.2
- Sodium: 1939
- Total Carbohydrate: 40.9
- Cholesterol: 88
- Protein: 39.7

---

350.   Tuscan Bean, Chicken, And Italian Sausage Soup

Serving: 6 | Prep: 20mins | Ready in:

Ingredients

- 3/4 pound Italian chicken sausage links, casings removed and sausages cut into 1/4-inch pieces
- 1 onion, chopped
- 1 yellow squash, sliced
- 2 cloves garlic, pressed
- 1 (32 ounce) carton chicken broth
- 2 (15 ounce) cans white beans, drained and rinsed
- 1 (15 ounce) can Italian-style diced tomatoes
- 2 cups baby spinach leaves
- 1/3 cup red wine
- 1 teaspoon Italian seasoning
- 3 tablespoons grated Pecorino-Romano cheese

Direction

- Cook sausage for 5-7 minutes till fully browned and cooked through in a big pot on medium high heat. Drain; discard grease.
- Mix and cook sausage and onion for 5 minutes till translucent. Add garlic and squash; mix

and cook for another minute till the garlic is fragrant.

- Put diced tomatoes, white beans and chicken broth into the pot; mix. Add Italian seasoning, red wine and spinach; simmer. Cook for 15 minutes till hot. Ladle the soup into bowls; using Pecorino-Romano cheese to garnish before serving.

Nutrition Information

- Calories: 365 calories;
- Sodium: 1338
- Total Carbohydrate: 40.8
- Cholesterol: 27
- Protein: 20.7
- Total Fat: 12

---

351. Tuscan Smoked Turkey Bean Soup

Serving: 6 | Prep: 20mins | Ready in:

Ingredients

- 1 pound dry white beans
- 2 smoked turkey legs
- 1/2 onion, diced
- 2 bay leaves
- 2 stalks celery, diced
- 4 large carrots, sliced
- 1 (14.5 ounce) can petite diced tomatoes, undrained
- 2 tablespoons Italian seasoning
- salt and ground black pepper to taste
- 2 tablespoons grated Parmesan cheese, divided

Direction

- In a large bowl, cover the beans with water. Use a cloth to cover the bowl and let the beans soak overnight. Let the beans drain; rinse.

- In a large soup pot, combine the turkey legs, bay leaves, onion, and soaked beans. Cover the mixture with water. Let it boil over medium heat. Adjust the heat to medium-low. Simmer the mixture for 3 hours. Remove and discard the bay leaves. Get the turkey legs from the broth and separate its meat from its bones. Place the meat back into the broth. Mix in diced tomatoes, salt, pepper, Italian seasoning, celery, and carrots. Simmer the mixture for 1 hour until the carrots and celery are tender. Distribute the soup in bowls. Sprinkle each bowl with 1 tsp. of Parmesan cheese. Serve.

Nutrition Information

- Calories: 454 calories;
- Sodium: 939
- Total Carbohydrate: 53.8
- Cholesterol: 66
- Protein: 40.1
- Total Fat: 8.8

---

352. Ukrainian Red Borscht Soup

Serving: 10 | Prep: 25mins | Ready in:

Ingredients

- 1 (16 ounce) package pork sausage
- 3 medium beets, peeled and shredded
- 3 carrots, peeled and shredded
- 3 medium baking potatoes, peeled and cubed
- 1 tablespoon vegetable oil
- 1 medium onion, chopped
- 1 (6 ounce) can tomato paste
- 3/4 cup water
- 1/2 medium head cabbage, cored and shredded
- 1 (8 ounce) can diced tomatoes, drained
- 3 cloves garlic, minced
- salt and pepper to taste

- 1 teaspoon white sugar, or to taste
- 1/2 cup sour cream, for topping
- 1 tablespoon chopped fresh parsley for garnish

Direction

- If using sausage, crumble it into a skillet over medium-high heat. Cook and stir the sausage until no longer pink. Remove from the heat; put aside.
- In a large pot filled halfway with water (about 2 quarts), boil the water first before adding the sausage. Cover the pot and continue to boil. Add the beets and cook until their color is lost. Add the potatoes and carrots. Cook for about 15 minutes until tender. Add the cabbage and a can of diced tomatoes.
- Put oil in a skillet and heat it over medium heat. Add in onion and cook until tender. Mix in water and tomato paste until well-combined. Pour the mixture into the pot. Add the raw garlic into the soup. Cover the pot and switch off the heat. Allow the soup to stand for 5 minutes. Taste before adding the sugar, pepper and salt to season.
- Ladle the soup into serving bowls. Garnish each with sour cream and fresh parsley, if desired.

Nutrition Information

- Calories: 257 calories;
- Protein: 10.1
- Total Fat: 13.8
- Sodium: 626
- Total Carbohydrate: 24.4
- Cholesterol: 31

353.   Ukrainian Salat Vinaigrette (Beet Salad)

Serving: 16 | Prep: 30mins | Ready in:

Ingredients

- 1 pound beets
- 1 pound carrots
- 1 pound potatoes
- 2 large dill pickles, diced
- 1 onion, minced
- 1 (8 ounce) can peas, drained
- 2 tablespoons olive oil
- 1/2 teaspoon ground black pepper
- 1 tablespoon chopped fresh parsley (optional)
- 1/2 teaspoon salt

Direction

- In a big pot, put the beets and pour water to cover. Let it boil on high heat, then lower the heat to medium-low, put cover and let it simmer for approximately 20 minutes. Add potatoes and carrots, then boil for another 10 minutes, cover the pot and leave it overnight.
- On the next day, peel and dice the potatoes, carrots and beets into even, small pieces. Put the vegetables in a big bowl, then stir in the pepper, salt, olive oil, peas, onion and pickles. Put parsley on top to garnish prior to serving.

Nutrition Information

- Calories: 68 calories;
- Total Carbohydrate: 12
- Cholesterol: 0
- Protein: 1.6
- Total Fat: 1.9
- Sodium: 337

354.   VELVEETA® Cheesy Broccoli Soup

Serving: 6 | Prep: 10mins | Ready in:

Ingredients

- 2 tablespoons butter or margarine
- 1/4 cup chopped onion
- 2 tablespoons flour

- 2 1/2 cups milk
- 3/4 pound VELVEETA®, cut up
- 1 (10 ounce) package frozen chopped broccoli, thawed, drained
- 1/8 teaspoon pepper

Direction

- In a large saucepan, melt the butter on medium. Put in the onion; stir and cook until the onion becomes tender for 5 minutes. Put in flour; cook and stir constantly until bubbling for a minute.
- Pour in milk and stir. Boil. Turn down the heat to medium-low; then allow to simmer for a minute.
- Put in the remaining ingredients. Cook and stir from time to time until the soup is heated completely and the Velveeta melts.

Nutrition Information

- Calories: 279 calories;
- Total Fat: 18.3
- Sodium: 920
- Total Carbohydrate: 15.2
- Cholesterol: 63
- Protein: 14.2

355.   Vegan Black Bean Quesadillas

Serving: 4 | Prep: 10mins | Ready in:

Ingredients

- 1 (15 ounce) can great Northern beans, drained and rinsed
- 3/4 cup diced tomatoes
- 1 clove garlic
- 1/3 cup nutritional yeast
- 1 teaspoon ground cumin
- 1/4 teaspoon chili powder
- salt to taste

- 1 pinch cayenne pepper, or to taste
- 1/2 cup black beans, drained and rinsed
- 1/4 cup diced tomatoes
- 1 tablespoon olive oil, or as needed
- 8 whole grain tortillas
- cooking spray

Direction

- In a food processor, blend garlic, 3/4 cup tomatoes, and great Northern beans until smooth. Add in red pepper flakes, salt, chili powder, cumin, and nutritional yeast; blend again.
- Remove bean mixture to a bowl, mix in 1/4 cup tomatoes and black beans.
- In a skillet, heat olive oil over medium-high heat.
- In the hot oil, place a tortilla; arrange 1/4 cup filling on the tortilla.
- On top of filling, put another tortilla. Cook for 10 minutes until filling is warmed.
- Spray cooking spray over the top of tortilla; flip quesadilla to cook the other side, about 3-5 minutes, until slightly browned. Repeat with the rest filling and tortilla.

Nutrition Information

- Calories: 416 calories;
- Sodium: 616
- Total Carbohydrate: 85.6
- Cholesterol: 0
- Protein: 23.2
- Total Fat: 5.8

356.   Vegan Carrot Curry Soup

Serving: 8 | Prep: 10mins | Ready in:

Ingredients

- 4 cups vegetable broth
- 2 teaspoons curry powder

- 1 teaspoon ground cumin
- 1/2 teaspoon ground cinnamon
- 1/2 teaspoon ground ginger
- 2 pounds carrots, peeled and chopped
- 1 (14 ounce) can coconut milk
- 14 ounces water
- 1 teaspoon chopped fresh cilantro (optional)

Direction

- In a soup pot, add vegetable broth and cook over medium heat. Let it boil. Mix cumin, ginger, curry powder, and cinnamon. Add carrots. Lower the heat and let it simmer. Cook for 20 more minutes or until the carrots are softened. Stir often.
- Drain the carrots from the soup and transfer them to a blender. Fill the blender halfway. Add 1/4 cup of vegetable broth to the blender. Put the lid on and hold it down using a towel or pot holder. Start to blend carefully, starting with a few short pulses to move the carrots around before leaving it on to puree. Blend in batches until smooth if needed. Return pureed carrots to veggie broth. You can also use a stick blender to puree the vegetables directly in the soup pot.
- Pour in water and coconut milk, use can from coconut milk to measure. Cook to simmer. Top with cilantro as garnish. Serve.

Nutrition Information

- Calories: 161 calories;
- Sodium: 317
- Total Carbohydrate: 15.4
- Cholesterol: 0
- Protein: 2.7
- Total Fat: 11.1

---

357.   Veggie Bulgur Salad (Kisir)

Serving: 6 | Prep: 15mins | Ready in:

Ingredients

- 1 cup fine bulgur
- 1 cup boiling water
- 2 tablespoons olive oil
- 1 onion, finely chopped
- 2 large tomatoes, finely chopped
- 1 cucumber, diced
- 2 green bell peppers, finely chopped
- 1 red bell pepper, finely chopped
- 7 green onions, finely chopped
- 1/2 cup minced fresh parsley
- 1/2 cup minced fresh mint leaves
- 1 teaspoon red pepper flakes, or to taste
- 2 tablespoons olive oil
- juice of 1 fresh lemon
- 2 tablespoons pomegranate molasses

Direction

- Add the bulgur to a bowl and stir in boiling water. Cover the bulgur and set aside for 20 minutes.
- Meanwhile, in a skillet heat 2 tablespoons olive oil over medium heat. Toss in chopped onion; simmer for about 5 minutes stirring until the onion becomes translucent and softened.
- Drain the excess water from the bulgur and place it back in the bowl. Toss in chopped tomatoes, green and red bell peppers, cucumber, mint, parsley, red pepper flakes, green onions, and cooked onion. Sprinkle with 2 tablespoons olive oil, pomegranate molasses, and lemon juice. Gently mix until the salad is evenly combined. Can be served immediately, or refrigerated.

Nutrition Information

- Calories: 216 calories;
- Cholesterol: 0
- Protein: 5.3
- Total Fat: 9.8
- Sodium: 19
- Total Carbohydrate: 30.4

358.   Veggie Pasta Salad

Serving: 8 | Prep: 20mins | Ready in:

Ingredients

- 1 (8 ounce) package pasta spirals
- 1/4 cup diced sweet onion
- 1 green bell pepper, seeded and minced
- 1/2 fresh hot chile pepper, seeded and minced
- 2 tomatoes, seeded and chopped
- 1 cucumber, seeded and chopped
- 1/4 cup olive oil
- 1/4 cup tomato sauce
- 1/4 cup lime juice
- 3 tablespoons red wine vinegar
- 1 teaspoon garlic powder
- 1 teaspoon salt
- ground black pepper to taste

Direction

- In a large pot, pour in water and a little salt. Bring it to a boil. Put in the pasta spirals in the boiling water and cook for about 8 minutes until it gets tender but still firm when bitten. Drain. Use cold water to rinse the pasta to cool, drain.
- In a large bowl, combine cucumber, tomatoes, chile pepper, green bell pepper, sweet onion and the drained pasta.
- In a separate bowl, add black pepper, salt, garlic powder, red wine vinegar, lime juice, tomato sauce and olive oil. Whisk well. Pour it slightly over the pasta mixture and toss to coat.
- Put in the refrigerator for 2 hours for chilling. Stir when served.

Nutrition Information

- Calories: 190 calories;
- Sodium: 336
- Total Carbohydrate: 27.1
- Cholesterol: 0

- Protein: 4.7
- Total Fat: 7.4

359.   Waldorf Goat Cheese Salad

Serving: 1 | Prep: 10mins | Ready in:

Ingredients

- 2 cups red leaf lettuce - rinsed, dried and torn
- 2 tablespoons raspberry walnut vinaigrette
- 1/2 cup seedless red grapes, halved
- 2 tablespoons crumbled goat cheese
- 2 tablespoons chopped pecans

Direction

- In a mixing bowl, toss lettuce together with the dressing; place into a serving dish. Use pecans, goat cheese, and grapes to dust on top and serve.

Nutrition Information

- Calories: 266 calories;
- Total Fat: 15.4
- Sodium: 515
- Total Carbohydrate: 29.7
- Cholesterol: 11
- Protein: 6.4

360.   Warm Greek Pita Sandwiches With Turkey And Cucumber Yogurt Sauce

Serving: 4 | Prep: | Ready in:

Ingredients

- 1/2 cup sour cream
- 1/2 cup plain low-fat yogurt

- 1/2 cup cucumber, peeled, grated and squeezed as dry as possible
- 2 teaspoons red or rice wine vinegar
- 2 garlic cloves, minced
- 1/2 teaspoon Salt and pepper, to taste
- 4 large pitas
- 2 tablespoons olive oil
- 1 large onion, peeled, halved and cut into chunky wedges
- 3 cups leftover roast turkey, pulled into bite-sized pieces
- 1 teaspoon oregano
- 1 1/2 cups shredded lettuce (preferably romaine)
- 1 cup cherry tomatoes, halved and lightly salted

Direction

- Place the oven rack in the middle part; preheat the oven to 300°.
- Combine one minced garlic clove, sour cream, vinegar, cucumber, yogurt, and pepper and salt to taste in a small bowl; set aside.
- Bake pitas for 7 minutes in the oven until pliable and warm; slice in half. In the meantime, heat oil on high heat in a big pan; add and sauté onion for 2-3 minutes until brown on spots yet remain crisp. Put the remaining minced garlic, oregano, and turkey; sauté for another 2 minutes until completely heated.
- Serve. Let the guests make their own pitas, lettuce first then turkey, cucumber sauce, and tomatoes.

Nutrition Information

- Calories: 517 calories;
- Cholesterol: 94
- Protein: 40
- Total Fat: 19.5
- Sodium: 730
- Total Carbohydrate: 44.2

361.   White Bean Chicken Breast Chili

Serving: 4 | Prep: 20mins | Ready in:

Ingredients

- 1 teaspoon vegetable oil
- 2 boneless, skinless chicken breast halves
- 1 teaspoon vegetable oil
- 1 large onion, diced
- salt and freshly ground black pepper to taste
- 4 cloves garlic, chopped
- 1 tablespoon ancho chile powder
- 1 teaspoon ground cumin
- 1 teaspoon all-purpose flour
- 1/2 teaspoon chipotle pepper powder
- 1/4 teaspoon dried oregano
- 1 teaspoon fine cornmeal
- 2 cups chicken broth, divided
- 2 (15 ounce) cans white beans, drained
- 1 cup chicken broth
- 1/4 teaspoon white sugar, or to taste
- 1 pinch cayenne pepper, or to taste
- 1/3 cup chopped green onions
- 1/3 cup sour cream
- 1/3 cup chopped fresh cilantro

Direction

- In a big, deep skillet over medium-high heat, heat a teaspoon vegetable oil. Put in chicken breasts and cook for 4 minutes till browned. Turn heat to medium, turn breasts over, put on the pan cover, and cook for 5 minutes till browned on the other side. Move to a plate and let cool down prior to cutting into cubes.
- Bring skillet back to medium heat, put in black pepper, salt, onion and a teaspoon vegetable oil. Cook and mix for 4 to 5 minutes till onion becomes translucent. Mix in garlic and cook for a minute till aromatic.
- Into the onion mixture, mix oregano, chipotle pepper powder, flour, cumin and ancho chili powder; cook and mix for 2 to 3 minutes. Add a cup of the chicken broth and mix, getting rid

of any brown bits in the bottom of the pan. Mix in cornmeal and let it simmer.

- Mix in another cup chicken broth and beans. Into cubes, slice cooled chicken breasts, mix to the chili and let simmer. Put in leftover cup of chicken broth, put cayenne pepper, sugar, black pepper and salt to taste; cook till heated through. Garnish with cilantro, sour cream, and green onions, serve.

Nutrition Information

- Calories: 410 calories;
- Sodium: 772
- Total Carbohydrate: 54.7
- Cholesterol: 41
- Protein: 29.1
- Total Fat: 8.9

---

362.   White And Gold Pizza

Serving: 6 | Prep: 40mins | Ready in:

Ingredients

- 3 tablespoons olive oil, divided
- 1 large sweet onion, thinly sliced, separated into rings
- 1 pound frozen pizza dough, thawed
- 1 large clove garlic, minced
- 4 ounces PHILADELPHIA Cream Cheese, softened
- 3/4 cup KRAFT Shredded Mozzarella Cheese
- 1/2 cup DIGIORNO Grated Romano Cheese
- 1/2 teaspoon crushed red pepper

Direction

- Heat the oven to 425°F.
- In big skillet, heat a tablespoon oil over moderate heat. Add and cook onions till golden brown and soft, for 15 to 20 minutes, occasionally mixing.

- On slightly floured baking sheet, put the pizza dough; expand to suit in baking sheet, 16 x 12-inch in size. Stir leftover oil and the garlic; smear onto the dough. Bake for 10 minutes.
- Slather cream cheese on crust; put the rest of the red pepper, onions and cheeses on top. Bake till crust is browned slightly for 10 to 12 minutes.

Nutrition Information

- Calories: 377 calories;
- Total Fat: 18.1
- Sodium: 728
- Total Carbohydrate: 40.1
- Cholesterol: 33
- Protein: 12.9

---

363.   Wild Rocket (Arugula) And Parmesan Salad

Serving: 4 | Prep: 20mins | Ready in:

Ingredients

- 2 (5 ounce) packages arugula
- 1/4 cup roughly chopped cilantro
- 1 teaspoon fresh lemon juice
- 1 teaspoon olive oil
- 1 teaspoon balsamic vinegar
- 1 teaspoon red pepper flakes
- 1 pinch ground black pepper
- 1/4 cup shaved Parmesan cheese

Direction

- In a large salad bowl, toss cilantro and arugula together. Drizzle balsamic vinegar, olive oil and lemon juice over the arugula mixture. Sprinkle black pepper and red pepper flakes over then toss again. Season with more black pepper, red pepper flakes, balsamic vinegar, olive oil and lemon juice, if preferred.

- Sprinkle Parmesan cheese shavings over the salad. Toss again and serve.

Nutrition Information

- Calories: 54 calories;
- Total Fat: 3.2
- Sodium: 106
- Total Carbohydrate: 3.7
- Cholesterol: 4
- Protein: 3.9

---

364.   Winter Green Salad

Serving: 4 | Prep: 30mins | Ready in:

Ingredients

- Salad:
- 4 collard leaves, trimmed and finely chopped
- 1/3 bunch kale, trimmed and chopped
- 1 head romaine lettuce, chopped
- 1/4 small head red cabbage, chopped
- 1 Bosc pear, cubed
- 1/2 Bermuda onion, finely diced
- 1/2 orange bell pepper, diced
- 1/2 Florida avocado - peeled, pitted, and diced
- 1/2 carrot, grated
- 5 cherry tomatoes, halved
- 7 walnut halves, crushed
- 2 tablespoons raisins, or to taste
- Dressing:
- 6 tablespoons olive oil
- 3 tablespoons balsamic vinegar
- 1 tablespoon wildflower honey
- 1 tablespoon oregano, crushed
- 1 1/2 teaspoons chili powder
- 1 teaspoon Dijon mustard
- 1 clove garlic, minced
- 1/2 teaspoon salt
- 1/4 teaspoon crushed black peppercorns

Direction

- In a large bowl, mix raisins, walnuts, tomatoes, carrot, avocado, orange bell pepper, onion, pear, cabbage, romaine, kale and collard greens together.
- In a glass jar with a lid, combine black pepper, salt, garlic, mustard, chili powder, oregano, honey, vinegar and olive oil. Use lid to cover the jar then shake vigorously to mix the dressing well. Top the salad with dressing and toss till coated.

Nutrition Information

- Calories: 421 calories;
- Total Fat: 27.8
- Sodium: 394
- Total Carbohydrate: 43.8
- Cholesterol: 0
- Protein: 7.5

---

365.   Zesty Quinoa Salad

Serving: 6 | Prep: 20mins | Ready in:

Ingredients

- 1 cup quinoa
- 2 cups water
- 1/4 cup extra-virgin olive oil
- 2 limes, juiced
- 2 teaspoons ground cumin
- 1 teaspoon salt
- 1/2 teaspoon red pepper flakes, or more to taste
- 1 1/2 cups halved cherry tomatoes
- 1 (15 ounce) can black beans, drained and rinsed
- 5 green onions, finely chopped
- 1/4 cup chopped fresh cilantro
- salt and ground black pepper to taste

Direction

- Boil water and quinoa in a pot. Lower heat to medium-low. Put the lid on. Let it simmer for 10-15 minutes, until the water is absorbed, and the quinoa is softened. Let it rest to cool.
- Mix lime juice, olive oil, cumin, red pepper flakes, and a teaspoon of salt in a bowl.
- Mix quinoa, black beans, tomatoes and green onions in a bowl. Drizzle the dressing over the quinoa mix. Toss until coated. Add cilantro. Add salt and pepper to taste. Serve as it is, or store in the fridge to cool.

Nutrition Information

- Calories: 270 calories;
- Sodium: 675
- Total Carbohydrate: 33.8
- Cholesterol: 0
- Protein: 8.9
- Total Fat: 11.5

Index

Conclusion

Thank you again for downloading this book!

I hope you enjoyed reading about my book!

If you enjoyed this book, please take the time to share your thoughts and post a review on Amazon. It'd be greatly appreciated!

Write me an honest review about the book – I truly value your opinion and thoughts and I will incorporate them into my next book, which is already underway.

Thank you!

If you have any questions, **feel free to contact at:** _author@spiritrecipes.com_

Kathy Parker

spiritrecipes.com

Printed in Great Britain
by Amazon

Bond
No.1 for exam success

Verbal Reasoning

Assessment Papers

Challenge

10–11+ years

OXFORD
UNIVERSITY PRESS

Great Clarendon Street, Oxford, OX2 6DP, United Kingdom

Oxford University Press is a department of the University of Oxford.
It furthers the University's objective of excellence in research,
scholarship, and education by publishing worldwide. Oxford is
a registered trade mark of Oxford University Press in the UK
and in certain other countries

British Library Cataloguing in Publication Data
Data available

978-0-19-277833-8

10 9 8 7 6 5 4 3 2 1

Paper used in the production of this book is a natural, recyclable
product made from wood grown in sustainable forests.
The manufacturing process conforms to the environmental
regulations of the country of origin.

Printed in China

Acknowledgements

The publishers would like to thank the following for permissions
to use copyright material:

Page make-up: GreenGate Publishing Services, Tonbridge, Kent
Cover illustrations: Lo Cole

Although we have made every effort to trace and contact all
copyright holders before publication this has not been possible in all
cases. If notified, the publisher will rectify any errors or omissions at
the earliest opportunity.

Links to third party websites are provided by Oxford in good faith
and for information only. Oxford disclaims any responsibility for
the materials contained in any third party website referenced in
this work.

Introduction

What is Bond?

The Bond *Challenge* titles are the most stretching of the Bond Assessment papers, the number one series for the 11+, selective exams and general practice. Bond *Challenge* is carefully designed to stretch above and beyond the level provided in the regular Bond assessment range.

How does this book work?

The book contains two distinct sets of papers, along with full answers and a Progress Chart:

- Focus tests, accompanied by advice and directions, which are focused on particular (and age-appropriate) Verbal Reasoning question types encountered in the 11+ and other exams, but devised at a higher level than the standard Assessment papers. Each Focus test is designed to help raise a child's skills in the question type as well as offer plenty of practice for the necessary techniques.

- Mixed tests, which are full-length tests containing a full range of Verbal Reasoning question types. These are designed to provide rigorous practice, perhaps against the clock, for children working at a level higher than that required to pass the 11+ and other Verbal Reasoning tests.

- Fully explained answers are provided for both types of test in the middle of the book.

- At the back of the book, there is a Progress Chart which allows you to track your child's progress.

How much time should the tests take?

The tests are for practice and to reinforce learning, and you may wish to test exam techniques and working to a set time limit. We would recommend your child spends 50 minutes to answer the 85 questions in each Mixed paper. You can reduce the suggested time by five minutes to practise working at speed.

Using the Progress Chart

The Progress Chart can be used to track Focus test and Mixed paper results over time to monitor how well your child is doing and identify any repeated problems in tackling the different question types.

Focus test 1   Similars and opposites

> Always read this type of question carefully, as most of them will have similar **and** opposite options.

Underline the pair of words which are the most similar in meaning.

Example   come, go   <u>roams, wanders</u>   fear, fare

> More than one set of answers may apply.
> Look for the most appropriate.

1 how, why   in, on   <u>by, near</u>
2 aunt, grandchild   niece, father   <u>brother, sister</u>
3 advance, reduce   <u>enhance, boost</u>   augment, austere
4 comprised, contained persuasive, urgent <u>covert, secret</u>
5 maltreat, misuse   ravage, repair   construct, construe   ○ 5

Find the word that is opposite in meaning to the word in capital letters and that rhymes with the second word.

Example SHARP   front   <u>blunt</u>

6 LOWER   graze   *raze*

7 IMMENSE   cute   _____

> If you cannot find a suitable opposite word, try experimenting with rhyming words.

Find the word that is similar in meaning to the word in capital letters and that rhymes with the second word.

8 PAINFUL   splendour   *tender*

9 IMMATURE   sprung   _____

10 REPULSIVE   towel   _____   ○ 5

Underline the one word in the brackets which will go equally well with each of the words outside the brackets.

Example word, paragraph, sentence   (pen, cap, <u>letter</u>, top, stop)

11 page, chapter, index   (writer, <u>contents</u>, capital, pencil)

12 ramshackle, dilapidated, ruined (castle, <u>messy</u>, derelict, derisive)

13 quiver, flicker, tremble   (arrow, <u>quake</u>, rumble, propel)

14 fervent, zealous, ardent   (<u>vehement</u>, different, stubborn, vicious)

15 malicious, malevolent, vindictive   (rational, <u>spiteful</u>, benevolent, irrational)   ◯ 5

Underline the two words, one from each group, which are the most opposite in meaning.

Example   (dawn, <u>early</u>, wake)   (<u>late</u>, stop, sunrise)

16 (quieten, <u>plentiful</u>, exacting)   (<u>meagre</u>, difficult, pacify)

17 (joyful, <u>juvenile</u>, craggy)   (<u>elderly</u>, youthful, ecstatic)

18 (<u>genuine</u>, fake, obvious)   (certain, constant, <u>bogus</u>)

> Remember: opposites, not similar.

19 (now, <u>simultaneously</u>, instantly)   (concurrently, <u>consecutively</u>, today)

20 (<u>soothe</u>, penitent, blatant)   (<u>aggravate</u>, appease, extend)   ◯ 5

Underline the one word in the brackets that will go with the word outside the brackets in the same way as the first two words go together.

Example   good, better   bad, (naughty, worst, <u>worse</u>, nasty)

21 tired, sleepy   awake, (daytime, alert, bed, up)

22 mystery, solve   task, (perform, relax, brain, reach)

23 affluent, wealthy   destitute, (poverty, impoverished, lonely)

24 dearth, lack   abundance, (choice, nuisance, plethora, prudence)

25 threatened, intimidated   menaced, (terrorised, protected, guarded, patronised)   ◯ 5

Work out the missing synonym. Spell the new word correctly, one letter in each space.

Example   strange   p e __ __ l __ __ r   (peculiar)

26 disjointed   f r a __ __ e n __ __ d

27 glue   f i __ __ __ __ v e

28 magnificent   __ __ __ __ __ n d i d

29 frivolous   i n __ o n s __ __ __ e n t i a l

30 enthralled   m e s __ __ __ i s e __   ◯ 5

Focus test 2   Sorting words

Underline the one word in the brackets which will go equally well with both the pairs of words outside the brackets.

Example   rush, attack   cost, fee   (price, hasten, strike, <u>charge</u>, money)

> Take care. Often each word in the brackets will go well with one lot of words. Look for one that goes well with both.

1 command, control   law, guideline   (measure, rule, govern, call, lead)

2 timepiece, clock   observe, monitor   (time, look, pay attention, regard, watch)

3 cut, trim   slap, smack   (clip, prune, strike, slice, cuff)

4 pale, not dark   gentle, soft   (faint, delicate, flimsy, light, bright)

5 adorable, charming sugary, honeyed   (cute, lovable, sweet, pleasant, fine)

6 movement, flow   modern, present   (push, now, river, current, run)

Find the three-letter word which can be added to the letters in capitals to make a new word. The new word will complete the sentence sensibly.

Example   The cat sprang onto the MO. <u>USE</u>

> For these questions, use the sense of the sentence to help you make a sensible guess.

7 Our weather seems to be wetter and warmer due to CLIE change.

_____

8 My older brother had difficulty finding a MORTE to buy his house.

_____

9 My mother cut the pie into QUERS so we each had a slice. _____

10 Our school GOVERS had a meeting last night. _____

11 Little Monica is too NG to learn to tie her shoelaces. _____

12 All the cars, lorries and BS drove more slowly in the heavy rain.

_____

Rearrange the muddled words in capital letters so that each sentence makes sense.

Example There are sixty SNODCES <u>seconds</u> in a UTMINE <u>minute</u>.

13 Use the BZRAE _____ crossing to FESLAY _____ cross the road.

14 The CCIRKTE _____ match was stopped as it REPODU _____ with rain.

15 The High ETSRET _____ shops were full of sale GRABNSAI _____.

16 The RNHCABSE _____ of the trees were GNIMVO _____ in the wind.

17 The mayor DESRPETEN _____ the medals to the NNWIGIN _____ competitors.

18 To EEVPTRN _____ infection, we must wash our hands GRUELLYAR.

6

Underline two words, one from each group, that go together to form a new word. The word in the first group always comes first.

Example (hand, <u>green</u>, for)   (light, <u>house</u>, sure)

19 (in, post, hill)   (stance, stamp, steep)

20 (thin, fat, part)   (nor, her, nets)

21 (up, ape, can)   (pear, start, down)

22 (care, plea, ease)   (full, sing, sure)

23 (climb, temper, ten) (meant, ate, shone)

24 (off, of, on)   (sit, put, ten)

> Take one word at a time from the left bracket and put it in front of each of the right bracket words.

6

Find a word that can be put either in front or at the end of each of the following words to make new, compound words.

Example	cast	fall	ward	pour	<u>down</u>
25	right	load	roar	stairs	_____
26	corn	pies	pet	per	_____
27	stream	shed	shot	thirsty	_____
28	knock	black	wash	patient	_____
29	false	brother	child	mother	_____
30	dove	pin	back	spin	_____

6

Which one letter can be added to the front of all of these words to make new words?

> Experiment with putting various letters in front of each of the words until you hit on the correct one.

Example <u>c</u>are   <u>c</u>at   <u>c</u>rate   <u>c</u>all

1 __ear   __row   __rip   __lad

2 __utter   __read   __east   __ladder

3 __ridge   __ear   __our   __lower

4 __bout   __board   __round   __tone

5 __lever   __able   __oast   __rate

5

Find the letter that will end the first word and start the second word.

Example drow (<u>n</u>) ought

6 ho (__) ater   8 bette (__) ose

7 gree (__) ever   9 danc (__) ver

4

> Look at the word on the left and find various letters that could finish that word. Then see which one you can use to start the word on the right.

Find the two letters that will end the first word and start the second word.

Example pas (<u>ta</u>) ste

10 becau (__ __) at   12 traff (__ __) icle

11 ga (__ __) ner   13 chur (__ __) icken

4

Find the letter which will complete both pairs of words, ending the first word and starting the second. The same letter must be used for both pairs of words.

Example mea (<u>t</u>) able   fi (<u>t</u>) ub

14 carro (__) iger   burn (__) ry

15 gre (___) ellow   tr (___) et

16 cur (___) est   or (___) end

17 stic (___) nit   struc (___) ing

> If you don't succeed with one pair, look at the other.

◯ 4

Move one letter from the first word and add it to the second word to make two new words.

Example hunt	sip	<u>hut</u>	<u>snip</u>
18 plane	last	_____	_____
19 drift	hear	_____	_____
20 treason	seam	_____	_____
21 platter	pear	_____	_____
22 freight	fed	_____	_____

◯ 5

Add one letter to the word in capital letters to make a new word. The meaning of the new word is given in the clue.

Example PLAN	simple	<u>plain</u>
23 HARD	listened	_____
24 BITER	sour	_____
25 SUCK	glued	_____
26 BOAT	brag	_____

> Keep an eye on the meaning to help you.

◯ 4

Remove one letter from the word in capital letters to leave a new word. The meaning of the new word is given in the clue.

Example AUNT an insect <u>ant</u>

> Approach this in the same way as above but take a letter away rather than add one.

27 PLOTTER	clay worker	_____
28 DANGER	fury	_____
29 PRICKLE	chutney	_____
30 WARY	droll	_____

◯ 4

Now go to the Progress Chart to record your score!   Total ◯ 30

⑨

Focus test 4   Finding words

Underline the two words which are the odd ones out in the following groups of words.

Example   black <u>king</u> purple green <u>house</u>

> Three of the words have something in common. Look for the link.
> Above, it is colours.

1 cleansed	fouled	sullied	unkind	stained
2 hasten	hurry	proceed	drive	accelerate
3 pristine	faultless	blameless	immaculate	sincere
4 knowledgeable	scholarly	academic	understood	impeccable
5 contemplate	reflection	ponder	cogitate	coagulate
6 genius	unanimous	prowess	ambience	brilliance

6

Change the first word of the third pair in the same way as the other pairs to give a new word.

Example   bind, hind   bare, hare   but, <u>hut</u>

7 climb, limb	plate, late	drain, _____
8 boat, beat	moan, mean	load, _____
9 said, aids	shear, hears	slime, _____
10 card, dark	leap, peak	fool, _____
11 plea, leap	near, earn	mite, _____
12 sold, sale	moth, mate	pony, _____

6

Underline the one word in each group that **cannot be made** from the letters of the word in capital letters.

Example   STATIONERY   stone   tyres   ration   <u>nation</u>   noisy

13 CHARACTER	tracer	carer	chart	church	cheat
14 BREAKING	baking	grain	banker	brink	engine
15 PLASTERER	plates	treats	please	pester	repast

3

Underline the one word in each group that **can be made** from the letters of the word in capital letters.

Example CHAMPION   camping   notch   peach   cramp   <u>chimp</u>

16 WANDERING   dangers   dawning   raining   drawer   window

17 DRAGONFLY   lagoon   grandly   found   larder   fondle

18 TROMBONE   noble   broth   number   broom   tremor   (3)

Underline the two words in each line which are made from the same letters.

Example TAP   PET   <u>TEA</u>   POT   <u>EAT</u>

Scan the words quickly and see if a pair jumps out. If you don't see the answer, look through word by word at individual letters.

19 DUSTY   DIRTY   RADIO   RODEO   STUDY

20 BLASTS   STABLE   BLADES   BLEATS   LABELS

21 TOWELS   STROLL   LOWEST   SWELLS   TEASEL

22 PRICES   PRINCE   PRIEST   CENTRE   STRIPE

23 STORES   SOREST   TRUSTS   STROKE   STRAIT

24 TREATS   LEARNT   STEERS   TRAILS   ANTLER   (6)

Find the four-letter word hidden in each sentence. Each begins at the end of one word and ends at the beginning of another word, and can cover two or three words. The order of the letters may not be changed.

Example We had bat<u>s and</u> balls.   <u>sand</u>

Scan quickly to see if you can spot the answer. Check the vowels. Then work through the sentence, word by word.

25 I saw her as I was walking down the road. _____

26 As I am tall, I can reach every book on the shelf. _____

27 Today the weather is cold for the time of year. _____

28 Mudit's hands were cold as he had forgotten his gloves. _____

29 Do not forget that the mayor is coming to school tomorrow.

_____

30 Mondays are my worst days of the week in term time. _____   (6)

Focus test 5 Word progressions

Look at the first group of three words. The word in the middle has been made from the two other words. Complete the second group of three words in the same way, making a new word in the middle.

Example PAIN INTO TOOK   ALSO <u>SOON</u> ONLY

> Look carefully at the first set of three words. Sometimes the pattern is straightforward, as in these:

1	CARE	RENT	WANT	FIRE	_____	MOST
2	PAID	PATH	THIN	STEM	_____	OPAL
3	BARE	CARE	COMB	TIME	_____	MAUL
4	ICED	WISH	WASH	OPEN	_____	BATH
5	LIFE	TAIL	ATOM	DISH	_____	ARCH

5

> Sometimes, letters have to be worked out individually or there are several options with repeat letters:

6	PAIN	PANE	ENDS	CROP	_____	WORK
7	BALL	BABY	BUOY	TIME	_____	SUNS
8	DRAW	WIND	WINK	MUFF	_____	GROW
9	POLE	LATE	TALL	KIND	_____	RACE
10	BOAT	COMB	COME	KNIT	_____	PEAR
11	TREE	BEAT	BOAT	EVIL	_____	MUCH
12	BOAT	ATOM	MATE	FATE	_____	RUSK
13	TOAD	COAT	ACTS	TINY	_____	SPIN
14	EACH	AREA	ARCH	ANTS	_____	BEAK
15	LEAF	FOIL	LION	LASH	_____	DRUM

10

Change the first word into the last word, by changing one letter at a time and making a new, different word in the middle.

Example	CASE	<u>CASH</u>	LASH
16	CRAB	_____	GRUB
17	PRIM	_____	PRAY
18	SAKE	_____	BIKE
19	CAGE	_____	BAKE
20	FIRM	_____	TIRE

> Write down the letters that remain the same. Substitute the remaining letters one at a time.

⬭ 5

Change the first word into the last word, by changing one letter at a time and making two new, different words in the middle.

> Do these in the same way. Work out which letter needs to be replaced first to make a word to lead to the next missing word.

Example	CASE	<u>CASH</u>	<u>WASH</u>	WISH
21	WICK	_____	_____	SUCH
22	ROAD	_____	_____	LARD
23	WIDE	_____	_____	FIRM
24	SOFT	_____	_____	LOUD
25	BOOK	_____	_____	LUCK
26	TALL	_____	_____	TOAD
27	DRIP	_____	_____	TRAY
28	COOL	_____	_____	FOUR
29	LANE	_____	_____	FIND
30	FULL	_____	_____	FAIR

⬭ 10

Now go to the Progress Chart to record your score! Total ⬭ 30

Focus test 6　Substitution and logic

If A = 6, B = 3, C = 11, D = 5 and E = 2, what are the values of these calculations? Write each answer as a letter.

> Replace the letters with numbers and work out the calculations.

1 C − (A + B)　　= _____　　2 DE − (B + E)　　= _____

3 EA ÷ E²　　　　= _____　　4 (D + E + A) − C　= _____

5 BC − CE　　　　= _____　　6 (A + C) − DB　　= _____

7 (C + D) − DE　= _____

7

If T = 4, B = 7, R = 3, A = 1, D = 5 and O = 2, find the sum of these words when the letters are added together.

8 BOAT　_____　　9 TOAD　_____　　10 ROOT　_____

3

Read the first two statements and then underline one of the four options below that must be true.

> **More than one statement may be true, but you must look for the only one that has to be true, given the information.**

11 'Maya loves going on holiday. This year she is going to Greece.'

    A Last year Maya went to France.

    B Maya likes Greece best.

    C Maya is going to Greece.

    D Greece is a popular place to go on holiday.

12 'Beetles are a type of insect. Insects have six legs.'

    A All animals are insects.

    B Beetles are small.

    C Animals have six legs.

    D Beetles have six legs.

2

In a test at school out of a total of 40 marks, Jo got half of them right. Kate got only 14 out of 40, while Tina only made seven mistakes. Anya made 11 mistakes and Dhruv got five more right than Jo.

Before you answer, write down the marks each child received.

13 Who got the most marks? _____

14 Who got less than Dhruv but more than Kate? _____

15 Who got 4 more marks than Dhruv? _____

〇 3

In French, Adrian sat somewhere to the left of Jasmine who sat somewhere to the left of Robert. Saskia and Jasmine did not sit next to each other. Connor sat next to Mo but not Robert. Mo sat somewhere to the right of Jasmine.

1	2	3	Robert	4	5

LEFT   RIGHT

Write a list of the children's names. Then write down their possible places beside the names as you read through sentence by sentence and eliminate the places as you progress.

Where did each child sit?

16 Adrian _____   **17** Jasmine _____   **18** Saskia _____

19 Connor _____   **20** Mo _____

〇 5

SWAFFHAM   SWANLEY   SWANSEA   SWINDON   SWANAGE

If these towns are put into alphabetical order, which comes:

21 second _____   **22** fourth _____

23 If the months with thirty days are put into alphabetical order, which comes second? _____

24 If the days of the week are put into alphabetical order, which day comes directly before Thursday? _____

EMAIL   LETTER   NOTE   TWEET   TEXT

25 Take all the vowels from the words. Put the remaining consonants in alphabetical order. Which comes tenth? _____

〇 4

〇 1

15

MELON   MANGO   ORANGE   LEMON   LYCHEE

26 Write the letters of each word in alphabetical order. Which fruit comes second? _____

27 Using the same words, write their letters in reverse alphabetical order. Ordering these letter groups into reverse alphabetical order, which fruit comes second? _____

28 If the letters of COPENHAGEN are written in alphabetical order, which comes in sixth place? _____

3

Put the letters of each of these colours in reverse alphabetical order:

CRIMSON   AZURE   SIENNA   KHAKI

29 Ordering these letter groups into alphabetical order, which word comes second? _____

30 From your answer to the previous question, what is the third letter?____

2

Focus test 7   Codes

First line up the code with the word:

G R A T E F U L
5 8 7 3 9 2 1 6

Then substitute the letters for numbers.

If the code for GRATEFUL is 5 8 7 3 9 2 1 6.
Encode each of these words using the same codes.

1 GATE _____   2 FURL _____

Decode these words using the same code as above.

3 3 9 7 8 _____   4 3 8 1 9 _____

5 If the code for SHEPHERD is K T O N T O Z L, what is the code for DRESS? _____

6 Using the same code, what does K N O O L stand for? _____

7 If the code for TOMORROW is ↑ ← → ← ↓ ↓ ← ↙, what is the code for WORM? _____

8 Using the same code, what does ↓ ← ← ↑ stand for? _____

9 If the code for FOUNTAIN is c X 9 P 8 e @ P, what does P X 9 P stand for? _____

10 Using the same code, what is the code for INTO? _____   ○10

Match the right word to each code given below.

REED   BARE   BEAR   BARB

11 X V W Z   _____

12 X W Z X   _____

13 Z V V Y   _____

14 X W Z V   _____

> Look for some letters that stand out. In this case, all the words begin with B except one and REED also has double E.

15 Using the same code, what does z v w y stand for? _____   ○5

Solve the problems by working out the letter code. The alphabet has been written out the help you.

A B C D E F G H I J K L M N O P Q R S T U V W X Y Z

Example   If the code for CAT is D B U, what is the code for DOG? <u>E P H</u>

16 If the code for TABLE is V C D N G, what is the code for CHAIR?

_____

17 If the code for PAPER is Q B Q F S, what does C P P L T mean?

_____

18 If the code for HEDGE is F C B E C, what is the code for TREES? _____

19 If the code for SHELF is O D A H B, what does C N E H H mean? _____

Look at the relationship between each of the letters and its code.

○ 4

Example If the code for CAB is 3 1 2, what is the code for EGG? <u>5 7 7</u>

Is there a link in the numbers? A is the first letter, C is the third.

20 If the code for DEAF is 4 5 1 6, what is the code for HIGH? _____

21 If the code for CHAFF is 3 8 1 6 6, what does 1 2 9 4 5 stand for?

_____

○ 2

Example If the code for PEACH is O F Z D G, what is the code for APPLE? <u>Z Q O M D</u>

This time the pattern alternates, letter by letter. If two letters in a word are the same, they are not necessarily the same code letter.

22 If the code for DRESS is E Q F R T, what is the code for SHIRT? _____

23 If the code for TREBLE is V Q G A N D, what is the code for VOICE? _____

Think of the alphabet as a continuous line, so YZ leads to AB etc.

24 If the code for STYLE is Q U W M C, what does T P E V C stand for? _____

25 If the code for MATHS is N B S G T, what does U J L D T stand for?

_____

26 If the code for TIGER is U H H D S, what is the code for ZEBRA?

_____

27 If the code for LAUGH is J Y S E F, what does F Y N N W stand for?

_____

28 If the code for SORRY is R Q Q T X, what is the code for TEARS?

_____

29 If the code for WATER is A Z X D V, what does Z Z P T I stand for?

_____

30 If the code for DIVE is C G S A, what is the code for BEAD?

_____

○ 9

Complete the following sentences in the best way by underlining one word from each set of brackets.

Example Tall is to (tree, <u>short</u>, colour) as narrow is to (thin, white, <u>wide</u>).

> Look for the relationship between the pairs of statements. The second pairing must be completed in the same way.

1 Impulsive is to (pleased, fast, cautious) as impetuous is to (rash, hasty, considered).

2 Curtail is to (restrict, allow, resume) as strike is to (beat, point, retain).

3 Diamond is to (necklace, heart, jewel) as (giant, spade, sports) is to club.

4 Vivid is to (important, bright, tranquil) as dull is to (quiet, muted, severe).

4

Find the missing letters. The alphabet has been written out to help you.

A B C D E F G H I J K L M N O P Q R S T U V W X Y Z

> Do these in the same way. Look for the pattern. Use the alphabet line to help you.

Example AB is to CD as PQ is to <u>RS</u>.

5 FG is to JK as PQ is to _____.

6 ZY is to YX as ON is to _____.

7 MK is to IG as EC is to _____.

8 CN is to GK is to NC is to _____.

9 HL is to JJ as RV is to _____.

10 Ta is to Ya as Za is to _____.

11 AZ is to BY as CX is to _____.

12 UN is to WP as YR is to _____.

8

> Most of the time in these sequences, the letters work independently, like these.

Find the two missing pairs of letters in the following sequences. The alphabet has been written out to help you.

A B C D E F G H I J K L M N O P Q R S T U V W X Y Z

Example CQ   DP   EQ   FP   <u>GQ</u>   <u>HP</u>

> There are two ways of tackling these sequences. Check to see if the letters are working together (as below) or independently as on the previous page.

13 AB   DE   GH   JK   ___   ___

14 ___   ___   WW   RT   MQ   HN

15 RS   VW   ___   DE   ___   LM

16 JH   FD   ___   ___   TR   PN

17 MA   NC   ME   ___   MI   ___

> Look at the letters separately with these ones.

18 GV   ___   CV   AW   ___   WW

19 AK   DI   GG   JE   ___   ___

20 ___   XG   VH   ___   RJ   PK

21 CHu   Plv   CJw   ___   ___   PMz

9

Find the two missing numbers in the following sequences.

Example 2 4 6 8 <u>10</u> <u>12</u>

22 23 25 __ 32 __ 43

23 16 __ 10 __ 4 1

24 21 26 __ __ 47 56

25 2 __ 8 __ 32 64

26 18 17 15 12 __ __

27 __ __ 19 22 24 25

28 20 __ 25 9 30 6 __ 3

29 6 4 6 6 __ __ 6 10

30 17 __ 14 9 __ 10 8 11

> Look for the pattern between the numbers.

> Sometimes, in these questions, the increase/decrease is irregular.

> Check for numbers going up and down. If this is the case, look at alternate numbers.

9

Now go to the Progress Chart to record your score!   Total   30

20

Underline the pair of words which are the most similar in meaning.

Example   come, go   <u>roams, wanders</u>   fear, fare

   1 soar, swoop   create, master   pendulous, dangling

   2 supple, lithe   brandish, banish   wavering, certain

   3 heartening, hastening   callous, heartless   heartfelt, sickening

   4 authorise, sanction   consent, refusal   subscribe, disagree

   5 sympathetic, apologetic caustic, corrosive   combine, contain   5

Find the three-letter word which can be added to the letters in capitals to make a new word. The new word will complete the sentence sensibly.

Example   The cat sprang onto the MO. <u>USE</u>

   6 Dad put the tools back into the garden D. _____

   7 "Ready, SDY, go!" shouted the starter at Sports Day. _____

   8 The puddles were so deep, I got my socks and SS wet.

       _____

   9 I felt guilty because I GOT my friend's birthday. _____

   10 We studied the Tudors in TORY lessons. _____   5

Which one letter can be added to the front of all of these words to make new words?

Example <u>c</u>are   <u>c</u>at   <u>c</u>rate   <u>c</u>all

   11 __pine   __hut   __lit   __will

   12 __lag   __arming   __light   __ill

   13 __ear   __hinge   __rite   __on

   14 __at   __aster   __we   __vent

   15 __ink   __otter   __eel   __udder   5

Underline the two words which are the odd ones out in the following groups of words.

Example black   <u>king</u>   purple   green   <u>house</u>

16 adjacent   beneath   bordering   flanking   contrary

17 support   condone   endorse   scold   castigate

18 tentative   fluent   assured   affluent   glib

19 definite   obstinate   preserve   defiant   perverse

20 assemble   flock   heard   pasture   congregate   (5)

Look at the first group of three words. The word in the middle has been made from the two other words. Complete the second group of three words in the same way, making a new word in the middle.

Example PA**IN** INTO <u>TO</u>OK   ALSO <u>SOON</u> ONLY

21 JUMP   JUST   MOST   DOOR _____ PIGS

22 BRIM   BITE   FATE   SLIP _____ GONG

23 COIN   INTO   TOMB   BAKE _____ EPIC

24 ZIPS   SPIN   CORN   BINS _____ JEEP

25 STUD   DUST   STOP   GLUM _____ USED   (5)

If a = 4, b = 2, c = 7, d = 3 and e = 5, work out the values of these calculations. Give your answer as a letter.

26 $(a + b + c) - (d + e)$ = _____

27 $ae - de$ = _____

28 $(e + c) \div a$ = _____

29 $d^2 - b^2$ = _____

30 $(c - a) + (d - b)$ = _____   (5)

If the code for SHOPPING is 7 6 1 3 3 5 2 4, what are the codes for the following words?

31 PINS   _____   32 SING   _____

33 GOSSIP   _____   (3)

Using the same code, what do the following codes stand for?

34 6 1 3 5 2 4 _____   **35** 6 5 4 6 _____

2

Complete the following sentences in the best way by choosing one word from each set of brackets.

Example Tall is to (tree, <u>short</u>, colour) as narrow is to (thin, white, <u>wide</u>).

36 Deceased is to (finished, lifeless, sensitive) as retorted is to (responded, risked, restricted).

37 Chilled is to (frozen, agitated, cold) as perturbed is to (unflustered, settled, icy).

38 Marmoset is to (France, monkey, trees) as eland is to (herbivore, Africa, antelope).

39 Billowing is to (sagging, sinking, wafting) as dicing is to (hazarding, changing, trembling).

40 Genteel is to (impolite, gracious, respectful) as coarse is to (route, curriculum, refined).

5

Add one letter to the word in capital letters to make a new word. The meaning of the new word is given in the clue.

Example PLAN   simple   <u>plain</u>

41 RIGHT   a scare   _____

42 SPOT   game   _____

43 BEAR   facial hair   _____

44 PEAT   fold   _____

45 CAVE   cut, slice   _____

5

Underline two words, one from each group, that go together to form a new word. The word in the first group always comes first.

Example (hand, <u>green</u>, for)   (light, <u>house</u>, sure)

46 (cub, surf, live)   (bend, board, belt)

47 (white, water, green)   (home, proof, cloud)

48 (back, from, sum)   (wood, were, ward)

(23)

49 (be, in, on)	(gun, end, sett)
50 (cap, free, card)	(land, oil, able)

5

Change the first word into the last word, by changing one letter at a time and making a new, different word in the middle.

Example CASE   <u>CASH</u>   LASH

51 FARM   _____   HARK

52 SNUB   _____   SNAG

53 LIKE   _____   WIFE

54 SNOW   _____   GLOW

55 MANE   _____   MUTE

5

In a sports shop, different types of balls were placed in a row of containers. From the information, work out where each type of balls were.

A	B	TABLE TENNIS	C	D	E

The tennis balls were at one end of the display.

The rugby balls and hockey balls were next to each other.

The cricket balls were next to the table tennis balls and the hockey balls.

The footballs were in the spare place.

56 A = _____   57 B = _____

58 C = _____   59 D = _____

60 E = _____

5

Find the word that is opposite in meaning to the word in capital letters and that rhymes with the second word.

Example SHARP   front   <u>blunt</u>

61 CLEAR   paint   _____

62 KIND   stool   _____

63 FLIMSY   trout   _____

64 TIMID   knave   _____

65 ADORE   wait   _____

5

24

Find the letter that will end the first word and start the second word.

Example drow (<u>n</u>) ought

66 dat (__) very

67 scow (__) avish

68 brea (__) ite

69 spil (__) iver

70 lur (__) ra

5

Underline the one word in each group that **cannot be made** from the letters of the word in capital letters.

Example STATIONERY   stone   tyres   ration   <u>nation</u>   noisy

71 DISTANCE   stand   dance   stain   caned   nasty

72 STARVING   grand   grants   strain   saving   string

73 SQUEALED   sealed   duels   ladles   deals   eased

74 TRUNCHEON   trench   torch   chant   tenor   thorn

75 SPURTING   spurn   trump   grins   spring   grunts

5

If the code for GARDEN is * @ ? # $ ~, what do the following codes stand for?

76 # ? @ *   _____

77 ? @ ~ *   _____

78 ~ $ @ ?   _____

79 * ? $ $ ~   _____

80 * ? @ # $ _____

5

Find the two missing numbers in the following sequences.

Example 2 4 6 8 <u>10</u> <u>12</u>

81 7 17 ___ 37 ___ 57

82 ___ ___ 8 16 32 64

83 33 ___ 27 24 21 ___

84 3 4 6 ___ 13 ___

85 40 32 ___ 19 ___ 10

5

Mixed paper 2

Find the two letters that will end the first word and start the second word.

Example   pas (<u>ta</u>) ste

1 befo (__ __) ason   2 clo (__ __) ere

3 oli (__ __) st   4 lem (__ __) ly

5 prin (__ __) iling

5

If the code for HEALTHY is ? & * % ^ ? ! what do the following codes stand for?

6 ? & * ^   _____   7 ^ * % %   _____

8 % * ^ & % !   _____

3

Using the same code, what are the codes for the following words?

9 ALLY   _____   10 TEETH   _____

2

Underline the one word in the brackets which will go equally well with each of the words outside the brackets.

Example   word, paragraph, sentence   (pen, cap, <u>letter</u>, top, stop)

11 frolic, caper, cavort   (gambol, amble, clatter, electrify, consent)

12 prepare, limb, equip   (furnish, leg, arm, bake, supply)

13 tract, merge, lime   (line, join, sub, mix, juice)

14 follower, silhouette, pursue   (stalk, outline, observer, tracker, shadow)

15 precise, appropriate, honourable (suitable, fair, justice, right, claim)

5

Find the missing letters. The alphabet has been written out to help you.

A B C D E F G H I J K L M N O P Q R S T U V W X Y Z

Example   AB is to CD as PQ is to <u>RS</u>.

16 GH is to KL as OP is to ____.   17 NL is to JH as FD is to ____.

18 EV is to GT as DW is to ____.   19 AQ is to XU as NY is to ____.

20 EC is to DB as CA is to ____.

5

Match these words to the codes below:

FEET   FATE   FINE   NEAT   NINE

21 ⑥⑨⑥⑩ _____

22 ⑤⑨⑥⑩ _____

23 ⑥⑩⑥④ _____

24 ⑤⑩⑩④ _____

25 ⑤⑥④⑩ _____

5

Fill in the crosswords so that all the given words are included. You have been given one or two letters as a clue in each crossword.

26

27

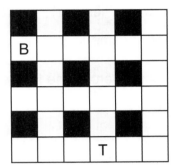

ROLLER   RATHER   RAREST
FATHER   FARMER   THRILL

CRATER   BUTTER   ATTEND
MUTTER   STREET   TRADER

2

Work out the missing synonym. Spell the new word correctly, one letter in each space.

Example strange   p e __ __ l __ __ r   (peculiar)

28 hollow   f__ __ i __ __

29 fragile   __ __ __ t t l __

30 spacious   c a __ __ r __ __ u s

3

Remove one letter from the word in capital letters to leave a new word. The meaning of the new word is given in the clue.

Example AUNT   an insect   <u>ant</u>

31 PRECLUDE   opening   _____

32 SPRING   stem   _____

33 GRAIN   obtain   _____

34 BLEAKER   cup   _____

35 PAINTS   aches   _____   ◯ 5

Underline the two words, one from each group, which are the most opposite in meaning.

Example (dawn, <u>early</u>, wake)   (<u>late,</u> stop, sunrise)

  36 (frail, robust, dumbfound)   (astound, delicate, fickle)

  37 (courage, splendour, cowardice)   (valour, strength, willpower)

  38 (migration, multitude, variety)   (handful, swarm, category)

  39 (distend, disturb, dismember)   (deflate, swell, inflate)

  40 (cushion, cradle, belittle)   (enlarge, bolster, demean)   ◯ 5

Find the two missing numbers in the following sequences.

Example 2 4 6 8 <u>10</u> <u>12</u>

  41 3 6 12 __ __ 96   **42** 1 2 __ 7 __ 16

  43 66 __ 44 33 __ 11   **44** 18 3 18 5 __ __

  45 6 4 __ 3 8 __   ◯ 5

Rearrange the muddled words in capital letters so that each sentence makes sense.

Example There are sixty SNODCES <u>seconds</u> in a UTMINE <u>minute</u>.

  46 Why can't you SECLO _____ the door YLTUQIE

              _____ ?

  47 My REFTHA _____ went to the KTEMASPREUR

              _____ after work.

  48 In the DSYAHLOI _____, Petra NDEJIO _____ a
      swimming club.

  49 The RATIN _____ stopped at many NSATTIOS

              _____ before we reached London.

  50 After KRAEB _____, we have double YRHSOTI _____.   ◯ 5

Underline two words, one from each group, that go together to form a new word. The word in the first group always comes first.

Example (hand, <u>green</u>, for)   (light, <u>house</u>, sure)

51 (bike, round, cart)   (form, board, wheel)

52 (good, bad, by)   (bye, by, buy)

53 (sail, law, fry)   (or, day, year)

54 (were, there, three)   (four, for, fore)

55 (for, in, out)   (cyst, cars, cast)   5

Underline the one word in each group which **can be made** from the letters of the word in capital letters.

Example CHAMPION   camping   notch   peach   cramp   <u>chimp</u>

56 CARDINAL   larder   danger   cranial   cradle   crayon

57 PREJUDICE   priced   justice   prelude   juicier   erudite

58 PARTICULAR   article   carpal   claret   particle   plural

59 GREATNESS   secret   nastier   agrees   stains   treats

60 YESTERDAY   sturdy   Saturday   strays   starry   trades   5

Look at the first group of three words. The word in the middle has been made from the two other words. Complete the second group of three words in the same way, making a new word in the middle.

Example PA<u>IN</u> INTO <u>TO</u>OK   ALSO   <u>SOON</u>   ONLY

61 KERB   BRAN   NAPE   SOUP   _____   AMID

62 TALK   LATE   LOBE   LEFT   _____   NAIL

63 BONE   BEST   DUST   CURL   _____   BLUE

64 MIST   FIST   FISH   BEAM   _____   CALF

65 LIVE   LOVE   VOLE   ZOOM   _____   LIME   5

Read the first two statements and then underline one of the four options below that must be true.

66 'Not all trees have green leaves. The ash tree has green leaves.'

   A Leaves fall from the trees in winter.

   B Not all trees are ash trees.

(29)

C Beech trees may have copper leaves.

D Ash trees may have many leaves.

67 'Animals are either tame or wild. If animals are scared, they may bite.'

   A Wild animals always bite.

   B Tame animals never bite.

   C Wild animals may bite.

   D Wild animals are scared.

   2

68 If the letters in the word NECESSARY were put into reverse alphabetical order, which would be the middle letter? _____

69 Put these words in alphabetical order: sprite, springbok, spirit, sprinkle, springer. Which word is third? _____

70 If the alphabet is written like this: AZ, BY, CX, DW and so on, what is the final pair? _____

   3

Change the first word into the last word, by changing one letter at a time and making a new, different word in the middle.

Example	CASE	<u>CASH</u>	LASH
71	KING	_____	FIND
72	SPOT	_____	HOOT
73	PURR	_____	CURE
74	SIFT	_____ _____	LINE
75	CORK	_____ _____	BOLD

> You'll need two word steps for these questions

   5

If T = 3, L = 6, R = 5, B = 2, E = 1 and A = 4, find the sum of these words when the letters are added together.

76 TABLE _____   77 LABEL _____   78 RABBLE _____

79 Using the same code, if the total of BLADDER is 34, work out the value of D. _____

80 Using the same code, if the total of TRAILER is 31, work out the value of I. _____

   5

Underline the two words in each line which are made from the same letters.

Example TAP   PET   <u>TEA</u>   POT   <u>EAT</u>

81 ASLEEP   PLATER   TAILOR   LAPSES   PLEASE

82 TESTER   TASTER   STREET   STEERS   ASTERS

83 SNAILS   SPINAL   PLAINS   PALEST   STABLE

84 BITERS   STRIPE   PRISES   SPORES   TRIBES

85 BLEEPS   CHAPEL   PEBBLE   PLEACH   BLEACH   (5)

Now go to the Progress Chart to record your score!   Total   (85)

Mixed paper 3

Underline the one word in the brackets which will go with the word outside the brackets in the same way as the first two words go together.

Example good, better   bad, (naughty, worst, <u>worse</u>, nasty)

1 practical, theoretical   unrealistic, (level-headed, unreliable, impractical, spiteful)

2 transmit, impart   conceal, (realise, repress, pilfer, pompous)

3 expert, novice   master, (wizard, solve, teacher, apprentice)

4 stilted, fluent   halting (trotting, standstill, articulate, artificial)

5 provident, prudent   profligate, (upright, dissolute, discreet, waste)   (5)

If $p = 6$, $q = 3$, $r = 2$, $s = 5$, $t = 4$ and $u = 12$, work out the values of these calculations. Write each answer as a letter.

6 $pq - qr$ = _____   **7** $(s + t) - p$ = _____

8 $(u \div t) + (s - r)$ = _____   **9** $p^2 \div q$ = _____

10 $tp - st$ = _____   (5)

Match these codes to the words below.

a y i u   u i a a   a o u i   u o a y

11 STEM   _____   **12** MAST   _____

13 SAME   _____   **14** MESS   _____

15 Using the same code, what does y i o u stand for? _____   (5)

Find the four-letter word which can be added to the letters in capitals to make a new word. The new word will complete the sentence sensibly.

Example They enjoyed the BCAST. <u>ROAD</u>

16 Mrs Blunt took her shopping ET and went off to the shops. _____

17 The little mouse SERED quickly back to its hole. _____

18 That coat is not yours; it BES to Yumi. _____

19 Mr Brown is angry as he is having trouble TING his car. _____

20 On her birthday, Dad gave Mum a huge bunch of ERS. _____ ⑤

Find the letter which will complete both pairs of words, ending the first word and starting the second. The same letter must be used for both pairs of words.

Example mea (<u>t</u>) able   fi (<u>t</u>) ub

21 bit (_) ach   hat (_) very   22 fla (_) ony   tra (_) et

23 qui (_) ip   buz (_) oo   24 sea (_) op   mea (_) win

25 dra (_) host   sin (_) et ⑤

Which one letter can be added to the front of all of these words to make new words?

Example <u>c</u>are   <u>c</u>at   <u>c</u>rate   <u>c</u>all

26 ___art   ___each   ___arched   ___ink

27 ___asp   ___rate   ___lad   ___row

28 ___and   ___ink   ___ate   ___imp

29 ___we   ___sleep   ___cross   ___head

30 ___lock   ___low   ___ear   ___army ⑤

Rearrange the muddled words in capital letters so that each sentence makes sense.

Example There are sixty SNODCES <u>seconds</u> in a UTMINE <u>minute</u>.

31 HTEIG _____ plus seven QLSUEA _____ fifteen.

32 The green CTRIAFF _____ light allows cars to move WFRODSAR _____.

Focus test 1: Similars and opposites (pages 4–5)

1 **by, near** 'By' and 'near' both mean next to.
2 **brother, sister** 'Brother' and 'sister' are both sibling relationships whereas the others are different generations and more removed.
3 **enhance, boost** Both words mean to improve.
4 **covert, secret** Both words mean hidden.
5 **maltreat, misuse** Both words mean to abuse.
6 **raise**
7 **minute**
8 **tender**
9 **young**
10 **foul**
11 **contents** All the words can be found in a book.
12 **derelict** All the words mean in disrepair.
13 **quake** All the words mean to shake.
14 **vehement** All the words mean very keen or passionate.
15 **spiteful** All the words mean vicious or hurtful.
16 **plentiful, meagre** 'Plentiful' means lots of something whereas 'meagre' means in short supply.
17 **juvenile, elderly** 'Juvenile' is young or immature whereas 'elderly' means old.
18 **genuine, bogus** 'Genuine' means real whereas 'bogus' means fake.
19 **simultaneously, consecutively** 'Simultaneously' means at the same time whereas 'consecutively' means one after the other.
20 **soothe, aggravate** 'Soothe' is to calm whereas 'aggravate' is to agitate or excite.
21 **alert** 'Tired' and 'sleepy' both mean drowsy whereas 'awake' and 'alert' both mean ready for action.
22 **perform** You 'perform' a 'task' in the same way you 'solve' a 'mystery.'
23 **impoverished** 'affluent' and 'wealthy' both mean rich whereas 'destitute' and 'impoverished' both mean penniless.
24 **plethora** 'dearth' and 'lack' both mean not having enough of something whereas 'abundance' and 'plethora' both mean having more than enough of something.
25 **terrorised** All of the words mean bullied or pressurised.
26 **fragmented** Both words mean broken up or fall to pieces.
27 **fixative** Both words mean adhesive.
28 **splendid** Both words mean superb, impressive.
29 **inconsequential** Both words mean trivial, thoughtless, unimportant.
30 **mesmerised** Both words mean awestruck, spellbound.

Focus test 2: Sorting words (pages 6–7)

1 **rule** 'Rule' means to govern as well as a regulation or an instruction.
2 **watch** A 'watch' is a clock you wear on your wrist as well as meaning to pay attention to or regard.
3 **clip** 'Clip' means to prune as well as to hit or cuff.
4 **light** 'Light' means a pale colour as well as dainty or flimsy.
5 **sweet** 'Sweet' means lovable and considerate as well as sugary.
6 **current** 'Current' is the flow of water in a river as well as meaning up-to-date.
7 **MAT** climate
8 **GAG** mortgage
9 **ART** quarters
10 **NOR** governors
11 **YOU** young
12 **USE** buses
13 **zebra, safely**
14 **cricket, poured**
15 **Street, bargains**
16 **branches, moving**
17 **presented, winning**
18 **prevent, regularly**
19 **instance**
20 **father**
21 **upstart**
22 **pleasure**
23 **temperate**
24 **often**
25 **up** upright, upload, uproar, upstairs
26 **pop** popcorn, poppies, poppet, popper
27 **blood** bloodstream, bloodshed, bloodshot, bloodthirsty
28 **out** knockout, blackout, washout, outpatient
29 **hood** falsehood, brotherhood, childhood, motherhood
30 **tail** dovetail, pintail, tailback, tailspin

Focus test 3: Selecting letters (pages 8–9)

1 **g** gear, grow, grip, glad
2 **b** butter, bread, beast, bladder
3 **f** fridge, fear, four, flower
4 **a** about, aboard, around, atone
5 **c** clever, cable, coast, crate
6 **w** how, water
7 **n** green, never
8 **r** better, rose
9 **e** dance, ever

EXPANDED ANSWERS

Bond Verbal Reasoning Assessment Papers Challenge 10–11+ years

10 **se** because, seat
11 **in** gain, inner
12 **ic** traffic, icicle
13 **ch** church, chicken
14 **t** carrot, tiger; burnt, try
15 **y** grey, yellow; try, yet
16 **b** curb, best; orb, bend
17 **k** stick, knit; struck, king
18 **e** plan, least
19 **d** rift, heard
20 **t** reason, steam
21 **l** patter, pearl
22 **e** fright, feed
23 **hea̱rd**
24 **bitter**
25 **s̱tuck**
26 **boas̱t**
27 **potter**
28 **anger**
29 **pickle**
30 **wry**

Focus test 4: Finding words
(pages 10–11)

1 **cleansed, unkind** All the other words mean grubby or mucky.
2 **proceed, drive** All the other words mean to rush or speed up.
3 **blameless, sincere** All the other words mean perfect or unspoiled.
4 **understood, impeccable** All the other words mean well-educated.
5 **reflection, coagulate** All the other words mean to consider.
6 **ambiguous, ambience** The other words all mean exceptional talent.
7 **rain** The pattern is to remove the first letter of the first word.
8 **lead** The pattern is to remove the 'o' from the first word and replace it with 'e'.
9 **limes** The pattern is to move the first letter to the end of the word.
10 **look** The pattern is to remove the first letter and replace it with the last letter. The second and third letters remain the same. The last letter is replaced by 'k'.
11 **item** The pattern is to move the first letter to the end, keeping the other letters in order.
12 **pane** The pattern is to change the second letter from 'o' to 'a'. The last letter changes to 'e'.
13 **church** There is only one 'h' and no 'u' in 'CHARACTER'.
14 **engine** There is only one 'e' and one 'n' in 'BREAKING'.
15 **treats** There is only one 't' in 'PLASTERER'.

16 **dawning**
17 **grandly**
18 **broom**
19 **DUSTY, STUDY**
20 **STABLE, BLEATS**
21 **TOWELS, LOWEST**
22 **PRIEST, STRIPE**
23 **STORES, SOREST**
24 **LEARNT, ANTLER**
25 **hero** I saw her as I was walking down **the ro**ad.
26 **ache** As I am tall, I can re**ach e**very book on the shelf.
27 **fort** Today the weather is cold **for t**he time of year.
28 **dash** Mudit's hands were col**d as h**e had forgotten his gloves.
29 **them** Do not forget that **the m**ayor is coming to school tomorrow.
30 **soft** Mondays are my worst day**s of t**he week in term time.

Focus test 5: Word progressions
(pages 12–13)

1–15 Use grids as shown below to help work out the missing word.

1 **REST**

		1	2			3	4
C	A	R	E	W	A	N	T

		1	2			3	4
F	I	R	E	M	O	S	T

2 **STOP**

1	2			3	4		
P	A	I	D	T	H	I	N

1	2			3	4		
S	T	E	M	O	P	A	L

3 **MIME**

	2	3	4	1			
B	A	R	E	C	O	M	B

	2	3	4	1			
T	I	M	E	M	A	U	L

4 **BOTH**

2				1		3	4
I	C	E	D	W	A	S	H

2				1		3	4
O	P	E	N	B	A	T	H

5 RAID

4	3			2	1		
L	I	F	E	A	T	O	M

4	3			2	1		
D	I	S	H	A	R	C	H

6 CROW

1	2		3?	4	3?		
P	A	I	N	E	N	D	S

1	2		3?	4	3?		
C	R	O	P	W	O	R	K

7 SITS

1/3	2			1/3			4
B	A	L	L	B	U	O	Y

1/3	2			1/3			4
T	I	M	E	S	U	N	S

8 FROM

4			1?	1?	2	3	
D	R	A	W	W	I	N	K

4			1?	1?	2	3	
M	U	F	F	G	R	O	W

9 CARD

		1?	4	3	2	1?	1?
P	O	L	E	T	A	L	L

		1?	4	3	2	1?	1?
K	I	N	D	R	A	C	E

10 PEAK

4	2?			1	2?	3	
B	O	A	T	C	O	M	E

4	2?			1	2?	3	
K	N	I	T	P	E	A	R

11 MICE

4?		2?	2?	1		3	4?
T	R	E	E	B	O	A	T

4?		2?	2?	1		3	4?
E	V	I	L	M	U	C	H

12 TEAR

	3	1?	2?	4	1?	2?	
B	O	A	T	M	A	T	E

	3	1?	2?	4	1?	2?	
F	A	T	E	R	U	S	K

13 PINT

4?	2	3?		3?	1	4?	
T	O	A	D	A	C	T	S

4?	2	3?		3?	1	4?	
T	I	N	Y	S	P	I	N

14 BEAN

3	1/4			1/4	2		
E	A	C	H	A	R	C	H

3	1/4			1/4	2		
A	N	T	S	B	E	A	K

15 HURL

4?			1	4?	3	2	
L	E	A	F	L	I	O	N

4?			1	4?	3	2	
L	A	S	H	D	R	U	M

16 GRAB
17 PRAM
18 BAKE
19 CAKE
20 FIRE
21 SICK, SUCK
22 LOAD, LORD
23 WIRE, FIRE
24 LOFT, LOUT
25 LOOK, LOCK
26 TOLL, TOLD
27 TRIP, TRAP
28 FOOL, FOUL
29 LINE, FINE
30 FALL, FAIL

Focus test 6: Substitution and logic (pages 14–16)

1 **E** $11 - (6 + 3) = 2$
2 **D** $(5 \times 2) - (3 + 2) = 5$
3 **B** $(2 \times 6) \div (2 \times 2) = 3$

4 **E** $(5 + 2 + 6) - 11 = 2$

5 **C** $(3 \times 11) - (11 \times 2) = 11$

6 **E** $(6 + 11) - (5 \times 3) = 2$; $2 = E$

7 **A** $(11 + 5) - (5 \times 2) = 6$; $6 = A$

8 **14** $7 + 2 + 1 + 4 = 14$

9 **12** $4 + 2 + 1 + 5 = 12$

10 **11** $3 + 2 + 2 + 4 = 11$

11 **C** You must use only the information you are given. A, B, D may or may not be true. Only 'Maya is going to Greece' must be true in this case.

12 **D** You must use only the information you are given. A, B, C may or may not be true. Only 'Beetles have six legs' must be true in this case.

13–15 A table is the easiest way to sort the information.

CHILDREN	MARKS
Jo	$(40 \div 2) = 20$
Kate	14
Tina	$(40 - 7) = 33$
Anya	$(40 - 11) = 29$
Dhruv	$(20 + 5) = 25$

13 **Tina**

14 **Jo**

15 **Anya**

16–20 A table is the easiest way to sort the information.

Adrian	1, 2
Jasmine	2, 3
Saskia	Not next to Jasmine
Connor	5
Mo	4

Jasmine cannot be 2, otherwise she would be next to Saskia. So, Jasmine = 3, Adrian = 2 and Saskia = 1.

16 **2**

17 **3**

18 **1**

19 **5**

20 **4**

21–22 Arrange the words in a grid to make it easier to put them in the correct alphabetical order.

S	W	A	F	F	H	A	M	1st
S	W	A	N	L	E	Y		3rd
S	W	A	N	S	E	A		4th
S	W	I	N	D	O	N		5th
S	W	A	N	A	G	E		2nd

21 **SWANAGE**

22 **SWANSEA**

23 **June** The months with 30 days in alphabetical order are: April, June, November, September.

24 **Sunday** The days of the week in alphabetical order are: Friday, Monday, Saturday, Sunday, Thursday, Tuesday, Wednesday.

25 **T** ML, LTTR, NT, TWT, TXT = LLMNRTTTTTTTXW

26 **MANGO** Arrange the words in a grid to make it easier to put them in the correct alphabetical order.

MELON	E	L	M	N	O		4th=
MANGO	A	G	M	N	O		2nd
ORANGE	A	E	G	N	O	R	1st
LEMON	E	L	M	N	O		4th=
LYCHEE	C	E	E	H	L	Y	3rd

27 **ORANGE** Arrange the words in a grid – remember reverse alphabetical order.

MELON	O	N	M	L	E		3rd =
MANGO	O	N	M	G	A		5th
ORANGE	R	O	N	G	E	A	2nd
LEMON	O	N	M	L	E		3rd =
LYCHEE	Y	L	H	E	E	C	1st

28 **H** COPENHAGEN = ACEEGHNNOP

29–30 Arrange the words in a grid to make it easier to put them in the correct alphabetical order.

CRIMSON	S	R	O	N	M	I	C	3rd
AZURE	Z	U	R	E	A			4th
SIENNA	S	N	N	I	E	A		2nd
KHAKI	K	K	I	H	A			1st

29 **SIENNA**

30 **N** S N N I E A

Focus test 7: Codes (pages 17–18)

1 **5 7 3 9** G = 5, A = 7, T = 3, E = 9

2 **2 1 8 6** F = 2, U = 1, R = 8, L = 6

3 **TEAR** 3 = T, 9 = E, 7 = A, 8 = R

4 **TRUE** 3 = F, 8 = R, 1 = U, 9 = E

5 **L Z O K K** D = L, R = Z, E = O, S = K, S = K

6 **SPEED** K = S, N = P, O = E, O = E, L = D

7 ↙ ← ↓ → W = ↙, O = ←, R = ↓ = M = →

8 **ROOT** ↓ = R, ← = O, ← = O, ↑ = T

9 **NOUN** P = N, X = O, 9 = U, P = N

10 **@ P 8 X** I = @, N = P, T = X, O = I

11–15 Only one of the words starts with R so 'REED' = z v v y. B must = x and BARB = x w z x. From this, you can work out all the coded letters.

11 **BEAR** x = B, v = E, w = A, z = R

12 **BARB** x = B, w = A, z = R, x = B

13 **REED** z = R, v = E, v = E, y = D

14 **BARE** x = B, w = A, z = R, v = E

15 **READ** z = R, v = E, w = A, y = D

16 **E J C K T** To get from the word to the code, move each letter forwards two places.
17 **BOOKS** To get from the code to the word, move each letter backwards one place.
18 **R P C C Q** To get from the word to the code, move each letter backwards two places.
19 **GRILL** To get from the code to the word, move each letter forwards four places.
20 **8978** The code here is A = 1, B = 2, C = 3, and so on. H = 8, I = 9, G = 7, H = 8.
21 **ABIDE** The code here is A = 1, B = 2, C = 3, and so on. 1 = A, 2 = B, 9 = I, 4 = D, 5 = E.
22 **T G J Q U** The code alternates. To get from the word to the code, move the first, third and fifth letters forwards one place. Move the second and fourth letter backwards one place.
23 **X N K B G** The code alternates. To get from the word to the code, move the first, third and fifth letter forwards two places. Move the second and fourth letters backwards one place.
24 **VOGUE** The code alternates. To get from the code to the word, move the first, third and fifth letter forwards two places. Move the second and fourth letters backwards one place.
25 **TIMES** The code alternates in a different manner. To get from the code to the word, move the first and second letters backwards one place. Move the third and fourth letters forwards one place. Move the fifth letter backwards one place.
26 **A D C Q B** The code alternates. To get from the word to the code, move the first, third and fifth letters forwards one place. Move the second and fourth letters backwards one place. (Think of the alphabet as a continuous line, so XYZ leads to ABC, etc.)
27 **HAPPY** To get from the code to the word, move each letter forwards two places.
28 **S G Z T R** The code alternates. To get from the word to the code, move the first, third and fifth letters backwards one place. Move the second and fourth letters forwards two places.
29 **VALUE** The code alternates. To get from the code to the word, move the first, third and fifth letters backwards four places. Move the second and fourth letters forwards one place.
30 **A C X Z** The code changes. To get from the word to the code, move back one extra place each time: move the first letter backwards one place, the second letter backwards two places, the third letter backwards three places and the fourth letter backwards four places.

Focus test 8: Sequences
(pages 19–20)

1 **cautious, considered** 'Impulsive' and 'cautious' are antonyms, as are 'impetuous' and 'considered'.
2 **restrict, beat** 'Curtail' and 'restrict' are synonyms meaning to limit in the same way as 'strike' is another word for 'beat' or hit.
3 **heart, spade** In cards, 'diamonds' and 'hearts' are the red suits whereas 'spades' and 'clubs' are the black suits.
4 **bright, muted** 'Vivid' and 'bright' are synonyms in the same way that 'dull' and 'muted' are synonyms.
5 **TU** Each letter in the first pair moves forwards four places in the second pair.
6 **NM** Each letter in the first pair moves backwards one place in the second pair.
7 **AY** Each letter in the first pair moves backwards four places in the second pair.
8 **RZ** The first letter in the first pair moves forwards four places. The second letter moves backwards three places. (Think of the alphabet as a continuous line, so YZ leads to AB, etc.)
9 **TT** The first letter in the first pair moves forwards two places. The second letter moves backwards two places.
10 **Ea** The capital letters move forwards five places. The lower case letters remain as 'a'.
11 **DW** The first letter in the first pair moves forwards one place. The second letter moves backwards one place.
12 **AT** Each letter in the first pair moves forwards two places. (When you reach the end of the alphabet, start from the beginning again so, XYZABC)
13 **MN, PQ** The letters are all in alphabetical order with a letter being missed out each time between the pairs.
14 **GC, BZ** The first letter in each pair moves backwards five places. The second letter moves backwards three places.
15 **ZA, HI** The letters are in alphabetical order with two letters being missed out each time between the pairs.
16 **BZ, XV** Each letter moves backwards four places.
17 **NG, NK** The first letters alternate between 'M' and 'N'. The second letter in each pair moves forwards two places.
18 **EW, YV** The first letter in each pair moves backwards two places. The second letters are in an alternating pattern (VWVWVW).
19 **MC, PA** The first letter in each pair moves forwards three places. The second letter moves backwards two places.

EXPANDED ANSWERS

Bond Verbal Reasoning Assessment Papers Challenge 10–11+ years

20 ZF, TI The first letter in each pair moves backwards two places. The second letter moves forwards one place.

21 PKx, CLy The first letters are a repeating pattern: CPCPCP. The second letter in each trio moves forwards one place. The lower case letter moves forwards one place.

22 28, 37 The number added increases by 1 each time: +2, +3, +4, +5, +6.

23 13, 7 The numbers decrease by 3 each time.

24 32, 39 The number added increases by 1 each time: +5, +6, +7, +8, +9.

25 4, 16 The numbers double each time.

26 8, 3 The number subtracted increases by 1 each time: −1, −2, −3, −4, −5.

27 10, 15 The number added decreases by 1 each time: +5, +4, +3, +2, +1.

28 12, 35 This is an alternating pattern. The first, third, fifth and seventh numbers increase by 5 each time. The second, fourth, sixth and eighth numbers decrease by 3 each time.

29 6, 8 This is an alternating pattern. The first, third, fifth and seventh numbers are always 6. The second, fourth, sixth and eighth numbers increase by 2 each time.

30 8, 11 This is an alternating pattern. The first, third, fifth and seventh numbers decrease by 3 each time. The second, fourth, sixth and eighth numbers increase by 1 each time.

Mixed paper 1 (pages 21–25)

1 **pendulous, dangling** Both words mean hanging or sagging.

2 **supple, lithe** Both words mean pliant and flexible.

3 **callous, heartless** Both words mean unfeeling or cold-hearted.

4 **authorise, sanction** Both words mean to allow or permit.

5 **caustic, corrosive** Both words mean acidic or burning.

6 **SHE** shed

7 **TEA** steady

8 **HOE** shoes

9 **FOR** forgot

10 **HIS** history

11 **s** spine, shut, slit, swill

12 **f** flag, farming, flight, fill

13 **w** wear, whinge, write, won

14 **e** eat, easter, ewe, event

15 **r** rink, rotter, reel, rudder

16 **beneath, contrary** All the other words mean neighbouring.

17 **scold, castigate** All the other words mean to agree with.

18 **tentative, affluent** All the other words mean confident or effortless.

19 **definite, preserve** All the other words mean rebellious or disobedient.

20 **heard, pasture** All the other words mean collect or gather.

21–25 Use grids as shown below to help work out the missing word.

21 DOGS

1	2						3	4
J	U	M	P		M	O	S	T

1	2						3	4
D	O	O	R		P	I	G	S

22 SING

1		2					3	4
B	R	I	M		F	A	T	E

1		2					3	4
S	L	I	P		G	O	N	G

23 KEEP

		1	2		3	4		
C	O	I	N		T	O	M	B

		1	2		3	4		
B	A	K	E		E	P	I	C

24 SNIP

	3	2	1					4
Z	I	P	S		C	O	R	N

	3	2	1					4
B	I	N	S		J	E	E	P

25 MUGS

3?	4?	2	1		3?	4?		
S	T	U	D		S	T	O	P

3?	4?	2	1		3?	4?		
G	L	U	M		U	S	E	D

26 **e** $(4 + 2 + 7) − (3 + 5) = 5$

27 **e** $(4 × 5) − (3 × 5) = 5$

28 **d** $(5 + 7) ÷ 4 = 3$

29 **e** $(3 × 3) − (2 × 2) = 5$

30 **a** $(7 − 4) + (3 − 2) = 4$

31 **3 5 2 7** P = 3, I = 5, N = 2, S = 7

32 **7 5 2 4** S = 7, I = 5, N = 2, G = 4

33 **4 1 7 7 5 3** G = 4, O = 1, S = 7, S = 7, I = 5, P = 3

34 **HOPING** 6 = H, 1 = O, 3 = P, 5 = I, 2 = N, 4 = G

35 **HIGH** 6 = H, 5 = I, 4 = G, 6 = H

36 **lifeless, responded** 'Deceased and 'lifeless' both mean dead in the same way as 'retorted' and 'responded' both mean replied.

37 **agitated, unflustered** 'Chilled' means relaxed and the opposite is 'agitated' which means ruffled or uptight. The second pair are antonyms too. 'Perturbed' means distressed whereas 'unflustered' means not bothered.

38 **monkey, antelope** A 'marmoset' is a type of monkey in the same way as an 'eland' is a type of antelope.

39 **wafting, hazarding** 'Billowing and 'wafting' both mean fluttering in the same way as 'dicing' and 'hazarding' both mean risking or gambling.

40 **impolite, refined** 'Genteel' and 'impolite' are antonyms as are 'coarse' and 'refined'.

41 f<u>r</u>ight
42 spo<u>r</u>t
43 bear<u>d</u>
44 p<u>l</u>eat
45 ca<u>r</u>ve
46 surfboard
47 waterproof
48 backward
49 begun
50 capable
51 HARM
52 SNUG
53 LIFE
54 SLOW
55 MATE

56–60 If the cricket balls are next to the table tennis balls and the hockey balls, then the cricket balls must be B or C and the hockey balls either A or D. Because the hockey balls and rugby balls are next to each other, cricket must be C, hockey D and rugby E. The tennis balls must be A as they are at the end of the display, leaving footballs in B.

56 **A = tennis balls**
57 **B = footballs**
58 **C = cricket balls**
59 **D = hockey balls**
60 **E = rugby balls**
61 faint
62 cruel
63 stout
64 brave
65 hate
66 **e** date, every
67 **l** scowl, lavish
68 **k** break, kite
69 **l** spill, liver
70 **e** lure, era
71 **nasty** There is no 'y' in 'DISTANCE'.

72 **grand** There is no 'd' in 'STARVING'.
73 **ladles** There is only one 'l' in 'SQUEALED'.
74 **chant** There is no 'a' in 'TRUNCHEON'.
75 **trump** There is no 'm' in 'SPURTING'.
76 **DRAG** # = D, ? = R, @ = A, * = G
77 **RANG** ? = R, @ = A, ~ = N, * = G
78 **NEAR** ~ = N, $ = E, @ = A, ? = R
79 **GREEN** * = G, ? = R, $ = E, $ = E, ~ = N
80 **GRADE** * = G, ? = R, @ = A, # = D, $ = E
81 **27, 47** The numbers increase by 10 each time.
82 **2, 4** The numbers double each time.
83 **30, 18** The numbers decrease by 3 each time.
84 **9, 18** The number added increases by 1 each time: +1, +2, +3 +4, +5.
85 **25, 14** The number subtracted decreases by 1 each time: −8, −7, −6, −5, −4.

Mixed paper 2 (pages 26–31)

1 **re** before, reason
2 **th** cloth, there
3 **ve** olive, vest
4 **on** lemon, only
5 **ce** prince, ceiling
6 **HEAT** ? = H, & = E, * = A, ^ = T
7 **TALL** ^ = T, * = A, % = L, % = L
8 **LATELY** % = L,* = A, ^ = T, & = E, % = L, ! = Y
9 *** % % !** A = *, L = %, L = %, Y = !
10 **^ & & ^ ?** T = ^, E = %, E = %, T = ^, H = ?
11 **gambol** All the words mean frisk and romp.
12 **arm** An 'arm' is a limb as well as meaning to 'prepare' a weapon, or to 'equip' oneself with something.
13 **sub** All the words can have the prefix 'sub' attached to them: subtract, submerge, sublime.
14 **shadow** A 'shadow' is an outline or someone who tracks another. To 'shadow' is to trail or stalk.
15 **right** 'Right' can mean exact as well as the correct or moral thing to do.
16 **ST** Each letter in the first pair moves forwards four places in the second pair.
17 **BZ** Each letter in the first pair moves backwards four places in the second pair. (Think of the alphabet as a continuous line, so BA leads to ZY, etc.)
18 **FU** The first letter in the first pair moves forwards two places. The second letter moves backwards two places.
19 **KC** The first letters move backwards three alphabetical places. The second letters move forwards four alphabetical places.
20 **BZ** Each letter in the first pair moves backwards one place in the second pair.

EXPANDED ANSWERS

Bond Verbal Reasoning Assessment Papers Challenge 10–11+ years

21–25 Three of the words begin with 'F' therefore F = ❺. 'FEET' must be ❺ ❿ ❿ ❹ because of the double 'E'. 'NINE' must be ❻ ❾ ❻ ❿ because of the repeated '6'. Now you can work out all the codes.

21 **NINE** ❻ = N, ❾ = I, ❻ = N, ❿ = E
22 **FINE** ❺ = F, ❾ = I, ❻ = N, ❿ = E
23 **NEAT** ❻ = N, ❿ = E, ❸ = A, ❹ = T
24 **FEET** ❺ = F, ❿ = E, ❿ = E, ❹ = T
25 **FATE** ❺ = F, ❸ = A, ❹ = T, ❿ = E

26

F	A	T	H	E	R
A		H			A
R	A	R	E	S	T
M		I			H
E		L			E
R	O	L	L	E	R

Check meanings of any words you do not know.

27

	M		S		T
B	U	T	T	E	R
	T		R		A
A	T	T	E	N	D
	E		E		E
C	R	A	T	E	R

28 **futile** Both words mean pointless.
29 **brittle** Both words mean delicate.
30 **cavernous** Both words mean vast.
31 **prelude**
32 **sprig**
33 **gain**
34 **beaker**
35 **pains**
36 **robust, delicate** 'Robust' means hard to break whereas 'delicate' is easily broken.
37 **cowardice, valour** 'Cowardice' means a lack of bravery whereas 'valour' is bravery.
38 **multitude, handful** A 'multitude' is a vast number gathered together whereas a 'handful' is very few.
39 **distend, deflate** 'Distend' is to swell up whereas 'deflate' is to get smaller and shrink.
40 **belittle, bolster** If you 'belittle' someone you demean them. If you 'bolster' them, you build them up, praise them.
41 **24, 48** The numbers double each time.
42 **4, 11** The numbers increase by 1 more each time, +1, +2, +3, +4, +5
43 **55, 22** The numbers decrease by 11 each time.

44 **18, 7** This is an alternating pattern. The first, third and fifth numbers are 18 each time. The second, fourth and sixth numbers increase by 2 each time.
45 **7, 2** This is an alternating pattern. The first, third and fifth numbers increase by 1 each time. The second, fourth and sixth numbers decrease by 1 each time.
46 **close, quietly**
47 **father, supermarket**
48 **holidays, joined**
49 **train, stations**
50 **break, history**
51 **cartwheel**
52 **goodbye**
53 **sailor**
54 **therefore**
55 **outcast**
56 **cranial**
57 **priced**
58 **carpal**
59 **agrees**
60 **trades**
61–65 Use grids as shown below to help work out the missing word.

61 **PUMA**

		2	1	4	3		
K	E	R	B	N	A	P	E

		2	1	4	3		
S	O	U	P	A	M	I	D

62 **FELL**

3	2	1?		1?			4
T	A	L	K	L	O	B	E

3	2	1?		1?			4
L	E	F	T	N	A	I	L

63 **CLUE**

1			2			3	4
B	O	N	E	D	U	S	T

1			2			3	4
C	U	R	L	B	L	U	E

64 **CALM**

	2?	3?	4	1	2?	3?	
M	I	S	T	F	I	S	H

	2?	3?	4	1	2?	3?	
B	E	A	M	C	A	L	F

A8

65 MILE

1?		3?	4?		3?	2	1?	4?
L	I	V	E		V	O	L	E

1?		3?	4?		3?	2	1?	4?
Z	O	O	M		L	I	M	E

66 B You must use only the information you have been given. A, C, D may or may not be true. Only 'Not all trees are ash trees' must be true in this case.

67 C You must use only the information you have been given. A, B, D may or may not be true. Only 'Wild animals may bite' must be true in this case.

68 N NECESSARY in reverse alphabetical order is: YSSRNEECA. The middle letter is 'N'.

69 springer Arrange the words in a grid to make it easier to put them in the correct alphabetical order.

s	p	r	i	t	e				5th
s	p	r	i	n	g	b	o	k	2nd
s	p	i	r	i	t				1st
s	p	r	i	n	k	l	e		4th
s	p	r	i	n	g	e	r		3rd

70 MN AZ, BY, CX, DW, EV, FU, GT, HS, IR, JQ, KP, LO, MN

71 KIND

72 SOOT

73 PURE

74 LIFT, LINT

75 CORD, COLD

76 16 $3 + 4 + 2 + 6 + 1 = 16$

77 19 $6 + 4 + 2 + 1 + 6 = 19$

78 20 $5 + 4 + 2 + 2 + 6 + 1 = 20$

79 8 B = 2, L = 6, A = 4, E = 1, R = 5. Total so far = 18. $34 - 18 = 16$, so each D = 8.

80 7 T = 3, R = 5, A = 4, L = 6, E = 1, R = 5. Total so far = 24. $31 - 24 = 7$, so I = 7.

81 ASLEEP, PLEASE

82 TESTER, STREET

83 SPINAL, PLAINS

84 BITERS, TRIBES

85 CHAPEL, PLEACH

Mixed paper 3 (pages 31–36)

1 levelheaded These are antonyms. 'Practical' is applied knowledge whereas 'theoretical' is learned, academic knowledge. In the same way, 'unrealistic' means not reflected in real life, whereas 'levelheaded' is sensible and reliable.

2 repress 'Transmit' and 'impart' both mean pass on or send. 'Conceal' and 'repress' mean to hide.

3 apprentice An 'expert' is someone who has acquired skill and knowledge through experience, whereas a 'novice' is someone who has just started learning. Similarly a 'master' has mastered a skill whereas an 'apprentice' is learning it.

4 articulate These are antonyms. 'Stilted' means jerky and awkward whereas 'fluent' means smoothly-spoken. 'Halting' has a similar meaning to 'stilted', while 'articulate' means the same as 'fluent'.

5 dissolute Both 'provident' and 'prudent' mean well prepared and careful whereas 'profligate' and 'dissolute' mean wasteful.

6 u $(6 \times 3) - (3 \times 2) = 12$, 12 = u

7 q $(5 + 4) - 6 = 3$, 3 = q

8 p $(12 \div 4) + (5 - 2) = 6$, 6 = p

9 u $(6 \times 6) \div 3 = 12$, 12 = u

10 t $(4 \times 6) - (5 \times 4) = 4$, 4 = t

11–15 MESS must be u i a a because of the double 'S'. Once you know this, you can match all the codes, starting with u o a y = MAST.

11 a y i u S = a, T = y, E = i, M = u

12 u o a y M = u, A = o, S = a, T = y

13 a o u i S = a, A = o, M = u, E = i

14 u i a a M = u, E = i, S = a, S = a

15 TEAM y = T, i = E, o = A, u = M

16 BASK basket

17 CAMP scampered

18 LONG belongs

19 STAR starting

20 FLOW flowers

21 e bite, each; hate, every

22 p flap, pony; trap, pet

23 z quiz, zip; buzz, zoo

24 t seat, top; meat, twin

25 g drag, ghost; sing, get

26 p part, peach, parched, pink

27 g gasp, grate, glad, grow

28 l land, link, late, limp

29 a awe, asleep, across, ahead

30 b block, blow, bear, barmy

31 eight, equals

32 traffic, forwards

33 killed, chickens

34 rained, muddy

35 haircut, older

36 r 4 c 8 L = r, A = 4, S = c, T = 8

37 b r = 4 c = P = b, L = r, E = =, A = 4, S = c, E = =

38 b 4 r = c 8 P = b, A = 4, L = r, E = =, S = c, T = 8

39 LAPSE r = L, 4 = A, b = P, c = S, = = E

40 APPLES 4 = A, b = P, b = P, r = L, = = E, c = S

41 **14, 16** The number added increases by 1 each time: +1, +2, +3, +4, +5.

42 **21, 15** This is an alternating pattern. The first, third and fifth numbers increase by 4 each time. The second, fourth and sixth numbers decrease by 6 each time.

43 **ZZ, QE** The first letters are in a repeating pattern: QRZQRZ. The second letters move forwards five places each time. (Think of the alphabet as a continuous line, so YZ leads to AB, etc.)

44 **JW, OU** The first letter in each pair moves forwards in an increasing pattern: +2, +3, +4, +5, +6. The second letter moves backwards two places each time.

45 **YG, EU** The first letter in each pair moves forwards three places. The second letter moves backwards six places.

46 **58zQ, 23jF** The two-digit numbers decrease by 7 each time. The lower case letters move forwards 2 places each time. The capitals move forwards 3 places each time.

47 **trivial** Both words mean unimportant.

48 **quarantine** Both words mean in (perhaps solitary) confinement

49 **integrate** Both words mean to join in, participate.

50 **ambiguous** Both words mean unclear.

51–55 Try each of the words in the first set of brackets. Do they make sense with any words in the second and third set of brackets? Only one combination of three words make sense. Also check the verb tense.

51 **playground, rain, wet**
52 **Yesterday, visit, hospital**
53 **types, fish, sea**
54 **car, car park, shops**
55 **door, open, inside**
56 **seem** Please **se em**pty your rubbish bin over here.
57 **best** The cat is asleep and doesn't want to **be st**roked.
58 **hall** At break time we played wit**h all** the little children.
59 **tour** We me**t our** new next door neighbours at the party.
60 **very** I could see your swing o**ver y**our garden fence.
61 **p** lay, purge
62 **e** quit, every
63 **s** ample, hairs
64 **r** beak, drove
65 **l** water, fiend
66 **ignorance, cunning** The other words mean learnedness.

67 **artery, muscle** The other words are internal organs of the body.

68 **continuous, welcome** The other words mean agreeable.

69 **stinginess, interest** The other words mean generosity.

70 **pirouette, ballet** The other words mean graceful, supple, elegant.

71–75 The woodlice have to be B, C or D because they are not under the snails (E) and they are below the beetles (A, B or C). The worms must be D or E as they are in the same row as the centipedes. The slugs must be B (as they are in the same row as the earwigs and closer to the centipedes) and the earwigs C (as they are in the same row as the slugs and further away from the centipedes). This means the beetles are A and the woodlice D and the worms E.

71 **C** earwigs
72 **E** worms
73 **A** beetles
74 **D** woodlice
75 **B** slugs
76 **DOTE, DOVE**
77 **DAMP, DAME**
78 **ROSY, ROSE**
79 **LANE, LAND**
80 **MILE, MALE**
81 **chest** A 'chest' can be a coffer or container as well as the upper part of your body.
82 **content** 'Content' (noun) means the matter or gist of something as well as (adjective) happy and at ease.
83 **break** 'Break' means to smash something as well as a gap in activity.
84 **match** A 'match' is a competition as well as a balance or equal. To 'match' means to equal or complement something.
85 **consume** 'Consume' means to destroy or use up (particularly with a fire) as well as to eat.

Mixed paper 4 (pages 36–41)

1 **bran**
2 **stained**
3 **bought**
4 **hated**
5 **stand**
6 **tribe**
7 **flower**
8 **dances**
9 **chives**
10 **solvent**
11 **18** $7 + 3 + 1 + 2 + 5 = 18$
12 **24** $7 + 3 + 1 + 4 + 6 + 3 = 24$
13 **23** $2 + 1 + 5 + 5 + 6 + 4 = 23$

14 **A** You must use only the information you are given. B, C or D may or may not be true. Only 'Madrid is a European city' must be true in this case.

15 **C** You must use only the information you are given. A, B or D may or may not be true. Only 'Robins have feathers' must be true in this case.

16 **brawl, tussle** Both words mean to scuffle or argue.

17 **ditch, abandon** Both words mean to scrap or leave.

18 **remote, isolated** Both words mean inaccessible, out of the way.

19 **brighten, animate** Both words mean to cheer up, revitalise.

20 **morsel, fragment** Both words mean a scrap or piece.

21 **strong**

22 **evil**

23 **cooled**

24 **lean**

25 **sane**

26 **godfather**

27 **background**

28 **into**

29 **overboard**

30 **behold**

31–35 Look at the relationship of STORM to its code. To get from the word to the code, move the first, third and fifth letters forwards one place, and move the second and fourth letters back one place. Then look at the first letters of the words and the first letters of the codes. ZERO must begin with 'A', FOUR and FIVE with 'G' and NINE with 'O'. The next letter moves backwards one place so FOUR = G N V Q and FIVE = G H W D. EIGHT can be worked out in the same way, letter by letter.

31 **FOUR**

32 **NINE**

33 **ZERO**

34 **FIVE**

35 **F H H G U**

36 **blew** Calm down and try explaining in a quiet and sensi**ble w**ay.

37 **them** As the weather worsened, **the m**ountains disappeared from view.

38 **feel** Tea and cof**fee l**eave me feeling thirsty.

39 **chap** We looked carefully for blemishes on ea**ch ap**ple.

40 **this** Conrad lef**t his** jacket on the floor of the gym.

41 **fire** firecracker, fireball, firefighter, fireside

42 **ward** forward, backward, inward, upward

43 **out** outdoors, outback, outlook, outgrow

44 **gold** goldfinch, goldfish, goldsmith, goldfield

45 **man** manage, mankind, manhood, manor

46 **BLOW**

47 **TINT**

48 **GOLD**

49 **HOLE**

50 **HARD**

51 **unattractive, vital** 'Picturesque' (pretty) is the opposite of 'unattractive' (ugly) in the same way that 'trivial' (petty) is the opposite of 'vital'.

52 **forthright, sincere** All these words are synonyms meaning frank, open or truthful.

53 **Zambia, Argentina** 'Zambia' is a country in 'Africa' as 'Argentina' is a country in 'South America'.

54 **anxious, plentiful** 'Carefree' (unconcerned) is the opposite of 'anxious' (concerned) in the same way as 'meagre' (sparse) is the opposite of 'plentiful' (lots of something).

55 **curt, terse** All these words are synonyms meaning crisp, sharp or gruff.

56 **62, 102** The numbers increase by 20 each time.

57 **2, 15** This is an alternating pattern. The first, third and fifth numbers increase by 4 each time. The second, fourth and sixth numbers decrease by 2 each time.

58 **5, 7** This is an alternating pattern. The first, third and fifth numbers decrease by 1 each time. The second, fourth and sixth numbers increase by 2 each time.

59 **15, 8** The number subtracted decreases by 1 each time: –6, –5, –4, –3 –2.

60 **25, 17** The numbers decrease by 4 each time.

61–65 Use grids as shown below to help work out the missing word.

61 **JOKE**

		3	4		1	2	
J	E	R	K		P	O	N	Y

		3	4		1	2	
M	A	K	E		J	O	I	N

62 **EARN**

	1	2	3		4		
C	L	A	W		N	O	T	E

	1	2	3		4		
W	E	A	R		N	A	I	L

63 GRIT

4			1?
H	O	O	F

3	2	1?	
S	I	F	T

4			1?
T	A	N	G

3	2	1?	
I	R	O	N

64 HALO

1	2?	2?	
C	A	L	L

3	4	2?	
S	O	L	D

1	2?	2?	
W	H	A	T

3	4	2?	
L	O	O	K

65 KING

			1
L	I	M	B

2	3	4
Z	O	N	E

			1
H	U	S	K

2	3	4
W	I	N	G

66 **en** broken, enjoy
67 **er** tender, erect
68 **ee** agree, eerie
69 **st** first, stamp
70 **es** buses, essay
71 **preferred** Both words mean much loved or most wanted.
72 **liquify** Both words mean to dissolve or soften.
73 **camouflage** Both words mean to conceal or hide.
74 **beneficial** Both words mean useful or helpful.
75 **particle** Both words mean a fleck, spot or crumb.
76 **V J T Q Y** To get from the word to the code, move each letter forwards two places.
77 **N Y Q R Y** To get from the word to the code, move each letter backwards two places. (Think of the alphabet as a continuous line, so YZ leads to AB, etc.)
78 **YEARN** To get from the code to the word, move each letter backwards three places.
79–80 This is an alternating pattern. To get from the code to the word, move the first, third and fifth letters forwards one place, and move the second and fourth letters backwards one place.
79 **APRIL**
80 **MARCH**

81 **Botswana** Arrange the words in a grid to make it easier to put them in the correct alphabetical order.

B	U	L	G	A	R	I	A		4ᵗʰ
B	E	L	G	I	U	M			1ˢᵗ
B	O	T	S	W	A	N	A		3ʳᵈ
B	O	L	I	V	I	A			2ⁿᵈ
B	U	R	U	N	D	I			5ᵗʰ

82–83 Arrange the words in a grid to make it easier to put them in the correct alphabetical order.

J	A	N	U	A	R	Y			5ᵗʰ
F	E	B	R	U	A	R	Y		4ᵗʰ
M	A	R	C	H					8ᵗʰ
A	P	R	I	L					1ˢᵗ
M	A	Y							9ᵗʰ
J	U	N	E						7ᵗʰ
J	U	L	Y						6ᵗʰ
A	U	G	U	S	T				2ⁿᵈ
S	E	P	T	E	M	B	E	R	12ᵗʰ
O	C	T	O	B	E	R			11ᵗʰ
N	O	V	E	M	B	E	R		10ᵗʰ
D	E	C	E	M	B	E	R		3ʳᵈ

82 **November**
83 **January**
84 **8** spring, s<u>u</u>mmer, <u>au</u>tumn, w<u>i</u>nter
85 **Z** (8 × 4) − (12 ÷ 2) = 26, 26 = Z

Mixed paper 5 (pages 41–46)

1–5 Try each of the words in the first set of brackets. Do they make sense with any words in the second and third set of brackets? Only one combination of three words makes sense.
1 **leave, in, place**
2 **watched, programme, cities**
3 **shining, brightly, window**
4 **book, reading, exciting**
5 **shop, rotten, buy**
6 **same**
7 **beam**
8 **inner**
9 **low**
10 **vanish**
11 **autumn, leaves**
12 **bonfire, night**
13 **football, sport**
14 **pencil, working**
15 **capital, England**

16–20 Look at the relationship between the word and the code. The number matches the letter's place in the alphabet.

A	B	C	D	E	F	G	H	I
1	2	3	4	5	6	7	8	9

16 4 9 3 5 D = 4, I = 9, C = 3, E = 5
17 6 1 3 5 4 F = 6, A = 1, C = 3, E = 5, D = 4
18 2 1 4 7 5 B = 2, A = 1, D = 4, G = 7, E = 5
19 HEDGE 8 = H, 5 = E, 4 = D, 7 = G, 5 = E
20 CABBAGE 3 = C, 1 = A, 2 = B, 2 = B, 1 = A, 7 = G, 5 = E
21 n yearn, nor
22 h bush, horror
23 l veal, love
24 d heed, door
25 s was, wan
26 ROSE
27 SIRE
28 SHIP
29 HEAR
30 THIN
31 ignite There is no 'E' in 'LIGHTNING'.
32 dragon There is no 'O' in 'GRANDEUR'.
33 drained There is only one 'D' in 'SPRAINED'.
34 crusts There is only one 'S' in 'CREATURES'.
35 shelter There is no 'R' and only one 'E' in 'BATTLESHIP'.
36–40 A table is the easiest way to sort the information, like this:

A	24
B	35 − 17 = 18
C	22 − 10 = 12
D	18 + 4 = 22
E	24 ÷ 2 = 12

36 22
37 A
38 B
39 24
40 D
41 astute, shrewd 'Hasty' and rash are synonyms meaning thoughtless or impulsive in the same way as 'astute' and 'shrewd' are synonyms meaning wise or smart.
42 courteous, genteel 'Courteous' and 'gracious' both mean well mannered in the same way as 'genteel' and 'elegant' both mean refined and cultured.
43 saturated, waterlogged 'Arid' and 'saturated' are antonyms in the same way as 'parched' and 'waterlogged'. The first word in each pair means very dry. The second means very wet.

44 bridge, agonise 'Connect' and 'bridge' both mean to link or join in the same way as 'fret' and 'agonise' both mean to worry.
45 perturbed, composed 'Tense' and 'untroubled' are antonyms in the same way as 'perturbed' and 'composed'. The first word in each pair means worried. The second means relaxed and calm.
46–48 TREADING in alphabetical order is ADEGINRT.
46 D
47 G
48 R
49–50 CHAMPION in alphabetical order is ACHIMNOP.
49 N
50 H
51 LICE slice
52 BEAR beard
53 FULL hopefully
54 RAIN rainfall
55 RAGE garage
56 C B P M W This is an alternating pattern. To get from the word to the code, move the first, third and fifth letters backwards two places. Move the second and fourth letters forwards one place.
57 NIGHT This is an alternating pattern. To get from the code to the word, move the first, third and fifth letters forwards two places. Move the second and fourth letters backwards one place.
58 AWAKE This is an alternating pattern. To get from the code to the word, move the first, third and fifth letters forwards one place. Move the second and fourth letters backwards one place. (Think of the alphabet as a continuous line, so YZ leads to AB, etc.)
59 M J F I S This is an alternating pattern. To get from the word to the code, move the first, third and fifth letters backwards one place. Move the second and fourth letters forwards one place.
60 Q N T S X To get from the word to the code, move each letter forwards five places.
61 reckless, cautious 'Reckless' is irresponsible whereas 'cautious' is thoughtful and careful.
62 elusive, obvious 'Elusive' means hard to pin down, subtle whereas 'obvious' means clear and describable.
63 linger, leave 'Linger' means to stay longer whereas 'leave' means to depart.
64 colossal, minuscule 'Colossal' is vast whereas 'minuscule' is tiny.
65 tragedy, triumph A 'tragedy' is a disaster whereas a 'triumph' is a great success.

66 **fore** The pattern is to replace the last letter of the first word with 'e'.

67 **wire** The pattern is to replace the third letter of the first word with 'p'.

68 **hub** The pattern is to start the second word with 'hu' and then add the third letter of the first word.

69 **suck** The pattern is to replace the 'a' of the first word with 'u'.

70 **dare** The pattern is to start with the fourth letter of the first word, add the third letter, and end with the first and second letters.

71–75 Use grids as shown below to help work out the missing word.

71 **CHIP**

		1	2		3	4	
B	A	T	H	W	I	N	D

		1	2		3	4	
R	I	C	H	W	I	P	E

72 **BRED**

		2	1			3	4
F	O	R	T	S	L	I	M

		2	1			3	4
K	E	R	B	S	P	E	D

73 **MEAN**

	2	3?	1	4	3?		
P	E	A	R	D	A	M	P

	2	3?	1	4	3?		
G	E	R	M	N	A	V	Y

74 **HUSH**

4?			1	2	3		4?
E	N	D	S	H	O	M	E

4?			1	2	3		4?
H	I	G	H	U	S	E	D

75 **CHAT**

		1	2?	4		3	2?
K	I	T	E	M	O	R	E

		1	2?	4		3	2?
M	U	C	H	T	R	A	P

76 **rear** Whe**re ar**e your clean clothes, Javin?

77 **mesh** Tania will not be allowed to co**me sh**opping with you on Friday.

78 **then** A train clattered by noisily through **the n**ew level crossing.

79 **tone** Paul pu**t one** of his paintings in an art exhibition.

80 **sour** A squirrel visit**s our** bird table to gobble all the bird food.

81 **UA, DD** The first letters are in a repeating pattern: LUDLUD. The second letter moves forwards three places.

82 **EW, ZZ** The first letter moves backwards five places. The second letter moves forwards three places.

83 **CZ, GX** The first letter moves forwards two places. The second letter moves backwards one place.

84 **UO, CI** The first letter moves forwards four places. The second letter moves backwards three places.

85 **sUs, yCr** The first letter moves forwards three places. The capital letter moves forwards four places. The final letters are in a repeating pattern: rsqrsq.

Mixed paper 6 (pages 46–51)

1–5 Use grids as shown below to help work out the missing word.

1 **LEAF**

4	2/3		1		2/3		
P	O	S	H	S	O	R	T

4	2/3		1		2/3		
F	A	I	L	F	E	R	N

2 **WASP**

	2	3		1			4
B	U	S	Y	M	I	N	T

	2	3		1			4
G	A	S	H	W	E	E	P

3 **DIRT**

			1?	4	2/3	2/3	1?
L	O	O	K	P	E	E	K

			1?	4	2/3	2/3	1?
L	O	A	D	T	R	I	P

4 **EACH**

4	2?	2?				3	1
R	E	E	L	L	O	A	F

4	2?	2?				3	1
H	O	A	X	N	I	C	E

5 PLEA

			4		3	2	1
S	N	A	P	B	I	R	D

			4		3	2	1
P	U	M	A	H	E	L	P

6

D	E	B	A	T	E
O	■	O	■	A	■
U	N	R	O	L	L
B	■	R	■	K	■
L	O	O	K	E	D
E	■	W	■	D	■

> Check meanings of any words you do not know.

7

T	A	L	E	N	T
A	■	E	■	I	■
V	O	T	I	N	G
E	■	H	■	E	■
R	E	A	C	T	S
N	■	L	■	Y	■

8–10 PICTURES in alphabetical order is CEIPRST.

8 **C**

9 **P**

10 **R**

11 **JO, AU** The first letter in each pair moves backwards three places. The second letter moves forwards two places. (Think of the alphabet as a continuous line, so YZ leads to AB, etc.)

12 **YL, CJ** The first letter in each pair moves forwards in an increasing pattern: +1, +2, +3, +4, +5 places. The second letter moves backwards two places.

13 **Fx, Rr** The first letters are in a repeating pattern: FWRFWR. The second letter moves forwards four places.

14 **HB, EZ** The first letter in each pair moves backwards three places. The second letter moves backwards two places.

15 **VY, PS** Each letter moves forwards ten places.

16 **SNOWY** This is an alternating pattern. To get from the code to the word, move the first, third and fifth letters backwards two places. Move the second and fourth letters forwards one place.

17 **H Z U D T** This is an alternating pattern. To get from the word to the code, move the first, third and fifth letters forwards one place. Move the second and fourth letters backwards one place.

18 **ROADS** To get from the code to the word, move each letter backwards one place.

19 **Z E B T P** To get from the code to the word, move each letter backwards three places.

20 **R T R H N** This is an alternating pattern. To get from the word to the code, move the first, third and fifth letters forwards two places. Move the second and fourth letters backwards one place.

21 **4, 4** This is an alternating pattern. The first, third, fifth, seventh numbers decrease by 2 each time. The second, fourth, sixth and eighth numbers increase by 1 each time.

22 **1, 2** The number added increases by 1 each time: +1, +2, +3, +4, +5, +6, +7.

23 **15, 27** The numbers increase by 6 each time.

24 **26, 26** This is an alternating pattern. The first, third, fifth and seventh numbers increase by 5 each time. The second, fourth, sixth and eighth numbers decrease by 3 each time.

25 **51, 60** This is an alternating pattern. For the first, third, fifth and seventh numbers, the number subtracted decreases by 1 each time: −9, −8, −7. The second, fourth, sixth and eighth numbers decrease by 3 each time.

26 **V** $(3 + 5) − (10 − 4) = 2$, $2 = V$

27 **W** $((4 \times 4) − (3 \times 3)) + 3 = 10$, $10 = W$

28 **Y** $(5 + 3 + 10 + 2) \div 4 = 5$, $5 = Y$

29 **Z** $(2 \times 5 \times 3) \div 10 = 3$, $3 = Z$

30 **W** $(3 \times 10) − (5 \times 4) = 10$, $10 = W$

31–35 A table is the easiest way to sort the information, like this:

	hat	scarf	flag	whistle
A	✓	x		✓
B	✓	x	✓	
C	✓	✓		✓
D	✓		✓	
E	✓	✓		
F	✓	✓	✓	

31 **A**

32 **2**

33 **D**

34 **C**

35 **one**

36 **pod** The pattern is to remove the third letter.

37 **grave** The pattern is to start with the first two letters of the first word and add '-ave'.

38 **won** The pattern is to reverse the letters of the first word.

39 **bake** The pattern is to remove 'oo' and replace it with 'a', then add 'e' as the final letter.

40 **than** The pattern is to start with the final two letters of the first word and add the suffix '-an'.
41 **charm, allure** Both words mean attraction.
42 **notable, significant** Both words mean remarkable or important.
43 **insane, senseless** Both words mean mad or ridiculous.
44 **sentimental, romantic** Both words mean emotional or starry-eyed.
45 **indulge, gratify** Both words mean to treat, pamper or spoil.
46 **side** outside, inside, beside, aside
47 **high** highlighter, highland, highball, highway
48 **dog** underdog, watchdog, doghouse, hotdog
49 **horse** horseplay, horsefly, horsepower, horseback
50 **slip** slipstream, slipper, slipping, slipway
51 **over** 'Done' and 'finished' mean completed or 'over'; six balls in cricket are called an 'over'.
52 **pet** A 'domestic animal' is a 'pet'; to 'stroke' or 'pat' is to 'pet'.
53 **quick** 'Quick' can mean 'fast' and 'swift'; it can also mean 'intelligent' or 'sharp'.
54 **incense** 'Incense' can mean to annoy greatly; 'incense' is also a 'perfume' that is often burned.
55 **lead** A 'lead' is a restraint for, say, a dog as well as a verb meaning to direct or be in charge.
56 **e** bacon, snipe
57 **c** with, chair
58 **b** stale, bringing
59 **a** chin, bread
60 **t** nigh, meant
61 **height** 'Wide' is the adjective that goes with the noun 'width'. 'High' is the adjective that goes with the noun 'height'.
62 **lessening** 'Replete' is full and 'filling' is on the way to being full. 'Least' is the smallest and 'lessening' is on the way to being the least.
63 **unoccupied** 'Flexible' and 'supple' both mean bendy and lithe. 'Vacant' and 'unoccupied' both mean not taken, empty.
64 **trap** Reverse 'tops' and it becomes 'spot'. Reverse 'part' and it becomes 'trap'.
65 **durable** 'Durable' is an antonym of 'brittle' in the same way that 'robust' is an antonym of 'fragile'. 'Durable' and 'robust' mean tough and sturdy whereas 'fragile' and 'brittle' mean easily broken.
66 **LAMENT, MENTAL**
67 **REPORT, PORTER**
68 **DRIEST, STRIDE**
69 **LATENT, TALENT**
70 **LEADER, DEALER**
71 **HARD**
72 **TALE**
73 **DISH**
74 **COME**
75 **DEAD**
76 **B B U F R** This is an alternating pattern. To get from the word to the code, move the first, third and fifth letters backwards one place. Move the second and fourth letters forwards one place.
77 **STEEP** To get from the code to the word, move the first, third and fifth letters forwards one place. Move the second and fourth letters backwards one place.
78 **F S Z J M** To get from the word to the code, move the first, third and fifth letters backwards one place. Move the second and fourth letters forwards one place.
79 **STALL** To get from the code to the word, move the first, third and fifth letters forwards one place. Move the second and fourth letters backwards one place.
80 **E V Y A X** To get from the word to the code, move the first, third and fifth letters backwards one place. Move the second and fourth letters forwards one place.
81 **they** To tremendous applause, **the y**oung players ran onto the pitch.
82 **down** We apologised when we broke the glass in the classroom win**dow n**ext to the playground.
83 **reel** I counted th**ree l**arge fish swimming slowly round the pond.
84 **oral** After working f**or a l**ong time in the baking sun, we had a break.
85 **chop** Please leave the door to the chur**ch op**en, when you leave.

Mixed paper 7 (pages 52–56)

1 **stale** The pattern is to move the 'e' to the end of the word.
2 **cat** The pattern is to use the first and last letters of the first word and put an 'a' between them.
3 **trait** The pattern is to remove the final letter of the first word and replaced it with 't'.
4 **to** The pattern is to start with the final letter of the first word, then add the second letter of the first word.
5 **chum** The pattern is to start with the third and fourth letters of the first word, then add the second letter and finally the first letter.
6 **way** A 'road' or 'path' can be described as a 'way'; a 'way' is also a 'method' or 'style' of doing something.

7 **light** 'Light' can mean 'pale' and 'faint'; a 'light' can also be a 'lamp' or a 'lantern'.

8 **pine** To 'pine' means to yearn or 'long for' or 'miss'; a 'pine' is also a type of coniferous tree.

9 **slack** 'Slack' means careless or 'slapdash' and 'lax'; it can also mean 'limp' and 'loose'.

10 **wind** 'Wind' is a current of air, or movement of air. Pronounced with a long 'i', and as a verb, it means to 'twist' or 'turn'.

11 **great** 'Great' means considerably above the average or 'excellent' and 'very good'. It can also mean very large or 'enormous' or 'vast'.

12 **desert** A 'desert' is a waterless place; to 'desert' means to 'abandon', 'forsake' or leave.

13 **direct** 'Direct' means straightforward, 'candid' or 'frank'; 'to direct' means to be in charge and issue instructions.

14 **meticulous, slapdash** 'Meticulous' means very careful whereas 'slapdash' means careless.

15 **scarce, abundant** 'scarce' means having too little, whereas 'abundant' means having plenty.

16–20 To get from the code to the word, move the first and third letters backwards one place. Move the second and fourth letters forwards one place.

16 **HAND** I = H, Z = A, O = N, C = D

17 **HARD** I = H, Z = A, S = R, C = D

18 **DASH** E = D, Z = A, T = S, G = H

19 **SAND** T = S, Z = A, O = N, C = D

20 **S Z T G** To get from the word to the code, move the first and third letters forwards one place. Move the second and fourth letters backwards one place. R = S, A = Z, S = T, H = G

21 **TALE, TALL**

22 **RIFT, RAFT**

23 **SHOW, SLOW**

24 **SPUR, SPUN**

25 **HARE, HIRE**

26 **disperse, scatter** Both words mean to separate or disband.

27 **responsive, alert** Both words mean reactive.

28 **permeate, saturate** Both words mean to soak or fill.

29 **indolent, slothful** Both words mean lazy or idle.

30 **fragrant, aromatic** Both words mean pleasantly scented.

31 **FF, JH** The first letter in each pair moves forwards two places. The second letter moves forwards one place.

32 **ZE, BE** The first letter in each pair moves forwards one place. The second letter moves forwards two places. (Think of the alphabet as a continuous line, so YZ leads to AB, etc.)

33 **TB, KA** The first letters are in a repeating pattern: TKTKTK. The second letter in each pair moves backwards one place.

34 **ZX, XA** The first letter in each pair moves backwards two places. The second letter moves forwards three places.

35 **ZA, AZ** The first letter in each pair moves forwards one place. The second letter moves backwards one place.

36 **care** carefree, careless, caretaker, careworn

37 **for** forbid, forgive, forgot, format

38 **house** household, housebreak, treehouse, housekeeper

39 **cart** cartridge, cartwheel, carton, carthorse

40 **leg** legend, legroom, legwork, legally

41 **E R A H V** To get from the word to the code, move each letter forwards three places.

42 **O N T D T** To get from the word to the code, move the first, third and fifth letters forwards one place. Move the second and fourth letters backwards one place.

43 **GIRLS** To get from the code to the word, move the first, third and fifth letters backwards two places. Move the second and fourth letters forwards one place.

44 **VILLA** To get from the code to the word, move each letter forwards three places.

45 **STRAW** To get from the code to the word, move each letter backwards four places.

46–47 Arrange the words in a grid to make it easier to put them in the correct alphabetical order.

S	T	O	R	K			3RD
S	W	A	L	L	O	W	4TH
S	W	I	F	T			5TH
S	P	A	R	R	O	W	1ST
S	T	A	R	L	I	N	G	2ND

46 **STORK**

47 **SWIFT**

48–50 BREAKING = ABEGIKNR

48 **A**

49 **G**

50 **N**

51 **RICK** cricket

52 **ABLE** table

53 **ICED** sliced

54 **RAKE** brakes

55 **EDGE** hedge

56 **bust** We went by **bus t**o the Houses of Parliament.

57 **also** Sixty-six divided by sixty-six equ**als o**ne.

58 **tour** We need to collec**t our** tickets from the bus station.

59 **them** The trees by the lake dropped their leaves into **the m**urky water.

60 **omit** I recycled my old jumper by turning it int**o mit**tens.
61 **distracted** 'Spellbound' and 'bored' are antonyms, in the same way as are 'enthralled' and 'distracted'.
62 **wrench** 'Grasp' and 'clutch' mean to grab. In the same way, 'yank' and 'wrench' mean to pull or twist violently.
63 **rotating** All the words mean turning or circling.
64 **populated** Antonyms are the key here. 'Mundane' means ordinary whereas 'bizarre' is peculiar. 'Sparse' means scarce whereas 'populated' has people in it.
65 **sultry** All the words mean clammy, damp, steamy.
66 **illustrate** Both words mean to show or describe.
67 **grief** Both words mean intense sorrow.
68 **clandestine** Both words mean furtive or surreptitious.
69 **apparel** Both words mean attire, clothing, dress.
70 **claustrophobic** Both words mean triggering a fear of being shut in.
71 **th** youth, than
72 **ex** flex, exit
73 **se** bruise, seal
74 **ea** area, earth
75 **al** opal, allow
76 **XW** Each letter in the first pair moves backwards two places.
77 **ID** Each letter in the first pair moves forwards one place.
78 **EH** The first letter moves backwards one place. The second letter moves forwards one place.
79 **MN** The first letter moves forwards three places. The second letter moves forwards four places.
80 **JQ** The first letter moves forwards one place. The second letter moves backwards one place.
81–85 Use grids as shown below to help work out the missing word.
81 **NODE**

	2		4		1			3
H	A	R	E		L	O	O	K

	2		4		1			3
B	O	N	E		N	E	E	D

82 **SALE**

1?	2	3			1?			4
V	A	S	E		V	E	N	T

1?	2	3			1?			4
S	A	L	T		F	A	Z	E

83 **SITE**

		2			1	3	4	
Q	U	I	Z		P	L	E	A

		2			1	3	4	
T	H	I	N		S	T	E	W

84 **FROG**

1?	2	3			1?			4
C	O	R	N		C	A	S	E

1?	2	3			1?			4
F	R	O	M		W	I	N	G

85 **SUCH**

3		1?	4			2		1?
T	I	M	E		C	A	L	M

3		1?	4			2		1?
C	A	S	H		B	U	S	H

Mixed paper 8 (pages 57–62)

1 **X Z U D S** To get from the word to the code, move the first, third and fifth letters forwards one place. Move the second and fourth letters backwards one place. (Think of the alphabet as a continuous line, so YZ leads to AB, etc.)
2 **HOSES** To get from the code to the word, move each letter forwards two places.
3 **BLACK** To get from the code to the word, move each letter backwards two places.
4 **Q J Y F C** To get from the word to the code, move the first, third and fifth letters backwards two places. Move the first and fourth letters forwards two places.
5 **G M P P E** To get from the words to the code, move each letter forwards one place.
6 **wing** Another name for a 'bird limb' is a 'wing'. In some team games, like football, rugby, hockey, a 'wing' is a player who plays near the edge of a pitch.
7 **blue** 'Feeling sad' is sometimes described as feeling 'blue; 'blue' is also a colour.

8 **hide** A 'hide' is another name for an 'animal skin'; to 'hide' means to 'shroud', 'conceal', 'camouflage' or 'disguise'.

9 **bolt** A 'bolt' can fasten a door with a sliding piece of metal; to 'bolt' means to 'run away' or 'escape' and also mean to eat food very quickly.

10 **key** 'Key' can mean 'vital', 'critical' or very important; a 'key' is also used to open a lock.

11 **FAME, FUME**

12 **TWIN, THIN**

13 **WASH, WISH**

14 **FACE, FADE**

15 **MOON, NOON**

16 **DE** Each letter in the first pair moves backwards two places in the second pair.

17 **DW** The first letter moves forwards one place. The second letter moves backwards one place.

18 **DH** The first letter moves forwards two places. The second letter moves forwards one place.

19 **VB** The first letter moves backwards two places. The second letter moves forwards two places.

20 **WB** Each letter moves forwards one place.

21 **R T F D O** To get from the word to the code, move the first, third and fifth letters forwards one place. Move the second and fourth letters backwards one place.

22 **H T W K V** To get from the word to the code, move each letter forwards two places.

23 **JEANS** To get from the code to the word, move each letter forwards four places.

24 **Q X M S B** To get from the word to the code, move the first, third and fifth letters backwards two places. Move the second and fourth letters forwards one place.

25 **LARGE** To get from the code to the word, move the first, third and fifth letters backwards two places. Move the second and fourth letters forwards one place.

26 **ate** The pattern is to start with the second letter of the first word, then add the fourth and fifth letters.

27 **lime** The pattern is to start with the third letter, then add the second and fourth letters and put an '-e' on the end.

28 **keep** The pattern is to double the 'e', then discard the last letter.

29 **slit** The pattern is to reverse the order of the second and third letters.

30 **overt** The pattern is to use the last four letters of the first word and add 't' to the end.

31 **sparkling** Antonyms are the key here. A 'clear' sky is opposite to a 'cloudy' sky. 'Still' water is ordinary or flat, whereas 'sparkling' water is bubbly.

32 **play** You 'fight' a 'battle' in the same way that you 'play' a 'game'.

33 **uneven** Antonyms again here. 'Patterned' cloth is decorated whereas 'plain' cloth has no pattern. 'Flat' is level whereas 'uneven' is varying in level.

34 **bruise** If you 'cut' your skin, it will 'bleed'. If you 'bump' your skin, it will 'bruise'.

35 **cut** The pattern here is to remove the second and fourth letters of the first word and this will create the second word.

36–40 Use grids as shown below to help work out the missing word.

36 **OMEN**

	3?	1	2		3?	4	
C	A	M	E	B	A	T	H

	3?	1	2		3?	4	
B	O	O	M	B	E	N	T

37 **WEEP**

	2	3	4	1			
B	A	C	K	J	U	R	Y

	2	3	4	1			
D	E	E	P	W	I	N	G

38 **VEST**

	2	3	4?	1			4?
B	E	N	T	D	I	R	T

	2	3	4?	1			4?
B	E	S	T	V	A	I	N

39 **TOMB**

	2	3?	1	4		3?	
H	A	R	M	K	E	R	B

	2	3?	1	4		3?	
B	O	A	T	B	O	M	B

40 **NAIL**

	3	1?	1?	2		4	
K	I	S	S	H	O	P	E

	3	1?	1?	2		4	
P	I	N	K	A	X	L	E

41 **TART** start
42 **LASH** flashing
43 **RIPE** striped
44 **AGED** damaged
45 **HOSE** those
46 **ours** Y**our s**kull protects your brain from harm.
47 **land** I think those exhibition pictures are colourfu**l and** attractive.
48 **herb** A fox chased a baby rabbit and scared **her b**adly.
49 **rest** Why a**re st**amps so expensive now?
50 **then** **The n**urse put a plaster cast on his broken arm.
51 **FW, NQ** The first letters are in a repeating pattern: FNCFNC. The second letter in each pair moves forwards five places.
52 **RA, ND** The first letter in each pair moves backwards four places. The second letter moves forwards three places.
53 **NA, YG** The first letter in each pair moves backwards five places. The second letter moves forwards two places.
54 **PdA, JvQ** The first capital letter moves backwards three places. The lower case letter moves backwards four places. The second capital letter moves backwards five places.
55 **atN, vqQ** The first lower case letter moves backwards five places. The second lower case letter moves backwards three places. The capital letter moves forwards three places.
56 **confined, spacious** 'Confined' means cramped whereas 'spacious' implies lots of room.
57 **scurry, saunter** To 'scurry' is to rush whereas to 'saunter' is to move slowly and casually.
58 **transparent, opaque** 'Transparent' is clear whereas 'opaque' is not clear.
59 **contradict, confirm** 'Contradict' is to dispute or argue with whereas 'confirm' is to agree with.
60 **laudable, loathsome** 'Laudable' means praiseworthy whereas 'loathsome' is detestable.
61 **con**tem**ptible** Both words mean disgraceful.
62 **ob**scu**re** Both words mean shadowy, vague, not clear.
63 **dim**inu**tive** Both words mean very small.
64 **br**andi**sh** Both words mean to flaunt or display.
65 **fur**row**ed** Both words mean bumpy, uneven.

66–70 A table is the easiest way to sort the information, like this:

CHILD	SHORTS: 2×B, 2×R, 1×G	SHIRT: 2×B, 1×R, 2×G	
JOHN	BLUE	BLUE	Only one to only have one colour.
LEENA	RED	*GREEN	Must have GREEN shirt as cannot have red.*
SAM	*RED	BLUE	Cannot have blue shorts so RED.*
SARAH	*BLUE	*GREEN	Only BLUE shorts left.* Only GREEN shirts left.*
MICAH	GREEN	*RED	Must have RED shirt as he cannot have green.*

66 **red**
67 **green**
68 **Micah**
69 **Sarah**
70 **Sam**
71 **ar** bear, arch
72 **op** shop, opened
73 **ch** much, child
74 **ce** mice, centre
75 **un** spun, under
76 **limit** All the words mean the edge of a designated area.
77 **checked** 'Checked' can mean a 'squared' pattern, to rein in or 'restrain' something and to 'investigate' or verify something.
78 **rest** 'Rest' can mean to relax or 'repose' as well as the leftovers or 'surplus'; it can also mean a 'holder' or stand for an object.
79 **charge** 'Charge' can mean to 'accuse' as well as the cost or 'price' of something; it can also mean a 'responsibility'.
80 **fine** 'Fine' can mean satisfactory or 'acceptable' as well as subtle or 'insubstantial'; a 'fine' can also be a charge or 'levy'.
81 **hound** greyhound, bloodhound, foxhound, wolfhound
82 **show** showjumping, showground, showdown, showcase
83 **side** sideburn, sideline, sideways, sidestep
84 **pay** payback, payable, payout, payroll
85 **back** backbone, backslap, backpack, background

33 Last night, a fox LDELKI _____ our HCCKNEIS _____.

34 As it has DRAINE _____ hard, the park will be very YDUMD

_____.

35 Maisy's new RCHTUIA _____ makes her look much DLORE

_____.

5

If the code for STAPLE is c 8 4 b r =, what are the codes for the following words?

36 LAST _____

37 PLEASE _____

38 PALEST _____

3

Using the same code, what do the following codes stand for?

39 r 4 b c = _____

40 4 b b r = c _____

2

Find the two missing letters/numbers in the following sequences.

A B C D E F G H I J K L M N O P Q R S T U V W X Y Z

Example	CQ	DP	EQ	FP	GQ	HP
41	13	__	__	19	23	28
42	17	27	__	21	25	__
43	QP	RU	__	__	RJ	ZO
44	AC	CA	FY	__	__	US
45	SS	VM	__	BA	__	HO
46	__	51bT	44dW	37fZ	30hC	__

6

Work out the missing synonym. Spell the new word correctly, one letter in each space.

Example strange   p e __ __ l __ __ r   (peculiar)

47 petty   t r i __ __ __ __ __

48 seclusion   q u __ __ a n t __ __ e

49 mix   i n t e __ __ __ t __

50 uncertain   a m __ __ __ __ o u s

4

Complete the following sentences by selecting the most sensible word from each group of words given in the brackets. Underline the words selected.

Example The (<u>children</u>, boxes, foxes) carried the (houses, <u>books</u>, steps) home from the (greengrocer, <u>library</u>, factory).

51 We cannot go out into the (playground, classroom, bedroom) as it is pouring with (fire, rain, snow) and we will get very (tired, hot, wet).

52 (Yesterday, Tomorrow, Today) afternoon we went to (annoy, climb, visit) a friend who is sick in (hospital, cinema, fire station).

53 There are many (types, cans, envelopes) of (cows, fish, paper) that live in the (house, sea, jar).

54 Mum parked the (horse, car, train) in the (pond, car park, hedge) next to the (shops, swan, kettle).

55 As the (book, door, mouth) was (wide, open, speaking) she went (inside, outside, over) without knocking.

5

Find the four-letter word hidden at the end of one word and the beginning of the next word. The order of the letters may not be changed.

Example We had bat<u>s and</u> balls. <u>sand</u>

56 Please empty your rubbish bin over here. _____

57 The cat is asleep and doesn't want to be stroked. _____

58 At break time we played with all the little children. _____

59 We met our new next door neighbours at the party. _____

60 I could see your swing over your garden fence. _____

5

Move one letter from the first word and add it to the second word to make two new words.

Example hunt   sip   <u>hut</u>   <u>snip</u>

61 play   urge   _____   _____

62 quite   very   _____   _____

63 sample   hair   _____   _____

64 break   dove   _____   _____

65 waiter   fend   _____   _____

5

Underline the two words which are the odd ones out in the following groups of words.

Example black   <u>king</u>   purple   green   <u>house</u>

66 knowledge   ignorance   wisdom   intellect   cunning

67 artery   muscle   heart   liver   kidney

68 congenial   continuous   amenable   compliant   welcome

69 stinginess   munificence   bounteousness   interest   liberality

70 willowy   nimble   pirouette   ballet   lissome

◯ 5

On a garden rockery, there were seven stones. Under each stone lived a different type of small animal. From the clues and the diagram, work out where each type of animal lived.

LEFT				RIGHT	
A				SNAILS	TOP
	B		C		
CENTIPEDES		D		E	BOTTOM

The snails were not directly above the woodlice.

The beetles were on a row somewhere above the woodlice.

The centipedes were on the same row as the worms.

The earwigs were on the same row as the slugs, which are closer to the centipedes than the earwigs.

71 earwigs   _____

72 worms   _____

73 beetles   _____

74 woodlice   _____

75 slugs   _____

◯ 5

Change the first word into the last word, by changing one letter at a time and making two new, different words in the middle.

Example CASE   <u>CASH</u>   <u>WASH</u>   WISH

76 VOTE   _____   _____   DIVE

77 RAMP   _____   _____   DIME

78 COSY   _____   _____   ROVE

79 LATE   _____   _____   LEND

80 MILK   _____   _____   KALE

◯ 5

(35)

Underline the one word in the brackets which will go equally well with each of the words outside the brackets.

Example word, paragraph, sentence   (pen, cap, <u>letter</u>, top, stop)

81 crate, strongbox, torso   (body, container, chest, ribs, suitcase)

82 subject, substance, comfortable   (content, satisfied, matter, gladden, pleased)

83 fragment, interval, respite   (shatter, rest, interim, break, fasten)

84 equivalent, coordinate, bout   (balance, contest, tally, equal, match)

85 devastate, devour, absorb   (drink, exhaust, consume, raze, pilfer)   5

Now go to the Progress Chart to record your score!   Total 85

Mixed paper 4

Remove one letter from the word in capital letters to leave a new word. The meaning of the new word is given in the clue.

Example AUNT   an insect   <u>ant</u>

1 BRAND   fibre   _____

2 STRAINED   marked   _____

3 BROUGHT   purchased   _____

4 HEATED   loathed   _____

5 STRAND   upright   _____   5

Underline the one word in each group which **can be made** from the letters of the word in capital letters.

Example CHAMPION camping notch   peach   cramp   <u>chimp</u>

6 BRIGHTEN   gender   rights   tribe   better   nightie

7 POWERFUL   flower   proof   parole   leper   prefer

8 DISTANCE   canter   stains   dances   stands   insist

9 VEHICLES   sieves   sleek   leaves   wheels   chives

10 TELEVISION notelet hotels   notice   solvent noises   5

(36)

If t = 4, c = 7, r = 3, a = 1, l = 5, e = 6 and w = 2, find the sum of these words when the letters are added together.

11 crawl _____   12 crater _____

13 wallet _____

3

Read the first two statements and then underline one of the four options below that must be true.

14 'Madrid is the capital of Spain. Spain is in Europe.'

    A Madrid is a European city.

    B England is in Europe.

    C The euro is the currency for much of Europe.

    D People from Spain speak Spanish.

15 'A robin is a type of bird. Birds have feathers.'

    A Robins are good at flying.   C Robins have feathers.

    B Robins have red breasts.   D All birds are robins.

2

Underline the pair of words which are the most similar in meaning.

Example come, go   roams, wanders   fear, fare

16 brawl, tussle   wrestle, waste   clash, brash

17 chasm, furrow   ditch, abandon   restart, cancel

18 popular, companion   stimulate, pacify   remote, isolated

19 illuminate, clear   depress, enhance   brighten, animate

20 identical, similar   morsel, fragment   repeat, refer

5

Find the word that is opposite in meaning to the word in capital letters and that rhymes with the second word.

Example SHARP   front   blunt

21 FRAIL   long   _____

22 GOOD   weevil   _____

23 HEATED   ruled   _____

24 PLUMP   seen   _____

25 CRAZY   drain   _____

5

Underline two words, one from each group, that go together to form a new word. The word in the first group always comes first.

Example (hand, <u>green</u>, for)   (light, <u>house</u>, sure)

26 (good, god, grade)   (further, father, future)

27 (back, four, head)   (plain, ground, grass)

28 (in, and, who)   (to, be, how)

29 (over, oven, order)   (line, law, board)

30 (in, out, be)   (hold, hive, port)   ⬭ 5

If the code for STORM is T S P Q N, match the right code to each word given below.

ZERO   FOUR   FIVE   NINE

31 G N V Q   _____   32 O H O D   _____

33 A D S N   _____   34 G H W D   _____

35 What would EIGHT be, using the same code? _____   ⬭ 5

Find the four-letter word hidden at the end of one word and the beginning of the next word. The order of the letters may not be changed.

Example We had bat<u>s and</u> balls. <u>sand</u>

36 Calm down and try explaining in a quiet and sensible way.

_____

37 As the weather worsened, the mountains disappeared from view.

_____

38 Tea and coffee leave me feeling thirsty. _____

39 We looked carefully for blemishes on each apple. _____

40 Conrad left his jacket on the floor of the gym. _____   ⬭ 5

Find a word that can be put either in front or at the end of each of the following words to make new, compound words.

Example cast   fall   ward   pour   <u>down</u>

41 cracker   ball   fighter   side   _____

42 for   back   in   up   _____

43 doors   back   look   grow   _____

(38)

44	finch	fish	smith	field	_____	
45	age	kind	hood	or	_____	5

Change the first word into the last word, by changing one letter at a time and making a new, different word in the middle.

Example CASE   <u>CASH</u>   LASH

46 BROW   _____   SLOW

47 TINY   _____   TILT

48 GOOD   _____   BOLD

49 HOME   _____   HOLT

50 YARD   _____   HARK   5

Complete the following sentences in the best way by choosing one word from each set of brackets.

Example Tall is to (tree, <u>short</u>, colour) as narrow is to (thin, white, <u>wide</u>).

51 Picturesque is to (scenic, unattractive, quaint) as trivial is to (vital, expensive, indolent).

52 Candid is to (guarded, forthright, sugared) as honest is to (sincere, fragrant, blithe).

53 (India, Peru, Zambia) is to Africa as (Argentina, Kenya, Poland) is to South America.

54 Carefree is to (careless, careful, anxious) as meagre is to (scanty, plentiful, insufficient).

55 Blunt is to (sharp, curt, watchful) as brusque is to (lazy, written, terse).   5

Find the two missing numbers in the following sequences.

Example 2 4 6 8 <u>10</u> <u>12</u>

56 2 22 42 ___ 82 ___   57 ___ ___ 6 13 10 11

58 ___ 3 4 5 3 ___   59 26 20 ___ 11 ___ 6

60 29 ___ 21 ___ 13 9   5

Look at the first group of three words. The word in the middle has been made from the two other words. Complete the second group of three words in the same way, making a new word in the middle.

Example PAIN INTO T<u>OO</u>K   ALSO   <u>SOON</u>   ONLY

61 JERK   PORK   PONY   MAKE _____   JOIN

62 CLAW   LAWN   NOTE   WEAR _____   NAIL

63 HOOF   FISH   SIFT   TANG _____   IRON

64 CALL   ALSO   SOLD   WHAT _____   LOOK

65 LIMB   BONE   ZONE   HUSK _____   WING   **(5)**

Find the two letters that will end the first word and start the second word.

Example pas (<u>ta</u>) ste

66 brok (__ __) joy   67 tend (__ __) ect

68 agr (__ __) rie   69 fir (__ __) amp

70 bus (__ __) say   **(5)**

Work out the missing synonym. Spell the new word correctly, one letter in each space.

Example strange   p e __ __ l __ __ r   (peculiar)

71 favourite   p r __ __ __ __ r e d

72 melt   l __ q __ __ __ y

73 disguise   c a m __ __ __ __ a g e

74 advantageous   b e __ __ f __ __ i a l

75 speck   __ __ __ __ i c l e   **(5)**

76 If the code for CATCH is E C V E J, what is the code for THROW?

_____

77 If the code for LUNCH is J S L A F, what is the code for PASTA?

_____

78 If the code for WANTS is Z D Q W V, what does B H D U Q stand for?

_____   **(3)**

If the code for AUGUST is Z V F V R U, what do the following codes stand for?

79 Z Q Q J K _____   80 L B Q D G _____   **(2)**

BULGARIA   BELGIUM   BOTSWANA   BOLIVIA   BURUNDI

81 If these countries are put in alphabetical order, which comes third?

_____

82 If all the months of the year are put in alphabetical order, which comes tenth? _____

83 If all the months of the year are put into alphabetical order, which comes fifth? _____

84 How many vowels are there in the four seasons of the year?

_____

85 If the letters of the alphabet are matched with increasing numbers so A = 1, B = 2, C = 3 and so on, work out this sum and write your answer as a letter of the alphabet:

HD – (L ÷ B) = _____

5

Now go to the Progress Chart to record your score!   Total   85

Mixed paper 5

Complete the following sentences by selecting the most sensible word from each group of words given in the brackets. Underline the words selected.

Example   The (<u>children</u>, boxes, foxes) carried the (houses, <u>books</u>, steps) home from the (greengrocer, <u>library</u>, factory).

1 Please don't (leave, find, jump) me alone (in, through, over) this strange (place, colour, wolf).

2 Yesterday we (ate, watched, threw) an interesting (pizza, programme, spear) on animals living in our (cities, buckets, socks).

3 The moon is (shining, calling, falling) really (suddenly, brightly, quickly) through my bedroom (wall, road, window).

4 The (book, garage, bird) I am (reading, flying, mending) at the moment is very (exciting, swimming, driving).

5 The fruit in the (shop, bridge, cage) was either unripe or (rotten, unkind, pink) so we did not (eat, buy, wish) it.

5

Find the word that is opposite in meaning to the word in capital letters and that rhymes with the second word.

Example SHARP   front   <u>blunt</u>

  6 DIFFERENT   blame   _____

  7 SCOWL   dream   _____

  8 OUTER   dinner   _____

  9 HIGH   sew   _____

10 APPEAR   banish   _____   ⬤ 5

Rearrange the muddled words in capital letters so that each sentence makes sense.

Example There are sixty SNODCES <u>seconds</u> in a UTMINE <u>minute</u>.

11 In AUUMNT _____ many trees lose their VSELAE

  _____.

12 The BFRENIO _____ burned brightly against the INHGT

  _____ sky.

13 BFLTOALO _____ is my favourite PTORS _____ at
our school.

14 Her CLIPNE _____ kept breaking as she was GNIWRKO

  _____.

15 London is the PTLACAI _____ city of GLAENDN

  _____.   ⬤ 5

If the code for BEAD is 2 5 1 4, what are the codes for the following words?

16 DICE   _____   **17** FACED   _____

18 BADGE   _____   ⬤ 3

Using the same code, what do the following codes stand for?

19 8 5 4 7 5 _____   **20** 3 1 2 2 1 7 5 _____   ⬤ 2

Find the letter that will end the first word and start the second word.

Example drow (<u>n</u>) ought

21 year (__) or   **22** bus (__) orror

23 vea (__) ove   **24** hee (__) oor

25 wa (__) wan   (42)   ⬤ 5

Change the first word into the last word, by changing one letter at a time and making a new, different word in the middle.

Example CASE   <u>CASH</u>   LASH

26 HOSE   _____   ROBE

27 SURE   _____   FIRE

28 WHIP   _____   SLIP

29 GEAR   _____   HEAP

30 CHIN   _____   THAN   5

Underline the one word in each group that **cannot be made** from the letters of the word in capital letters.

Example STATIONERY   stone   tyres   ration   <u>nation</u>   noisy

31 LIGHTNING   glint   night   ignite   thing   tiling

32 GRANDEUR   danger   gander   ranger   dragon   grader

33 SPRAINED   drapes   rinsed   rained   drained   spared

34 CREATURES   steer   crusts   curate   traces   secret

35 BATTLESHIP   spittle   thistle   shape   tables   shelter   5

In a test at school out of 35, pupil A got 24 right while pupil B got 17 wrong. C got 10 less than D who got 4 more than B. E got half of A's score.

36 How many did D get right? _____

37 Who did the best? _____

38 Who got 6 more marks than C? _____

39 How many marks did C and E score when their totals are added together? _____

40 Who did better than B but not as well as A? _____   5

Complete the following sentences in the best way by choosing one word from each set of brackets.

Example Tall is to (tree, <u>short</u>, colour) as narrow is to (thin, white, <u>wide</u>).

41 Hasty is to rash as (astute, angry, sympathetic) is to (constant, thoughtless, shrewd).

42 (Spotless, Courteous, Spacious) is to gracious as (elaborate, genteel, kind) is to elegant.

43 Arid is to (desert, climate, saturated) as parched is to (streams, thirsty, waterlogged).

44 Connect is to (bridge, ascend, undo) as fret is to (lurch, frame, agonise).

45 Tense is to untroubled as (frightened, perturbed, fabricated) is to (apprehensive, composed, terrified).

5

If the letters of the word TREADING are put into alphabetical order, which comes:

46 second? _____   47 fourth? _____

48 seventh? _____

3

If the letters of the word CHAMPION are put into alphabetical order, which comes:

49 sixth? _____   50 third? _____

2

Find the four-letter word which can be added to the letters in capitals to make a new word. The new word will complete the sentence sensibly.

Example They enjoyed the BCAST. <u>ROAD</u>

51 Please may I have another S of cake? _____

52 Father Christmas is pictured with a bushy white D. _____

53 HOPEY it will stop raining soon. _____

54 Deserts are dry, arid places with little FALL. _____

55 The mechanic has a workshop in the GA. _____

5

56 If the code for SLEEP is Q M C F N, what is the code for EARLY?

_____

57 Using the same code, what does L J E I R stand for? _____

58 If the code for DREAM is C S D B L, what does Z X Z L D stand for?

_____

59 Using the same code, what is the code for NIGHT? _____

60 If the code for TIGER is Y N L J W, what is the code for LIONS?

_____

5

Underline the two words, one from each group, which are the most opposite in meaning.

Example (dawn, <u>early</u>, wake)   (<u>late</u>, stop, sunrise)

61 (reckless, chaste, sparse)   (imprudent, intelligent, cautious)

62 (heartfelt, linear, elusive)   (vague, oblivious, obvious)

63 (linger, gather, find)   (protract, leave, mingle)

64 (fatuous, colossal, strategic)   (minuscule, gigantic, vast)

65 (accident, tragedy, party)   (sorrow, heart-rending, triumph)

5

Change the first word of the third pair in the same way as the other pairs to give a new word.

Example bind, hind   bare, hare   but, <u>hut</u>

66 comb, come   wand, wane   form, _____

67 type, tyre   pant, part   wine, _____

68 come, hum   with, hut   jibe, _____

69 lack, luck   tack, tuck   sack, _____

70 leap, pale   deaf, fade   read, _____

5

Look at the first group of three words. The word in the middle has been made from the two other words. Complete the second group of three words in the same way, making a new word in the middle.

Example PA<u>IN</u> INTO <u>TO</u>OK   ALSO   <u>SOON</u>   ONLY

71 BATH THIN WIND   RICH _____ WIPE

72 FORT TRIM SLIM   KERB _____ SPED

73 PEAR READ DAMP   GERM _____ NAVY

74 ENDS SHOE HOME   HIGH _____ USED

75 KITE TERM MORE   MUCH _____ TRAP

5

Find the four-letter word hidden at the end of one word and the beginning of the next word. The order of the letters may not be changed.

Example We had ba<u>ts and</u> balls. <u>sand</u>

76 Where are your clean clothes, Javin? _____

77 Tania will not be allowed to come shopping with you on Friday.

_____

78 A train clattered by noisily through the new level crossing.

_____

79 Paul put one of his paintings in an art exhibition. _____

80 A squirrel visits our bird table to gobble all the bird food. _____ ⚪ 5

Find the two missing pairs of letters in the following sequences.

A B C D E F G H I J K L M N O P Q R S T U V W X Y Z

Example	CQ	DP	EQ	FP	GQ	HP
81 LO	UR	DU	LX	__	__
82 __	__	UC	PF	KI	FL
83 AA	__	EY	__	IW	KV
84 MU	QR	__	YL	__	GF
85 pQr	__	vYq	__	bGs	eKq

⚪ 5

Now go to the Progress Chart to record your score!   Total ⚪ 85

Mixed paper 6

Look at the first group of three words. The word in the middle has been made from the two other words. Complete the second group of three words in the same way, making a new word in the middle.

Example	PAIN	INTO	TOOK	ALSO	SOON	ONLY
1	POSH	HOOP	SORT	FAIL	_____	FERN
2	BUSY	MUST	MINT	GASH	_____	WEEP
3	LOOK	KEEP	PEEK	LOAD	_____	TRIP
4	REEL	FEAR	LOAF	HOAX	_____	NICE
5	SNAP	DRIP	BIRD	PUMA	_____	HELP

⚪ 5

Fill in the crosswords so that all the given words are included. You have been given one letter as a clue in each crossword.

6

7

BORROW LOOKED UNROLL

TALKED DOUBLE DEBATE

REACTS TAVERN TALENT

VOTING NINETY LETHAL

If the letters of the word PICTURES are put into alphabetical order, which comes:

8 first? _____   **9** fourth? _____   **10** fifth? _____

Find the two missing pairs of letters in the following sequences.

A B C D E F G H I J K L M N O P Q R S T U V W X Y Z

Example CQ   DP   EQ   FP   <u>GQ</u>   <u>HP</u>

11 MM   ___   GQ   DS   ___   XW

12 SR   TP   VN   ___   ___   HH

13 ___   Wb   Rf   Fj   Wn   ___

14 KD   ___   ___   BX   YV   VT

15 RU   BE   LO   ___   FI   ___

16 If the code for IGLOO is K F N N Q, what does U M Q V A stand for?

_____

17 If the code for FENCE is G D O B F, what is the code for GATES?

_____

18 If the code for CROSS is D S P T T, what does S P B E T stand for?

_____

19 If the code for BITES is Y F Q B P, what is the code for CHEWS?

_____

20 If the code for TEACH is V D C B J, what is the code for PUPIL?

_____

Find the two missing numbers in the following sequences.

Example 2 4 6 8 <u>10</u> <u>12</u>

21 8 2 6 3 ___ ___ 2 5

22 ___ ___ 4 7 11 16 22 29

23 3 9 ___ 21 ___ 33

24 16 32 21 29 ___ ___ 31 23

25 75 69 66 66 58 63 ___ ___

If Z = 3, Y = 5, W = 10, V = 2 and U = 4, what are the values of these calculations? Write each answer as a letter.

26 (Z + Y) − (W − U) = _____

27 (U² − Z²) + Z = _____

28 $\dfrac{(Y + Z + W + V)}{U}$ = _____

29 (VYZ) ÷ W = _____

30 ZW − YU = _____

At a football match, six friends all wore their red supporters' shirts. A and B wore hats but no scarves. C, F and E wore hats and scarves. B and D and E had flags and hats. A and C carried whistles.

31 Who had a whistle but no scarf? _____

32 How many friends wore hats and scarves but no whistles?

_____

33 Who, besides A and B, did not have a scarf? _____

34 Who had a hat, scarf and whistle? _____

35 How many wore scarves and carried flags? _____

Change the first word of the third pair in the same way as the other pairs to give a new word.

Example bind, hind   bare, hare   but, <u>hut</u>

36 gasp, gap   camp, cap   pond, _____

37 knit, knave   slow, slave   gruel, _____

38 pot, top   nit, tin   now, _____

39 food, fade   moon, mane   book, _____

40 crime, mean   stale, lean   broth, _____

Underline the pair of words which are the most similar in meaning.

Example come, go   <u>roams, wanders</u>   fear, fare

41 charm, allure   repel, avoid   dazzle, subdue

42 notable, significant   realistic, dreamy   caustic, celebrated

43 mad, sane   insane, senseless   common, sense

44 historical, famous   sentimental, romantic   colourful, patterned

45 ponder, decide   deny, displease   indulge, gratify   (5

Find a word that can be put either in front or at the end of each of the following words to make new, compound words.

Example cast   fall   ward   pour   <u>down</u>

46 out   in   be   a   _____

47 lighter   land   ball   way   _____

48 under   watch   house   hot   _____

49 play   fly   power   back   _____

50 stream   per   ping   way   _____   (5

Underline the one word in the brackets which will go equally well with both sets of words outside the brackets.

Example rush, attack   cost, fee   (price, hasten, strike, <u>charge</u>, money)

51 done, finished   cricketing term   (over, complete, wicket, century, ball)

52 domestic animal   stroke, pat   (cat, rabbit, fondle, pet, dog)

53 fast, swift   intelligent, sharp   (quick, rapid, clever, bright, cool)

54 aggravate, enrage   sweet spice, perfume   (infuriate, light, incense, scent, antagonise)

55 strap, cord   command, control   (martial, walk, ribbon, lead, rope)   (5

(49)

Move one letter from the first word and add it to the second word to make two new words.

Example hunt   sip   <u>hut</u>   <u>snip</u>

56 beacon   snip   _____   _____

57 witch   hair   _____   _____

58 stable   ringing   _____   _____

59 chain   bred   _____   _____

60 night   mean   _____   _____   5

Underline the one word in the brackets which will go with the word outside the brackets in the same way as the first two words go together.

Example good, better   bad, (naughty, worst, <u>worse</u>, nasty)

61 wide, width   high, (height, higher, highest, low)

62 replete, filling   least, (increasing, spending, lessening, most)

63 flexible, supple   vacant, (engaged, unoccupied, expressive, different)

64 tops, spot   part, (past, trap, rapt, step)

65 robust, fragile   brittle, (durable, frail, delicate, spirited)   5

Underline the two words in each line which are made from the same letters.

Example TAP   PET   <u>TEA</u>   POT   <u>EAT</u>

66 PARADE   DEARER   LAMENT   MENTAL   PARENT

67 REPORT   PORTER   TREATS   STREET   STRIPE

68 UGLIER   GRUELS   DRIEST   STRIDE   GUESTS

69 LATENT   TALENT   STALER   RESTED   TRUEST

70 LEADER   DREAMS   SMEARED   INDEED   DEALER   5

Change the first word into the last word, by changing one letter at a time and making a new, different word in the middle.

Example CASE   <u>CASH</u>   LASH

71 YARD   _____   HAND

72 TAPE   _____   TALK

(50)

73	FISH	_____	DASH
74	COMB	_____	CORE
75	DEAF	_____	READ

5

The code for BREAK is A S D B J. Use this code to answer the following questions.

76 Which of these codes is the right one for CAVES: B B U F R or B B W D T? _____

77 Which of these words is the right one for R U D F O: STEEP or STEER? _____

78 Which of these codes is the right one for GRAIN: F S Z J M or F S Z J O? _____

79 Which of these words is the right one for R U Z M K: STALK or STALL?

_____

80 Which of these codes is the right one for FUZZY: E V Y Y X or E V Y A X? _____

5

Find the four-letter word hidden in each sentence. Each begins at the end of one word and the beginning of another word, and can cover two or three words. The order of the letters may not be changed.

Example We had bat<u>s and</u> balls. <u>sand</u>

81 To tremendous applause, the young players ran onto the pitch.

_____

82 We apologised when we broke the glass in the classroom window next to the playground. _____

83 I counted three large fish swimming slowly round the pond.

_____

84 After working for a long time in the baking sun, we had a break.

_____

85 Please leave the door to the church open, when you leave.

_____

5

Mixed paper 7

Change the first word of the third pair in the same way as the other pairs to give a new word.

Example   bind, hind   bare, hare   but, <u>hut</u>

  1 great, grate   fear, fare   steal, _____

  2 drum, dam   begin, ban   closet, _____

  3 bend, bent   form, fort   trail, _____

  4 beam, me   mesh, he   cost, _____

  5 dust, stud   dame, mead   much, _____

5

Underline the one word in the brackets which will go equally well with both sets of words outside the brackets.

Example   rush, attack   cost, fee   (price, hasten, strike, <u>charge</u>, money)

  6 road, path   method, style   (track, way, route, distance, manner)

  7 pale, faint   lamp, lantern   (torch, soft, gentle, light, candle)

  8 long for, miss   evergreen tree   (fir, yew, pine, yearn, ache)

  9 slapdash, lax   limp, loose   (sagging, slack, slow, negligent, careless)

10 air movement   twist, turn   (current, air, wind, loop, snake)

11 excellent, very good   enormous, vast   (large, huge, great, wonderful, fat)

12 arid land, waterless   abandon, forsake   (leave, desert, desolate, sand dune)

13 candid, frank   order, command   (clear, control, direct, open)

8

Circle two words, one from each group, that are most opposite in meaning.

Example (good   better   luck)   (charm   poor   bad)

Answer: good, bad

14 (meticulous, wasteful, prosperous)   (silly, slapdash, tidy)

15 (tiny, scarce, crop)   (minuscule, grow, abundant)

If the code for GARAGE is H Z S Z H D, match the right word to each code given below.

SAND   HAND   HARD   DASH

16 I Z O C   _____   18 E Z T G   _____

17 I Z S C   _____   19 T Z O C   _____

20 Using the same code, what is the code for RASH?   _____

Change the first word into the last word, by changing one letter at a time and making two new, different words in the middle.

Example CASE   <u>CASH</u>   <u>WASH</u>   WISH

21 TAPE   _____   _____   TOLL

22 GIFT   _____   _____   RAPT

23 SHOD   _____   _____   FLOW

24 SLUR   _____   _____   SPIN

25 RARE   _____   _____   HIVE

Underline the pair of words which are the most similar in meaning.

Example come, go   <u>roams, wanders</u>   fear, fare

26 disperse, scatter   penetrate, seal   gore, gauge

27 reactive, sluggish   responsive, alert   alive, inert

28 pervade, permit   contribute, dispel   permeate, saturate

29 torpid, industrious   indolent, slothful   lax, vigilant

30 fragrant, aromatic   foul-smelling, sweet-smelling   rancid, fresh

Find the two missing pairs of letters in the following sequences.

A B C D E F G H I J K L M N O P Q R S T U V W X Y Z

Example	CQ	DP	EQ	FP	<u>GQ</u>	<u>HP</u>
31	___	HG	___	LI	NJ	PK
32	XA	YC	___	AG	___	CK
33	___	___	TZ	KY	TX	KW
34	DR	BU	___	___	VD	TG
35	VE	WD	XC	YB	___	___

◯ 5

Find a word that can be put either in front or at the end of each of the following words to make new, compound words.

Example	cast	fall	ward	pour	<u>down</u>
36	free	less	taker	worn	_____
37	bid	give	got	mat	_____
38	hold	break	tree	keeper	_____
39	ridge	wheel	on	horse	_____
40	end	room	work	ally	_____

◯ 5

41 If the code for CRATE is F U D W H, what is the code for BOXES?

_____

42 If the code for MOUTH is N N V S I, what is the code for NOSES?

_____

43 If the code for CHILD is E G K K F, what does I H T K U stand for?

_____

44 If the code for HOUSE is E L R P B, what does S F I I X stand for?

_____

45 If the code for BERRY is F I V V C, what does W X V E A stand for?

_____

◯ 5

STORK   SWALLOW   SWIFT   SPARROW   STARLING

If these birds are put into alphabetical order, which comes:

46 third? _____   **47** fifth? _____

◯ 2

If the letters of the word BREAKING are put into alphabetical order, which comes:

48 first? _____   **50** fourth? _____   **49** seventh? _____

◯ 3

54

Find the four-letter word which can be added to the letters in capitals to make a new word. The new word will complete the sentence sensibly.

Example They enjoyed the BCAST. <u>ROAD</u>

51 Matt scored fifty runs in the CET match at school. _____

52 Supper's ready, so please lay the T! _____

53 Aidan SL his birthday cake into twelve pieces with a sharp knife.

_____

54 Although she slammed on the BS, Aisha's bike crashed into the wall.

_____

55 Our garden H badly needs clipping. _____

5

Find the four-letter word hidden at the end of one word and the beginning of the next word. The order of the letters may not be changed.

Example We had bat<u>s and</u> balls. <u>sand</u>

56 We went by bus to the Houses of Parliament. _____

57 Sixty six divided by sixty six equals one. _____

58 We need to collect our tickets from the bus station. _____

59 The trees by the lake dropped their leaves into the murky water.

_____

60 I recycled my old jumper by turning it into mittens. _____

5

Underline the one word in the brackets which will go with the word outside the brackets in the same way as the first two words go together.

Example good, better   bad, (naughty, worst, <u>worse</u>, nasty)

61 spellbound, bored   enthralled, (entranced, captivated, distracted, distraught)

62 grasp, clutch   yank, (collapse, wrench crush, spin)

63 whirling, revolving   gyrating, (cornering, curving, rotating, round)

64 mundane, bizarre   sparse, (populated, meagre, bare, treeless)

65 muggy, humid   tropical, (sultry, arid, dry, hot)

5

Work out the missing synonym. Spell the new word correctly, putting one letter in each space.

Example strange   p e __ __ l __ __ r   (peculiar)

66 portray   __ __ l u s __ __ a t e

67 anguish   g __ __ __ __ __

68 secretive   c l a __ __ __ __ t i n e

69 costume   a __ __ a r __ __

70 suffocating   __ __ __ __ s t r o p h o b i c

Find the two letters that will end the first word and start the second word.

Example pas (ta) ste

71 you (__ __) an   72 fl (__ __) it

73 brui (__ __) al   74 ar (__ __) rth

75 op (__ __) low

Find the missing letters. The alphabet has been written out to help you.

A B C D E F G H I J K L M N O P Q R S T U V W X Y Z

Example AB is to CD as PQ is to RS.

76 UT is to SR as ZY is to __.   77 FA is to GB as HC is to __.

78 MN is to LO as FG is to __.   79 BB to EF as JJ is to __.

80 GT is to HS as IR is to __.

Look at the first group of three words. The word in the middle has been made from the two other words. Complete the second group of three words in the same way, making a new word in the middle.

Example PAIN INTO TOOK   ALSO   SOON   ONLY

81 HARE LAKE LOOK   BONE _____ NEED

82 VASE VAST VENT   SALT _____ FAZE

83 QUIZ PILE PLEA   THIN _____ STEW

84 CORN CORE CASE   FROM _____ WING

85 TIME MATE CALM   CASH _____ BUSH

1 If the code for GLASS is H K B R T, what is the code for WATER?

   _____

2 If the code for SPRAY is Q N P Y W, what does F M Q C Q stand for?

   _____

3 If the code for GREEN is I T G G P, what does D N C E M stand for?

   _____

4 If the code for LAMPS is J C K R Q, what is the code for SHADE?

   _____

5 If the code for RIVER is S J W F S, what is the code for FLOOD?

   _____   5

Underline the one word in the brackets which will go equally well with both sets of words outside the brackets.

Example	rush, attack	cost, fee	(price, hasten, strike, <u>charge</u>, money)
6	bird limb	sport position	(leg, centre, half, wing, forearm)
7	feeling sad	a colour	(blue, grim, fateful, black, indigo)
8	animal skin	conceal, shroud	(leather, hide, camouflage, fur, cloak)
9	fastener, bar	run away or eat quickly	(gobble, escape, bolt, flee, gorge)
10	vital, critical	lock opener	(crucial, decisive, key, jemmy, bar)

5

Change the first word into the last word, by changing one letter at a time and making two new, different words in the middle.

Example	CASE	<u>CASH</u>	<u>WASH</u>	WISH
11	SAME	_____	_____	FUSE
12	TWIG	_____	_____	CHIN
13	BASH	_____	_____	WITH

| 14 | FACT | _____ | _____ | WADE |
| 15 | MOOD | _____ | _____ | NOUN |

Find the missing letters. The alphabet has been written out to help you.

A B C D E F G H I J K L M N O P Q R S T U V W X Y Z

Example   AB is to CD as PQ is to <u>RS</u>.

16 KL is to IJ as FG is to ___.   19 SU is to QW as XZ is to ___.

17 AZ is to BY as CX is to ___.   20 TY is to UZ as VA is to ___.

18 AF is to CG as BG is to ___.

21 If the code for CROWN is D Q P V O, what is the code for QUEEN?

_____

22 If the code for GRAPE is I T C R G, what is the code for FRUIT?

_____

23 If the code for SHIRT is O D E N P, what does F A W J O stand for?

_____

24 If the code for ARROW is Y S P P U, what is the code for SWORD?

_____

25 If the code for SMALL is U L C K N, what does N Z T F G stand for?

_____

Change the first word of the third pair in the same way as the other pairs to give a new word.

Example   bind, hind   bare, hare   but, <u>hut</u>

26	scrape, cap	cheats, hat	barter, _____
27	calm, lame	port, rote	film, _____
28	best, bees	felt, feel	kept, _____
29	swan, sawn	blot, bolt	silt, _____
30	churches, chest	larkspur, spurt	undercover, _____

58

Underline the one word in the brackets which will go with the word outside the brackets in the same way as the first two words go together.

Example good, better   bad, (naughty, worst, <u>worse</u>, nasty)

31 clear, cloudy   still, (almost, sparkling, gloomy, motionless)

32 battle, fight   game, (football, play, run, think, avoid)

33 plain, patterned   flat, (house, striped, brick, uneven)

34 cut, bleed   bump, (bruise, ramp, water, leg)

35 plump, pup   crust, (rust, rut, cut, cur)   ◯ 5

Look at the first group of three words. The word in the middle has been made from the two other words. Complete the second group of three words in the same way, making a new word in the middle.

Example PA<u>IN</u> INTO T<u>OO</u>K   ALSO   <u>SOON</u>   ONLY

36 CAME   MEAT BATH   BOOM _____   BENT

37 BACK   JACK JURY   DEEP _____   WING

38 BENT   DENT DIRT   BEST _____   VAIN

39 HARM   MARK KERB   BOAT _____   BOMB

40 KISS   SHIP HOPE   PINK _____   AXLE   ◯ 5

Find the four-letter word which can be added to the letters in capitals to make a new word. The new word will complete the sentence sensibly.

Example They enjoyed the BCAST. <u>ROAD</u>

41 The racehorses grouped together impatiently, ready to S the race.

_____

42 The blue FING light of the ambulance showed up clearly. _____

43 The rugby player wore a red and white STD shirt. _____

44 A tree fell on our house and DAM the roof. _____

45 T pencils you lent me were all blunt! _____   ◯ 5

Find the four-letter word hidden at the end of one word and the beginning of the next word. The order of the letters may not be changed.

Example   We had bat<u>s and</u> balls.   <u>sand</u>

46 Your skull protects your brain from harm. _____

47 I think those exhibition pictures are colourful and attractive. _____

48 A fox chased a baby rabbit and scared her badly. _____

49 Why are stamps so expensive now? _____

50 The nurse put a plaster cast on his broken arm. _____

(5)

Find the two missing pairs of letters in the following sequences.

A B C D E F G H I J K L M N O P Q R S T U V W X Y Z

Example	CQ	DP	EQ	FP	<u>GQ</u>	<u>HP</u>
51	__	NB	CG	FL	__	CV
52	VX	__	__	JG	FJ	BM
53	XW	SY	__	IC	DE	__
54	ShF	__	MzV	__	GrL	DnG
55	__	__	qnT	lkW	ghZ	beC

(5)

Underline the pair of words which are the most similar in meaning.

Example	come, go	<u>roams, wanders</u>	fear, fare
56	imprisoned, prisoned	confined, spacious	restricted, overcrowded
57	deviate, diverge	swerve, stray	scurry, saunter
58	transparent, opaque	flimsy, insubstantial	tenuous, unconvincing
59	refute, deny	contradict, confirm	oppose, challenge
60	brave, valiant	sturdy, steadfast	laudable, loathsome

(5)

Work out the missing synonym. Spell the new word correctly, one letter in each space.

Example   strange   p e __ __ l __ __ r   (peculiar)

61 despicable   c o n __ __ m p t __ __ l e

62 indistinct   o __ __ __ u r __

63 minute   d i __ __ __ u t __ v e

64 wield   b __ __ __ __ i s h

65 rutted   f u __ __ __ __ e d   5

At a summer camp, five children wore either blue, green or red shorts and either red, blue or green shirts.

Two children wore red shorts, two wore blue shorts and one wore green.

Two children wore green shirts, two wore blue shirts and one wore red.

John wore blue shorts and shirt. He was the only one to wear one colour.

Leena wore red shorts and Sam wore a blue shirt.

Sarah had one colour in common with Leena.

Micah wore green shorts.

From the information, work out which child wore which clothes and answer the questions.

66 What colour was Micah's shirt?_____

67 What was the colour Sarah had in common with Leena? _____

68 Who wore the red shirt? _____

69 Who, besides John, wore blue shorts? _____

70 Who wore red shorts and a blue shirt? _____   5

Find the two letters that will end the first word and start the second word.

Example   pas (ta) ste

71 be (__ __) ch   72 sh (__ __) ened

73 mu (__ __) ild   74 mi (__ __) ntre

75 sp (__ __) der   5

Underline the one word in the brackets which will go equally well with each of the words outside the brackets.

Example   word, paragraph, sentence   (pen, cap, <u>letter</u>, top, stop)

   76 perimeter, boundary, border   (limit, area, acreage, field)

   77 squared, restrained, investigated   (checked, caught, inspected, curbed)

   78 repose, surplus, holder   (time-out, balance, remainder, rest)

   79 accuse, price, responsibility   (attack, trust, charge, blame)

   80 acceptable, insubstantial, levy   (delicate, fine, penalty, select)   **5**

Find a word that can be put either in front or at the end of each of the following words to make new, compound words.

Example   cast   fall   ward   pour   <u>down</u>

   81 grey   blood   fox   wolf   _____

   82 jumping   ground   down   case   _____

   83 burn   line   ways   step   _____

   84 back   able   out   roll   _____

   85 bone   slap   pack   ground   _____   **5**

Now go to the Progress Chart to record your score!   Total   **85**

Bond

English

10 Minute Tests

9–10 years

OXFORD

UNIVERSITY PRESS

Add the missing commas to these sentences.

1–2 On her way to school, Carys realised she had forgotten her glasses, swimming things, reading book and recorder.

3–4 Dave and Tim struggled through the rain, slipping on rocks and stumbling through the mud as they hurried to reach cover.

Complete the word sums. Watch out for the spelling changes!

5 depend + able   *dependable*   **8** doubt + ful   *doubtful*

6 early + er   *earlier*   **9** likely + hood   *likelihood*

7 cord + less   *cordless*   **10** response + ible   *responsible*

Give one word for each of these *definitions*. Each word begins with the letter p.

11 A code of letters and numbers at the end of an address to help with the sorting and delivering of mail.

_____

12 A coin.

penny

13 A drawing or painting of someone, usually showing their head and shoulders.

Portrait

14 A male member of a royal family.

Prince

15 The sweet part of a meal.

_____

Write the following *adjectives* of comparison.

Example: quiet   *quieter*   *quietest*

16–17   heavy   heavier   heaviest

18–19   good   better   best

20–21   angry   angrier   angriest

Complete each sentence using a different *adverb*.

22   They screamed _quickly_ .

23   I swam _softly_ .

24   We giggled _loudly_ .

25   He whispered _slowly_ .

Write the *plural* forms of these words.

26   roof   roofs

27   circle   circles

28   lioness   lionesses

29   quantity   quantities

30   shelf   shelves

Total

TEST 2: **Spelling**

Write the *contraction* for each of these.

1 have not   *have'nt*
2 could have   *could've*
3 I will   *I'll*
4 will not   *Won't*

Write each of these words correctly.

5   temprature   *temperature*
6   mischivous   *mischievous*
7   ocurred   *Occured*
8   apreciate   *appreciate*
9   forign   *forgin*
10 existance   *existence*
11 familar   *familiar*
12 cemetry   *Symmetry*
13 aggresive   *aggressive*
14 garantee   *guarantee*

Add the missing double letters to each of these words.

15 a_c c_idental   18 courge_t t_e
16 begi_n n_ing   19 a_p p_earance
17 reco_m m_end   20 tomo_r r_ow

4

Add ary or ery to each of these to make a word.

21 nurs *ery*

25 diction *ary*

22 annivers *ary*

26 deliv *ery*

(23) scen *ery*

27 imagin *ary*

24 burgl *ary*

28 gloss *ary*

Each of these words has a missing silent letter. Rewrite each word correctly.

(29) reath — *wreath*

30 night — *Knight*

31 resin — *resign*

(32) sene — *scence*

33 autum — *autumn*

34 clim — *climb*

35 sord — *sword*

Add a different hyphenated prefix to each of these to make a new word.

bi-	ex-	re-	by-	cross-

36 weekly — *bi-weekly*

37 country — *cross-country*

(38) colleague — *ex colleague*

(39) election — *re-election*

40 enter — *re-enter*

Total

Read this extract carefully.

The Very Bloody History of Britain   *by John Farman*

1 **The Cunning Celts**

[The Celts] came here [Britain] in 650 BC from central Europe apparently looking for tin – please don't ask me
5 why! The Celts were tall, blond and blue-eyed and so got all the best girls right away. This, of course, annoyed the poor Britons even more, but there was not much they could do about it as they
10 only had sticks and fists to fight with. The Celts set up home in the south of England around Surrey and Kent – building flash wooden forts which the poor boneheaded locals could only mill
15 around in awe and envy.

Now England wasn't too bad a place to live for the next few hundred years (providing you were tall, blue-eyed and blond). Then in 55 BC the late Julius
20 Caesar – star of stage and screen – arrived with a couple of legions from Rome, Italy. The refined Romans were repelled, in more ways than one by the crude Celts, who by this time had turned
25 blue (from woad). They did, however, come back a year later with a much bigger, better-equipped army – and guess what – were repelled again.

55 BC – The Romans

30 You couldn't get away from the fact, however, that the Romans were much sharper than the Celts. They therefore decided that they'd infiltrate peacefully rather than invade; which was just a
35 sneaky Italian trick. How the Celts didn't notice the daftly-dressed Roman soldiers I'll never know.

AD 43 Boadicea

This gradual infiltration took longer
40 than expected and the Romans became rather impatient. Emperor Claudius sent another lot of legions to conquer us properly – which they did – properly! The only real trouble they encountered
45 was a strange woman warrior from somewhere near Norwich. Her name was Boadicea and, from the only available picture I've seen, she seemed to travel everywhere in a very snazzy horse-drawn
50 cart with blades sticking out of the wheels. This must have made parking in London rather tricky, which is probably why she burnt it to the ground. She went on to kill 70,000 Romans but, when
55 they started getting the better of things, poisoned herself.

**When In Britain Do As
The Romans Do**

If you can't beat a Roman, join him.
60 Gradually the hostile Brits came round to the Roman way of thinking. The smart ones even managed to make a few lire and live Hollywood-style, in centrally heated villas covered in naff mosaics.
65 The unsmart ones stayed in their hovels, being only serfs and slaves…. Soon everybody knew their place. Christianity was made the imperial religion and the first two centuries were to be among
70 the most prosperous and peaceful in England's history.

Answers these questions about the extract.

1 Where did the Celts originally come from?

Europe

2 How did the Britons react when the Celts arrived?

_____

3 When did the Romans first arrive on British soil?

_____

4 Describe one way the Romans were different from the Celts.

She was a strange _____

_____

5 Who was Boadicea?

She Was a Strange woman Warrior
from Somewhere near Norwich,

6 Why was Boadicea described in the extract as 'real trouble' (line 44)?

Because She Killed 70,000 Romans,

7 What is meant by 'the hostile Brits came round to the Roman way of thinking' (lines 61–62)?

They goined the Romans Without
even thinking,

8 What is the meaning of 'prosperous' in line 72?

having Success,

9 Describe what it was like in Britain during the period of Roman rule.

_____

_____

10 Why do you think John Farman has titled his book 'The Very Bloody History of Britain'?

because he wants to
tell us about them,

Total _____

Test 4: **Mixed**

Add a *verb* to these sentences.

1 _____*get*_____ my coat, it's raining.

2 _____*join*_____, Tariq is in the next race.

3 _____*quick*_____, we have to get the car out the mud!

4 _____*look*_____ on the carpet, Kate.

5 _____*eat*_____ your breakfast quickly, or you will be late.

Write the masculine gender of these words.

6 daughter _____*son*_____

7 cow _____*bull*_____

8 waitress _____*waiter*_____

9 duck _____*drake*_____

10 Mrs _____*Mr*_____

11 queen _____*king*_____

Underline one *clause* in each of these sentences.

12 The children wanted to walk to school even though it was pouring with rain.

13 Jess worked hard at her story and finished it just before playtime.

14 Although the sun was hidden by the clouds the sunbathers still got burnt.

15 Tom jumped with excitement when he was invited to David's party.

16 The chicken clucked loudly after laying an egg.

Write two *antonyms* for each of these words.

17–18 hot

cold (handwritten)   _freezing_ (handwritten)

19–20 hard

soft (handwritten)   _easy_ (handwritten)

21–22 love

hatred (handwritten)   _hate_ (handwritten)

Write a word with the same letter string and the same pronunciation.

23 rough   _____

24 dough   _____

25 thorough   _____

26 fought   _____

Complete these words using *tial* or *cial*.

27 confiden_tial_ (handwritten)

28 artifi_tial_ (handwritten)

29 finan_cial_ (handwritten)

30 ini_tial_ (handwritten)

TEST 5: **Vocabulary**

Write these *abbreviations* in full.

1 TV *television*

2 km *kilometre*

3 UK *United kingdom*

4 approx. *approxamitly*

5 UFO *unidentified flying object*

Circle the words that can be used for either gender.

6–10

lioness   teacher   farmer

husband   electrician   nurse

lord   mistress   uncle

doctor   niece   headmaster

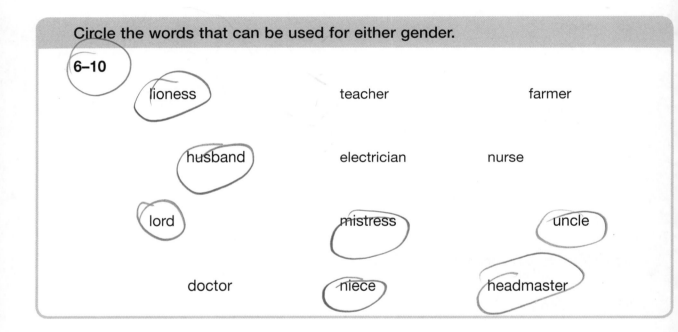

Write two *synonyms* for each word.

11–12 laugh *crack up* ✗ _____

13–14 shut *close* ✓ _____

15–16 frighten *scare* ✓ _____

17–18 drink _____ _____

10

Write the word for the young of each of these animals.

19 pig   _piglet_ ✓

20 owl   ✗

21 duck   _duckling_ ✓

22 goose   _gooseling_ ✗

Write a *definition* for each of these words.

23 purchase   _earn money_ ✗

24 supervise   _look after_ ✓

25 rehearse   _to practise_ ✓

26 grumpy   _moody_ ✓

Mix and match these words to make four *compound words*.

foot   snow   ball   man

27 _snow ball_ ✓

28 _snow man_ ✓

29 _foot ball_ ✓

30 _snow foot_ ✗

Total

Write six words using a word and a suffix from each box.

| observe | assist | confide |

| ant | ance | ent | ence |

1–6 _a ssistance assistant confident confidence obsevent observen_

Put a tick next to the words spelt correctly and a cross next to those spelt incorrectly.

7 height _✓_

8 weild _✗_

9 relieve _✓_

10 deceive _✓_

11 retreive _✗_

12 cieling _✗_

Write two sentences that use commas, brackets or dashes to indicate when something is in parenthesis.

13–14 _I like to run, skip and dance._

15–16 _I like to jog (run slowly.)_

12

Write two *onomatopoeic* words that describe the sounds that each of these make.

17–18 volcano   splash ✗   blop ✗

19–20 plug hole   gluy ✓   plut ✗

Complete the table of *nouns*.

21–28

jealousy   herd   jacket   China
Meena   lifetime   gaggle   hate

Common nouns	Proper nouns	Collective nouns	Abstract nouns
jacket	china	gaggle	hate
lifetime	Meena	herd	jealousy ✓

Add an *adjectival phrase* to complete each sentence.

29 The ___colorfull skined___ cockerel, protected his chickens from the fox.

30 The washing dried quickly in the ___strong fast___

___ wind.

Total

Change the *verbs* in each sentence into more powerful verbs.

1   The dog **ate** its food hungrily.   _____

2   The children **walked** to the park.   _____

3–4   Mum **said** it was time
      to **get** out of bed.   _____   _____

5–6   As the car **drove** past, it
      frightened the lollipop lady.   _____   _____

Write two *adjectives* to describe each of these *nouns*.

7–8   a _____, _____ baby

9–10   a _____, _____ car

11–12 a _____, _____ fish

13–14   _____, _____ sky

Write two examples of each of the following.

15–16   *proper noun*   _____   _____

17–18   *preposition*   _____   _____

19–20   *adverb*   _____   _____

21–22   *pronoun*   _____   _____

Use *adverbs* (for example perhaps, surely) or *modal verbs* (for example might, should) to write four sentences illustrating degrees of possibility. For example, *The shops might be open later.*

Underline the adverb or modal verb in each sentence.

23–24 _____

_____

_____

25–26 _____

_____

_____

27–28 _____

_____

_____

29–30 _____

_____

_____

Total _____

Read this extract carefully.

The Ghost of Tantony Pig

by Julia Jarman

1 *A house was being built in Hogsbottom Field, close to Laurie Gell's home.*

He strained to see in the darkness. There was definitely an animal in Hogsbottom
5 Field, peering into the trench. Its head was down and large ears covered most of its face, but clearly visible, glistening in the moonlight was the flat edge of a moist snout.

10 For a moment he wondered if he ought to do something about it, tell someone. But then he thought that a pig in a pigfield or an ex-pigfield wasn't exactly an earth shattering event, wasn't a reason to call
15 out the emergency services or even wake his mum and dad...But where had it come from, he wondered. Was it one of Arthur Ram's? Escaped from the new farm perhaps?

20 Now it was making its way along the bar of the H-shape, pausing every now and then to look into the trench and push with its snout.

'Yow!'

25 'No Gingie.'

The pig was deliberate and careful, skirting the other side of the H now, pausing from time to time to examine and push. Stop. Start. Stop. Start. Then left. Left again.
30 Then it was turning round, to come down the other side facing him. Its head swung up and it stood still for a moment, seemed to be looking at Laurie, straight at him, its eyes tawny-gold in the moonlight.

35 'YOW!'

'Gingie. Wait.'

It was walking again. *Walking*. His stomach lurched. He told himself not to be stupid. Of course it was walking. That was what
40 pigs did...And then it was running, not walking now, but rollicking towards the end of the field, where suddenly it vanished.

Vanished. That made it sound like a conjuring trick. Now you see it, now you
45 don't. Had he really seen a pig or was it a cement mixer which looked fat and round?

Who was he kidding? He caught sight of his white knuckles gripping the window sill. The silence was heavy. He felt as if he'd
50 been holding his breath for an impossibly long time. He opened his mouth and the air came out in a gush – and the wind began again, whipping up the soil.

Closing the window he made his way to
55 bed. Mrs Gingerbits pushed under the covers and settled herself in the curl of his stomach. She was comfortable, like a purring hot water-bottle, but he couldn't sleep. Just lay there listening to the wind.
60 Trembling.

...Shouts woke him. It was light. He'd slept late – and there was something wrong at the building site. A ready-mix truck had just drawn up. Laurie dressed and breakfasted
65 quickly, hurried over the road. The driver was still yelling at Charlie Hancock.

'You ordered a ton of concrete, mate, you're getting it!'

And Charlie, very agitated, was pointing at
70 the field. 'Where you gonna put it mate? Look at the so-called footings!'

Laurie was already looking. There was none. The site looked like a badly ploughed field...

Answers these questions about the extract.

1   How was Laurie able to see the pig in the darkness?

It Was glistening in the moonlight

2   Why was Laurie surprised to see the pig where it was?

He wondered where had it come from

3   Why didn't Laurie wake his Mum and Dad to tell them?

It wasn't a earth shattering event.

4   What colour were the pig's eyes? tawny-gold.

5   Copy a sentence in the extract that lets the reader know how Laurie is feeling.

Trembling.

6   What is 'Gingie'? The pig

7   Why in line 49 is the silence described as 'heavy'?

I way long and loud.

8   Who is Charlie Hancock?

9   What is the significance of the final sentence in the extract?

It shows that its is really messy.

10 Describe how you think Laurie is now feeling at the end of the extract.

I think he feels confused

TEST 9: **Mixed**

Underline the *connectives* in each sentence.

1   Thomas had a friend around for tea but Alex wasn't allowed one.

2   Kay was late for the party despite leaving home on time.

3   Bola lost his race when he tripped over his laces.

4   The dog barked and made the horse rear up.

Write a *definition* for each of these words.

5   opinion   _____

6   confide   _____

7   truce   _____

8   incident   _____

9   sudden   _____

Rewrite these sentences without the *double negatives*.

10   There wasn't no footballs to play with.

_____

11   They didn't wear no school uniform on the trip.

_____

12   There wasn't no recorder lesson today.

_____

13   The train didn't arrive early at no platform.

_____

Underline the correct *verb* form in each sentence.

14   The book (fell/fall) open at the page listing magic spells.

15   When it snowed Raj (sweeps/swept) the drive.

16–17 The groom (was/were) (drove/driven) to the church.

18   Hannah (found/find) her homework just in time to hand it in.

Circle the words which have a soft g.

19–24

geese   magic   legend

register   wrong

playground   enlarge   dragon

dungeon   disregard

mirage   ghost

Write whether these sentences are written in the past, present or future *tense*.

25   I am stroking my cat.   _____

26   I will eat my tea.   _____

27   I played football.   _____

28   I made pancakes.   _____

29   I might tidy my room.   _____

30   I am exhausted.   _____

Total

TEST 10: **Sentences**

Rewrite these sentences, adding the missing punctuation and capital letters.

1–6 did you get my e-mail gareth asked

_____

7–10 nina now she was feeling better had arranged to meet her friends

_____

_____

11–16 would you like some sweets asked deano

_____

_____

Add 'did' or 'done' to each sentence to make it correct.

17 Ivan _____ his homework as soon as he was given it.

18 "I'm sure we have _____ the right thing," confirmed Helen.

19 "_____ you know we had to bring a packed lunch today?" asked Tim.

20 They were sure they had _____ enough to win the competition.

Write these sentences as *reported speech*.

21 "I'm glad you are coming with us, Aunty Sue," said Alex.

_____

_____

22 "We must remember our coats," Mum reminded the children.

_____

_____

Write four sentences, each with a relative clause beginning with the following words.

23 who

_____

_____

_____

_____

24 which

_____

_____

_____

_____

25 that

_____

_____

_____

_____

26 where

_____

_____

_____

_____

Total

TEST 11: Mixed

Underline the correct *homophone* in each bracket.

1–2 The (bough/bow) of the boat collided with the (bow/bough) of the tree.

3–4 Aimee's cut on her (heal/heel) didn't take long to (heal/heel).

5–6 The (cellar/seller) sold his goods from the (cellar/seller).

Underline the *pronouns* in the following passage.

7–11

They rushed over the rocks, desperate to get to safety before the waves came in and cut them off from the path ahead. Henry cried as he slipped and hurt his arm. It was wrapped in a jumper, as there was no time for anything else.

Underline one word in each group which is <u>not</u> a *synonym* for the rest.

12	right	decent	honest	untrue	fair
13	quiet	direct	peaceful	calm	tranquil
14	guard	protect	defend	shield	pursue
15	convey	clever	intelligent	smart	brainy
16	offend	question	quiz	ask	interrogate

Rewrite these sentences changing them from *plural* to *singular*.

17–18 The puppies raced towards the balls.

_____

19–23 They ate the ice-creams quickly as they dripped down their arms.

_____

_____

Add a *suffix* to each of these to make new words.

24 end   _____

25 help   _____

26 colour   _____

Add *tious* or *cious* to complete the words.

27 scrump_____

28 mali_____

29 flirta_____

30 fero_____

23

Total _____

TEST 12: **Spelling**

Write the *root word* of each of these words.

1 redevelop   _____

2 unanswerable   _____

3 prejudge   _____

4 amusement   _____

5 untidy   _____

6 peaceful   _____

7 electrician   _____

8 interconnect   _____

Add able or ible to each of these to make a word.

9 excit_____   13 flex_____

10 poss_____   14 divis_____

11 inflat_____   15 reli_____

12 resist_____   16 excus_____

Each of these words has an unstressed vowel missing. Rewrite each word.

17 histry   _____

18 avalable   _____

19 lesure   _____

20 vegtable   _____

21 jewellry   _____

22 diffrent   _____

Answers

Answers will vary for questions that require children to answer in their own words. Possible answers to most of these questions are given in *italics*.

TEST 1: Mixed

1–2 On her way to school Carys realised she had forgotten her glasses, swimming things, reading book and recorder.

3–4 Dave and Tim struggled through the rain, slipping on rocks and stumbling through the mud, as they hurried to reach cover.

5 dependable **8** doubtful
6 earlier **9** likelihood
7 cordless **10** responsible
11 postcode
12 pound, penny
13 portrait
14 prince
15 pudding
16–17 heavier, heaviest
18–19 better, best
20–21 angrier, angriest
22 *loudly* **27** circles
23 *gracefully* **28** lionesses
24 *helplessly* **29** quantities
25 *quietly* **30** shelves
26 roofs

TEST 2: Spelling

1 haven't **17** recommend
2 could've **18** courgette
3 I'll **19** appearance
4 won't **20** tomorrow
5 temperature **21** nursery
6 mischievous **22** anniversary
7 occurred **23** scenery
8 appreciate **24** burglary
9 foreign **25** dictionary
10 existence **26** delivery
11 familiar **27** imaginary
12 cemetery **28** glossary
13 aggressive **29** wreath
14 guarantee **30** knight
15 accidental **31** resign
16 beginning **32** scene

33 autumn **37** cross-country
34 climb **38** ex-colleague
35 sword **39** by-election
36 bi-weekly **40** re-enter

TEST 3: Comprehension

1 The Celts came from central Europe.

2 *The Britons weren't happy about the arrival of the Celts, though were in awe of their superior skills.*

3 The Romans first arrived in 55 BC.

4 *The Romans were more intelligent / more organised / better equipped than the Celts.*

5 *Boadicea was a female Celt who was a threat to the Romans.*

6 *Boadicea is described as 'real trouble' as she managed to lead a force against the Romans that killed many of the Roman soldiers.*

7 *The unhappy Britains that were invaded by the Romans eventually decided it was better to work with the Romans than against them.*

8 *successful, especially with money*

9 *It was a peaceful period in history when general living conditions improved for many.*

10 *John Farman titled his book as he did, as there appear to have been many 'bloody' battles to win control of Britain through different periods in history.*

TEST 4: Mixed

1 *Grab* **7** bull
2 *Watch* **8** waiter
3 *Push* **9** drake
4 *Sit* **10** Mr
5 *Eat* **11** king
6 son
12 The children wanted to walk to school OR even though it was pouring with rain.

13 Jess worked hard at her story OR and finished it just before playtime.

14 Although the sun was hidden by the clouds OR the sunbathers still got burnt.

15 Tom jumped with excitement OR when he was invited to David's party.

16 The chicken clucked loudly OR after laying an egg.

17–18 *cold, freezing*
19–20 *soft, easy*
21–22 *hate, dislike*
23 *tough* **27** confidential
24 *though* **28** artificial
25 *borough* **29** financial
26 *thought* **30** initial

TEST 5: Vocabulary

1 television
2 kilometre
3 United Kingdom
4 approximately/approximate
5 unidentified flying object
6–10 teacher, farmer, electrician, nurse, doctor
11–12 *giggle, chuckle*
13–14 *block, close*
15–16 *scare, terrify*
17–18 *guzzle, gulp*
19 piglet **21** duckling
20 owlet **22** gosling
23 *to buy something*
24 *to watch over (a task, activity or person) to make sure everything runs well*
25 *to practise something*
26 *bad-tempered*
27–30 football, snowball, snowman, footman

TEST 6: Mixed

1–6 observant, observance, assistant, assistance, confident, confidence
7 ✔ **9** ✔ **11** ✗
8 ✗ **10** ✔ **12** ✗
13–16 Two sentences that use either commas, brackets or dashes to indicate something is in parenthesis.

17–18 *whoosh, crackle*
19–20 *glug, drip*
21–28

Common nouns	Proper nouns
jacket	China
lifetime	Meena
Collective nouns	**Abstract nouns**
herd	jealousy
gaggle	hate

29 *brave, fearless and determined*
30 *strong and warm*

TEST 7: **Grammar**

 1 *gulped, gobbled*
 2 *rushed*
 3–4 *yelled; struggle, jump*
 5–6 *raced; terrified*
 7–8 *beautiful, happy*
 9–10 *bright, shiny*
 11–12 *slippery, silvery*
 13–14 *blue, cloudy*
 15–16 *Wales, Queen Elizabeth*
 17–18 *in, after*
 19–20 *softly, suddenly*
 21–22 *she, they*
 23–30 Four sentences, each using an adverb or modal verb to illustrate degrees of possibility, e.g. The shops *should* be open tonight.

TEST 8: **Comprehension**

 1 *Laurie was able to see the pig because it glistened in the moonlight.*
 2 *He was surprised to see the pig because the pig was wandering around a building site.*
 3 *Although Laurie realised he was watching something out of the ordinary, he also realised that it wasn't so important that he needed to wake his parents.*

 4 tawny-gold
 5 *'His stomach lurched'; 'He caught sight of his white knuckles gripping the window-sill'.*
 6 Laurie's cat Mrs Gingerbits.
 7 *The silence is described as 'heavy' because it is an uncomfortable silence, loaded with worry and concern for Laurie.*
 8 the builder
 9 *It proved that Laurie had seen a pig because the land was destroyed by the pig's rooting around.*
 10 *Your child's description of how Laurie might now be feeling, e.g. frightened, worried, shocked.*

TEST 9: **Mixed**

 1 Thomas had a friend around for tea <u>but</u> Alex wasn't allowed one.
 2 Kay was late for the party <u>despite</u> leaving home on time.
 3 Bola lost his race <u>when</u> he tripped over his laces.
 4 The dog barked <u>and</u> made the horse rear up.
 5 *a statement of ideas or beliefs*
 6 *to trust someone with a secret*
 7 *an agreement between two parties to stop fighting for a certain length of time*
 8 *an event or happening*
 9 *happening quickly or unexpectedly*
 10 There were no footballs to play with / There weren't any footballs to play with.
 11 They didn't wear school uniform on the trip.
 12 There wasn't a recorder lesson today. / There was no recorder lesson today.
 13 The train didn't arrive early at the platform.
 14 fell   **15** swept
 16–17 was; driven
 18 found

 19–24 magic, legend, register, enlarge, dungeon, mirage
 25 present   **28** past
 26 future   **29** future
 27 past   **30** present

TEST 10: **Sentences**

 1–6 "Did you get my e-mail?" Gareth asked.
 7–10 Nina, now she was feeling better, had arranged to meet her friends.
 11–16 "Would you like some sweets?" asked Deano.
 17 did   **19** Did
 18 done   **20** done
 21 *Alex said he was glad Aunty Sue was coming with them.*
 22 *Mum reminded the children not to forget/to remember their coats.*
 23–26 Four sentences that include a relative clause using the listed words, e.g. That's the girl who lives near my uncle.

TEST 11: **Mixed**

 1–2 bow bough
 3–4 heel heal
 5–6 seller cellar
 7–11 <u>They</u> rushed over the rocks, desperate to get to safety before the waves came in and cut <u>them</u> off from the path ahead. Henry cried as <u>he</u> slipped and hurt his arm. <u>It</u> was wrapped in a jumper, as there was no time for <u>anything</u> else.
 12 untrue   **15** convey
 13 direct   **16** offend
 14 pursue
 17–18 The puppy raced towards the ball.
 19–23 S/he ate the ice-cream quickly as it dripped down his/her arm.
 24 *endless, ending*
 25 *helpful, helper, helping*
 26 *colourless, colourful*

27 scrumptious **29** flirtatious
28 malicious **30** ferocious

Test 12: **Spelling**

1 develop **21** jewellery
2 answer **22** different
3 judge **23** They're
4 amuse **24** there
5 tidy **25** their
6 peace **26** There
7 electric **27–28** They're
8 connect their
9 excitable **29** v**ei**l
10 possible **30** h**ei**ght
11 inflatable **31** for**ei**gn
12 resistible **32** cash**ier**
13 flexible **33** rel**ief**
14 divisible **34** rec**ei**pt
15 reliable **35** flatter
16 excusable **36** preferring
17 history **37** busier
18 available **38** transferred
19 leisure **39** referred
20 vegetable **40** relieved

Test 13:

1 We don't know. It was written anonymously.
2 They sang.
3 *She wanted to wear something more practical outside.*
4 white
5 caught sight of
6 *She wanted a freer, or more exciting life.*
7 *The lord felt upset and surprised. He wanted to try to persuade her to come back home.*
8 *messy, dirty, unclean, untidy*
9 *the language it is written in, the description of the servants, horse, home etc.*
10 *happy, relieved and free to have left the home where she obviously felt unhappy*

Test 14: **Mixed**

1 pizza – Italy
2 boomerang – Australia
3 restaurant – France
4 pyjamas – India
5 adverb
6 verb
7 preposition
8 abstract noun/noun/verb
9 pronoun
10 adjective/verb
11 *Chloe asked if they could go swimming.*
12 *The Bayliss family complained that they always have fish fingers for tea.*
13 *Dad suggested they drive past Buckingham Palace.*
14 *Elizabeth laughed, saying she loved pony riding.*
15 misquote **18** dislodge
16 mishandle **19** misspell
17 dismount
20–30 "I feel so tired," complained Jim.
"That's because it is one o'clock in the morning!" said the babysitter.

Test 15: **Vocabulary**

1 impossiblility **6** smart
2 irritable **7** smirk
3 island **8** smoke
4 ivy **9** smother
5 investigate **10** smuggle
11–14 *computer, compact disc, ipod, mobile phone, television*
15 *heehaw* **17** *honk*
16 *roar* **18** *cluck*
19–20 *untidy, messy*
21–22 *sad, unhappy*
23–24 *weak, feeble*
25–26 *damp, wet*
27 cloud **29** fence
28 cats **30** music

Test 16: **Mixed**

1 HRH **3** Dec
2 DIY **4** PM
5 OAP **9–10** to, to
6 PO **11** two
7 too **12** to
8 Too
13–16 "Time for your piano lesson," Mum called. (or!)
17–20 "Where have you put my phone?" asked Rebecca.
21 *sparkly, glamourous*
22 *terrified, prickly*
23 *mad, strict*
24 *empty, bustling*
25 *The rain poured but they still had a BBQ.*
26 *There was a fire in the school hall although it didn't do much damage.*
27 *Jake threw the ball and it landed in someone's garden.*
28 *disrespect* **30** *whisper*
29 *daft*

Test 17: **Grammar**

1–8

Common nouns	Proper nouns
insects	Jake
pets	Tyrone
Collective nouns	**Abstract nouns**
swarms	dislike
colonies	fear

9 *the old and musty book*
10 *the long, hot and busy summer*
11 *the fearless and amazing acrobat*
12 *the beautiful and interesting country of India*
13 *a lovely, old family photograph*
14 *because*
15 *although*
16 *but*
17 *as*
18 *so*
19–20 Everyone watched anxiously as the rope was lowered over the edge of the cliff.
21–22 The children wandered off gloomily despite being given some money to spend.

23–24 Nazar worked happily knowing as soon as he'd finished cleaning the car he could go <u>inside</u> to watch the rugby match.

25–30 *Three sentences, each sentence containing two possessive pronouns, e.g. <u>Ours</u> is bigger than <u>theirs</u>.*

11 suffixes
12 under
13 at
14 with
15 above
16 on
17 dramatise
18 solidify
19 thicken
20 fertilise
21 You'll
22 mustn't
23 Let's
24 could've
25 I'd
26 *though*
27 *weight*
28 *grown*
29 *hour*
30 *door*

Test 18: Comprehension

1 Nairobi
2 (1) *dirt instead of paved roads* (2) *background noise of cockerels and cows instead of car horns and radios*
3 *the daughter of Boniface and Pauline Kamaus*
4 *one's native language/ the language a person first learns to speak*
5 *Many of the plants grown in Murang'a differ to those grown here because of the different climate.*
6 *Pauline felt comfortable back home with her parents and possibly liked getting away from the busy city.*
7–8 *Joyce and Sharon's grandparents must get their water from a stream and grow their own food. Most grandparents in England get their water from taps in their house and buy food in shops.*
9 *If they moved back to the country, getting a job to earn enough money to take care of the young family would be much harder than it is in the city.*
10 *the watching of TV, enjoying time with cousins, staying with grandparents etc.*

Test 19: Mixed

1 *section*
2 *unoccupied, empty*
3 *selfish*
4 *obvious*
5 *recall*
6 torches
7 princesses
8 thieves
9 bikes
10 valleys

Test 20: Sentences

1–4 *Two sentences, each with two correctly marked commas, e.g. Katy put her pencil, pen, ruler and sharpener in her backpack.*
5 *It is time to meet in the park.*
6 *We are going on holiday to Devon.*
7 *Liverpool won the Premiership.*
8 *The school is closed because of the snow that fell last night.*
9 *The cows are milked twice a day.*
10 are   12 is   14 Is
11 are   13 is   15 are
16–28 "What time does the film start?" asked Brenna. She was worried they wouldn't have time to buy popcorn before it started. "We have plenty of time," her dad reassured her.

Puzzle ❶

sausage – usage, age, sage, us, sag, a
wardrobe – ward, robe, rob, war, be, a
mathematics – math, at, the, he, them, mat, hem, tic, tics, thematic, thematics, a
scarecrow – scar, scare, car, row, are, crow, care, a
coincidentally – coincide, coincidental, dent, dental, tall, den, ally, all, incident, incidental, incidentally, tally, in, coin, a

Puzzle ❷

An adjective beginning with each letter of the alphabet – 'x' will be the biggest challenge and a dictionary could be used to help with this one!

Puzzle ❸

Your child's own answers to a number of word problems e.g.
marmalade *maroon marry mask mass master match material maths matter mattress maximum mayor meadow mean measles* **measure**
A word with all vowels = *aeronautics*

Puzzle ❹

north = thorn
parties = pirates
vowels = wolves
team = meat, mate, tame
eighth = height
thicken = kitchen
Three anagrams chosen by your child

Puzzle ❺

silly – sensible
official – unofficial
dissatisfied – happy
huge – tiny
incorrect – right
unclear – legible
smooth – rough

Write there, their or they're in each gap.

23 _____ going to be late.

24 We must be nearly _____ by now!

25 We'll collect _____ sleeping bags on the way home.

26 _____ seems to be a problem with that car.

27–28 _____ great friends but they argue about _____ favourite football teams all the time!

Add ie or ei to each of these to make a word.

29 v__ __l

30 h__ __ght

31 for__ __gn

32 cash__ __r

33 rel__ __f

34 rec__ __pt

Complete these word sums. Watch out for the spelling changes!

35 flat + er = _____

36 prefer + ing = _____

37 busy + er = _____

38 transfer + ed = _____

39 refer + ed = _____

40 relief + ed = _____

Read this poem carefully.

The Wraggle Taggle Gypsies

1   There were three gypsies a-come to my
    door,
    And down-stairs ran this lady, O!
    One sang high, and another sang low,
5   And the other sang, Bonny, bonny,
    Biscay, O!

    Then she pulled off her silk finished
    gown
    And put on hose of leather, O!
10 The ragged, ragged rags about our door –
    She's gone with the wraggle taggle
    gypsies, O!

    It was late last night, when my lord
    came home,
15 Enquiring for his a-lady, O!
    The servants said on every hand:
    'She's gone with the wraggle taggle
    gypsies, O!'

    'O saddle to me my milk-white steed,
20 Go and fetch me my pony, O!
    That I may ride and seek my bride,
    Who is gone with the wraggle taggle
    gypsies, O!'

    O he rode high and he rode low,
25 He rode through woods and copses too,
    Until he came to an open field,
    And there he espied his a-lady, O!

    'What makes you leave your house and
    land?
30 What makes you leave your money, O!
    What makes you leave your new-wedded
    lord;
    To go with the wraggle taggle gypsies,
    O!'

35 'What care I for my house and my land?
    What care I for my money, O?
    What care I for my new-wedded lord?
    I'm off with the wraggle taggle gypsies,
    O!'

40 'Last night you slept on a goose-feather
    bed,
    With the sheet turned down so bravely,
    O!
    And to-night you'll sleep in a cold open
45 field,
    Along with the wraggle taggle gypsies,
    O!'

    'What care I for a goose-feather bed,
    With the sheet turned down so bravely,
50 O!
    For to-night I shall sleep in a cold open
    field,
    Along with the wraggle taggle gypsies,
    O!'

Anon.

Answer these questions about the poem.

1 Who wrote this poem? _____

2 What did the gypsies do at the lady's door?

_____

3 Why do you think the lady took off her silk gown?

_____

4 What colour was the lord's horse?

_____

5 What does the word 'espied' (line 27) mean?

_____

6 Why did the lady leave with the gypsies?

_____

_____

7 Describe how the lord felt about his wife leaving.

_____

_____

8 What impression does the phrase 'wraggle, taggle' give you about the gypsies?

_____

9 How do we know this poem was not written in the present day?

_____

10 At the end of the poem, how do you think the lady is feeling? Why?

_____

_____

Total

Draw lines to link each word with the country from which it is borrowed.

1 pizza   Australia

2 boomerang   India

3 restaurant   Italy

4 pyjamas   France

Which part of speech is each of these words?

5 beautifully   _____

6 wrote   _____

7 behind   _____

8 love   _____

9 they   _____

10 blunt   _____

Change these sentences into *reported speech*.

11 "Can we go swimming?" Chloe asked.

_____

12 "We always have fish fingers for tea," complained the Bayliss family.

_____

13 "Let's drive past Buckingham Palace," suggested Dad.

_____

14 "I love pony riding!" laughed Elizabeth.

_____

Select the *prefix* mis or dis for each of these words.

15 _____quote

16 _____handle

17 _____mount

18 _____lodge

19 _____spell

Rewrite the following correctly.

20–30 i feel so tired complained jim that's because it is one o'clock in the morning said the babysitter

_____

_____

_____

_____

_____

Total

Write one word for each *definition*. Each word begins with the letter i.

1 Something that cannot be done under any circumstances. _____

2 Grumpy and easily annoyed. _____

3 A piece of land surrounded by water. _____

4 A leafy, evergreen plant that can climb up walls. _____

5 To look into something or someone. _____

Write these words in *alphabetical order*.

smirk   smother   smart   smuggle   smoke

6 _____

7 _____

8 _____

9 _____

10 _____

Write four words that have been invented in the last 100 years.

11 _____

12 _____

13 _____

14 _____

Write an *onomatopoeic* word for the sound that each of these animals makes.

15   donkey   _____

16   lion   _____

17   goose   _____.

18   hen   _____

Write two *antonyms* for each of these words.

19–20   tidy   _____   _____

21–22   happy   _____   _____

23–24   strong   _____   _____

25–26   dry   _____   _____

Choose a word to complete each expression.

fence   cloud   music   cats

27   Every _____ has a silver lining.

28   It is raining _____ and dogs.

29   To sit on the _____.

30   To face the _____.

Total

Write the *abbreviations* of these words.

1   His Royal Highness   _____

2   do it yourself   _____

3   December   _____

4   Prime Minister   _____

5   old age pensioner   _____

6   Post Office   _____

Add 'to', 'too' or 'two' to each sentence to make it correct.

7   The chips were _____hot.

8   _____ many people were trying to get on the bus.

9–10 Danielle wanted _____ go _____ Rupa's party.

11   The _____ boys ran as fast as they could.

12   The teacher spoke sternly _____ the giggling children.

Rewrite these sentences with the missing punctuation.

13–16 Time for your piano lesson Mum called

_____

_____

17–20 Where have you put my phone asked Rebecca

_____

_____

Add an interesting *adjective* to describe each of these *nouns*.

21   the _____ dress

22   the _____ hedgehog

23   the _____ professor

24   the _____ restaurant

Use *connectives* to write each of these pairs of short sentences as one sentence.

25   The rain poured. They still had a BBQ.

_____

26   There was a fire in the school hall. It didn't do much damage.

_____

_____

27   Jake threw the ball. It landed in someone's garden.

_____

Write an *antonym* for each of these words.

28   respect   _____

29   clever   _____

30   scream   _____

Complete the table using some of the *nouns* in the short passage.

1–8 Jake had a dislike of insects. He worried that swarms or colonies might attack him! Tyrone wanted to help him get over his fear and so told him to think of them as pets!

Common nouns	Proper nouns	Collective nouns	Abstract nouns

Write an *adjectival phrase* about each of these *nouns*.

9 a book

_____

10 the summer

_____

11 an acrobat

_____

12 India

_____

13 a photograph

_____

Complete each sentence by adding a different *conjunction*.

14 Faye couldn't go to the party _____ she was unwell.

15 The flowers opened in the sun _____ there was a cold wind blowing.

16 Annie was painting in the kitchen _____ the cat had taken cover under the table!

17 Gareth was terrified _____ the spider made its way towards him.

18 They missed their train _____ they had to catch a bus.

Circle the *adverbs* and underline the *prepositions* in these sentences.

19–20 Everyone watched anxiously as the rope was lowered over the edge of the cliff.

21–22 The children wandered off gloomily despite being given some money to spend.

23–24 Nazar worked happily knowing as soon as he'd finished cleaning the car he could go inside to watch the rugby match.

Write three sentences, each including two *possessive pronouns*.

25–26 _____

_____

27–28 _____

_____

29–30 _____

_____

(35)

Total ⬭

Read this article carefully.

The Kamaus from Kenya   *by Xan Rice*

1 For the half-term holidays, the Kamaus went upcountry to the farming village where Pauline's parents live. Though just 60 miles from the Kenyan capital,
5 Nairobi, Murang'a is a very different world.

Tarred road gives way to dirt; concrete urban sprawl to rich red soil. The background noise comes from cockerels
10 and cows rather than the car hooters and blaring radios of the big city.

The children love visiting their grandparents. Though Joyce is something of a TV addict, she and
15 Sharon revel in the wide-open space and the chance to play all day with their cousins, who seldom make it to Nairobi.

They also practise speaking Kikuyu, which should be their mother tongue.
20 Boniface and Pauline are native Kikuyu speakers, but at home in Nairobi they communicate in Kiswahili, which together with English is Kenya's official national language and predominates in
25 the urban areas. At school, Joyce learns only the two national languages, and her Kikuyu is rusty at best....

Pauline also enjoys being home with her parents. As their first-born child, she
30 assumes the greatest responsibility of all her siblings for her parents' well-being. For now they are doing just fine.

On a hectare of land, they grow maize, beans, bananas, sugarcane, sweet
35 potatoes, avocados and coffee. They also have a cow, a few goats, chickens and rabbits. Some of the produce is eaten; the rest taken to the wholesale market.

40 Pauline quickly slipped back into the lifestyle of her youth. She fetched water from the nearby stream. She worked in the fields. In the evenings, she helped prepare dinner. It made her
45 nostalgic, and after the holiday Pauline told Boniface that they should think of moving to the countryside.

But Boniface was not tempted. Murang'a in particular, just a few miles from where
50 he was raised, holds too many memories of a difficult childhood. Then there is the issue of work. Being a taxi-driver in Nairobi is a tough job, but at least it provides a steady income – far more
55 than he could ever make as a small-scale farmer.

Article from the Guardian *by Xan Rice*

Answer these questions about the article.

1 Where do the Kamaus live in Kenya?

   _____

2 List two differences between life in Murang'a and life in Nairobi.

   _____

   _____

3 Who is Joyce?

   _____

4 What is a 'mother tongue' (line 19)?

   _____

5 What do you notice about the foods grown in Murang'a compared to in England?

   _____

6 Why do you think Pauline wanted to move back to the countryside?

   _____

7–8 Describe two ways the life of these children's grandparents differs from the lives of the grandparents of many children in the United Kingdom.

   _____

   _____

   _____

   _____

9 What is meant by the sentence 'Then there is the issue of work' (lines 51–52)?

   _____

   _____

10 How many similarities can you list between your family and the Kamaus family?

   _____

   _____

Total

TEST 19: **Mixed**

Test time: 0   5   10 minutes

Write a *synonym* for each of the words in bold.

1 Please pass me the **part** of the newspaper that is for children.

_____

2 The bungalow in our street has been **vacant** for a year. _____

3 She is so **stingy**, she never shares her colouring pens. _____

4 It was **clear** from his pale face that he had hurt his ankle badly.

_____

5 Gemma, can you **remember** what I asked you to do next?

_____

Write the *plural* forms of these words.

6 torch   _____   **9** bike   _____

7 princess   _____   **10** valley   _____

8 thief   _____   **11** suffix   _____

Circle the *preposition* in each of these sentences.

12 George's shoes were hidden under the sofa.

13 Tea will be ready at six-thirty.

14 Helen mended her broken tyre with a puncture repair kit.

15 The river flooded above the height of the fence posts.

16 The dog slept soundly on his owner's bed!

Change these words into *verbs* by adding a *suffix*.

en   ise   ify

17 drama _____

18 solid _____

19 thick _____

20 fertile _____

Add the missing apostrophes.

21 Youll have to learn your spellings for the test!

22 We mustnt be late.

23 Lets buy some sweets, please.

24 You couldve stayed longer.

25 I wish Id brought my bike to ride.

Write a word with the same letter string as underlined in each of these words, but a different pronunciation.

26 t<u>ough</u> _____

27 h<u>eight</u> _____

28 br<u>own</u> _____

29 f<u>our</u> _____

30 sp<u>oo</u>n _____

(39)

Write two sentences. Each sentence needs to have two commas.

1–2

Are emma, Katie, Luc and Sarah coming to your party?

3–4

I need to get an apple, banana, orange and pear from the shop.

Write these questions as statements.

5   Is it time to meet in the park?

Its time to meet in the park.

6   Are we going on holiday to Devon?

We are going on holiday to Devon.

7   Did Liverpool win the Premiership?

Liverpool won the Premiership.

8   Is the school closed because of the snow that fell last night?

The school is closed because of the snow that fell last night.

9   Are the cows milked twice a day?

The cows are milked twice a day.

Add 'is' or 'are' to each sentence to make it correct.

10 On Saturday, Kellie and Sarah __are__ coming for a sleepover.

11 We __are__ still waiting for the train!

12 Hussan __is__ working hard to improve his skateboarding.

13 Daniel __is__ going to walk the dog when he gets home.

14 __IS__ Sam's answer right?

15 Where __are__ your gloves?

Rewrite this short passage correctly.

16–28

what time does the film start asked brenna

she was worried they wouldn't have time to buy popcorn before it started

we have plenty of time her dad reassured her

"What time does the film start?" asked Brenna. She was worried they wouldn't have time to buy popcorn before it started. "We have plenty of time", her dad reassured her.

Total

Puzzle 1

Each of these words has within it a number of smaller words.
How many smaller words can you find in each word, without rearranging the letters or missing letters out?

sausage

_____

wardrobe

_____

mathematics

_____

scarecrow

_____

coincidentally

_____

Find your own word that has at least five smaller words within it.

Try it out on someone.

_____

Puzzle ❷

Can you find 26 different *adjectives*, each beginning with a different letter of the alphabet?

a _____   b _____   c _____

d _____   e _____   f _____

g _____   h _____   i _____

j _____   k _____   l _____

m _____   n _____   o _____

p _____   q _____   r _____

s _____   t _____   u _____

v _____   w _____   x _____

y _____   z _____

Circle the five most imaginative *adjectives* you have written.

Puzzle ❸

Answer these problems, then try again using a dictionary!

List as many words as you can that lie alphabetically between the words 'marmalade' and 'measure'.

My unaided answers

My answers with the help of a dictionary

Write the longest word you can think of.

_____

Write the longest word you can find in a dictionary.

_____

Write a word with as many vowels as possible.

_____

Write a word from the dictionary that uses as many vowels as possible.

_____

Can you find a word in the dictionary that uses all of the vowel letters?

_____

Puzzle ❹

Look carefully at these words.

spoon	**sister**	**petal**

If the letters in each word are rearranged they will make a new word.
These words are called anagrams.

spoon	**=**	**snoop**
sister	**=**	**resist**
petal	**=**	**plate**

Your challenge is to find the hidden words by rearranging the letters in these words, as quickly as possible!

north _____

parties _____

vowels _____

team _____

eighth _____

thicken _____

Now make three anagrams of your own.

_____ = _____

_____ = _____

_____ = _____

Puzzle ⑤

g	f	r	a	t	u	h	m	c	i
s	e	n	s	i	b	l	e	t	p
d	w	e	m	n	s	q	h	o	p
v	h	q	c	y	n	g	c	r	e
t	e	a	k	d	i	y	a	o	g
i	e	j	p	r	k	r	d	u	i
t	w	g	j	p	o	d	s	g	b
e	l	s	i	a	y	n	e	h	y
u	n	o	f	f	i	c	i	a	l
p	i	t	l	e	g	i	b	l	e

Look in the wordsearch to find *antonyms* for the following words.
Write the words you have found.

silly   _____

official   _____

dissatisfied   _____

huge   _____

incorrect   _____

unclear   _____

smooth   _____

Key words

abbreviation	a word that has been shortened
abstract noun	a noun referring to a concept or idea, for example love, beauty
adjectival phrase	a group of words describing a noun
adjective	a word that describes somebody or something
adverb	a word that gives extra meaning to a verb
alphabetical order	words arranged in the order of the letters in the alphabet
antonym	a word with a meaning opposite to another word, for example hot/cold
clause	a section of a sentence with a verb
collective noun	a word referring to a group or collection of things, for example a swarm of bees
common noun	a general name of a person, place or thing, for example boy, office
compound word	a word made up of two other words, for example football
conjunction	a word used to link sentences, phrases or words, for example and, but
connective	a word or words that join clauses or sentences
contraction	two words shortened into one with an apostrophe placed where the letter/s have been dropped, for example do not/don't
definition	the meaning of a word
double negative	two negative words in a sentence that make the idea in the sentence positive, for example I am <u>not</u> going to buy <u>no</u> bike (which means I am going to buy a bike)
homophone	a word that has the same sound as another but a different meaning or spelling, for example right/write
modal verb	a verb that changes the meaning of other verbs, for example can, will
noun	a naming word
onomatopoeic	a word that echoes a sound, associated with its meaning, for example hiss
parenthesis	this is a word or phrase that is separated off from the main sentence by brackets, commas or dashes usually because it contains additional information not essential to its understanding
phrase	a group of words that do not contain both a subject and a verb
plural	more than one, for example cats
possessive pronoun	a pronoun showing to whom something belongs, for example mine, ours
prefix	a group of letters added to the beginning of a word, for example un, dis
preposition	a word that links nouns and pronouns to other parts of a sentence, for example he sat *behind* the door
pronoun	a word that can be used instead of a noun
proper noun	the specific name or title of a person or a place, for example Ben, London
relative clause	a special type of clause that makes the meaning of a noun more specific, for example The prize *that I won* was a book
reported speech	what has been said without using the exact words or speech marks
root word	a word to which a prefix or suffix can be added to make another word, for example quick – *quickly*
singular	one of something, for example cat
suffix	a group of letters added to the end of a word, for example ly, ful
synonym	a word with a very similar meaning to another word, for example quick/fast
tense	tells when an action was done, for example past (I slept), present (I am sleeping) or future (I will sleep)
verb	a 'doing' or 'being' word

Total

Progress Grid

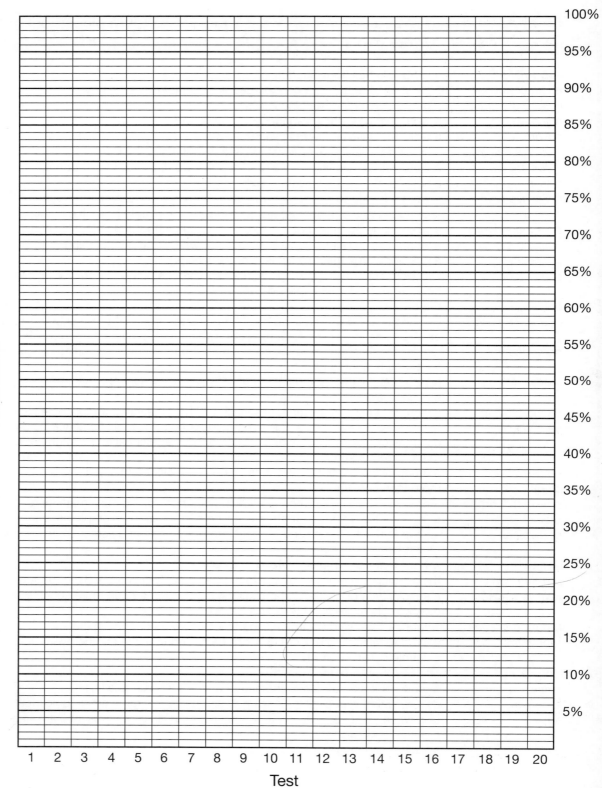

Total marks

Test

French Fortresses in North America 1535–1763

Québec, Montréal, Louisbourg and New Orleans

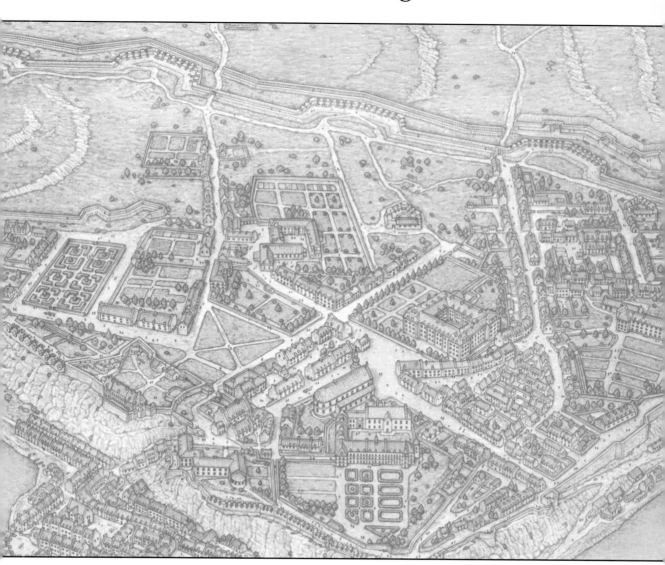

René Chartrand · Illustrated by Donato Spedaliere

Series editors Marcus Cowper and Nikolai Bogdanovic

First published in 2005 by Osprey Publishing
Midland House, West Way, Botley, Oxford OX2 0PH, UK
443 Park Avenue South, New York, NY 10016, USA
Email: info@ospreypublishing.com

ISBN 1 84176 714 X

Editorial: Ilios Publishing, Oxford, UK (www.iliospublishing.com)
Design: Ken Vail Graphic Design, Cambridge, UK
Index by David Worthington
Maps by The Map Studio Ltd
Originated by The Electronic Page Company, Cwmbran, UK
Printed and bound in China by L Rex Printing Company Ltd..

05 06 07 08 09   10 9 8 7 6 5 4 3 2 1

A CIP catalog record for this book is available from the British Library.

FOR A CATALOG OF ALL BOOKS PUBLISHED BY OSPREY MILITARY AND AVIATION PLEASE CONTACT:

NORTH AMERICA
Osprey Direct, 2427 Bond Street, University Park, IL 60466, USA
E-mail: info@ospreydirectusa.com

ALL OTHER REGIONS
Osprey Direct UK, P.O. Box 140, Wellingborough, Northants, NN8 2FA, UK
E-mail: info@ospreydirect.co.uk

www.ospreypublishing.com

The Fortress Study Group (FSG)

The object of the FSG is to advance the education of the public in the study of all aspects of fortifications and their armaments, especially works constructed to mount or resist artillery. The FSG holds an annual conference in September over a long weekend with visits and evening lectures, an annual tour abroad lasting about eight days, and an annual Members' Day.

The FSG journal *FORT* is published annually, and its newsletter *Casemate* is published three times a year. Membership is international. For further details, please contact:

The Secretary, c/o 6 Lanark Place, London W9 1BS, UK

Acknowledgments

The author is grateful to his many colleagues at Parks Canada, notably those at Fortress Louisbourg, the Fortifications of Québec and at the national HQ in Ottawa. Also Claire Mousseau, chief archaeologist of the City of Montréal, the staff of the National Archives and Library of Canada and of the Archives Nationales in France.

Artist's note

Our sincere thanks to all who have helped in the preparation of this book. We would like to dedicate this book to our dearest daughter Alina.
Readers may care to note that the original paintings from which the colour plates in this book were prepared are available for private sale. All reproduction copyright whatsoever is retained by the Publishers. All enquiries should be addressed to:

Sarah Sulemsohn
Tel-Fax: 00 39 0575 692210
info@alinaillustrazioni.com
alina@alinaillustrazioni.com
www.alinaillustrazioni.com

The Publishers regret that they can enter into no correspondence upon this matter.

Author's Note

"In the new colonies, the Spanish start by building a church, the English a tavern and the French a fort." There was some truth in this tongue-in-cheek remark by the great French author René de Chateaubriand (1768–1848); New France eventually had a North American network of numerous forts, big and small, extending from the Gulf of St. Lawrence to the Gulf of Mexico and west into the present-day Canadian and American prairies. There were also fortresses, the subject of this study, as the main towns were fortified. Fortresses such as Louisbourg and Québec have been rightly famed for their extensive fortifications, Québec having the advantage of a formidable natural site. However, few people today would guess that Montréal and New Orleans could also be termed fortresses, for they were once enclosed by bastioned walls and moats. Although their fortifications were relatively modest and meant to deter raiders rather than fully fledged armies, both cities were surrounded by numerous outlying forts. These provided early warning and acted as an outer buffer, a feature peculiar to the fortress cities situated at the hub of great North American rivers.

Measures

These have varied over the centuries and varied from one nation to another. In New France, weights and measures were those used by the mother country. It is most important to note that the French foot, used in New France, was longer (12.789 inches) than the British foot (12 inches). The official French measures from 1668 to 1840 were:

2 miles = 1 Lieue = 3.898 kilometers
1,000 Toises = 1 mile = 1.949 kilometers
       (British = 1.61 kilometers)
6 feet = 1 Toise = 1.949 meters
       (British Fathom = 1.83 meters)
12 inches = 1 foot = 32.484 centimeters
       (British = 30.48 centimeters)
12 lines = 1 inch = 2.707 centimeters
       (British = 2.54 centimeters)

Contents

Introduction

Following the discovery of America by Columbus in 1492, European colonists built their style of fortification in the New World in an attempt to ensure their safety and consolidate their conquests. The Spanish and Portuguese were the first to build sizeable forts, some of which evolved into fortified towns—fortresses—as their settlements grew. San Juan (Puerto Rico), Havana (Cuba), Cartagena de Indias (Colombia) and several others in the "Spanish Main" and South America were already renowned by the 17th century. The French and the British came later to North America and thus the establishment of their sizeable permanent settlements only got under way during the 17th century. The British colonists rapidly outgrew their small stockaded settlements along the North American coastline but did not build elaborate fortifications to protect their towns. Their French neighbors did.

From the early 17th century until the end of the Seven Years War in 1763, the greater part of North America came under the French realm and much of it was called *La Nouvelle-France* (New France). Thanks to relentless explorers and traders, the land mass of New France was enormous, extending from the Gulf of St. Lawrence to the Rocky Mountains in the west and from the Great Lakes to the Gulf of Mexico in the south. But as impressive as it may have looked on a map, New France remained a weak colony in terms of population, which was sparse and scattered. It had only about 500 French inhabitants in 1641, some 14,000 in 1689 and perhaps 80,000 of French origin by the 1750s.

In the early 17th century, New France was divided into two administrative entities. The largest and most important was the colony of Canada, which included the settled areas in the St. Lawrence Valley with the three towns of Montréal, Trois-Rivières and Québec. It also extended into the western wilderness as far as it had been explored, an ongoing process. On the Atlantic seaboard was the small colony of Acadia whose settlements were spread in parts of present-day Nova Scotia, New Brunswick and Maine. On the island of Newfoundland was the port of Placentia that formed a small colony. Following the cession of Acadia and Placentia to Britain by the Treaty of Utrecht in 1713, the garrisons and some of the settlers were moved to Cape Breton Island, subsequently renamed Isle Royale, where, from 1720, the fortress of Louisbourg was built.

Further south, the French had reached the Gulf of Mexico in 1682 by coming down the Mississippi River and, from 1699, settlements were established on the coast to make up the third entity, the colony of Louisiana, in the present-day states of Alabama, Mississippi and Louisiana. Today a relatively small American state, Louisiana in the 18th century covered an enormous territory extending from Canada to the Gulf of Mexico. Louisiana's population was modest and its settlements were concentrated on the Gulf Coast and in Les Illinois (also called Upper Louisiana), in the general area of present-day St. Louis.

The government of New France was patterned after that of a French province. The governor-general of New France, who resided in Québec, had overall authority and was commander-in-chief. He was assisted by the intendant in financial and civic matters and the bishop in religious issues, their respective powers being devolved to local governors, commissaries and senior priests. In Canada, there were local governors in Montréal and Québec. Isle Royale's governor was in Louisbourg and Louisiana's governor was in New Orleans. Although nominally subordinate to the governor-general in Québec,

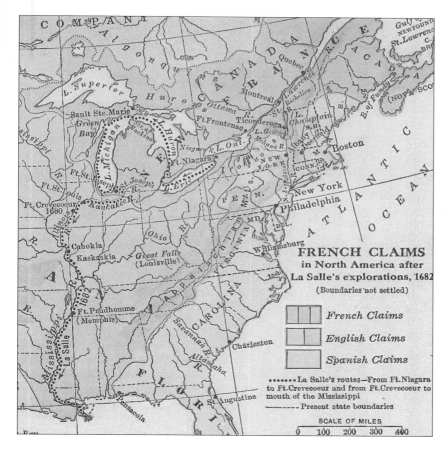

Detail of a map of French claims to North America following Robert Cavelier de La Salle's explorations (dotted line) from Canada to the Gulf of Mexico. It formed a great arc enclosing the British coastal colonies. Starting in the northeast (top right corner) with Cape Breton Island, where Fortress Louisbourg was built from 1720, it extended west along the St. Lawrence River, passing the fortresses of Québec and Montréal and continuing to the Great Lakes; then south on the Mississippi River to the Gulf of Mexico where New Orleans, also eventually enclosed by walls, would be built. The forts shown along the Mississippi River were mostly the early ones built by La Salle.

the governors of Isle Royale and Louisiana were independent as they reported directly to the minister responsible for naval and colonial affairs in Versailles. Canada, the Atlantic seaboard colonies and Louisiana each had their respective garrisons of colonial troops.

The fortresses of New France studied in this book—that is to say, substantial towns and cities enclosed by protective walls—were extraordinary in their variety. (The term *place forte* rather than *forteresse* was generally used by the French to denote a town surrounded by fortifications until the 1870s.) Québec was a formidable natural fortress; the defenses of Louisbourg were almost transposed from Vauban's textbooks; Montréal had a substantial wall and New Orleans was eventually also protected by moats and redoubts. Although quite different in fortification style and extent, Québec, Montréal, Louisbourg and New Orleans all had one thing in common: their strategic importance was tremendous and the fall of any one of them practically ensured the fall of their entire area.

Except for New Orleans, all were besieged during the 17th and 18th centuries. Québec resisted in 1690 but fell in 1759; its henceforth British garrison would resist in 1760, and again (against the Americans) in 1775–76. Louisbourg fell twice, in 1745 and 1758, after great sieges. Montréal held the last French army in Canada when it surrendered to three British armies in September 1760. Only New Orleans escaped being besieged although treaties signed in Europe passed it from France to Spain in 1763, to France again in 1802 and finally to the United States of America in 1803.

One town that never quite made it as a fortress was Trois-Rivières, although it was enclosed by a palisade wall. Founded in 1634, it quickly lost its strategic and economic importance after Montréal was settled in 1642. As will be seen

The Coat of Arms of France, c.1725–60. Traditionally, the royal coat of arms was put up above the gates of fortifications. In New France, this was not always the case and, according to Chief Engineer Chaussegros de Léry, they were nowhere to be seen "in this colony." In 1725, he had royal coats of arms made and put up at all government buildings, forts, gates, courtrooms and jails; and all new government buildings would have them henceforth (AC, C I IA, 47). This particular example was once displayed over the gates of Québec and may have been the work of Pierre-Noël Levasseur. It is now in the Canadian War Museum in Ottawa. A similar example is at the Musée de la Civilisation in Québec. (Author's photograph)

later, its meager defenses had become useless by the middle of the 18th century.

Each major town was capital to an area. Québec was simultaneously the capital of New France, the colony of Canada and the district of Québec. Trois-Rivières and Montréal were respectively the capitals of their districts of Trois-Rivières and Montréal. Louisbourg was the capital of the colony of Isle Royale (Cape Breton Island) and New Orleans was the capital of Louisiana.

Within the French colonial administrative system, these towns—Québec, Trois-Rivières, Montréal, Louisbourg and New Orleans—were the seats of governors and their retinues of garrison staff officers. Principal among these were the *Lieutenant du Roi* (King's Lieutenant, in effect the lieutenant governor), the *Major de Place* (Town Major, often assisted by an assistant major) and, in major cities, a *Capitaine des Portes* (Captain of the Gates, a medieval title to denote the officer in charge of security). In the case of Québec, the governor-general of New France resided there and was also the town's governor. His prestige was of the highest order and some of the honor due to him equaled that of marshals in France. Drum rolls greeted him when he came into or out of his château; he was allowed an escort of his own guards; he enjoyed cannon salutes when arriving in towns and he would be addressed as *Monseigneur* (My Lord). He had a staff of several officers including the senior *Ingénieur du Roi* (King's Engineer) in the colony and the captain of his guards acted as an aide-de-camp.

Next in line to the governor-general was the intendant, the most important civil official, who also resided in Québec City. By protocol a subordinate to the governor-general, the intendant was his equal regarding financial management (including military budgets), legal matters and commerce, all of which were his responsibility. His subalterns, the *Commissaire-ordonnateur*, were to be found in all fortress towns except Trois-Rivières. The intendant and a colony's *Commissaire-ordonnateur* ranked as high civil officials and enjoyed an escort of an *Archer* (police constable) on formal occasions.

Chronology

1534	Explorer Jacques Cartier takes possession of Canada for France. The area is named New France.
1535	Cartier and his men build a small fort in the area of Québec.
1541–43	Cartier and the Sieur de Roberval build several forts in the Québec area, but the colony is abandoned in 1543.
1608	Samuel de Champlain, explorer and first governor-general of New France, founds Québec and has the first of several forts built.
1620	Fort built on Cape Diamond at Québec. It eventually becomes the residence of the governor-general of New France.
1642	Montréal, originally called Ville-Marie, is founded.
1682	Explorer Robert Cavelier de La Salle descends the Mississippi River to the Gulf of Mexico, takes possession of the Mississippi Valley for France and names it Louisiana.
1660s–90s	String of outlying forts built in the Montréal area.
1687–89	Palisade built around Montréal.
1690	Québec is enclosed by a stockade with small bastions. A New England fleet and soldiers, led by Sir William Phips, are repulsed after a short siege in October.
1693	Ramparts with large bastions replace the stockade at Québec. Several inconclusive attempts to make better ramparts in following decades.
1699	First permanent French settlements established in Louisiana.
1717	Work commences on reveted rampart to enclose Montréal. The work goes on until 1744.
1720	Foundation stone is laid at Louisbourg and extensive fortifications are built there until 1743.
1722	New Orleans becomes the capital of Louisiana.
1730	Work commences on rampart at New Orleans, but it is left unfinished.
1745	Louisbourg falls to a New England army. Reveted walls are built to enclose the landward side of Québec.
1749	Louisbourg is returned to the French.
1758	Louisbourg falls to British army and fleet; its fortifications are blown up two years later and the remnants of the town are abandoned in the late 1760s.
1759	Fortifications of Québec are improved, notably artillery batteries and a series of redoubts built on the Beauport shore area up to the Montmorency River. After a summer-long siege by British forces and the French army's defeat on the Plains of Abraham, the city surrenders.
1760	French siege to retake Québec fails. Last French army in Canada surrenders at Montréal in September.
1760–61	Fortifications enclosing New Orleans are built and completed.
1763	Treaty of Paris: France cedes Canada, Isle Royale and Louisiana on east side of the Mississippi River to Britain; the rest of Louisiana is ceded to Spain.

The King's Engineers

The theoretical education of French engineers in the age of Louis XIV (1643–1715) and Louis XV (1715–74) was remarkably good by the standards of the day and covered aspects of engineering, tactics, architecture, fine arts and town planning. Geometry was the main element of European military architecture since the end of the Middle Ages and the introduction of artillery in siege warfare. The large castles with high walls and turrets were obsolete as they could be demolished by cannonballs. New ways had to be found to protect strongholds; obviously, the walls and towers would have to be lower and wider, made of stone frames filled with earth, so as to accommodate artillery for the defenders while making it much more difficult for the besieger to breech the walls. By the 1480s, Italian military engineers had conceived the corner bastion that became, quite literally, the cornerstone of fortifications for centuries to come. Renaissance engineers in Italy published a multitude of geometric designs with bastions and moats at all angles to enclose a city with fortifications as well as laying out city streets and squares in an orderly fashion. Some were fanciful but, on the whole, they offered effective ways to defend a city in a European military context. From the late 16th century and during the 17th century, major wars were often fought in mostly flat terrain of Flanders where geometric designs could be built almost flawlessly. The Dutch engineers now became leaders in military architecture, devising enormous earthworks that were surrounded by large water-filled moats thanks to the high water table of that area. Menno van Coehorn (1641–1704) was the leading Dutch engineer whose intricate fortification designs and the use of water as an obstacle were much admired.

The French were also keenly interested in fortifications and had, since the Renaissance, applied the "Italian tracing" to their fortress designs while adding features of their own. The French approach was more systematic than elsewhere and, as early as 1604, a nationwide administrative regulation concerning fortifications was put in place. This brought an increasing professionalization of military engineering, which coincided with the advent of Sébastien Le Preste de Vauban (1633–1707), one of the greatest engineers in military history. Part of Vauban's remarkable success was due to his pragmatic approach; he was not merely a theoretician with skills in geometry, he was also a veteran military engineer in the field who conducted some 48 sieges during his career. Vauban's elaborate systems of fortifications thus combined and enhanced designs proven effective in actual siege warfare, hence their renown. Louis XIV, recognizing Vauban's great talent, made him national superintendent of fortifications and tasked him with building or repairing a multitude of forts and fortresses all over France, but especially in Flanders, where the king wanted a line of fortresses built to prevent enemy incursions. This vast public works project, which went on for decades, required numbers of qualified engineers. Previously, more or less gifted amateurs had been somewhat self-proclaimed "engineers" who largely acquired their knowledge from engineering books published mostly in Italy and in Holland. Louis XIV felt that military engineering was a state secret and that Vauban's manuals on fortifications, on the ways to attack and defend fortresses should not be published. Thus, those selected to be military engineers had no printed manuals from Vauban; instead part of their training was to make a manuscript copy of Vauban's treatises, which they would keep as their main reference work afterwards.

In France, the men responsible for designing and building fortifications were the "King's Engineers" (*Ingénieurs du Roi*). These were highly skilled and educated individuals who held royal commissions—hence being called the "King's"—to practice their art in government service. They combined the present-day skills of architecture, military and civil engineering, and urban planning. While primarily concerned with fortifications, they could also be called upon to design churches, windmills, warehouses, etc. The King's Engineers also had military officers' commissions to provide them with a rank, usually that of captain, within the military structure. They were employed as staff officers and would also be found in the entourage of a colonial governor or governor-general.

Under Marshal Vauban's leadership, the King's Engineers formed a sort of small independent ministry whose staff was spread all over France and its colonies. This state of affairs continued following Vauban's death. The Marquis d'Asfeld, his successor, was a skilled soldier and courtier who, during his lifetime, managed to keep the engineers from being amalgamated. In 1732, he introduced a colorful uniform for the King's Engineers consisting of a scarlet coat with blue cuffs, scarlet waistcoat and breeches, gilt buttons set in pairs, a dress that certainly distinguished them from most officers in the armed forces.

In March 1743, the Marquis d'Asfeld passed away and the engineers' independence came to an end. Most were absorbed into the army in France with others going to the navy. As the navy was responsible for the colonies in America, there were hardly any changes for the engineers posted to the various towns who continued to be called the King's Engineers and wear their scarlet uniforms. From the time of the Seven Years War, metropolitan army engineers were sent to Canada and other colonies and served mostly in the field as with Montcalm's army. The colonial King's Engineers continued to be mostly preoccupied by fortifications, sometimes quite far into the wilderness interior of the continent.

Engineers were active in Canada from the early decades of the 17th century, most notably Jacques Bourdon, who was active in Québec from 1634 to 1668. A regular establishment of engineers under a chief engineer was set up in the late 17th century. Robert de Villeneuve first had the post from 1685 to 1693. Jacques Levasseur de Néré was named to succeed him but only arrived from France in 1694. In the meantime, Captain Josué Berthelot de Beaucours, an infantry officer with engineering talent, had filled in and supervised the construction of Québec's first line of ramparts. Both engineers were kept busy in the next decades with de Beaucours succeeding Levasseur de Néré as chief engineer of Canada in 1712 until transferred to Louisbourg in 1715. Two sub-engineers had been added from 1712. Gaspard Chaussegros de Léry arrived in 1716 to fill the post of chief engineer, which he had until his death in 1756. He was succeeded by Nicolas Sarrebrousse de Pontleroy.

The first chief engineer in Isle Royale was Jacques de Lhermitte, who was succeeded by de Beaucours in 1715. However, Joseph-François du Verger de Verville drafted the initial plans of the new fortress, followed by Étienne Verrier, chief engineer at Louisbourg from 1725 to 1745. Louis Franquet took on the post in 1750 as well as that of Inspector of Fortifications in Canada (which was done in 1752–53); he was an experienced engineer with the rank of colonel in 1751 and brigadier in 1754, the highest ranking engineer in New France. He served in Louisbourg until the fortress fell in 1758.

The early engineers in Louisiana were Paul de Perrier, Pinel de Boispinel, Jacques Le Blond de La Tour and Adrien de Paugé who all arrived in 1718 sponsored by the "Occident" monopoly company that then ruled the colony. In 1731, the French crown took over the administration and Broutin became Chief Engineer in Louisiana. He designed the first fortifications for New Orleans in the early 1730s but it was only in 1760 that the city was finally enclosed by a rampart laid out by Chief Engineer Vergès.

An *Ingénieur du Roi* (King's Engineer) c.1740. They were assigned a uniform from February 25, 1732, consisting of a scarlet coat with scarlet lining, waistcoat, breeches and stockings, blue cuffs, gold buttons (four set in pairs on cuffs), gold hat lace and, initially, a white plume border (not mentioned from the later 1730s onward). Colonial engineers continued to wear this uniform until the end of the Seven Years War in 1763. (Reconstruction by Michel Pétard; Parks Canada)

A French military engineer landing in New France came with an education suitable for siege warfare in Europe. He was now faced with a "New World" offering very different strategic and geographic conditions into which he simply had to adapt. A good example was Chief Engineer Chaussegros de Léry. A veteran of European campaigns during the War of the Spanish Succession, he landed at Québec in 1716 with a complete knowledge of Vauban's system and, in his baggage, his own multi-volume manuscript treatise on fortifications and architecture. This remarkable work, which has survived the ravages of time and is now preserved in the National Archives of Canada, shows the considerable extent of knowledge a senior military engineer would have arriving in a colonial setting. In a site such as Louisbourg, local topography allowed an engineer such as Verrier the building of Vauban-style fortifications. But in Canada, as de Léry quickly perceived, many elements rendered Vauban's system questionable. Distance and a sparse population meant that military forces would move by water rather than by land and that manpower to build enormous bastions and glacis was not available. Thus, his first major work, the design to enclose Montréal with a reveted rampart, was a radical departure from the ideal star-shaped fortress in Flanders and resembled far more an early 17th-century fortress without the extensive outworks. De Léry's plans to enclose the landward sides of Québec were in the typical Vauban style and built from 1745. The planned moats and glacis were only completed facing the Saint-Jean Bastion, no doubt due to labor and money shortages and perhaps to doubts as to the pertinence of having such works on the heights of Cape Diamond. On the other hand, New Orleans had the flat terrain and high water table ideal for a city surrounded by water-filled moats and large bastions. But, as Chief Engineer Broutin soon found, he was not dealing with calm waters as in Flanders but with the mighty Mississippi River and its tons of silt that might wash fortifications away and fill moats with silt. And New Orleans did not have sufficient labor to build such large works in the first place, although a good solution to the city's defenses was eventually put up by Engineer de Vergès.

Besides fortresses, as plans in the archives and remaining vestiges show, French engineers in North America had to alter their notion of what an outlying stone fort should be like. From the 17th until the mid-18th century, the main threat came from enemy Indian raids. Thus, stone forts more reminiscent of small medieval castles (see pages 38–39) were built near Montréal and also at Chambly and, as a huge tower, at Saint-Frédéric (Crown Point, NY). Thereafter, with an Anglo-American enemy looming, the more usual square plan with bastions, already common in wooden forts, was used for stone-walled strongholds such as Fort de Chartres (Illinois) and Fort Carillon (Ticonderoga, NY).

Québec

The mightiest site on the continent

The most formidable fortress in North America was the city of Québec. An Indian town was already there when, in 1535, French explorer Jacques Cartier arrived and named its imposing 300-foot cliff Cap Diamant (Cape Diamond). Cartier and his men decided to pass the winter in Canada. They feared "betrayal" on the part of the Indians and so they built a small fort "entirely enclosed with large pieces of wood standing on end" that was mounted "with artillery all around it." They reinforced it externally "with large moats, wide and deep, and a drawbridge gate." It was the first fort built in Canada, but the French abandoned it the following year.

In 1541, Cartier was back, leading a larger expedition. This time, two small forts were built, one at the foot of Cap Rouge (west of Cape Diamond) and the other, certainly smaller, on top of the cliff. Once again, however, the French left the area in the spring of 1542 after some fighting with Indians. Later that year, another French expedition led by the Sieur de Roberval arrived in the area and built a fort on the summit of Cap Rouge that was described as being "very strong" with "a large tower" and a main building inside. Another fort was built at the foot of Cap Rouge and featured "a two-storey tower, with two good main buildings." The new settlement was baptized France-Roy. During the winter of 1542–43, scurvy took the lives of a quarter of the French colonists. With his colony decimated and no gold found, Roberval gave up, and everyone went back to France in 1543. Sixty-five years were to pass before another settlement attempt was made.

On July 3, 1608, another French expedition under Samuel de Champlain landed at Québec and began the construction of a "Habitation" at the foot of Cape Diamond, on the site of the present-day city's lower town. Thus began the first permanent settlement in New France. Initially, it was a trading post, but missionaries and settlers joined the traders in the following years while the

The forts of France-Roy (at the present-day Cap Rouge, just west of Québec), built by Roberval and his men in 1542. One fort was near the shore at the estuary of the St. Lawrence River and the small Cap-Rouge River; the other was at the top of the height just behind. The settlement was abandoned in 1543. (National Film Board of Canada)

11

Ships before Cape Diamond in the early 17th century. Samuel de Champlain chose the magnificent site, called Québec by the Indians, in 1608 as the place at which to establish the first settlement in what would become Canada. (Author's photograph)

The "Habitation" was the first fort built by the French at Québec from July 1608. It featured high vertical walls, a ditch and platforms for artillery outside the castle-like structure. The structure was enlarged in 1616. (Print after Samuel de Champlain; National Library of Canada, L8769)

adventurous Champlain, also governor of the small establishment, started exploring the interior of the vast continent. Québec was his base and, in 1616, the Habitation was enlarged. In 1620, a new fort with a residence for the governor was built on top of Cape Diamond to replace his lodging in the decaying Habitation. This fort was built of timber with earthen embankments. The exceptional site of the fort gave a commanding view of the St. Lawrence River. In time the governor's residence grew and became the Château Saint-Louis, residence of the governor-generals of New France and, later, of British North America. Today, the governor-general of Canada has a summer residence in the citadel, not very far from the site of the original Château Saint-Louis.

Between 1624 and 1626, a new and larger Habitation featuring "a square wall with two little towers on the corners" was built "for the security of the place." In 1626, work started on reconstructing and expanding the fort on Cape Diamond. The work was to little avail, however, as Québec was blockaded from 1628 and captured without a fight in 1629 by English corsairs, the Kirke brothers.

Under the terms of the 1632 peace treaty between France and Britain, Canada was returned to France. When the French retook possession of Québec in 1633, it found the second Habitation burned down, and the fort on the cape and other public buildings ransacked by the Kirke brothers. Repairs were made over the next couple of years but, in 1636, the new governor, Jacques Huault de Montmagny, had major improvements made to the

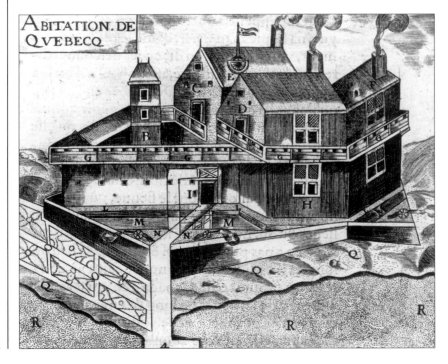

The second "Habitation" was built in 1624–26 and replaced the first one built in 1608. Situated at the foot of Cape Diamond, it was larger and featured two medieval-looking stone turrets at the corners of a large stone building enclosed by a wooden wall. At the time, Québec was primarily a fortified trading post. (Model at the Centre d'Interprétation de la Place Royale, Québec; Author's photograph)

fort on Cape Diamond; a parade ground and the first streets, named Saint-Louis, Sainte-Anne and Mont-Carmel, leading to the fort were laid out. In 1646–47, the fort and its château were rebuilt in stone.

As imposing as its site was, for many years Québec had practically no fortifications other than the Château Saint-Louis and its fort perched on Cape Diamond. It was impressive nonetheless, as indeed it still is today. In 1672, Governor-General Louis de Buade, Comte de Frontenac, wrote to Jean-Baptiste Colbert, Louis XIVs powerful minister of trade and the navy, that "nothing has seemed to me so beautiful and magnificent as the site of the city of Québec, it cannot be better situated, and is destined to one day become the capital of a great empire." These were prophetic words as the "great empire" was in the process of being discovered by explorers such as Marquette and La Salle who were exploring the Mississippi Valley.

Québec remained an open city until 1690. During the spring of that year, the fall of Port Royal in Acadia to a naval and military force from Massachusetts under Sir William Phips fueled concerns that Québec City would be the next target. Should a hostile force land, the whole landward side of the city to the north and west had no defenses at all and was totally exposed. An attack from those areas, and particularly from the flat western side known as the Plains of Abraham, would catch the defenders in the city from the rear. Nothing much could be done from the fort enclosing the Château Saint-Louis to prevent such an attack by a well-organized enemy. Governor-General Frontenac, who had just returned to Canada for a second term, immediately ordered that a wooden palisade be erected to enclose the city. This first wall, which featured 11 small stone redoubts, was sufficient to avoid any nasty surprises and gave a measure of protection against a force lacking siege artillery. Built under the direction of Town Major Provost, it extended from the château to the St. Charles River. The likelihood of an enemy getting its heavy siege guns on that side was correctly thought to be most unlikely. Besides the wall, a number of batteries were built and the existing batteries were

The Château Saint-Louis and its fort at Québec in 1683. The walls of the fort on Cap Diamant (Cape Diamond) were built from 1636 and stood until torn down in 1693. This first Château Saint-Louis was built in 1647. This was where, in 1690, Sir William Phips' messenger delivered the summons to surrender and received Count Frontenac's celebrated reply that he would answer with his cannons' muzzles. During the 1690 siege, the fort acted as the citadel of Québec's fortifications. The château was demolished in 1692 in order to build a larger one. The houses on the right side border the narrow way (now Petit-Champlain Street) down to the lower town. (Print after Jean-Baptiste Franquelin)

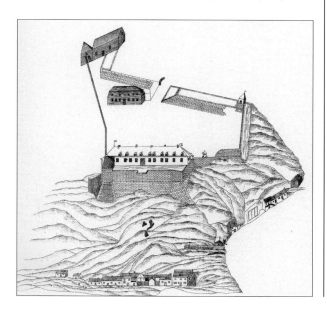

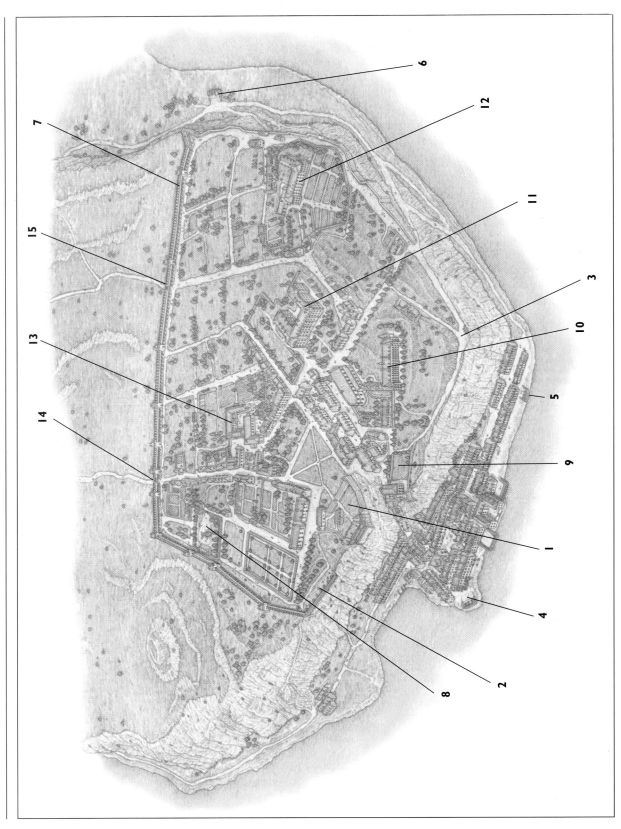

Québec , 1690

In 1690, the city of Québec did not have extensive fortifications. Instead it relied on the great strengths offered by its location. Not only did the city have outstanding and very visible cliffs and Cape Diamond, but also its whole eastern shore heading toward the St. Charles River to the north was very shallow and could not be approached by ships. The town's main man-made defenses consisted of batteries set up in both the lower town and upon the cliff, and a palisade to protect the landward side. Within the city, various temporary obstacles had also been erected, notably at the street leading to the upper town.

In the upper town, just west of the fort (1) and the Château Saint-Louis, residence of the governor-general, was an eight-gun battery (2). East of the Château Saint-Louis, at the turn of the cliff toward the north, was a three-gun battery (3).

On the shore of the lower town, at the site of the future Royal Battery, was a platform with three 18-pounder guns (4). Further east on the waterfront was another battery with three 18-pounder guns (5). Heading north, at the limit of the town near the intendant's palace, was another three-gun battery at water level (6). This area also had a large contingent of troops and, beyond, the west shore of the St. Charles River had been strenghened with field fortifications (not shown).

The landward side was enclosed by a palisade built shortly before the siege (7). It started west of the battery near the Château Saint-Louis and ended on the eastern side not very far from the hospital. This log wall featured 11 stone "redoubts" that seem to have been square towers. On the west side, facing the Plains of Abraham, was a windmill called Mont-Carmel where a three-gun battery was established to provide a strong point for the palisade line on the landward side (8). There may also have been individual guns at other locations all over the city. Other important sites in the city included the Bishop's palace (9), Québec Seminary (10), Jesuit's College and residence (11), Hospital (12), Ursuline Sisters College and residence (13), Saint-Louis Gate (14) and Saint-Jean Gate (15).

This bust of Louis XIV by Bernini was unveiled in 1686 at the Place Royale in Québec's lower town. Later removed and lost, another casting of the bust was installed when the area was renovated in the 1960s and 1970s; a fitting reminder of the "Sun King" whose policies fostered France's influence in North America. (Author's photograph)

improved. A battery of eight guns was erected next to the château and two more were built at the docks in the lower town, each having three 18-pounder cannons. Other batteries were sited at various points overlooking the river. All these batteries were meant to cover any enemy ship that got too close to the city.

The 1690 siege

While Québec did not have a real citadel, the construction of all these batteries sited on the finest spots of the city's commanding cape made it a difficult place for enemy ships to attack. On October 16, 1690, some 34 ships flying English ensigns came into view with 2,300 men on board. It was Sir William Phips, heading an expedition of New Englanders out to conquer New France. The colony of Massachusetts had sponsored the whole scheme and financed it by

issuing paper bonds set against the value of the booty that would be taken in the conquered colony. As his fleet came into view of Québec, Sir William and his senior officers realized that their objective was sited on the strongest natural position they likely had ever seen. Up in the château on Cape Diamond was Governor-General Frontenac, a crusty old soldier from ancient nobility, proud and temperamental, an experienced officer and shrewd man of action. He was looking forward to the coming fight.

Up to that point, Phips and his New Englanders were quite confident that the cowardly and effete French would be no match for their hardy men and the city was expected to surrender immediately. Phips wrote up a fairly curt summons with instruction to the French commander that he had one hour to comply. An officer was at once sent to the city to present the summons. He was blindfolded and brought to the Château Saint-Louis. There, the fiery Governor-

The 1690 defense of Québec. This 19th-century print shows the city as it would have appeared in the early 1700s rather than 1690, notably the Château Saint-Louis as rebuilt from 1692. Nevertheless, it gives an excellent sense of the commanding sites available to the French batteries on Cape Diamond when pitted against Sir William Phips' ships on the St. Lawrence River. (National Archives of Canada, C6022)

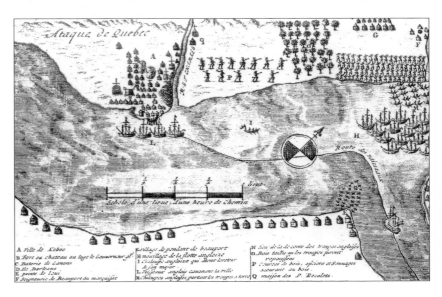

"Ataque de Québec" in 1690, showing the failed attack by Sir William Phips. The "English" ships (actually from New England) can be seen in the river (L and H). At the upper right, the Massachusetts troops have landed (M) below the village of Beauport (F) and are about to be met by French troops and Canadian militiamen (P) in the woods (O). Québec's fortifications are not shown in any detail, probably on purpose. (Print after La Hontan)

General Frontenac, with many of his officers in their best dress, listened to the summons. The New Englander then pulled out his watch. That was too much for Frontenac. He was so enraged that he wanted to have the messenger hanged at once in full view of the Massachusetts fleet! Calmed by the bishop and the intendant, he answered the summons with a line that has since become famous in Canadian history: "Tell your master I will answer him by the mouth of my cannons!"

Governor-General Frontenac had gathered at Québec about 900 regular soldiers of the colonial troops—the *Compagnies franches de la Marine*—out of the 1,400 in New France. In addition, some 1,100 Canadian militiamen were assembled. There were also approximately 100 allied Indians. The French defending force was thus about 2,100 men.

Possibly the weakest part of the French defenses was the city's northeastern side. Phips and his senior officers saw it as the only possibility to crack French defenses, while his ships would bombard the city. On October 18, about 1,200 New Englanders landed unopposed at Beauport. Frontenac expected the New Englanders' land attack to come from that area and so the banks of the St. Charles River had been built up with field fortifications on the southwestern side. He had already sent strong detachments of Canadian militiamen along with some Indians skilled in bush warfare into the wooded areas east of the river. Meanwhile, the bigger British ships had moved closer to bombard the city. The French shore batteries proved to be more than a match; their guns pounded four of the larger ships. Rigging and hulls were badly damaged, and,

at length, the battered vessels withdrew. During the artillery duel, the ensign of Phips' flagship was cut down and fell into the St. Lawrence River. A few hardy Canadians jumped into a canoe and paddled for it under a hail of musket shots from the ships. Their daring paid off and they triumphantly brought the prize back into the city unscathed.

After a couple of miserable days, the New Englanders on shore decided to attack. The plan was to cross the St. Charles River, carry the shore positions, overcome the earthworks and break into the city. They set out in the best European tradition

A 1690 view of Québec from the northeast. The logs of the hurriedly erected palisade helped seal the city against an attack from the landward side. (National Archives of Canada)

Map detail of the 1690 siege of Québec. Sir William Phips' fleet of 34 vessels is before the city. The French battery of eight guns in the lower town was the strongest element of the city's defenses. It was rebuilt as the permanent Royal Battery the following year. Other batteries (Nos. 11, 12, 15 and 16) each had three guns, while No. 17 indicates canoes stationed as lookouts along the coast. The New England land forces disembarked from 42 longboats at la Canardière, on the Beauport shore. (Map by Nicolas de Fer, 1694; National Archives of Canada)

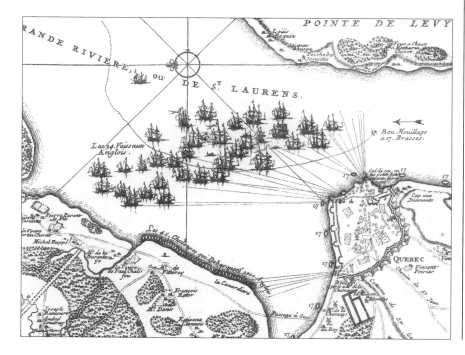

Québec:
The Royal Battery

This battery was situated on the waterfront of the lower town and, in spite of being relatively modest in size, was one of the most important fortifications in the city due to its strategic location. The Royal Battery's guns covered the city's dock area and a good part of the St. Lawrence River to its south shore.

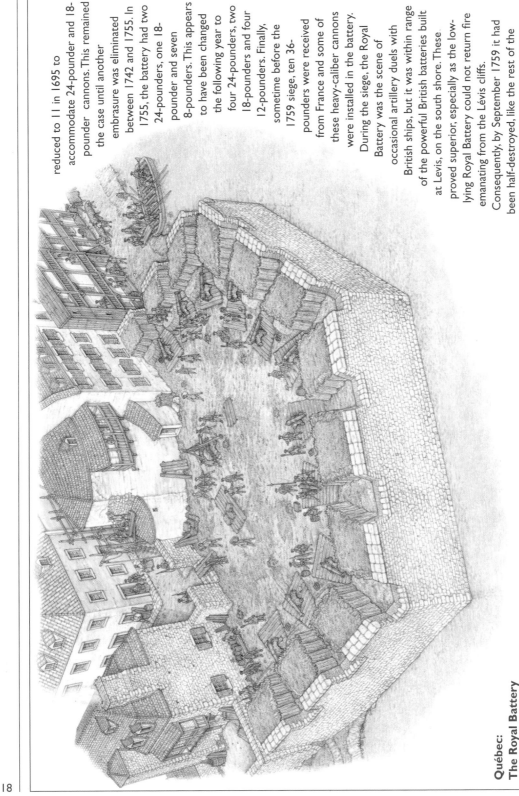

After the siege of 1690, Governor-General Frontenac ordered a fully fledged shore battery to be built there. It was shaped like a small bastion and featured 14 embrasures for guns to cover both sides of the shore as well as the river. Over the years, some features changed, notably the number of embrasures for guns; they were reduced to 11 in 1695 to accommodate 24-pounder and 18-pounder cannons. This remained the case until another embrasure was eliminated between 1742 and 1755. In 1755, the battery had two 24-pounders, one 18-pounder and seven 8-pounders. This appears to have been changed the following year to four 24-pounders, two 18-pounders and four 12-pounders. Finally, sometime before the 1759 siege, ten 36-pounders were received from France and some of these heavy-caliber cannons were installed in the battery. During the siege, the Royal Battery was the scene of occasional artillery duels with British ships, but it was within range of the powerful British batteries built at Lévis, on the south shore. These proved superior, especially as the low-lying Royal Battery could not return fire emanating from the Lévis cliffs. Consequently, by September 1759 it had been half-destroyed, like the rest of the lower town. After the Seven Years War (1756–63), the site of the battery was transformed into trade docks covered with warehouses. But the old battery was never quite forgotten and, in the 1970s, was restored to its mid-18th-century appearance by the Québec government.

The Royal Battery was built from 1691 on the waterside of the lower town. Buried and transformed into a dock in the late 18th century, the foundations of the battery were unearthed and restored in the 1970s. In the background are the castle-like Château Frontenac Hotel and the Dufferin Terrace where the governor-generals of New France had their fortified Château Saint-Louis. (Author's photograph)

with drums beating and colors unfurled. At the edges of the woods, plenty of Canadian militiamen were waiting for them. The New England militiamen could not cope with their heavy fire, wavered and fell back. Brass field guns were brought up and fired into the woods, but to no effect. At length, unable to advance further, the New Englanders retreated back to their camp. The Canadians and Indians maintained the pressure thereafter by skirmishing closer and closer to their camp. By the night of October 21–22, the New Englanders were utterly discouraged and made a spontaneous general retreat to their ships in a state of near panic, even leaving behind five of their field guns on the shore. Thus far, about 150 New Englanders had been killed or wounded in action and many more would die of exposure and sickness. The French and Canadians had suffered, at most, nine killed and 52 wounded (but only eight known wounded for certain). On October 23, Phips and his fleet sailed back to Boston. Thus ended the first siege of Québec.

The old and new fortifications, essentially the batteries, had proven more than a match for Phips' ships when they tried to bombard the city. The batteries on the waterfront had not been seriously damaged while those further

A plan of the works at Québec started in September 1693 by the engineer Berthelot de Beaucours. On the landward side was a new line of earthworks "at the top of which are stakes that join each other." Work on the line proceeded slowly and it was not completed until 1702. Another new feature built in 1693 was a square stone redoubt on top of Cape Diamond (visible at left), which commanded the whole area. Fort Saint-Louis remained the city's main fort. Various walls and batteries were built along the heights of the upper city. The lower city's main defense was the waterside Royal Battery. (National Archives of Canada)

up were unscathed. The weak point had been the Beauport shore where the New Englanders had landed; but they had been contained and driven back. However, if a stronger force landed there with siege artillery, the city could be attacked on the landward side. Obviously, the hastily built wall would have to be improved. For the New Englanders, a most important lesson had been learned: they could not, by themselves, take Québec; to achieve such an objective, the resources of Old England would have to be brought in.

Improvements

Although the attack had been repulsed, Governor-General Frontenac was well aware of Québec's weaknesses

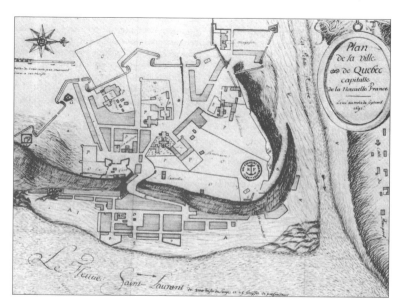

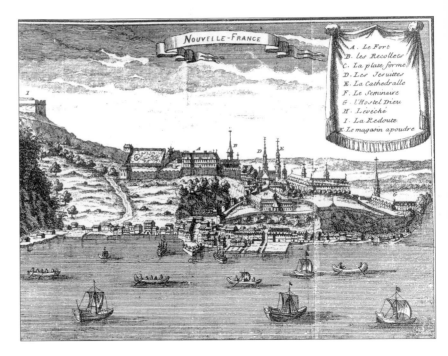

A view of Québec in 1700. The improvements made to the city's defenses since Phips' 1690 siege are shown in this print. The Royal Battery protects the harbor. To the left (or west) of the fort and the Château Saint-Louis (A) is a wall with cannon embrasures extending to a small stone tower with a palisade up the hill connecting to another tower; these are two of the redoubts built with the 1690 palisade that enclosed the city. On the height of Cape Diamond at left is the Cape Redoubt (I); built in 1693, it was the beginning of de Beaucours' rampart (invisible on this print) started that year. (Private collection)

and, in 1692, tasked Engineer Josué Berthelot de Beaucours with the design and construction of new fortifications on the landward side that could withstand a European-style siege. Work started in the summer of 1693 on an earth rampart with large bastions, which enclosed the city. Pointed wooden stakes were planted on top of the walls. Two masonry structures were also built: the Cape Diamond Redoubt on top of the highest spot on the cape and the *cavalier* du Moulin in the first bastion. The building work continued slowly for nine years. In the meantime, a new engineer, Jacques Levasseur de Néré, had arrived and disagreed with just about everything de Beaucours had constructed. The new fortifications did indeed have some defects; most could be enfiladed from various heights outside the fortifications. The resulting disputes put a stop to any major works for some time to come.

In 1711, during Queen Anne's War (1702–13), another attempt was made to capture Québec. This time, Royal Navy Admiral Hoveden Walker sailed for

Québec's ramparts just above the Saint-Jean gate. These are the walls constructed in 1745. (Author's photograph)

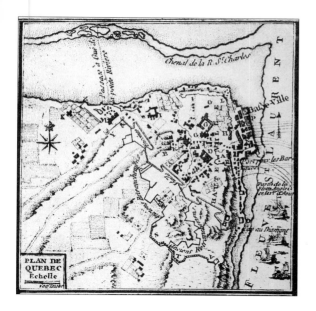

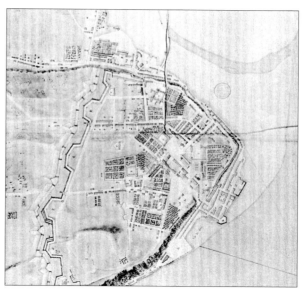

Québec leading nine warships, two bomb ketches, and 60 other vessels carrying eight British infantry regiments and two New England militia regiments; some 7,500 soldiers in all. But fate stepped in. On the night of August 22–23, the fleet was sailing north of Anticosti Island as it entered the St. Lawrence River. The weather was bad and eight transport vessels carrying troops ran onto the reefs of Egg Island with disastrous consequences: 29 officers and 705 soldiers belonging to four of the eight British regiments of regular troops were lost, as well as 35 soldiers' wives. Walker turned back and Québec was spared another siege. But because the British might return, in 1712 work started on the Dauphine and Royale redoubts to cover the north side of the city on the land side. In 1713, war ended; work on the Royale Redoubt was nearing completion but the Dauphine Redoubt was only half-finished and remained unusable for many years to come.

In 1716, Chief Engineer Gaspard Chaussegros de Léry arrived in Canada. He immediately submitted several plans to improve Québec's fortifications. A talented engineer, he at once saw that the city's weak point was in its western approaches and made plans for a new line of works on the western (landward) side of the city to replace de Beaucours' crumbling quarter-century-old earthworks. A regular bastioned wall faced with masonry was necessary. De Léry's main proposal to make the place almost impregnable was to build a citadel on the highest point of Cape Diamond. By 1720, he even had a scale model of Québec made and shipped to France for the minister of the navy and colonies to consider his proposals; this model featured the new fortifications that should be built. (De Léry's model has never been found and seems to have been destroyed. Another model of Québec was made in 1806–08 by J-B Duberger and Captain John By, RE, and is now on display at the Québec Fortifications National Historic Site in the Saint-Jean Bastion.)

De Léry's plans to improve Québec's defenses were rejected due to fiscal restraint. Besides, it was considered more urgent to fortify Montréal, which hardly had any defenses, and to build substantial forts at Pointe à la Chevelure (renamed Saint-Frédéric; Crown Point to the British and Americans) and Niagara. Québec was imposing enough for the time being, especially as France and Britain were at peace, and so practically nothing was done until war broke out again in 1744. The fall of Louisbourg, in the summer of 1745, came as a shock to people in Québec. Nothing now stood in the way to prevent a British force from sailing up and attacking the city.

ABOVE LEFT Québec, 1709. This is possibly the most famous map of Québec as it has been published in countless books, notably in Father Charlevoix's *Histoire de la Nouvelle-France* (1744). It was attributed to Chaussegros de Léry in 1720 and Royal Engineer Patrick Mackellar used it in 1759 as his main source for a map of Québec. Close examination reveals that the line of fortifications enclosing the city's western side is that put up in 1693 by de Beaucours. The unfinished line of ramparts further to the left are those built by Levasseur de Néré between 1700 and 1707. Because the second line of fortifications featuring the Dauphine and Royale redoubts started by Levasseur de Néré in 1712 is not shown, the map can be dated to 1709 as Father Charlevoix was in Canada between 1705 and 1709. (Private collection)

ABOVE RIGHT In 1745, a new line of fortifications further west was started and these are the present-day walls of Québec on the landward side. Except for the glacis and earthworks outside the wall that were never finished, this 1752 plan by Chief Engineer Chaussegros de Léry shows the city essentially as it was when General Wolfe's army besieged it in 1759. De Léry also drew in future streets and rectangular city blocks in the upper city's west side and future square city blocks bordered by walls and bastions in the vacant lots of the lower city's northeast area. (National Archives of Canada, C21779)

21

Québec
1759

The city's fortifications during the siege of 1759 were reasonably extensive but certainly not very elaborate.

From 1745, the city's landward side was enclosed by a line of bastioned ramparts that were reveted with stone, as planned by Chief Engineer Chaussegros de Léry (1). A small redoubt with a powder magazine was positioned at the highest point on Cape Diamond, on the emplacement where the present Québec Citadel was later built. It offered a magnificent view and was the ideal lookout point. In 1759, the walls extending from the Cape Diamond Redoubt to the Potasse Demi-bastion were completed and equipped with 52 guns, but they were mounted in the several bastions' flanks for enfilade fire and so could not fire at the enemy at long range. Furthermore, the ditch and glacis were only finished in front of the Saint-Jean bastion and the Potasse Demi-bastion facing north (2). The rest of the perimeter was unprotected by a ditch and glacis and was thus considered the city's weak side by the French commanders. Traces of the previous earthen wall, work on which started in 1693, were still visible, as were its unfinished Royale and Dauphine redoubts, but none of these features had any protective value in 1759 (3).

In the upper town, the batteries west of the fort and the Château Saint-Louis were rebuilt from 1693, improved during the 1740s and had 16 guns and two mortars in 1759 (4). The most extensive batteries, sometimes called the Grand Battery, had 42 cannons and seven mortars installed at the southern edge of the cliff from the Côte de la Montagne to beyond the turn of the cliff (5). Because the river level was very shallow, fewer guns were needed on the eastern side of the cliff heading north toward the Potasse Demi-bastion; but, in all, some 66 cannons and seven mortars were mounted between the Côte de la Montagne and the Potasse Demi-bastion. Near the intendant's palace was a narrow jetty (6) that, in 1759, had a chain going across to the Beauport shore so as to prevent enemy raids by longboats into the St.

Charles River. Slightly further north were the Saint-Roch and du Palais suburbs (7), which had 25 guns mounted in their newly built shore entrenchments.

The lower town featured five shore batteries facing south to sweep shipping on the narrows of the St. Lawrence River. The walls of the houses along the waterfront had also been strengthened. The most westerly battery was the small La Reine (Queen's) Battery (not visible); then, heading east, was the King's shipyard battery (8). Past the "Cul de Sac" (dead end)

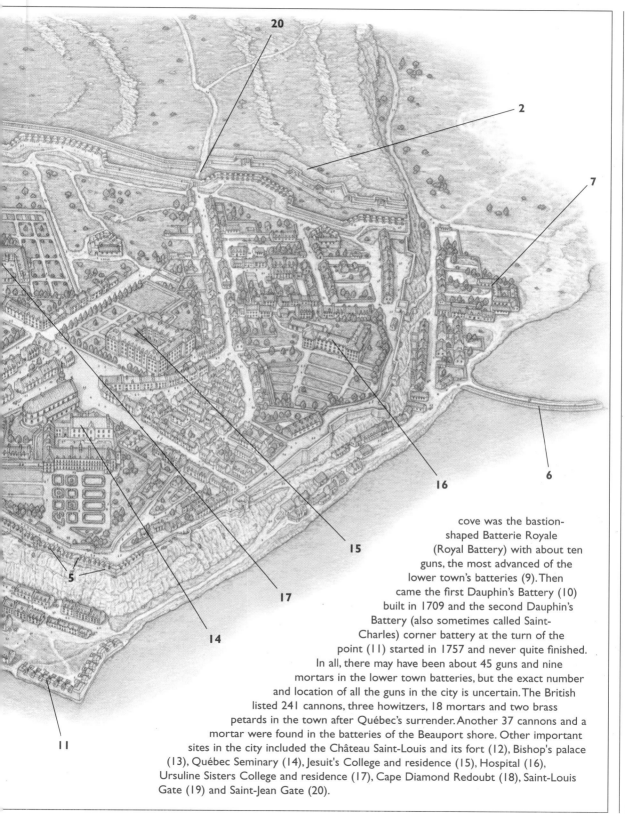

20

2

7

16

6

15

5

17

14

11

cove was the bastion-shaped Batterie Royale (Royal Battery) with about ten guns, the most advanced of the lower town's batteries (9). Then came the first Dauphin's Battery (10) built in 1709 and the second Dauphin's Battery (also sometimes called Saint-Charles) corner battery at the turn of the point (11) started in 1757 and never quite finished. In all, there may have been about 45 guns and nine mortars in the lower town batteries, but the exact number and location of all the guns in the city is uncertain. The British listed 241 cannons, three howitzers, 18 mortars and two brass petards in the town after Québec's surrender. Another 37 cannons and a mortar were found in the batteries of the Beauport shore. Other important sites in the city included the Château Saint-Louis and its fort (12), Bishop's palace (13), Québec Seminary (14), Jesuit's College and residence (15), Hospital (16), Ursuline Sisters College and residence (17), Cape Diamond Redoubt (18), Saint-Louis Gate (19) and Saint-Jean Gate (20).

Improving Québec's fortifications became the order of the day. De Léry's plans called for the construction of a classic Vauban-style wall with four large bastions and a demi-bastion at each end. The bastions provided for one of Vauban's basic principles in defensive works: the protection of the ditch by crossfire from the flanks of the bastions. By the fall of 1745, hundreds of men were busy constructing the ramparts. The contractor hired specialized craftsmen and their apprentices as well as some soldiers familiar with building trades, but they were much too few in number. To obtain the necessary manpower, the government decreed a *corvée*—compulsory labor for a public work—on every able-bodied man aged from 16 to 60 within a radius of 40 French miles to help construct the rampart. They put up the masonry stone wall with buttresses and filled the inside with earth to make up the rampart. Just outside the wall, a ditch with a glacis was planned but only a small portion of it was built, in front of the Saint-Jean Bastion.

In 1748, de Léry completed the unfinished Dauphine Redoubt originally designed by de Beaucours as an arms and ammunition storehouse. The following year, it was transformed into a barrack. Close by, the Nouvelle Casernes (New Barracks) were built from 1749 to 1752 to house the garrison. It was an imposing structure and, at over 520 feet from end to end, the longest building in North America at that time.

The 1759 siege

The Austrian Succession War ended in 1748 but another conflict was expected and, in 1754, it broke out in the wilderness of the Ohio Valley. By 1756, war had been formally declared between France, Britain and most other major European nations. Governor-General Vaudreuil worried about Québec's defenses and, in October 1756, noted that little had been done since the 1740s to improve the ramparts. Vaudreuil tasked the Engineer Nicolas Sarrebrousse de Pontleroy, transferred from Louisbourg to Québec, with improving the city's fortifications. The batteries of La Genouillère and du Clergé were built and a 6-foot-wide wall was started but left unfinished on the upper east side near the St. Charles River. In America, the British and Americans slowly gained the advantage over the French, thanks to their greatly superior forces. When Louisbourg fell in July 1758, it opened the way to Québec. It was now obvious that the city would be the next target.

A small battery still armed with two guns positioned along the rampart edging Québec's upper town. Batteries were built in that area and at various other points along this rampart from 1690. (Author's photograph)

Pontleroy, as well as many French army officers sent to Canada, had little confidence in the ramparts put up since 1745. As Louis-Antoine de Bougainville, General Montcalm's aide-de-camp, put it, Québec "was without fortifications" and would be difficult to fortify, adding, "if the approaches to the city were not defended, the place would have to surrender." General Montcalm thought much the same, as did Pontleroy. Perhaps their judgement on de Léry's ramparts was somewhat hasty but they saw it as an unfinished piece of work without ditches and glacis. By the standards of the day, the walls would thus have been easily breached by enemy siege artillery. It was therefore essential to deny the enemy a foothold on the north shore of the St. Lawrence

River. If such a thing occurred, it was expected that the British, with their superior resources and greater numbers of regular soldiers, would prevail and the city would be doomed. It was therefore essential to build redans and batteries along the whole length of the north shore, from the Montmorency River to the city. But everything else also had to be improved. It was a tall order.

By the spring of 1759, an attack on the city was daily expected and so the defenses were in the process of being strengthened. Thousands of men were employed building new fortifications and improving old ones all over the city. A strong barricade closed the Côte de la Montagne road to the upper city. The suburbs of Saint-Roch and du Palais were enclosed and armed with 25 cannons. Some 66 cannons and seven mortars were installed between the Côte de la Montagne and the Potasse Bastion and another 52 cannons were installed on the

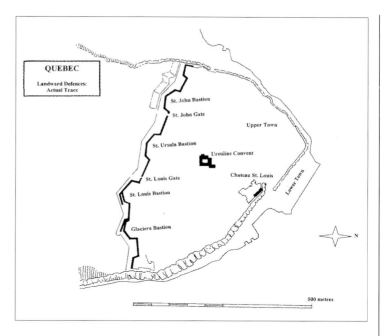

western side. Between the Château Saint-Louis and the Cape Diamond Redoubt, another two batteries holding 16 cannons and two mortars were built.

Perhaps the most impressive effort was to fortify the length of the Beauport shore, from the falls of the Montmorency River, which would act as the eastern (or left) side of the French army. Pontleroy felt that it was the weak point, especially in the area about La Canardière where Phips' men had landed in 1690. A first entrenchment line was built in May running along the St. Charles River up to the General Hospital. Pontleroy wanted to close access to the river and had two ships scuttled at its entrance. They were transformed into advanced batteries. Behind were more obstacles including a boat bridge and a floating battery called La Diable (The She-Devil) holding 18 cannons of 24-pound caliber. By the end of June 1759, many batteries, redoubts and redans had been built along the Beauport shore, both on the cliff and on the beach, some mounted with guns. General Montcalm listed the following on 27 June:

Québec's landward defenses in 1759. Chief Engineer Chaussegros de Léry was responsible for the design of the walls that had been built in 1745. A ditch with a glacis was planned but, by 1759, only a small portion of it had been built, in front of the Saint-Jean Bastion. (Osprey)

A view of the cliff separating the upper town from the lower town with the rampart edging it, occasionally punctuated by batteries. The large gray building with spires is a wing of the Québec Seminary of Laval University, built in the late 19th century but originating in 1664, the fourth oldest university in America. Further away is the Château Frontenac. On the highest point of Cape Diamond beyond is the redoubt first built in 1693 and later incorporated into the citadel when the latter was built in the 1820s. (Author's photograph)

The redoubts and redans built in 1759 on the Beauport shore east of Québec City up to the Montmorency River. They proved to be resilient enough to prevent the British from landing. General Wolfe's attempt to storm the defenses just west of the Montmorency River on July 31 ended in a near-disaster. The Johnstone and Sault shore batteries were occupied but the British grenadiers were mowed down as they charged up the cliff. (Osprey)

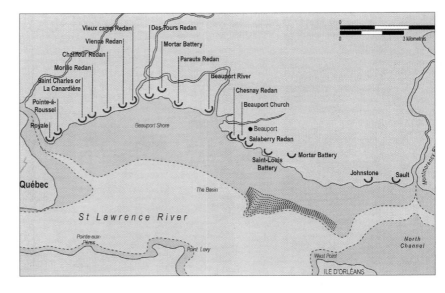

Pointe-à-Roussel Battery: three 12-pounder cannons, flanked by two redans
La Canardière Battery: three 12-pounders
Morille Redan
Chalifour Redan
Vienne Redan
Vieux camp Redan: three 8-pounders
Des Tours Redan
Parauts Redan: three 8-pounders
Redoubt of the mouth of the Beauport River
Chesnay Redan
Salaberry Redan
Redoubt below the church with two batteries: four 12-pounders
Saint-Louis Battery with two redans to be built
Sault Redoubt: three 8-pounders

The Sault Redoubt was the most easterly on the beach, just below the majestic-looking Montmorency falls. Another work, the Johnstone Battery, was also built on the beach, about 900 yards west of the Sault Redoubt. Behind all these works was a garrison of about 15,000 troops, mostly militiamen.

In late June, the anticipated invasion force came into sight as an enormous fleet made its way on the St. Lawrence River. On board were some 10,000 regular soldiers and 13,000 sailors with a powerful train of artillery. In the following months, part of the lower town was destroyed by the constant British bombardments. However, that area was considered much too strong a position to attack. Both the shore batteries and the ones

A composite view of the landing place at Anse-aux-Foulon showing the British longboats carrying troops, the ascent and subsequent skirmishing on the heights and the battle of the Plains of Abraham on September 13, 1759. Québec, with some of its fortifications, is in the middle ground and the Beauport shore is at the far right. (Print after Hervey Smith; Author's photograph)

dotting the cliffs were likely to inflict severe losses on landing boats full of redcoats while their ships would have only a slim chance of hitting anything important in the city. Once landed, the surviving troops would then be set upon by superior numbers of French soldiers and Canadian militiamen.

General Wolfe opted instead to land and attack just west of the Montmorency River and its majestic falls. He believed that if a breach could be made in the French fortifications on the Beauport shore, the army could assemble and roll over the French all the way into the city. Québec could then be invested and pounded into submission. In reality the assault, which took place on July 31, was a total failure. The French works on the Beauport shore, at the points attacked, proved to be quite resilient. Once the beachhead had been established, the British grenadiers found themselves to be within range of skirmishers hidden on the cliffs and at other points above the beachhead. A charge up the cliffs failed and, with heavy casualties being sustained, General Wolfe saw that it was no use and ordered a retreat.

For the next six weeks, the British prodded with no hope of piercing the defenses. Finally, in desperation, a daring plan was hatched. The only way to land on the north shore might be at a point west of the city. The cliff past Cape Diamond was quite high but there were no important field fortifications there.

A view of Québec from the north, 1759–60. At left is the unfinished Redoute Royale, built from 1712 and nearly completed on the unfinished line of fortifications started by de Beaucours. The Ursuline sisters' convent and college are in the center. The ramparts built from 1745 are behind the viewer and cannot be seen. What can be seen is that the area between the old and the 1745 ramparts was left largely vacant and used to keep livestock. (Print after Richard Short; National Archives of Canada, C358)

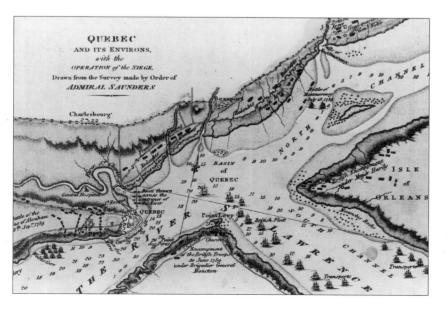

"Quebec and its environs, with the operation of the siege. Drawn from the Survey made by Order of Admiral Saunders" 1759. This plan shows the city, the British fleet in the St. Lawrence River and the French fortifications on the Beauport shore. The British camps are on the south shore, the Isle of Orleans and east of the Montmorency River. (National Archives of Canada, C14523)

27

The ramparts on the western side of the city did not seem to be in the best of conditions, according to Royal Engineer Patrick Mackellar, who had previously been detained as a prisoner of war in Québec. The amazing thing was that Mackellar was not aware of the new walls that had been built since 1745; his plans as submitted to General Wolfe still outlined the early-18th-century line of fortifications, not that it would have changed much in the final decision to attempt the landing.

On the night of September 12–13, thousands of troops were landed at Anse-aux-Foulons, west of the city, and managed to scale the cliffs and form up on the Plains of Abraham. During the siege of 1759, General Montcalm and other French officers often commented that the city's fortifications on the western side were in bad repair with gates that hardly closed shut. In some aspects, they were right; the ditch and glacis that were to provide for a parapet and a covered way outside the walls had not been completed. However, criticism concerning the adaptation of the defenses to the rolling terrain was unfounded. In any event, General Montcalm chose to come out with as many troops as he could gather to meet General Wolfe's redcoats. Both generals were mortally wounded in the ensuing battle, which was won by the British.

At the end of the September 13 battle on the Plains of Abraham, the pursuing British stopped at the walls and then retreated to a safe distance. Thus, the walls' weaknesses did not cause the city's subsequent surrender. It was more a question of discouragement amongst the defenders inside; not only had they lost the battle but their general had perished. The lower town had been under severe bombardment for months and was half-destroyed. No relief was forthcoming. Given these circumstances, and to avoid an assault by the British troops massing to the west, Québec surrendered on September 18, 1759, thus bringing to an end its second siege.

The 1760 siege

Following the surrender of Québec, the French troops retreated to Montréal. The British now settled themselves in Québec as best they could. Brigadier-General James Murray was in command with about 8,000 men to hold the city until the spring of 1760. They had to shore up the fortifications because General Lévis, Montcalm's successor, was rallying troops in Montréal and might try to retake Québec. Murray asked his engineers to see what could be done to reinforce the city's fortifications. Their report was none too encouraging. Mackellar estimated it would take a year of work to make the ramparts resistant to artillery, and that hardly any work could be done during a Canadian winter. Furthermore, some 700 of Murray's men died of sickness over the winter and many more were taken ill—hardly a suitable workforce. The best that could be done under the circumstances was to repair the damaged fortifications and install more artillery to increase the firepower. New embrasures were also made in the walls so that the guns could offer effective fire against siege batteries. Murray also ordered the demolition of houses that were too close to the ramparts so as to provide a clear field of fire. Finally, he had seven blockhouses built forward of the ramparts.

On April 26, 1760, General Lévis, at the head of about 7,000 French soldiers and Canadian militiamen, arrived on the western side of Québec. Brigadier-General Murray, like General Montcalm, regarded the city's fortifications as unable to withstand a siege by a regular force. He thus came out with about 4,000 men the next day, hoping to gain the initiative and beat Lévis on the spot in the open field. Both armies met at Sainte-Foy on the west end of the Plains of Abraham, just a few hundred yards from where Wolfe and Montcalm had fought. The battle of Sainte-Foy was a hard-fought affair in which the French finally prevailed; Murray had to spike all but two of his field guns but he managed an orderly retreat back into Québec.

Murray, now besieged in Québec, used the rampart effectively. For his part, Lévis did not have much heavy artillery and little gunpowder. He knew the weakest point to be the Glacière Bastion and what guns he had concentrated their fire on that target. The bastion's walls started to crumble, threatening a breach; the British gunners now reacted with a heavy cannonade on the French batteries. With little ammunition available to them, the French besiegers could hardly reply and had to limit themselves to a mere 20 shots a day. Both General Lévis and Brigadier-General Murray knew that under such circumstances, the first French or British ships bearing reinforcements to reach Québec would decide the issue. On May 9, a single British warship arrived, but Lévis still hoped for relief and continued the siege. On May 15, two warships, HMS *Vanguard* and HMS *Diana*, appeared on the river; the next day, the French army retreated to Montréal. Thus, Québec had successfully withstood its third siege, its ramparts never actually being breached and assaulted.

Years of peace followed until the American Revolution. In 1775–76, the existing walls discouraged the besieging Americans from attacking on the western side of the city. On December 31, 1775, they attempted an assault through the lower town, but were repulsed with heavy losses caused by the Canadian militiamen and a small force of British regulars. The Americans finally withdrew in June 1776. This fourth siege by the Americans was destined to be the last siege Québec would have to endure.

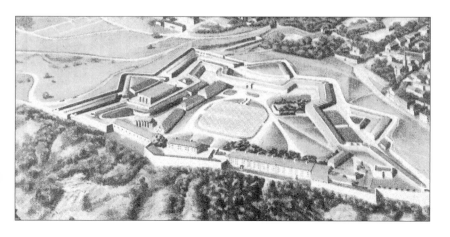

The present-day Québec Citadel was built between 1820 and 1832. Designed by Lieutenant-Colonel Elias Walker Durnford of the Royal Engineers, it incorporated the 1693 Cape Diamond Redoubt and battery into the King's Bastion (lower right), the buttressed French powder magazine behind the barracks in the Prince of Wales' Bastion (lower left) and a section of the 1745 wall with the citadel. The citadel is now both a national monument (incorporating the summer residence of the governor-general of Canada) and an active army base as the headquarters of the Royal 22e Régiment. (*Canadian Army Journal*, July 1952)

Trois-Rivières

The town of Trois-Rivières, while not an important fortress as such, was more substantial than a fortified village or an outlying fort. As early as 1615, a mission for Indians had been set up there by Franciscan lay brother Pacifique Duplessis. Because of this, a few notes are given here on the development of the town, its fortifications and its ironworks.

Following the return of Québec to the French in 1633, Governor Samuel de Champlain wished to have a post further west to support penetration further into the interior. In 1634, a party of settlers led by Louis de La Violette landed where the Saint-Maurice River flowed into the St. Lawrence River from the north and founded a town. At the mouth of the Saint-Maurice River were two large islands, giving the impression that three rivers flowed into the St. Lawrence, hence the site's name of Trois-Rivières (Three Rivers). There the settlers built a "Habitation" to which two more buildings for lodgings, a magazine and a "platform garnished with cannon" had been added by 1636. Early on, Trois-Rivières was established as a distinct entity with its own governor and garrison staff. Like Québec and eventually Montréal, Trois-Rivières became the capital of the settlements in its immediate area. It was the military and civil administrative headquarters for the District of Trois-Rivières, one of three districts, comprising the French town and villages in the St. Lawrence River Valley.

Trois-Rivières did not remain Canada's most westerly settlement for very long. In 1642, Montréal was founded and because of its strategic position at the crossroads of the St. Lawrence, Ottawa and Richelieu rivers, it soon surpassed Trois-Rivières in importance as a commercial and military town. Nevertheless,

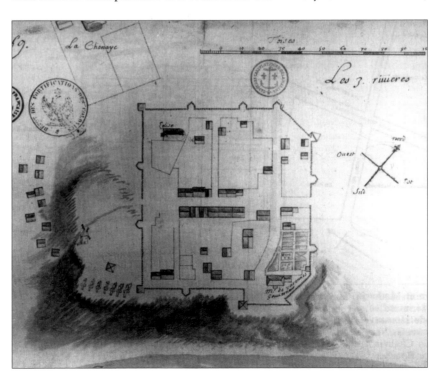

A plan of Trois-Rivières in 1685. Since 1650, the town had been protected by a stockade that grew with the city. An eight-gun open battery is on the cliff just outside the southwest corner. (National Archives of Canada, C16055)

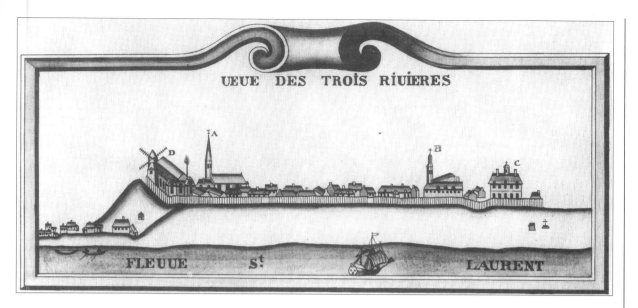

UEUE DES TROIS RIUIERES

FLEUUE St LAURENT

Trois-Rivières thrived; but, by the late 1640s, it was exposed to relentless attacks by Iroquois raiders. Inhabitants carried arms when going out and, beginning in the spring of 1650, a palisade was built to enclose the settlement. This turned out to be a very wise measure when, in August 1652, a very large war party of Iroquois ambushed and killed the town's governor and 15 of his men near Trois-Rivières. In April of the following year, some 600 Iroquois surrounded and attacked the town. Fortunately its fortifications, which now featured a redoubt, withstood the assault and, under the leadership of Captain Pierre Boucher, a seasoned soldier and fighter, the garrison of 46 soldiers and inhabitants repulsed the Iroquois attackers.

The Iroquois menace became far less acute from the later 1660s, but the palisade wall was kept up and an artillery battery was located just outside overlooking the river. An order of January 1706 called for cedar logs for the palisade and they could be seen still in good repair in 1721. Each log was 10–12 inches in diameter and some 12 feet in height. They enclosed the town until May 19–21, 1752, when a major fire consumed several buildings and the town's log palisade. When Engineer Colonel Franquet inspected Trois-Rivières in July and August 1752, he recommended rebuilding the fortifications with an earth and masonry wall; but by then the town was of minor strategic importance and so there was no sense of urgency to carry out his recommendations. Nothing was done and, from then on, Trois-Rivières was an open city without fortifications. The British occupied Trois-Rivières in the summer of 1760, followed by the Americans during their 1775–76 invasion.

Another feature of Trois-Rivières was the rich deposits of iron ore located a short distance north of the town. These began to be exploited from 1733 as the Forges du Saint-Maurice. These substantial ironworks, the first such industry in Canada, were sponsored by the French government mainly to provide the various iron implements required by the shipyard in Québec, in particular for the construction of warships there at the royal dockyards. In 1748, a few small-caliber naval iron guns were also cast at the Forges du Saint-Maurice, but they were found to be defective when inspected in France. This was due to the absence of an experienced gun founder at the ironworks. In any event, there was no lack of naval iron ordnance sent from France to Canada. However, getting ammunition could be a problem in Canada, with the result that cannonballs and mortar bombs were cast in quantity at the Forges du Saint-Maurice for many years.

A view of Trois-Rivières in 1704 as seen from the St. Lawrence River. The part of the town enclosed by walls is at the centre of the image. The letter "A" denotes the parish church; "B" is the mission of the Recollet fathers; the large building with a spire is the Ursuline sisters' convent, hospital and school, built in 1697 (and still active today), and "D" is the powder magazine. (National Archives of Canada, C15784)

Montréal

Montréal was founded on 18 May 1642 by a group of fervent Catholic settlers led by the Sieur Paul Chomedey de Maisonneuve who became the nascent town's first governor. Originally called Ville-Marie (City of Mary), the settlement initially consisted of a fort that contained a "Habitation." This was soon joined by a chapel and small houses built of squared logs, all of which were constructed at the same time by de Maisonneuve's order for fear of Iroquois attacks which began that year. Thereafter, Iroquois warriors were lurking everywhere and the settlement's inhabitants rarely ventured outside without being fully armed. The settlers and members of religious orders remained clustered in the fort which, in 1645, was substantially improved by Engineer Jean Bourdon. It seems bastions were also added at that time. For many years, the garrison usually consisted of about a dozen soldiers. It was only in 1653 that, thanks to the arrival of 100 new settlers, a great clearing of the forest was undertaken and houses began to be built in numbers outside the fort.

The new settlement was sited on relatively flat ground near the river but had in the background to the north the majestic Mont-Royal mountain. In time, the name Ville-Marie was replaced by Montréal as the original religious purpose of the settlement was overtaken by the activities of traders and, eventually, of soldiers as Montréal became the main military garrison in Canada. All this activity was a consequence of Montréal's exceptional strategic position; it was situated where the Ottawa River, flowing from the northwest, joined the St. Lawrence River. Not far to the east, the Richelieu River, flowing from Lake Champlain to the south, joined the St. Lawrence. This provided exceptional river highways to the heart of the continent.

Montréal's first quarter century was marked by the constant fear of raids by the Iroquois who controlled the rivers leading to the town. This changed drastically from 1665 with the arrival of the Carignan-Salières Regiment. The French, who now had the upper hand militarily, used these same rivers to attack Iroquois villages and expand their trade westward. The town's population shot up from about 75 to 600, plus soldiers.

Up to 1672, Montréal was an ill-assorted cluster of various structures built not far from the river and the fort. That year, some city planning occurred when the main streets (Saint-Paul, Notre-Dame, etc.) were laid out, giving the town an elongated rectangle form running from east to west with a relatively narrow span north to south. Apart from the fort built near the small Saint-Pierre River in 1642–43, Montréal's defenses were practically nonexistent. The town depended on the several outlying forts on the island and on the south shore for its protection. Renewed warfare

The fort of Ville-Marie in 1645; it was built from 1642 and demolished in 1672. This 19th-century drawing is a conjecture of its possible appearance. The fort is known to have been bastioned but the appearance of the buildings shown is much more uncertain.

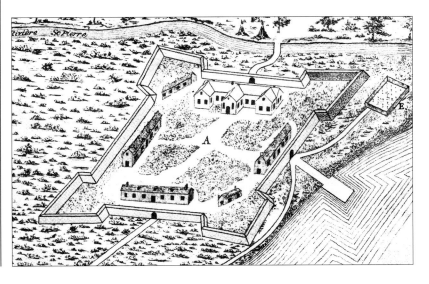

Building the walls at Montréal, 1717–44. In the foreground, a large raft brings stones to be used to face the wall under construction from the west (left). The small citadel is at the eastern end (right). Mount Royal is visible in the background. (Painting by L.R. Batchelor c.1933; National Archives of Canada, C1540)

with the Iroquois from 1682 did not immediately rouse Montréalers, but over time the raids got increasingly closer. The appearance of Iroquois raiding parties at the western end of the island must have contributed to a decision being made to build a picket "wall" around Montréal.

Palisades and ramparts

In 1687–89, a palisade was built by ordering the inhabitants to compulsory labour; this wooden wall enclosed the city for the first time. The wall was rebuilt in 1697–98 with large "cedar logs of 15 or 16 feet high fixed together with large nails and wooden joint," according to Sister Marie Morin's memoirs. This wall had five gates. A redoubt was also needed; during 1693 a small log fort was built atop the *coteau* (a little hill) to the east where a windmill had been built in 1685. In 1709, the growth of the city—by now its population had doubled to over 1,200—required the palisade to be extended east. The *coteau* fort was now within the picket walls but the Bonsecour suburb was still left outside its perimeter.

The next step aimed to make Montréal much stronger. In 1713, Intendant Bégon issued an order requiring Montréal to be protected by a stone rampart.

A plan of Montréal in 1724 by Gaspard Chaussegros de Léry. Begun in 1717, work to build the walls surrounding the city had been completed. There is little evidence of earthworks outside, nor were they much needed: the north side of the city walls sat high on a long east-to-west bluff; the south side bordered the St. Lawrence River; the northeast side (right) had two strong bastions and the small citadel. Only the southwest side (left) was weaker and, indeed, a suburb was already being built there outside the wall of the thriving fur trade business center of Canada. (Print after C. Bertrand, *Histoire de Montréal*, 1933)

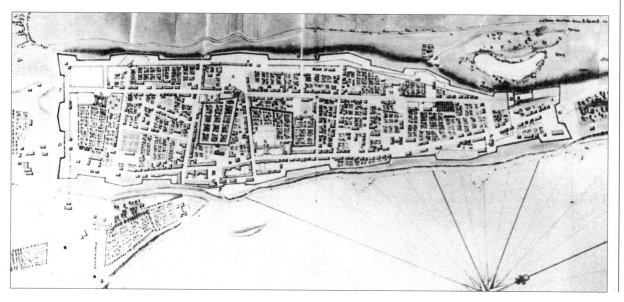

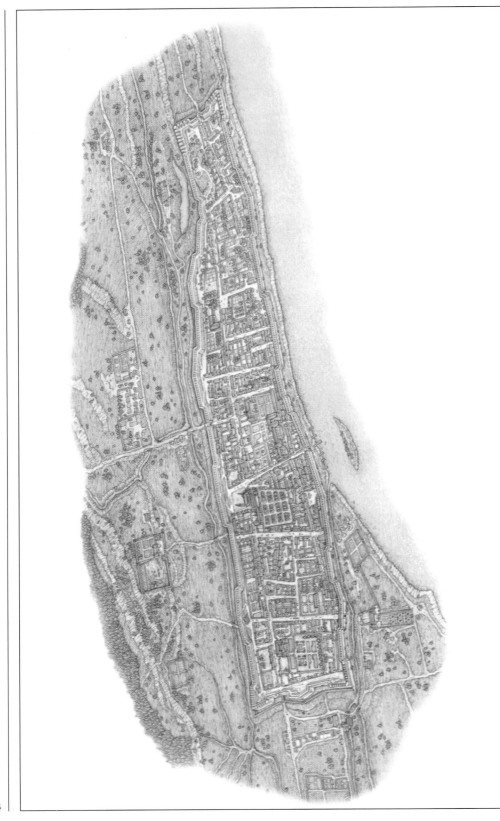

Montréal 1760

Chief Engineer Chaussegros de Léry chose to follow the previous outlines of the city, which formed a very long and narrow rectangle. Under such circumstances, a Vauban-style fortress design was impossible but de Léry may have been influenced by some of the town fortifications erected in the 16th and 17th centuries in his native Provence. At Montréal the ramparts took the form of long and narrow bastions with a modest ditch was dug on three sides. On the north side of the eastern end was the small hill with the little "citadel" on top. The gates and sally ports on the edge of the St. Lawrence River must have been the busiest as this was the main trading place in Canada. Fortress Montréal was thus well protected against any strong raiding party, rather than against a European-style siege.

34

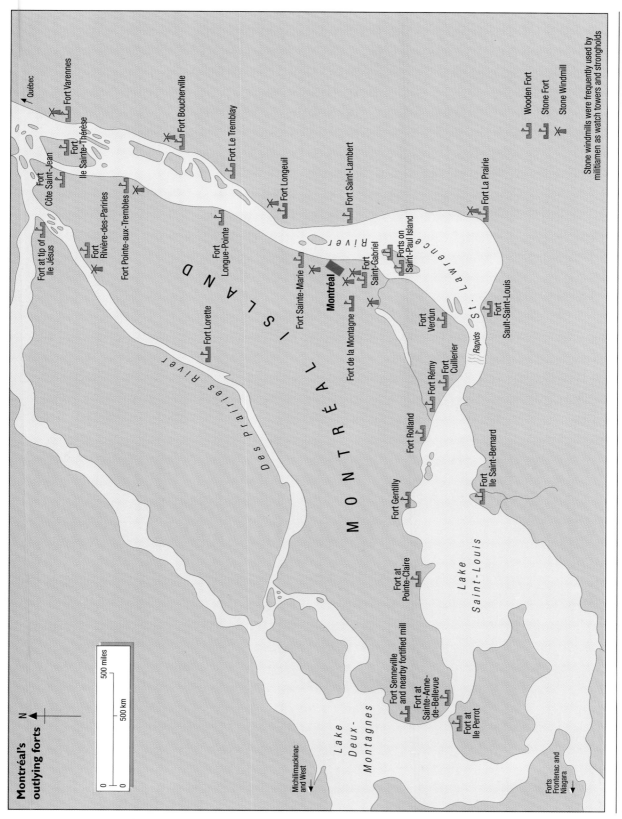

Montréal's outlying forts

N

500 miles
500 km

Stone windmills were frequently used by militiamen as watch towers and strongholds

Wooden Fort
Stone Fort
Stone Windmill

Québec

Fort Varennes
Fort Sainte-Thérèse
Île Sainte-Jean
Fort Côte Saint-Jean
Fort Boucherville
Île Sainte-Jean
Fort Le Tremblay
Fort Longeuil
Fort Saint-Lambert
Fort at tip of Île Jésus
Fort Rivière-des-Prairies
Fort Pointe-aux-Trembles
Fort La Prairie
Fort Longue-Pointe
Forts on Saint-Paul Island
Fort Sainte-Marie
Fort Saint-Gabriel
Fort Lorette
Montréal
Fort de la Montagne
Fort Verdun
Fort Sault-Saint-Louis
Fort Rémy
Fort Cuillerier
Rapids
Fort Rolland
M O N T R É A L   I S L A N D
Fort Gentilly
Fort Île Saint-Bernard
Des Prairies River
St. Lawrence River
Fort at Pointe-Claire
Lake Saint-Louis
Fort Senneville and nearby fortified mill
Fort at Sainte-Anne-de-Bellevue
Lake Deux-Montagnes
Michilimackinac and West
Fort at Île Perrot
Forts Frontenac and Niagara

35

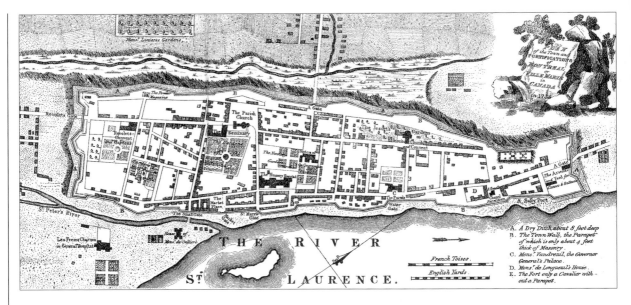

A plan of Montréal, 1745. First published in London during 1758, this document was a close copy from a French map of 1745 now in the King's Maps of the British Library. The French map appears to have been drawn by Chaussegros de Léry and might have been captured by the British on a French ship or copied by a spy. (Print after T. Jefferys)

"An East View of Montreal, in Canada" c.1760. This is one of the best views of Montréal as it appeared in the middle of the 18th century. (Print by P. Canot after a drawing by Thomas Patten; National Archives of Canada, C2433)

This heralded four years of bureaucratic wrangling between government officials, religious orders and property owners over land titles and who would pay for the work. Chief Engineer Josué Dubois Berthelot de Beaucours drew up a first plan and some work started, albeit rather timidly, but it was interrupted following disapproval of the plans in France. However, the government confirmed its order to build the fortifications by a special tax levied on May 5, 1716. That year, Gaspard Chaussegros de Léry arrived as chief engineer and duly submitted a revised plan for the new fortifications that was approved. Work started in 1717 and continued until 1744.

De Léry's design for Montréal's fortifications followed the former log palisade as much as possible, so as to avoid going through privately owned land, as that would require costly demolitions and expropriations. The lengthy perimeter was therefore kept with the ends redesigned so as to enclose the Bonsecour suburb. In all, the new design added 20 percent to the city within the walls at a cost of only six houses and a brick-making work demolished. The new perimeter extended to about 10,800 feet of wall featuring 14 large bastions. It ran from the present McGill Street, its western end, to Saint-Hubert Street, its eastern end. The walls were 18 feet high and had embrasures at about every 6 feet. The wall on the landward sides was wider than that on the waterside as an attack from the river was considered most unlikely. There were eight gates, some with drawbridges, and eight smaller postern doors. A ditch with a glacis of about 80 feet was to be built outside the wall on the landward sides. As conceived by de Léry, the relatively narrow rampart was not meant to withstand heavy artillery fire as the chances of an enemy appearing with heavy siege cannons were thought to be very unlikely. However, its parapets with

embrasures could provide exceptionally heavy fire to repulse any mixed raiding force of New Englanders and Indians that might attempt an assault.

The work to strengthen Montréal's fortifications continued slowly in the ensuing decades, sometimes due to budget constraints, sometimes because of the occasional resistance of Montréalers to paying taxes or to working on the fortifications. A notable incident occurred in 1717 when the inhabitants of Longueuil, on the south shore, refused to provide statute labor to build the Montréal wall, arguing that they should be improving their own defenses instead. Troops were sent to enforce the order but were met by armed Longueuil militiamen on the outskirts of the village. Fortunately, cooler heads prevailed and, after a two-day standoff between the troops and the militia, officials canceled the decree. The work therefore progressed slowly, all the more so as this was during a long period of peace. Nevertheless, by 1738, the bastions and curtain walls were complete, the last gate was erected in 1741 and, after another three years to complete various details, the wall was finally finished in 1744. Montréal was thus a fortress with a reveted stone wall. The small *coteau* fort was also improved when, in 1723, artillery was installed there and it effectively became Montréal's small citadel and military headquarters.

Montréal island's outlying forts

An unusual feature of the defenses of Montréal was the string of about 30 outlying forts erected in the second half of the 17th century when the Iroquois staged many successful raids (see map of these forts in 1702, after a plan by M. Vachon de Belmont, on page 35). The forts were built all around the town to control its approaches as well as on the south shore of the St. Lawrence River. The great majority of the forts were fairly modest with wooden stockade walls. However, four of them were substantial stone structures featuring masonry walls and medieval-looking round or square towers at the corners. None of these fortifications were meant to resist an attack by a European enemy equipped with siege artillery. Rather, they were meant to provide shelter for settlers in the vicinity and to resist attacks by Indians (and, on very rare occasions, New England militiamen). Many of these forts had detachments of regular soldiers until the early 18th century as well as guards of militiamen. Stone windmills also acted as small strongholds. Near each fort, at the river's shore, was a spot to make an alarm bonfire if the enemy was sighted. This alarm would be relayed in succession to Montréal where a cannon would be fired to warn soldiers and militiamen to prepare for action.

A peculiar fort, just a few hundred yards to the northwest outside the town of Montréal, was **Fort de la Montagne**, also called **Fort des Messieurs** and

37

Fort de la Montagne, 1690s

Built from 1685 just a few hundred yards outside
of Montréal on the flanks of Mount Royal,
the fort is shown as it appeared
in the 1690s. The two
turrets on the most
exposed northern side
had no roof and were
open at the top. The
two southern turrets
were also used as
a school by the
Sisters of the
Congrégation.
The stone walls
and turrets had
loopholes. The
mission priest's
house was at the
center, the chapel
of Notre-Dame-des-
Neiges was at the
south wall, and a barn
that doubled as a shelter for
allied Indian women and children during attacks was at the north wall. An
Indian village (not shown) was just outside on the west side.

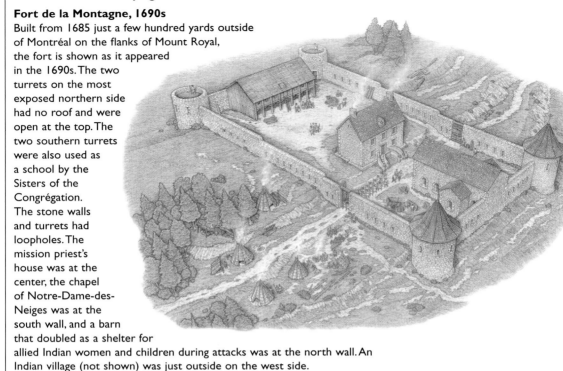

Fort Senneville, 1700–1750s

The stone walls and corner tower/bastions were built at the western
end of Montréal island from 1692 and Jacque Le Ber, the local *seigneur*,
had his manor built against the wall before 1706. At the end of the 17th
century, this was the area most exposed
to Iroquois attacks. Therefore, Fort
Senneville was possibly the most
substantial castle-like fort built in
the Montréal area. It could offer
heavy musket fire from two-
tier rows of loopholes in
its walls and crossfire
from its
tower/bastions,
which would
have also
featured small-
caliber
cannons and
swivel guns.

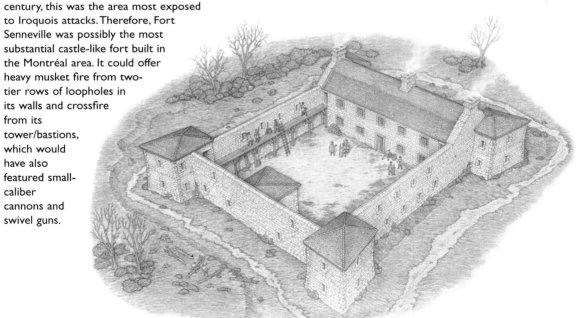

38

Fort Longueuil
Built between 1695 and 1698 on the south shore of the St. Lawrence River, facing the town of Montréal, this large stone structure was constructed more as a fortified manor house for the Baron de Longueuil than as a powerful fort. Against its walls were built a manor house, a large chapel, a barn, stables and other smaller structures. It was the most medieval-looking fort built in Canada, with the tall round turret at each corner having its own pointed roof.

Fort de Belmont. It was built by the Sulpicians, a religious order devoted to the education of the settlers and Indians. Military sciences seem to have been among the subjects taught there, and, while details are still obscure, it seems that Canadian officer-cadets in the *Compagnies franches de la Marine* attended courses given by the Sulpicians from the mid-1680s. It is not known if any buildings were used for a specific military academy, but it would appear that the officer-cadets' activities took place in a small citadel and that classes were held in the Sulpicians' seminary. The Sulpician Order, which had come to Montréal in 1657, built a substantial seminary in the city center from 1684.

The recently excavated foundations of some of Montréal's walls in a park behind City Hall, once the area of the Jesuits' bastion. In this view looking east, the ditch between the glacis (left) and the ramparts (right) can be seen. (Author's photograph)

Led by Father de Belmont, the missionaries were often called the Messieurs de l'Ordre de Saint Sulpice by early Montréalers, hence the fort's nicknames. A first mission consisting of lodgings and a chapel was built in 1679 at the foot of Mount Royal. Because of renewed hostilities with the Iroquois, it was deemed wise to fortify the mission and, in about 1682, a rectangular wooden stockade 230 feet long by 114 feet wide

with earthen bastions at the corners was built to enclose the mission. Another stockade enclosed the village of friendly Indians next to the mission.

In 1685, Father de Belmont, who was also something of a military engineer, came up with a design for a stone wall 200 feet long by 140 feet wide with round turrets at each corner. This was immediately built. The wall was 11 feet high and the stone turrets were 43 feet high, the two south towers each having a pointed roof of timber and cedar shingles. It proved to be a wise precaution when, on May 17, 1694, a band of Iroquois partly destroyed the Indians' settlement while the mission fort resisted the raid. However, on September 11, 1694, a drunken mission Indian accidentally set fire to the adjacent Indian village with the result that the mission's wooden buildings suffered much damage. They were rebuilt in stone during the following years while the Indian village was moved and eventually resettled at Oka from 1721. The Sulpician mission's military role ended in the early 18th century and, after various transformations, the remaining mission buildings and walls were demolished during the 1860s. The two attractive southern turrets with their medieval-looking cone-shaped roofs were retained and still stand today in a little park surrounded by modern city buildings.

The western part of the island of Montréal was one of the most important strategic areas of Canada. Here the St. Lawrence River, flowing west to east from Lake Ontario, meets the waters of the Ottawa River coming from the northwest and the upper Great Lakes. Most of the vital fur trade was carried out on the Ottawa River route. Great convoys of canoes bearing all sorts of manufactured goods for the Great Lakes Indians who were assembled at Michilimackinac, would come back laden with valuable furs. As the convoys came down the Ottawa River they passed by the settlements of Senneville and Sainte-Anne-de-Bellevue and landed at Lachine, the traders' village west of Montréal. Other convoys going to and from Lake Ontario would also arrive at Lachine. It was impossible to go on further to Montréal because of the great rapids that lay between Lachine and the city.

The area west of Montréal was greatly exposed to attacks by the Iroquois in the second half of the 17th century and, in 1662, a stockaded outpost, **Fort Verdun**, was built west of the city. Slightly further west was Lachine, which was seemingly given its oriental name (it means China in French) in 1667 by explorer Robert Cavelier de La Salle, who later went on to great fame by descending the Mississippi River to the Gulf of Mexico. In 1671, a settlement cum fur trade post was established there. It initially consisted of a strongly built stone windmill (which also acted as a redoubt), a chapel, the house of the *seigneur* (roughly a squire), a trade store, barracks and several smaller buildings, all of which were surrounded by a wooden stockade with small bastions. It was called **Fort Lachine** and also, from 1680, **Fort Rémy**, after the arrival of Father Pierre Rémy, the parish priest. Settlers meanwhile built the village of Lachine some distance to the northwest, outside the fort, during the 1670s and 1680s. A small outlying stockaded fort was **Fort Cuillerier**, built to the east on the land of René Cuillerier in 1676. In 1670, **Fort Rolland** rose as a stockaded fur traders' fort west of Lachine and eventually had a garrison of regular colonial troops in the later 1680s. Further west was **Fort Présentation** (not to be confused with Fort La Présentation at present-day Ogdensburg, NY), also called **Fort Gentilly** or **Fort La Grande Anse**, which was built in 1674 at present-day Dorval.

Encouraged by the British in the New York colony, Lachine was attacked and many of its inhabitants horribly slaughtered by Iroquois warriors on the night of August 4–5, 1689. The attackers ignored the outlying forts and went right into the undefended village. At that time, there were soldiers in Fort Rolland and a column rushed out but arrived too late. This event had a tremendous impact for generations thereafter; henceforth the Canadians, with their superior tactics and woodcraft, wreaked havoc among enemy Indians and American colonists. Following the raid, Fort Rolland was vacated for Fort

Lachine (or Rémy) which was closer to the village; its garrison was increased. Detachments were posted there until the end of the French Regime.

Fort Senneville originated as a trading post built in about 1671, just above the western tip of the island of Montréal, about half a mile above the rapids at Sainte-Anne-de-Bellevue. By late 1686, Fort Senneville also featured a high stone windmill that doubled as a watch tower, its position on a hill offering a commanding view of the Ottawa River, the Lake of Two Mountains and the mouth of the smaller Des Prairies River. This windmill was like no other in New France: it had very thick walls, small square loopholes for muskets and, at the top, projections of masonry facing down— the machicolations of medieval castles in Europe—to enable lethal liquids and rocks to be dropped onto any attackers.

In October 1687, the nearby village of Sainte-Anne-de-Bellevue (a stockade called **Fort Sainte-Anne** had been there since about 1683) and the Senneville mill were attacked by marauding Iroquois; several settlers were killed in the area but the enemy was beaten off. In 1691, another Iroquois party was more successful and Fort Senneville was burned down; only the fortified stone windmill remained standing.

An enraged Governor-General Frontenac ordered the immediate construction of another **Fort Senneville**, this time to be built of stone and made more imposing so as to discourage any future incursions. Work began in 1692. This new fort was a castle-like structure having stone, bastion-like, small elongated square towers at each corner of its square perimeter connected by thick stone walls. Obviously built to defeat hostile Iroquois incursions as well as to impress any other Indians, it also featured cannons and wall guns.

The new Fort Senneville guarded the western approaches to Montréal for many decades and was never attacked during the French Regime. Following the Great Peace of 1701 with the Indians, the northwestern area became much safer and, a few years later, Jacque Le Ber, the *seigneur* of Senneville, had his manor house built within the fort. In the following decades, its military importance decreased considerably. Nevertheless, a small detachment seems to have been posted at the fort right up to the end of the French Regime. The fortified windmill/watch tower was restored in 1700 and appears to have been in use until the 1780s. The fort itself was abandoned after 1760 but on May 25, 1776, it was occupied by American troops under the command of General Benedict Arnold. A small force of Canadians and Indians defeated the Americans further west at Cedars and, in their retreat, they set fire to whatever could be burned in the fort. As its defensive value was just about nil, their actions were "something of the aspect of vandalism," to quote Alexander D. Angus, the historian of Fort Senneville.

There were also small stockaded forts on the northern side of the island of Montréal, bordering the Rivière-des-Prairies. Heading east from Fort Senneville, one came successively upon **Fort Sainte-Geneviève**, **Fort Nouvelle Lorette** (or **du Sault-aux-Récollets**) made of stone, **Fort de la Rivière-des-Prairies**, the fort

The defense of Montréal was largely dependent on outlying forts. In 1660, Adam Dollard des Ormeaux, the young commandant of the small garrison of Montréal, went up the Ottawa River with 16 French companions and 44 Indian allies. Meeting a large party of Iroquois warriors descending the river to attack Montréal, Dollard and his men put up an heroic defense in a ramshackle Indian picket fort at Long Sault. Most of the Indian allies defected. In the final assault, a powder barrel thrown out by Dollard hit a branch and fell back into the fort; most of the defenders were killed in the resulting explosion. It was said that the Iroquois were so impressed by the defense that they went no further, making Dollard and his companions the "saviors of New France;" a version of events that has since been contested. It nevertheless shows how important outlying forts were to Montréal's safety. (Print after René Bombled; Author's photograph)

The two southern turrets of the Sulpicians' "Fort de la Montagne" are still extant in what is now downtown Montréal, although the walls and original buildings have long since vanished. (Print after a *c.*1920 painting by Paul Caron)

at the tip of **Ile Jésus** and **Fort Côte Saint-Jean** (or **des Roches**) at the eastern end of the island. Not far from the eastern end, on its southern side was **Le Petit Fort Gervais** with another fort on nearby **Sainte-Thérèse** island; then, heading west, **Fort Pointe-aux-Trembles**, **Fort de la Longue-Pointe** and **Fort Sainte-Marie** just before arriving at Montréal. In the 18th century, these smaller forts were used as lookout stations and had no regular garrisons, but they would be manned and maintained by local militiamen as there was always a village nearby.

Montréal also had a number of outlying stockaded forts on the south shore of the St. Lawrence River. Approaching Montréal from the east on the river, one would see, after the mouth of the Richelieu River at Sorel, **Fort Contrecoeur** and **Fort Verchères**, **Fort Varennes** built in 1693, **Fort Boucherville** built in 1668 and **Fort Le Tremblay**. At Longueuil, just across the river from Montréal, stood a remarkable structure, the combined château and fort of the Le Moyne family. This was **Fort Longueuil**, built between 1695 and 1698 by Charles Le Moyne, scion of one of the most powerful and wealthy families in New France. It consisted of a large stone wall rectangle measuring some 226 x 153 feet with, at each corner, a turret about 18 feet in diameter. The height of each wall is unknown but they were at least two storeys high and 3 to 3$\frac{1}{2}$ feet thick. Within the rectangle was a fine manor house of about 76 x 25 feet, a chapel of about 48 x 23 feet, a stable for 12 horses and 40 cattle, a barn, a dairy and a few other dependencies. It was, according to Governor-General Frontenac, very similar to the "fortified châteaux in France" within one of the finest *seigneuries*

Fort Lachine (also called Fort Rémy), built from 1671, was typical of the log palisade forts erected to protect settlements around Montréal. It featured a windmill (1), a priest's house (2), a chapel (3), the house of Jean Millot which had previously been that of explorer Robert Cavelier de La Salle (4), a barn (5), palisades (6), bastions (7), barracks (8) and a powder magazine (9). (Reconstruction from a plan by G. de Catalogne; print from Girouard, *Le vieux Lachine*, 1889)

in Canada. Indeed, a pleased Louis XIV ennobled Charles Le Moyne as first baron of Longueuil in 1700. Besides numerous servants, a small detachment of troops was based at the fort in the early 1700s, but they were withdrawn thereafter until 1755–60, when some of General Montcalm's metropolitan regiments were quartered in the area.

Further west, just across from the town of Montréal, was **Fort Saint-Lambert** and then **Fort Laprairie**. The latter originated in a settlement founded around 1670. Because of the increasing frequency of Iroquois raids, a stockade was built around the village in 1684, making a large irregular enclosure with two bastions at the river shore. The wisdom of this measure was highlighted on August 11, 1691, when a raiding party of some 300 Iroquois and New York militiamen led by Major Peter Schuyler attacked the fort. They were repulsed after having caused substantial losses to the defenders and destroying everything they could outside the fort.

WATCH TOWER.

The remains of the fortified windmill and watch tower at Fort Senneville as seen in the 1870s. (*Picturesque Canada…*1882)

Relatively content and feeling they had nothing to fear, Schuyler and his men started back toward Albany. But the alarm had been raised and some 700 French troops and Canadian militiamen caught up with them. The ensuing battle was disastrous for Schuyler, who lost 83 killed (including 17 Indians) besides the wounded, while the French only had five or six wounded. The incident showed that, while the forts could not guarantee total safety for the settlers, they did provide protection for those within while the alarm system could muster a sizeable relief force fairly quickly. Iroquois warriors continued to lurk near the French settlements, but in decreasing numbers, while New York militiamen preferred to stay home.

Further west was **Fort Sault-Saint-Louis**, a mission reserve of Iroquois who had been converted to Christianity by French missionaries. Initially situated at the site of Laprairie in 1667, the reserve moved several times until it settled on the shore of the great Sault-Saint-Louis rapids in 1689. In 1724, a guardhouse and a house to lodge the garrison were built. At first a stockade fort, it was rebuilt in stone around 1729 but only half-finished on its southern and western sides as the Indians objected to stone walls facing their adjacent town just a few yards east of the fort. This Indian town was also protected by a bastioned stockade.

Following Queen Anne's War, many of the wooden forts around Montréal decayed. The inhabitants rebuilt them in stone during 1729–30, under the direction of Sub-Engineer de La Morandière who was following orders from the governor-general. As was the case previously, these forts were mainly intended to provide nearby inhabitants with a refuge against attacks by Indians. For the most part, the forts were very simple affairs consisting of a square stone-walled structure laid out by de La Morandière, probably pierced with loopholes. Such forts had no regular troops and would be manned by militiamen in an emergency. The forts with detachments of regular soldiers were more substantial and had bastions and artillery. By the mid-18th century, only Fort Senneville, Fort Sault-Saint-Louis and Fort Laprairie had small detachments of regular soldiers of the *Compagnies franches de la Marine*.

The 1760 capitulation

Many more troops were in and around Montréal from 1755 but, by the late summer of 1760, it was clear that the city (and its outlying forts) was doomed as three British armies converged on it. In early September, some 17,000 British and American provincial troops under the command of General Jeffery Amherst surrounded Montréal. Inside, General Lévis and his 3,000 men knew that any further resistance was futile, especially as Amherst had siege artillery at his disposal. In spite of the French regiment's gallant fighting record in the last five years, Amherst refused to grant them the honors of war so they could march out with drums beating, their colors flying and holding their muskets. Mortified and angered by Amherst's pettiness, General Lévis and many of his officers and men gathered together that night, reputedly on Sainte-Hélène Island. There, the old and glorious battle-worn silk colors were brought around a fire, held high for all to see, and then slowly lowered into the flames. It is said that many a French soldier and Canadian militiaman angrily broke his musket that night. The next day, September 8, 1760, the troops lined up in Montréal's Place d'Armes and the last French army in Canada surrendered.

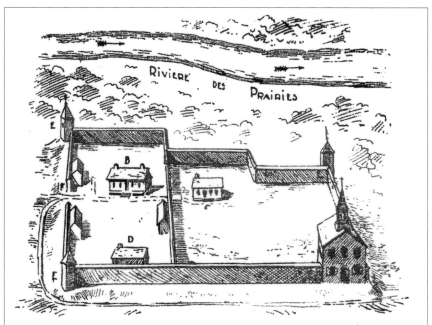

Louisbourg

During the 17th century, France also had two small colonies on the Atlantic Coast: Acadia, which was essentially in the western part of present-day Nova Scotia with outposts in New Brunswick and the American state of Maine; and the harbor of Placentia in Newfoundland. The Treaty of Utrecht, signed by Britain and France in 1713, conceded Acadia (which confirmed it as Nova Scotia) and Newfoundland to Britain. France, however, kept Cape Breton Island and Isle Saint-Jean (the future Prince Edward Island). That year, French colonists arrived at Isle Royale, as Cape Breton Island was now known. In 1719, one of the island's best harbors was selected to become a fortress and naval base called Louisbourg. It was inaugurated in 1720 and, for the next 23 years, a town rose surrounded by substantial fortifications. It has often been told how Louis XV had once remarked, when presented with more bills to pay for Louisbourg's construction, that he expected to see its spires from Versailles! The story is, no doubt, apocryphal. In fact, it cost only a small part of France's vast recurring expenses for works on dozens of other fortresses at the time. Indeed, Louisbourg never even had a real citadel.

Building Louisbourg was nevertheless an expensive undertaking largely due to its remote location. However, it was a commercial success. It provided French Grand Banks fishermen with a secure harbor; their activities, which had been ruined during Queen Anne's War, were totally redressed by 1718 and expanded thereafter. Louisbourg's harbor also became the scene of intense maritime traffic from France, Canada and the West Indies; and from Britain's 13 colonies, which included a fair amount of smuggling.

A view of Louisbourg in 1731. Just over a decade after its foundation, the town had flourished and achieved the general appearance it would keep until July 1758. (Print after Verrier)

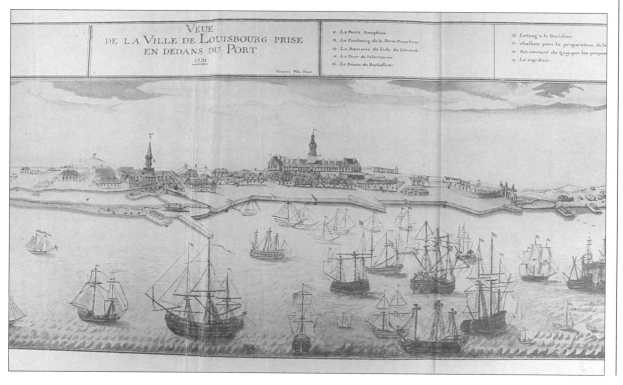

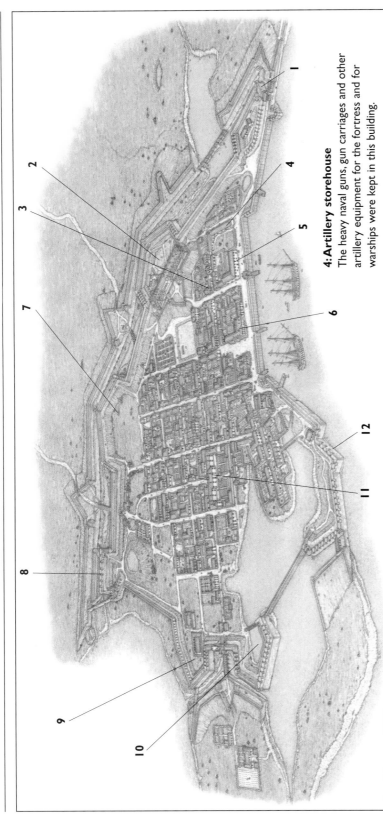

Louisbourg 1745

1: Dauphin Demi-bastion

This structure was mounted with heavy guns intended to protect the town's port as well as to provide crossfire with the Royal Battery on any enemy ship that might get this far upriver. It would also provide crossfire with guns on the landward side in conjunction with the guns in the King's Bastion. Its basic flaw was that it did not have sufficient firepower to cover the landward side.

2: King's Bastion

This was the military headquarters and "citadel" of Louisbourg. Its large building, the longest in North America at the time, housed the governor's residence, the Saint-Louis chapel that served as the town's main church, and the barracks of the garrison. While each flank had emplacements for six guns, the front of the bastion remained without artillery emplacements. It was thought, mistakenly as it turned out, that the marshes and swamps beyond would deter any attackers.

3: Engineer's house

The King's Engineer was one of the most important officials in Louisbourg, especially during its construction, and he had a large house that also served as an office.

4: Artillery storehouse

The heavy naval guns, gun carriages and other artillery equipment for the fortress and for warships were kept in this building.

5: King's storehouse

The *magasin du Roi* was a warehouse in which government supplies of all sorts were kept.

6: Residence of the Commissaire-Ordonnateur

The senior civil official in the colony lived here. Charged with responsibility for the finances and the administration of justice,

7: Queen's Bastion
8: Princess Bastion
9: Brouillan Bastion
10: Maurepas Bastion
11: Hospital
12: Piece de la Grave

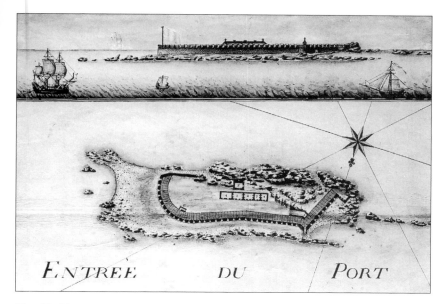

ENTREE   DU   PORT

Building the fortress

The designs of Louisbourg's fortifications were the most "European" of the fortresses built in New France. Marshal Vauban's manuals were practically transposed on the relatively flat and low-lying site of Louisbourg. The ramparts and bastions were finished with ravelins, redans, glacis, etc., very much as they would have been in a fortress in Flanders. Indeed, some of the cut stone came from the Rochefort area in France, shipped as ballast on vessels heading for Isle Royale. (Along with Brest and Toulon, Rochefort was one of the main naval bases of 18th-century France. Its built heritage has largely been preserved and displays remarkable similarities with the structures built in Louisbourg.)

In 1719, construction started on the King's Bastion, the foundation stone of which was officially laid in 1720, and which was completed in 1726–27. This bastion was the largest in the town and was meant to act as a small citadel as it was the only one featuring a covered way and glacis facing in toward the town as well as out and away from it. Inside this bastion stood the longest building in North America, the left (or east) wing of which contained the governor's residence and the Saint-Louis chapel while the right (or west) wing consisted of soldiers' barracks.

Between 1728 and 1730, the Dauphin Demi-bastion with its gate and powder magazine were built. Work went on from 1731 on the La Reine (Queen's) and Princesse (Princess) bastions. In 1737, construction work started on the Brouillan, Maurepas and Pièce de la Grave bastions facing Rochefort Point to the east. The Pièce de la Grave area also featured a wall that was mounted with guns, edging the water and extending toward the harbor.

Louisbourg's harbor entrance in 1731. The Island Battery is at the center with the tip of Rochefort Point to the right. (Print after Verrier)

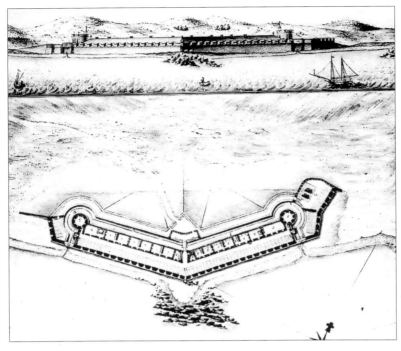

In 1743, the ramparts, bastions and glacis enclosing the town were reported as having been completed.

Batteries were also built outside the town to provide protection for the harbor. The most imposing was the Royal Battery, built between 1724 and 1732 at the far end of the harbor. It had some 40 embrasures for heavy 36-pounder guns as well as a dozen 6-pounders on its turrets. The Island Battery, built between 1726 and 1731, was, as its name implies, located on a small island at the harbor's entrance. Following modifications made in 1734, this battery featured 39 cannons of 24-pounder caliber. When joined in crossfire with the guns of the Dauphin Demi-bastion, it was reckoned that any enemy ship entering the harbor had only the slimmest chance of surviving the onslaught.

ABOVE A plan of the Royal Battery built between 1724 and 1732 at the far end of Louisbourg Harbor. It had some 40 embrasures for heavy 36-pounder guns as well as a dozen 6-pounders on its turrets. It was the strongest of Louisbourg's batteries up to 1745 and was designed to pulverize any enemy ship that succeeded in getting into the harbor. (Archives Nationales, DFC)

The 1745 siege

By the 1740s, the town had grown to about 4,000 inhabitants and had become the fourth busiest harbor in North America. Merchants and officials in American ports were worried by its success. When war broke out between Britain and France in 1744, New Englanders were quite concerned about the French fortress to the north and consequently some 4,000 volunteers attacked it with the help of the Royal Navy. The 1745 siege revealed the vulnerability of the outer batteries. The Royal Battery proved utterly useless and, worse, a menace to the town itself. Having poor landward defenses, it was abandoned without a fight to the New Englanders, who used its guns to bombard the town. The New Englanders' attack on the Island Battery was a costly failure but this battery was also at a disadvantage, being dominated by the heights of Lighthouse Point; the attackers built a battery there and bombarded the Island Battery until it surrendered.

With the fall of its outer batteries, the town was doomed and it duly capitulated on June 17, 1745. The population was deported to France and Britain immediately posted a strong regular garrison at Louisbourg. France wanted Louisbourg back and, in 1746, sent out a fleet under the Duke d'Anville carrying five battalions and a train of siege artillery. The expedition was beset by misfortune and dispersed by a hurricane. D'Anville and many men subsequently died of sickness and the remnants of the fleet limped back to France. Meanwhile, once in possession of Louisbourg, the British sought to repair and improve its works. Wooden barracks were built in the Queen's Bastion. Most

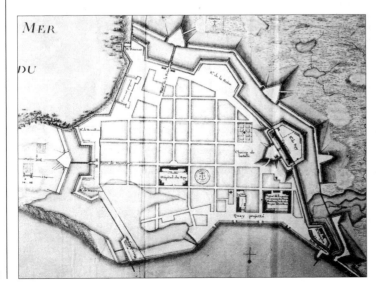

notably, the Dauphin Demi-bastion was strengthened by directing its main firepower out of the ramparts rather than into the harbor and adding a cavalier on the battery, thus creating two superimposed rows of cannon emplacements.

Returned to French possession

Under the terms of the Treaty of Aix-la-Chapelle signed in 1748, Louisbourg was returned to France. Needless to say, the New Englanders were quite upset about Britain's view that Madras in India was more important than the menacing fortress just to the north of them. Back in French possession in 1749, the fortress looked formidable but was in fact in poor condition. By the early 1750s, its fortifications had many defects. The masonry was crumbling and needed repair. The engineers' efforts were generally ineffective as a great deal of money—far more than the French treasury was willing to spend—was needed to put things right. To be truly safe, the Royal Battery required the addition of major defenses on its landward side. A strong fort needed to be built on Lighthouse Point to fully secure the harbor's entrance and prevent the Island Battery from being bombarded from that high point. The town's ramparts and bastions needed counterguards, ravelins and demi-lunes. Most of all, if it was going to be a truly powerful fortress that could repulse a major besieging force, Louisbourg needed a large citadel. Such a project seemed so hopeless, insofar as official approval in Versailles was concerned that engineers in Louisbourg did not even propose detailed plans because they knew that they would be rejected.

The French government's emphasis was on rebuilding trade and commerce and, within a few years, Louisbourg was flourishing again with a population of about 4,500. Nevertheless, some improvements were made in the Queen's Bastion with a demi-lune built there from 1754. A battery was also built at Rochefort Point. Overall, however, the town's defenses had not been improved significantly by the time war broke out again in 1756, nor would they be two

Louisbourg, reconstructed as it looked in 1744–45. During the 1960s and 1970s, part of the fortress was rebuilt as a heritage site. The town's main battery, the Dauphin Demi-bastion, is in the foreground with the Dauphin gate. (Parks Canada)

OPPOSITE A plan of Louisbourg in 1741. Most of the construction work had been completed by that date except at the Pièce de la Grave (lower left). (Archives Nationales, DFC)

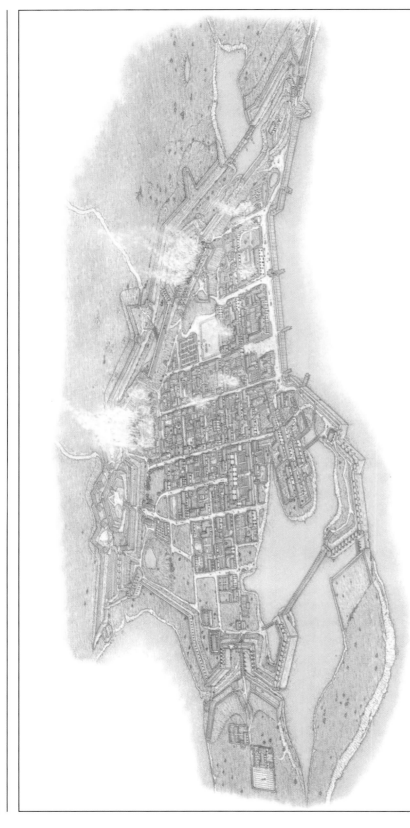

Louisbourg 1758

The main features of Louisbourg during its second siege in 1758 were broadly similar to those in 1745 (see page 46). The walls and buildings were much the same except for improvements in the Dauphin Demi-bastion, which had been rebuilt with a cavalier so as to cover the land side with artillery fire.

Despite the spirited counter-fire by the French gunners, the relentless bombardment of the fortress by General Amherst's and Admiral Boscawen's gunners had inflicted heavy damage on the fortifications by the last week of July 1758. By July 24–25, the top of the cavalier and the walls of the Dauphin Demi-bastion and the King's Bastion had been reduced to rubble; part of the King's Bastion and the barracks in the Queen's Bastion were burning, as were some houses in the town.

Even more critical was the breach in the curtain wall between the Dauphin Demi-bastion and the King's Bastion. This gave the British the option of attempting an assault into the town. In spite of its partially filled moat (see foreground), storming the town via this large breach had every chance of success. The consequences of such assaults were costly in lives for both sides and likely meant a dire fate for the civilians at the hands of enemy soldiers half-crazed from the fighting. When fortresses reached the point of being partly destroyed and breached, further fighting was considered useless and negotiations leading to surrender were held. This is what happened at Louisbourg, which surrendered on July 26, after its walls had been breached.

years later when a large British fleet carrying over 10,000 troops led by Sir Jeffery Amherst was sighted off Louisbourg.

Less expensive but necessary work that had been done concerned building field fortifications at the most likely landing site for an enemy army. The shores around Louisbourg were very rocky and the only real landing beach nearby was at La Comorandière (later renamed Kennington Cove). This was where the New Englanders had landed in 1745. In 1757, parapets and fascines were positioned on the beach at La Comorandière. A trench behind the parapets and fascines ran the length of the site, punctuated by the occasional battery of 6-pounders and swivel guns.

The 1758 siege

Rough weather and the field fortifications at Kennington Cove initially caused difficulties for the British when they tried to land troops on June 8, 1758. Brigadier James Wolfe managed to land with his men, rush up a cliff and outflank the defenders, who retreated into town. The second siege of Louisbourg was a hard-fought affair lasting seven weeks. Outnumbered, the French garrison put up an outstanding fight to delay the British as much as possible so that it would be too late for them to go on and attack Québec. This time, the French rendered the Royal Battery largely useless before the siege, but General Amherst had plenty of guns and pioneers to build his own powerful siege batteries. As a fort had not been built on Lighthouse Point, the British again built a battery there that battled for days with the French colonial artillery gunners in the Island Battery below. Finally, on July 26, after a breach had been made near the Dauphin Demi-bastion, the much-battered fortress surrendered.

Although the fortifications were badly damaged and the town partly in ruins as a result of the bombardments, there was still a chance that it might be rendered a viable fortress again with some determined repairs. In Britain as in New England, many worried that Louisbourg might be recaptured by the French or, as in 1748, returned to France at the end of the war. The menace simply had to be removed. Thus, in February 1760, it was "His Majesty's orders and Mr. Pitt's" that "all the Fortifications, Works and Deffences whatever shall be totally demolished and Razed."

Louisbourg's harbor walls were covered with heavy wood planking as shown in this 1752 plan. (Archives Nationales, DFC)

Colonel Bastide, Royal Engineers, who had supervised the 1758 siege operations, was put in charge of the demolition work. A Company of Miners, especially raised in England for the purpose, arrived in May and started blowing up the defenses. The summer was spent destroying all the walls, batteries and bastions. By late fall, the town's fortifications had been reduced to piles of rubble. Some of the better-quarried stones were taken to Halifax, Nova Scotia, to be used in buildings erected there. With the demolition work complete, Colonel Bastide and the Company of Miners sailed back to England in January 1761. Louisbourg was a fortress no more. Thereafter, small detachments of regulars were posted there until 1768 when its small garrison was withdrawn and what remained of the town's site was eventually abandoned.

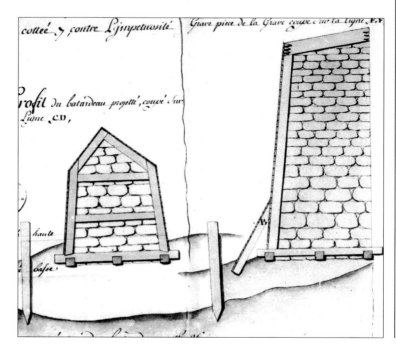

New Orleans

The city of New Orleans was the capital of the huge but sparsely settled French colony of Louisiana. Now reduced to a small-sized American state, Louisiana's original area was enormous, covering the whole of the American Midwest to the Canadian border and the territories bordering the Gulf of Mexico from Texas to Florida. France ceded Louisiana to Spain and Britain in 1763, Britain getting the land east of the Mississippi River and Spain getting the lion's share including New Orleans, territories bordering the Gulf of Mexico and all land west of the Mississippi. However, Spanish troops only replaced the small French garrison in 1769. The new Republic of the United States of America took over Britain's territory in 1783 while Spain, keeping only the present-day Gulf states of Mississippi and Alabama, returned all the rest of Louisiana to France by secret treaty in 1800 that was made public in 1802. Thus, once again for a short while, New Orleans was the capital of French Louisiana. It was in New Orleans, on December 20, 1803, at the Place d'Armes (now Jackson Square), first laid out in 1722, that the official transfer of Louisiana from France to the United States of America took place. (For more details on events, personalities and Spanish and French troops, including uniforms and artillery, during 1803, see René Chartrand, "Napoleonic Louisiana 1803," *Military Collector & Historian: Journal of the Company of Military Historians*, Winter 2000.)

France's claim originated in 1682 when explorer Robert Cavelier de La Salle traveled down the Mississippi River and planted a cross with the arms of King Louis XIV, claiming the whole area for France when he reached the Gulf of Mexico. He named the area Louisiane after the Louis XIV. After a failed attempt by La Salle to establish a settlement in 1685, the French were back in 1699 under the command of Pierre Le Moyne d'Iberville and his brother Jean-Baptiste Le Moyne de Bienville. They established permanent settlements at Biloxi and Mobile further east (in the present-day states of Mississippi and Alabama).

From 1719, a wave of wild speculation on the settlement of Louisiana swept France and several thousand settlers, many seeking gold and diamonds, flowed in. Once in the Biloxi area, at the unhealthy site of Nouveau Biloxi (New Biloxi), many succumbed to tropical diseases at a very alarming rate and, by May 1721, some 900 settlers had reportedly died. Another settlement at the mouth of the Mississippi River had been planned in

Robert Cavelier de La Salle and his exploration party formally take possession of Louisiana in the name of King Louis XIV in 1682 upon reaching the Gulf of Mexico. (Print after a *c.*1900 painting by T. de Thulstrup)

1719 and concerned colonial authorities rushed an engineer to the spot to lay out a plan for the town. The new town was to be called Nouvelle-Orléans (New Orleans), named after the Duke of Orléans, who was regent of France while King Louis XV was still a child. In August 1722, Governor Bienville moved the capital of Louisiana from Biloxi to New Orleans, having just received approval for the move from France. The new capital was about 100 miles north of the Mississippi River Delta, where the Mississippi enters the Gulf of Mexico and the open sea.

Outlying forts and batteries

New Orleans, somewhat like Montréal, depended on a number of outlying forts and batteries that were critical to its security. Work on a fortified post started in early 1722 at **La Balise**, a low-lying island of mud, sand and pine trees at the point where the Mississippi River flows into the Gulf of Mexico. This post was really a shore battery to check the progress of any ship heading up the river. Vessels coming into the Mississippi would stop there to confirm their identity and take a pilot before heading further upriver. Construction work continued

Governor Jean-Baptiste Le Moyne de Bienville founding New Orleans in August 1722. (Print after a c.1920s painting by A. Alaux)

A plan of a semicircular artillery battery at La Balise, 1722. This post was at the entrance of the Mississippi River (still called "Fleuve St. Louis" on the plan) on the Gulf of Mexico. Any ship going up the river to New Orleans would stop there. It was the first of several outlying forts on the river before reaching the city. Note the mast with the large lantern to guide ships at night. (Archives Nationales, DFC, Louisiane)

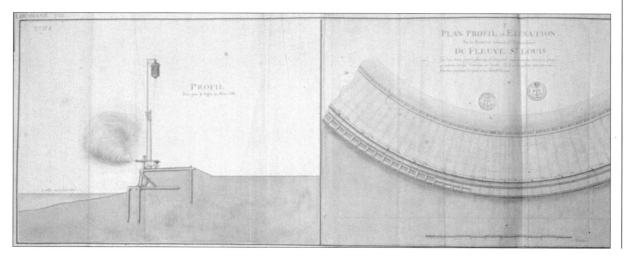

A plan of the barracks of New Orleans dated March 30, 1729. This side view shows the musket racks. (Archives Nationales, DFC, Louisiane)

intermittently for decades thereafter. There were two batteries with barracks for the detachment of troops, a powder magazine built on pilings to keep it dry, and a protective palisade on the landward side.

As elsewhere on the Mississippi, the great floods of the mighty river with its strong current played havoc with such shore fortifications. Except for the two batteries, which were higher up, the land was often flooded when there were high winds. By 1746, La Balise was too silted up and most of its garrison moved to Détour à l'Anglois. Captain Bossu's impression of the place in 1752 was that it was "isolated and surrounded by swamps filled with snakes and alligators." Indeed, La Balise had practically been washed away by the end of the French Regime. British Captain Philip Pittman saw little more than the barracks there in the mid-1760s.

From September 1766, the Spanish administration built a pilot station slightly to the north on higher ground. In 1803, when French colonial prefect Pierre de Laussat saw the pilot station, he noted that it featured "quarters for

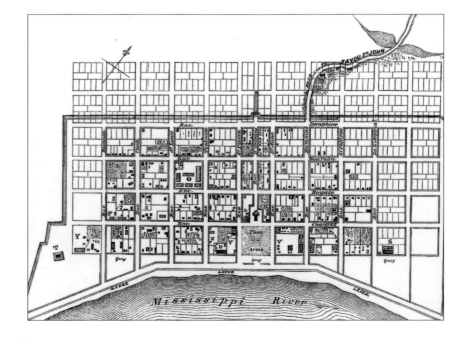

A plan of New Orleans, c.1730–31, by which time the town was being enclosed for the first time by a narrow ditch with a palisade and a small earthen wall. The powder magazine ("T") is shown to the lower left. (Print after a c.1730–31 plan in Cable, *The Creoles of Louisiana*, 1885)

The guardhouse of the New Orleans garrison originally built facing the Place d'Armes (the present-day Jackson Square). This 1970s exhibit re-created the guardhouse's appearance in the mid-18th century although the French soldiers' uniforms should have been gray-white faced with blue rather than blue faced with red. The floors and walls are from the original structure and are the only vestiges left from the French military works. In the late 1790s, the guardhouse was incorporated into the much larger Cabildo government house built by the Spanish and reoccupied briefly by French Napoleonic administrators in 1803. It is now the main location of the Louisiana State Museum. (Author's photograph)

sixteen student pilots, the customs house; barracks for the soldiers and officers [one sub-lieutenant and ten men of the Luisiana Regiment at the time]; and a guardhouse." There was also a tower "constructed of grating and lattice work to cut out the wind" about 45 feet high "with a spire in the form of a steeple, atop of which a flag was raised. One can see it out on the ocean five leagues [10 miles] away." All that remained on the site of the abandoned French fort were "orange groves, orchards, and the ruins of the arsenal." During December 1803, the French *tricolor* replaced the Spanish flag on the tower and, in turn, was replaced by the American Stars and Stripes from January 1804.

As La Balise was so vulnerable to being ruined by the forces of nature, other fortifications were erected at **Détour à l'Anglois** (English Turn) at a bend on the Mississippi about 17 miles south of New Orleans in 1746–47. These fortifications would provide the main defenses against ships coming upriver from the south. Two forts were built, one on each side of the river at this bend, which were "enclosures of stockade and defences against small arms" on the land side and batteries facing the river. According to Captain Pittman, each battery was mounted by ten 12-pounders, which was "more than sufficient to stop the progress of any vessel." The garrison was much stronger at Détour à l'Anglois with 56 men there against only 18 at La Balise in 1752. The Spanish succeeded the French until the 1790s when Détour à l'Anglois was abandoned in favor of the new Fort San Felipe and Fort Bourbon at Plaquemines.

The French and the Spanish had realized that additional fortifications were necessary south of New Orleans. As early as 1767, plans were made for the construction of a small fort on the river about 60 miles south of New Orleans at **Plaquemines**. Twenty years later, plans were drawn up to build a substantial fort that could pulverize ships at Plaquemines and, in 1790, construction started on Fort St. Philip (or San Felipe), with the smaller adjoining Fort Bourbon across the river. In 1803, when the French retook possession, Fort St. Philip had 18 iron guns and Fort Bourbon had a garrison of about 100 men and "several iron cannons that crossfired" with those across the river.

Ramparts and batteries

New Orleans, capital of Louisiana from 1722, was laid out on low-lying flat land in a rectangular plan with city blocks but without, initially, fortifications. Thought was nevertheless given to the matter of defense. A plan of 1724 outlined a suggested wall with bastions but nothing was done until 1729 when the uprising of the Natchez Indians and the fall of Fort Rosalie (Natchez), where nearly all the French perished, spread much fear among the inhabitants of defenseless New Orleans. Governor Périer at once ordered that a palisade and a moat be built to enclose the town. By 1731–32, the ditch and earth wall then being built enclosed most of the town. However, the northeast side remained open except for a moat. The Natchez did not move to attack New Orleans and

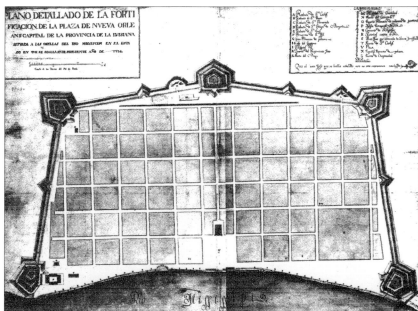

TOP A plan of New Orleans showing the new pentagon-shaped walls with bastions built to enclose the city in 1759. (Map from Pittman, *The Present State...*, 1770)

BOTTOM A plan of New Orleans in 1794 showing the rebuilt walls and added redoubts erected in 1793–94. (Servicio Historico Militar, Madrid)

56

were defeated in the field, with the result that the sense of urgency concerning matters of defense lessened. There was thus less interest in finishing the work, especially as settlers complained they had too few slaves to do this government work as well as till their plantations for crops. Another factor was the Mississippi River itself which, when it rose, as it often did, washed its silt and sand into the moat. Thus, Governor Bienville reported, in May 1733, that the moat, planned to be 60 feet wide, had a mere 2 feet of width.

There was also a lack of funds for fortifications as other military structures had to take priority. Louisiana had come directly under the government's administration since 1731 and the garrison had been increased from eight to 13 companies of colonial infantry. Up until then, the soldiers were lodged in "barracks" made of wooden "stakes planted in the ground, roofed with bad tree bark, ready to collapse, without flooring, without chimneys" and which were thus very humid, reported Chief Engineer Broutin (AC, C13A, 16). With such poor housing, the soldiers frequently became ill. It thus became crucial to have a proper barrack building, which was built from 1734 with various finishing touches being added until 1743. This large building, consisting of a wide main block to house the NCOs and men with pavilions at each end for the Officers' Quarters, was erected on the western side of the Place d'Armes. The site of the barrack building is now occupied by the notable Pontalba buildings constructed in 1850.

Another important work was the powder magazine in a large bastion-shaped area at the southwest angle near the river. The original magazine was built of framed squared timbers filled in with bricks and mortar and surrounded by a log palisade. Chief Engineer Broutin had a new magazine made of brick, which featured elegant corner turrets to replace the rotting logs, the whole structure being designed to look like a small fort. It also featured a gate decorated with the royal arms in wrought iron. It was constructed this way, he explained to the minister of the navy, to impress the Indians and to reassure the inhabitants that, in the event of an attack, the women and children of New Orleans could find refuge within its walls. In effect, the powder magazine doubled as a small citadel. It was completed in early 1736.

Insofar as the walls surrounding New Orleans were concerned, little seems to have been done during the following decades despite calls from time to time to improve the fortifications. The city, although it had some military works such as the fortified powder magazine and the barracks, remained just about defenseless. Its only salvation was its fairly large garrison. As late as 1755, it was not thought necessary to have fortifications to protect the city. However, with the outbreak of the Seven Years War in 1756, opinions began to change as news of the war went from bad to worse. By 1759, Governor Louis de Kerlérec was getting worried about New Orleans's safety and had the existing fortifications repaired. This work, although denounced as expensive by Commissary Rochemore, only consisted of erecting a palisade and digging a ditch around the city. It was insufficient. In the event of an attack by Indians or the British, such works could not offer much protection.

The ceremony marking the transfer of Louisiana from France to the United States, New Orleans, December 20, 1803. This print after a c.1900 painting by T. de Thulstrup reconstructs fairly well the general scene that occurred on the Place d'Armes. In the background is the Cabildo government house built by the Spanish in 1795–99 and the St. Louis cathedral as it looked in 1803 before its spires were added. At right is what appears to be French Prefect Laussat. To his left, a few French officers, the one with the hand on his sword guard seemingly Battalion Chief Vinache, an engineer officer. The smaller figures standing to attention further back are likely meant to represent the Company of French Citizens. An American soldier is raising the Stars and Stripes while two figures in French uniforms are gathering the French *tricolor*. The Americans are uniformed according to plates by Henry Ogden published in 1888. (Print after a c.1900 painting by T. de Thulstrup)

In March 1760, more bad news reached New Orleans regarding French defeats in Canada and elsewhere. The governor and his senior officers convened a War Council and resolved that New Orleans had to have fortifications erected immediately. The work started in April 1760. Slaves were drafted in to build the fortifications, head taxes on slaves were raised and government property was sold to pay for the new fortifications. News of the fall of Québec reached New Orleans only in August 1760, 11 months after the event, and must have added to the sense of urgency in building the fortifications. They were erected rapidly under the direction of Chief Engineer Vergès, who finished construction in mid-December 1760.

Although by no means a formidable fortress, New Orleans was at last surrounded by walls featuring six wide bastions and two smaller bastions. Instead of a rectangular plan as was the case previously, Vergès laid out the expanding city in a large pentagon. The wall itself was simply, as an official noted, a palisade with a small ditch. There were "two or three batteries" on the shore of the Mississippi River. The town had about 100 cannons mounted *en barbette* for lack of carriages. The highest-caliber guns were 24-pounders, all the guns no doubt being old naval iron artillery pieces. However, there was very little ammunition available. In January 1764, British Captain Philip Pittman saw a "stockade with a banquette and a very trifling ditch without; these can answer no end but against Indians, or Negroes, in the case of an insurrection." Facing the river, Pittman counted "twenty-one pieces of ordnance, *en barbette*." (These were only the guns at the riverside. There would have been others in the bastions and some more in store.)

The Spanish, who occupied the city from 1769, maintained the existing works until early 1792 when the Governor, Baron Carondelet, ordered that the walls of New Orleans be rebuilt. He was often to be seen on horseback with his suite of officers supervising the construction work. Gilbert Guillemard, major of the Luisiana Regiment and occasional engineer, designed the new fortifications. The work was undertaken from 1792 to 1794. The previous walls in the pentagon plan designed by Vergès were kept to enclose the city, but all the bastions were removed. The town's fortifications now featured five redoubts at the angles of the straight curtain walls and a large battery on the waterfront. Each redoubt also had the pentagon shape and was armed with artillery so as to

Québec lit up at night. Now a UNESCO World Heritage site, Québec is the only walled city in North America. (Author's photograph)

The foundations of Montréal's 18th-century ramparts toward the Saint-Laurent Bastion with part of the city's center as a backdrop. (Author's photograph)

provide crossfire on an attacking enemy. The two redoubts on the banks of the Mississippi River, St. Charles and St. Louis (San Carlos and San Luis), were both larger and stronger. They had 18-foot-thick parapets and ditches 8 feet deep by 20 feet wide. Their parapets' interiors were reveted with masonry, the outside with grass sod, and the scarp and counterscarp with boards. Inside were barracks capable of lodging 150 men. The three smaller redoubts on the land side, named San Juan, San Felipe de Borgoña and San Fernando by the Spanish, were connected by an earth rampart featuring a line of pickets in front of a ditch 7 feet deep by 40 feet wide. Great damage by hurricanes and floods, and a sense that the wall could not offer much protection, led to the fortifications being neglected and they eventually vanished in the early 19th century.

With such modest fortifications, New Orleans could not be defined as a fortress in the usually accepted sense of the word in Europe, with extensive masonry-faced ramparts and glacis and citadels. Although this colonial town was far from being a strong position defensively, it was surrounded by a protective wall, partially from 1730 and completely from 1760, which was and remains the basic definition of a fortress. It was never put to the test of an attack but perhaps, in the low-lying and swampy terrain, its works were much more formidable than they seemed. When the British attacked New Orleans in January 1815, the defensive line built at Chalmette was similar in style to the old city walls: a ditch, a thick earthen rampart and some pickets. It was enough to provide New Orleans's defenders with one of the most outstanding triumphs in the history of the United States of America.

New Orleans had no outlying defenses to the north on the Mississippi River until 1748 when some Choctaw warriors attacked the village of the **Côte des Allemands** (German Coast), 40 miles to the north. Although troops sent from New Orleans subsequently defeated and routed the Choctaws, the attacks led some frightened settlers to depart, with the result that a small regular garrison was henceforth posted there. A fort was built consisting of a square palisade, with 35 yards of one side facing the Mississippi River. A timber and fill main building within served as officers' and men's barracks and as a guardhouse. The fort was abandoned in 1759.

The sites today

Following the cession of Canada to Britain and the American siege of 1775–76, Québec's fortifications were steadily improved and a large citadel was finally built in the 1820s, thus truly rendering it the "Gibraltar of North America." Three large forts were also built on the south shore in the 1860s. Following the withdrawal of the British garrison in 1871, there was pressure to demolish the walls and batteries. Thanks to the efforts of the heritage-conscious Lord Dufferin, governor-general of Canada in the 1870s, the ramparts were preserved and today, Québec is the only walled city in North America. The rampart that was erected is essentially the same that can be seen in present-day Québec. Since the end of the 19th century, Québec has become a favorite destination for tourists and great efforts have been made to preserve the heritage of this exceptional city. In 1985, UNESCO declared it a World Heritage Site.

After 1760, Montréal's walls seemed less relevant to a successful defense and more of an obstacle to businessmen as the city expanded rapidly, there being twice as many inhabitants outside its ramparts by the beginning of the 19th century. In 1801, legislation authorized the walls' demolition, which started in 1804 and continued until 1817, although most of it had been leveled by 1810. Montréal is now Canada's second largest city and one of the main business centers in the northeast of North America. In the last two decades, small parts of its ramparts' foundations have been rediscovered and preserved. The network of outlying forts also fell into ruin and disappeared except for a few stone vestiges.

At Louisbourg, what had once been a sizeable fortress was reduced to little more than a pile of rubble on an abandoned peninsula. Further back in the bay, a fishing village was established and carried on the name of Louisbourg. In the late 19th century, with the advent of a railroad, tourists started to visit the rather haunting and barren area strewn with evocative ruins. In time, it became a national historic site with a small museum. In 1961, over two centuries after the second siege, the Government of Canada ordered "The Fortress of Louisbourg is to be reconstructed partially so that future generations can thereby see and understand the role of the fortress as a hinge of History. The restoration is to be carried out so that the lessons of History can be animated." The reconstruction work was carried out over the next two decades. Incredibly, the fortress town of Louisbourg lives again today as it was in the mid-18th century!

New Orleans's earthen ramparts disappeared with the city's rapid growth following the cession of Louisiana to the United States. Thereafter, the Americans built strong outlying forts rather than trying to enclose its most important business city and port on the Gulf Coast. Nothing today hints that New Orleans's old and famous "French Quarter," with its many historic buildings and jazz halls, was once surrounded by ramparts.

Select bibliography

Archives

Myriad maps and plans have been consulted at the National Archives of Canada, in Ottawa, which holds, as well as originals in its collections, handmade copies, photos (a negative is indicated by a "C" and its number), photostats and photocopies of nearly all known original examples pertaining to Canada held in other archives. For New France, the vast majority of originals are held at the French Archives Nationales, Centre des archives d'outre-mer at Aix-en-Provence in the Dépôt des Fortifications des Colonies (DFC) section. The colonial correspondence in the Archives des Colonies (AC) sections, series B (outward letters), C11A (Canada), C11B (Louisbourg) and C13A (Louisiana) has many useful documents. For Spanish New Orleans, correspondence in the Papeles de Cuba for the appropriate years as well as maps and plans are preserved at the Archivo General de Indias in Seville.

Books and articles:

Angus, Alexander David, *Old Quebec in the days before our day* (Montréal, 1949)

Bosworth, Newton, *Hochelaga Depicta: the early history and present state of the city and island of Montreal* (Montréal, 1839)

Charbonneau, André, with Desloges, Yvon, and Lafrance, Marc, *Québec: ville fortifiée* (Québec, 1982)
The definitive work on Québec's fortifications.

Fry, Bruce W., *An Appearance of Strength: The Fortifications of Louisbourg* (Ottawa, 1984; 2 volumes)
An essential study.

Gauthier, Raymonde, *Trois-Rivières disparue, ou presque* (Québec, 1978)

Girouard, Désiré, *Le vieux Lachine et le massacre du 5 août 1689* (Montréal, 1889)

Gonzalez, Julio, *Catalogo de Mapas y Planos de la Florida y la Luisiana en el Archivo General de Indias* (Madrid, 1979)
Guide to Louisiana maps and plans.

Grant, George Monro, *Picturesque Canada; the country as it was and is* (Toronto, 1882; 2 volumes)

Hinshelwood, N.M., *Montreal and Viscinity* (Montréal, 1903)

Laussat, Pierre Clément de, *Memoirs of my Life* (Baton Rouge, 1977)

Lemoine, Louis, *Le château fort de Longueuil* (Longueuil, 1987)

McDermott, John Francis (ed.), *Frenchmen and French Ways in the Mississippi Valley* (Urbana, 1969)

McLennan, Stewart, *Louisbourg: From its Foundation to its Fall 1713–1758* (London, 1918)

Montréal, ville fortifiée au XVIIIe siècle (Montréal, 1992)
Studies by several authors. An essential source.

Noppen, Luc, with Paulette, Claude and Tremblay, Michel, *Québec: trois siècles d'architecture* (Montréal, 1979)

Parker, Gilbert, and Bryan, Claude G., *Old Quebec* (New York, 1903)

Québec: ville et capitale (Sainte-Foy, 2001)
Studies by several authors. An essential source.

Robert, Jean-Claude, *Atlas historique de Montréal* (Montréal, 1994)
Essential for maps and plans.

Robinson, Willard B., "Maritime Frontier Engineering: the Defense of New Orleans" in *Louisiana History* (winter 1977)
An essential study.

Vidal, Laurent and d'Orgeix, Emilie (ed.), *Les villes françaises du Nouveau Monde* (Paris, 1998)

Wilson, Samuel, Jr., "Gulf Coast Architecture" in *Spain and her Rivals on the Gulf Coast* (Pensacola, 1971)
Good overview; well illustrated.

Glossary

abbatis A defensive barricade or row of obstructions made up of closely spaced felled trees, their tops toward the enemy, their branches trimmed to points and interlaced where possible.

banquette A continuous step or ledge at the interior base of a **parapet** on which defenders stood to direct musket fire over the top of the wall. A fire step.

barbette Said of cannons placed over a **rampart** without the protective **embrasures**.

bastion A projection in the **enceinte**, made up of four sides (two faces and two flanks), which better enabled a garrison to defend the ground adjacent to the main or **curtain** walls.

battery An emplacement for artillery.

breastwork See **parapet**.

casemate A mortar-bomb or shell-proof chamber located within the walls of defensive works; generally pierced with openings for weapons; **loopholes** for muskets or **embrasures** for cannon.

cavalier A raised construction, usually in a fortress, holding a second tier of guns in a **battery**.

citadel A strong fort within (or a part of) a larger fortification. No true citadels were built in New France.

cordon The coping or top course of a **scarp** or a **rampart**, sometimes of different-colored stone and set proud from the rest of the wall. The point where a **rampart** stops and a **parapet** starts.

counterguard A defensive work built in a **ditch** in front of a **bastion** to give it better protection.

covered way A depression, road or path in the outer edge of a fort's **moat** or **ditch**, generally protected from enemy fire by a **parapet**, at the foot of which might be a **banquette** enabling the coverage of the **glacis** with musketry.

cunette A furrow located in the bottom of a dry **ditch** for the purpose of drainage.

curtain The wall of a fort between two **bastions**.

demi-bastion A half-bastion with only one face and one flank.

demi-lune A triangular-shaped defensive work built in a **ditch** in front of a **bastion** or a **curtain** wall.

ditch A wide, deep trench around a defensive work. When filled with water it was termed a **moat** or wet ditch; otherwise a dry ditch or foss.

embrasure An opening in a wall or **parapet** allowing cannon to fire through it, the gunners remaining under cover. The sides of the embrasure were called cheeks, the bottom was the sole, the narrow part of the opening was the throat and the wide part was the splay.

en barbette An arrangement for cannon to be fired directly over the top of a low wall instead of through **embrasures**.

enfilade fire Fire directed from the flank or side of a body of troops, or along the length of a **ditch**, **parapet** or wall. Guns in the flank of a **bastion** can direct enfilade fire along the face of the **curtain**.

epaulement A **parapet** or work protecting against **enfilade fire**.

fascines Long bundles of sticks or small-diameter tree branches bound together for use in **revetments**, for stabilizing earthworks, filling ditches, etc.

fossé or foss See under **ditch**.

fraise A defense of closely placed stakes or logs, 6–8 feet long, driven or dug into the ground and sharpened; arranged to point horizontally or obliquely outward from a defensive position.

gabion A large, round, woven wicker cylinder intended to be set in place and filled with earth, sand or stones.

gallery An interior passageway or corridor that ran along the base of a fort's walls.

gate A main entrance of a fortress.

glacis A broad, gently sloped earthwork or natural slope in front of a fort, separated from the fort proper by a **ditch** and outworks and so arranged as to be swept with musket or cannon fire.

gorge The interval or space between the two curtain angles of a **bastion**. In a **ravelin**, the area formed by the flanked angle and either left open or enclosed.

guardhouse The headquarters for the daily guard.

guérite A small lookout watch tower, usually located on the upper outer corner of a **bastion**.

half bastion See **demi-bastion**.

hornwork A work made up of a **bastion** front; two half-bastions and a **curtain** and two long sides termed "branches." It functioned to enclose an area immediately adjacent to a fort or **citadel** and create another layer of defense. None were built in New France's fortresses.

loopholes Small openings in walls or **stockades** through which muskets were fired.

magazine A place for the storage of gunpowder, arms or goods generally related to ordnance.

merlon The solid feature between **embrasures** in a **parapet**.

moat See **ditch**.

orgue See **portcullis**.

outwork An outer defense, inside the **glacis** but outside the body of the place. A **ravelin** is an outwork.

palisade A high fence made of stakes, poles, palings, or pickets, supported by rails and set endwise in the ground from six to nine inches apart. See **stockade**.

parapet A **breastwork** or protective wall over which defenders, standing on **banquettes**, fired their weapons. The parapet was usually built on top of the fort's **rampart**.

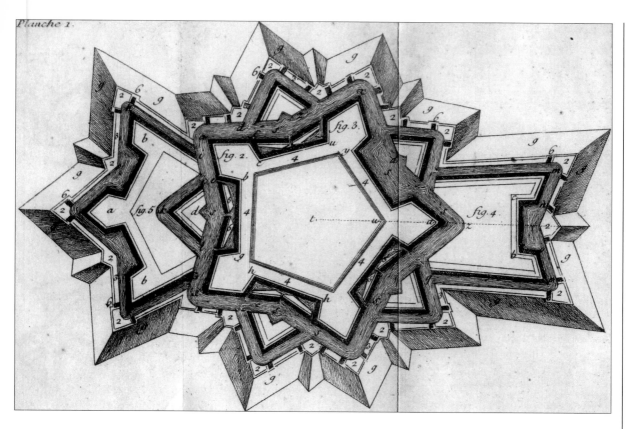

portcullis A timber or iron grating that can be lowered to close the gates of a fortress. Called *orgue* (organ) in French.

postern A passage leading from the interior of a fortification to the **ditch**.

rampart The mass of earth, usually faced with masonry, formed to protect an enclosed area. The main wall of a fortress.

ravelin An outwork consisting of two faces forming a salient angle at the front and a flank angle to the rear that was usually closed at the **gorge**. Ravelins were separated from the main body of the place by **ditches** and functioned to protect **curtains**.

redoubt An enclosed fortification without **bastions**.

revetment The sloping wall of stone or brick supporting the outer face of a **rampart**.

sallyport A passageway within the **rampart**, usually vaulted, leading from the interior of a fort to the exterior, primarily to provide for sorties.

sap A trench and **parapet** constructed by besiegers to protect their approaches toward a fortification.

scarp The interior side of a ditch or the outer slope of a **rampart**.

stockade A line or enclosure of logs or stakes set upright in the earth with no separation between them, to form a barrier eight or more feet high. Stockades were generally provided with **loopholes**. The loopholes were reached by **banquettes** or elevated walks. See also **palisades**.

A fortifications plate from *Le petit dictionnaire du tems, pour l'intelligence des nouvelles de la guerre* (Paris, 1757). The letters and numbers on this theoretical plan refer to various fortification terms in the Glossary.

traverse A **parapet** or wall thrown across a covered way, a terreplein, **ditch** or other location to prevent **enfilade fire** or reverse fire along a work.

63

Index